George Breckenridge Davis

Outlines of International Law

With an Account of it Origin and Sources and of its Historical Development

George Breckenridge Davis

Outlines of International Law
With an Account of it Origin and Sources and of its Historical Development

ISBN/EAN: 9783337232245

Printed in Europe, USA, Canada, Australia, Japan

Cover: Foto ©Suzi / pixelio.de

More available books at **www.hansebooks.com**

OUTLINES

OF

INTERNATIONAL LAW

WITH

AN ACCOUNT OF ITS ORIGIN AND SOURCES AND

OF ITS HISTORICAL DEVELOPMENT

BY

GEORGE B. DAVIS

MAJOR AND JUDGE-ADVOCATE U.S.A.

NEW YORK

HARPER & BROTHERS, FRANKLIN SQUARE

Copyright, 1887, by HARPER & BROTHERS.

All rights reserved.

PREFACE.

It has been my purpose in the preparation of this volume to provide a work sufficiently elementary in character to be within the reach of students and others who may desire to gain some knowledge of the general principles of International Law. It is intended to be used as a text-book, rather than as a book of formal reference. To that end the use of citations, and of terms technical to the law, has been avoided wherever it was possible to do so, and the effort has been made to express the fundamental principles of the science as concisely as possible and in the English language.

Where quotations have been found necessary they have been acknowledged in the text, and the student will find, at the end of each chapter, a list of references to state papers, or to the works of writers of standard authority, where the subjects discussed in the text will be found treated at greater length and in more elaborate detail.

WEST POINT, N. Y.

TABLE OF CONTENTS.

	PAGE
List of Authorities Cited.	xix

CHAPTER I.
DEFINITION AND HISTORY.

Of Law in General	1
Classification of Public Law	1
Municipal Law	1
International Law	1
International and Municipal Law Compared	2
History of the Science of International Law.	3
The Oriental Monarchies	3
Greece	3
Rome	4
The International Law of the Middle Ages	4
Effects of the Revival of Commerce	5
Early Codes of Maritime Law	5
The "Jugements of Oleron"	5
The "Consolato del Mare"	6
The "Guidon de la Mar"	6
Other Early Codes	7
Comparison of the Sea Laws	7
Effects upon International Law of—	
The Feudal System	8
The Institution of Chivalry	10
The Roman Church	11
The Church and the Emperor	11
Œcumenical Councils	13
The Rise of the European Monarchies	14
The Influence of Grotius	15
The Sources of International Law	18
Treaties and Conventions	18
The Judgments of International Courts and Boards of Arbitration	19
The Diplomatic Correspondence of States	19

TABLE OF CONTENTS.

	PAGE
The Roman Law	19
The Works of Text Writers	22
Decisions of Courts upon Questions of International Law	23
The Municipal Law of States	24
General Histories, Histories of Important Epochs, Biographies, etc.	24
The Divine Law	24
Divisions of International Law	24
The Natural Law of Nations	25
The Positive Law of Nations	25
(a) The Customary Law of Nations	25
(b) The Conventional Law of Nations	25
The Parties to International Law	26
References	26

CHAPTER II.
STATES AND THEIR ESSENTIAL ATTRIBUTES.

Definition of a State	28
The Sovereignty of a State	28
The Government of a State	28
Classification of Governments	29
Classification of Governmental Powers	30
Governments *de facto* and *de jure*	30
The Essential Attributes of Sovereignty	31
Sovereignty	31
Independence	31
Equality	31
Sovereign States	32
Dependent or Semi-sovereign States	32
Confederations	32
Rule for Determining the Strength of a Confederation	33
Right of a State to Change its Constitution and Laws	33
Sovereignty, how Acquired, how Lost	34
Territory	35
Definition of the Term	35
River Boundaries	35
What Constitutes the Territory of a State	36
Jurisdiction over Closed Seas	37
Rights of Ownership and Jurisdiction in the case of Straits	37
The Danish Sound Dues	38
Ship Canals	39
Jurisdiction over a Portion of the Coast Sea, the Marine League	40
Case of the Franconia	41

TABLE OF CONTENTS.

	PAGE
The High Seas	42
Freedom of the Seas	43
Claims to Exclusive Dominion	43
Right of River Navigation	44
Action of the Congress of Vienna	44
Cases of the Rhine, Main, Moselle, Neckar, Meuse, and Scheldt	44
Cases of the Elbe, Vistula, Weser, and Po	45
Case of the Douro	45
Case of the Danube	45
Case of the Mississippi	46
Case of the St. Lawrence	49
Servitudes	52
Origin and Definition of the Term	52
Its Application in International Law	52
How Created and Terminated	53
Examples of Servitudes	54
The Right of Territorial Jurisdiction	54
Classification of Jurisdictional Powers	54
In Whom Vested	55
The Legislative Power	55
The Executive Power	56
The Judicial Power	56
Extra-territorial Jurisdiction of a State	57
Over the Officers and Crews of Ships of War	57
Over its Merchant Vessels on the High Seas	57
Over its Armies in the Field	59
Over Crimes Committed by its Subjects in Unoccupied Territory	59
Over the Crime of Piracy	59
The Principle of Exterritoriality	59
Origin and Definition of the Term	59
Application to Ships of War in Foreign Ports	60
Application to Armies in Transit	63
Application to the Person of a Sovereign, to his Retinue and Train, while Passing through, or Sojourning in, Foreign Territory	65
Application to Ambassadors, etc.	67
Application to Consuls, and to Foreigners in Certain Eastern Countries	67
References	68

CHAPTER III.
PERFECT AND IMPERFECT RIGHTS.

	PAGE
Perfect Rights	70
Classification of	70
The Right of Self-preservation	70
Duty of a State to Protect its Subjects	72
The Right of Reputation	73
The Enforcement of Treaty Stipulations	74
Duty of Non-interference	74
The Right of Interference	74
(a) To Assist a State in Suppressing an Insurrection or Rebellion	75
(b) Interference in Accordance with Treaty Stipulations	76
(c) In Self-defence	77
(d) Interference in Behalf of the Balance of Power	77
De Marten's Statement of the Principle of Balance of Power	80
Vattel's Rules	81
Senior's Limitation of the Right	81
(e) Interference in Behalf of Oppressed Populations	82
The Duty of Mutual Respect	83
Forms of Mutual Courtesy	85
Maritime Ceremonial	87
Ceremonial in Foreign Ports	88
International Agreement as to Salutes	90
Observance of National Anniversaries	91
Ceremonial on Land	91
The Formalities of Diplomatic Intercourse	92
Imperfect Rights, or Moral Claims	92
The Duty of Humanity	93
The Duty of Comity	94
The Duty of Intercourse	94
(a) Interstate	94
(b) Commercial	95

CHAPTER IV.
NATIONAL CHARACTER.

National Character of an Individual, how Determined	98
Definition of the Terms Citizen and Subject	98
Classification of Citizens	99
Native-born Citizens	99
Naturalized Citizens	100

TABLE OF CONTENTS. ix

	PAGE
Naturalization	100
Conditions of Naturalization	101
Heinrich's Case	102
Koszta's Case	103
Largomarsini's Case	105
Ungar's Case	106
Naturalization Treaties of the United States	107
Expatriation	108
Conditions of	108
Policy of States in the Matter of	109
Aliens and Domicile	110
History of the Treatment of Aliens	110
Definition of the Term	112
(a) Aliens, or Aliens Proper	112
(b) Domiciled Strangers	112
Legal Situation of Aliens	112
Domicile	116
Distinction between Citizenship and Domicile	117
Conditions of Domicile	118
Importance of the Rules of Domicile	121
References	121

CHAPTER V.
EXTRADITION.

The Right of Criminal Jurisdiction	123
Duty of a State as to Crimes Committed Abroad.	123
Extradition by Comity and Treaty	124
Difference of View as to Criminal Jurisdiction.	124
Definition of the Term Extradition.	126
Methods of Extradition.	126
(a) By Treaty	126
(b) In Accordance with Municipal Law	126
(c) By Comity	126
Extraditable Offences	126
Requisitions for Extradition, by Whom Made	127
Conditions of Extradition	127
Extradition Treaties of the United States	128
Interstate Extradition in the United States.	129
References	131

CHAPTER VI.
PRIVATE INTERNATIONAL LAW.

Relations of States and Individuals at International Law	132
Definition of Private International Law.	132

TABLE OF CONTENTS.

	PAGE
Practice of International Law Based on Comity or Consent.	132
Origin of the Practice	133
Subjects Discussed in Private International Law	136
Limitations upon the Practice of Private International Law	137
Foreign Judgments	138
Effect of.	138
Conditions to be Fulfilled in Order that Effect may be Given to	138
Condition of Reciprocity.	138
Why Produced before the Courts of a State.	139
Practice of States in the Matter of	139
References	140

CHAPTER VII.
THE RIGHT OF LEGATION.

Origin of the Right	141
The Right of Legation	142
Classification of Diplomatic Agents	143
Rank of Ambassadors	144
Titles of Ambassadors.	145
Manner of Sending and Receiving Ambassadors	146
Reception of Ambassadors	146
Duties of Ambassadors	147
Diplomatic Language.	147
Functions of, how Suspended and Terminated.	148
Privileges and Immunities of Ambassadors.	149
Necessity of Immunities.	149
The Principle of Exterritoriality.	150
Immunity from Criminal Jurisdiction.	150
Immunity from Civil Jurisdiction	151
Immunity of Hotel.	152
Privilege of Religious Worship	153
Exemption from Customs Dues	153
Consuls, their Duties and Privileges	154
Origin of the Consular Function	154
The Duties of Consuls.	156
Classification of Consular Employees	157
Privileges and Immunities of Consuls	157
By whom Appointed	158
How Recognized in Foreign States	158
The Exequatur	158
Manner of Appointment in the United States	160
Consular Jurisdiction	161
Extent and Character of.	162

TABLE OF CONTENTS. xi

Jurisdiction of U. S. Consuls 162
References 164

CHAPTER VIII.
TREATIES AND CONVENTIONS.

Definition and Purpose. 165
The Right of Making Treaties 165
Contracts and Agreements with Individuals 166
The Treaty-Making Power 166
    Limitations upon the Treaty-Making Power. 167
Conditions Essential to the Validity of Treaties 167
    The Power of the Contracting Parties 167
    The Consent of the Contracting Parties 168
    Possibility of Execution 168
Binding Force of Treaties. 169
Manner of Negotiating Treaties. 169
    Language Used 170
    Form and Signature 171
    Ratification of Treaties 172
Classification of Treaties 173
    Transitory Agreements or Conventions 174
    Permanent Treaties 174
    Cartels 174
    Capitulations 174
    Treaties of Alliance 175
    Treaties of Guarantee 176
    Reciprocity Treaties 178
Treaties, how Terminated 179
    How Violated 179
Rules for Interpreting Treaties 180
    Strict Interpretation 182
    Liberal Interpretation. 182
Terms Used 183
    Protocol. 183
    Recez 183
    Separate Articles 183
    The Most Favored Nation Clause 183
References 184

CHAPTER IX.
THE CONFLICT OF INTERNATIONAL RIGHTS.

Causes of Conflict. 186
Methods of Adjusting International Differences 186
    Amicable Adjustment. 186

TABLE OF CONTENTS.

	PAGE
The Duty of Moderation	189
Mediation	190
Arbitration	191
Conditions of Arbitration	191
Binding Effect of Decision	192
Mediation and Arbitration Compared	192
Measures of Redress	193
Retorsion	194
Reprisals	195
References	197

CHAPTER X.
WAR.

The Right of Redress	198
Definition and Purpose of War	198
Rightfulness of War	199
Classification of Wars	199
Internal Wars	199
(a) Civil Wars	199
(b) Insurrections and Rebellions	199
Belligerents	200
The Laws of War	200
Right of Declaring War, in Whom Vested	201
Causes of War	201
Responsibility for a Resort to War	202
Moral Considerations Involved	202
Declaration of War, Ancient and Modern Rule	203
Official Notification of an Intended Resort to War	204
Effect of War upon Treaties of Alliance, Guarantee, and Subsidy	204
Effects of a State of War	205
(a) Upon the Belligerent States	205
(b) Upon the Subjects of the Belligerent States	205
(c) Upon the Property of Enemy Subjects	207
The Laws of War	208
Their Character and Tendency	208
Subjects Treated of	210
Amount and Kind of Force that may be Used	210
Legal Effects of a State of War upon the Subjects of the Belligerent States	210
Who may Lawfully Carry on War	211
Partisans	211
Levees *en masse*	212

TABLE OF CONTENTS.

	PAGE
Guerillas	214
Forces that may not be Employed in War	214
Wars with Savages	215
Forces Employed at Sea	215
Privateers	216
Letters of Marque	216
Letters of Marque and Reprisal	216
Effect of Modern Inventions	218
Methods of Carrying on War	218
Rule of Good Faith	219
Use of Deceit	219
Attack of Places	219
Duty of the Commander of a Besieged Place in the Matter of Surrender	221
Use of the Enemy's Uniform and Flag	222
Giving and Receiving Quarter	222
Treatment of Individuals of the Enemy	223
Forbidden Practices	223
Instruments of War	223
Rule for Determining whether a Particular Instrument may, or may not, be Used in War	224
Torpedoes, and Torpedo Warfare	225
Usages of War at Sea	226
The Public and Private Property of the Enemy	226
Treatment of Property on Land	226
Requisitions	228
Contributions	230
Captured Property on Land	230
Treatment of Non-combatants in the Theatre of War	232
Combatant, Defined	232
Non-combatant, Defined	233
Prisoners of War	233
Who may be Made Prisoners of War	233
Treatment of	234
Exchange of	235
Paroles	236
From Whom Received	236
Breach of Parole	237
Intercourse between Belligerents	237
Flags of Truce	238
Cartels and Capitulations	239
Safe-conducts and Safeguards	239
Licenses to Trade	240

TABLE OF CONTENTS.

	PAGE
Offences Against the Laws of War	241
By Whom Punished	241
Spies	241
Guerillas	242
Pillaging	243
Crimes of Violence, etc.	243
Temporary Occupation	244
History of the Different Views of	245
Present View of Military Occupation	246
Rights of Occupation	247
Martial Law	247
The State of Siege	247
Differences of Opinion as to the Meaning of the Term Occupation	250
Opposing Views	250
Permanent Occupation	251
Retaliation	251
How Exercised in War	252
The Termination of War	253
Truces	253
What may be Done during a Special Truce	253
General Truces, Armistice	254
Treaties of Peace	255
How Different from Ordinary Treaties	255
Binding Character of	256
How Made	256
Preliminary and Definitive Treaties	257
When Binding	257
Effects of Treaties of Peace	257
Treatment of Occupied Territory	258
The Rules of Maritime Capture	259
Tendency and Character of	259
Forces Employed in Maritime War	260
Definition of Prize	261
Title to Prize, in Whom Vested	261
Duty of Captor	261
Ransom of Captured Vessels	263
Ransom Contracts	264
Hostages	265
Recapture and Postliminy	266
Prize Courts and their Jurisdiction	268
Character of Prize Jurisdiction	269
Law Applied in Cases of Prize	270
Procedure in Prize Cases	270
Right of Appeal in Prize Cases	272

TABLE OF CONTENTS. xv

Rules for Determining the Nationality of Ships and Goods 272
References 274

CHAPTER XI.
NEUTRALITY.—THE RIGHTS AND DUTIES OF NEUTRALS.

Definition of the Term 276
Character of the Neutral Relation 276
History of Neutrality 276
  Origin and Development of the Modern Theory of Neutral
    Obligation 277
  Rule of the "Consolato del Mare" 279
  General Acceptance of the Rule 279
  The Principle of "Free Ships, Free Goods" 281
  Rules of the Declaration of Paris 284
  Binding Force of the Declaration 286
  Effect of Claims to Exclusive Dominion upon the Develop-
    ment of the Neutral Theory 288
  The Monopoly of Colonial Trade 291
  The Rule of 1756 292
  Development of the Theory of Neutrality among the Non-
    Maritime States of Europe 292
  Influence of England 293
  General Acceptance of the Modern Theory in the Seven-
    teenth Century; its Later History 294
Gradations of Neutrality 295
  Permanent Neutrality 296
  Armed Neutrality 296
  Strict Neutrality 297
Neutral Duty of a State 297
Duties of Neutrals to Belligerents 299
  Asylum to Troops and Ships 299
  Asylum in the Case of Public and Private Vessels . . . 299
  Neutral Territory, Immunity of from Acts of Belligerency 300
Responsibility of a Neutral State for the Acts of its Subjects . 302
  View of England and the United States 303
  Continental View of the Same Subject 305
Neutral Rights 306
  Their Character and Extent 306
  Case of the Chesapeake 307
  Case of the Florida 308
Neutrality Laws 309
  Neutral Obligation of a State Determined by International,
    not Municipal, Law 310
  English Neutrality Laws 311

Neutrality Laws of the United States 313
Neutrality Laws of other States 314
Case of the Alabama. 315
The Geneva Arbitration 327
References 335

CHAPTER XII.
CONTRABAND OF WAR.

History of the Practice 336
Power of a Belligerent over Neutral Commerce in Time of
    War 338
    General Character of the Restrictions 338
    The Rules of Contraband Affect Chiefly the Acts of Individuals 339
    Character of Contraband Trade 339
Rules for Determining Contraband 340
    Difficulty of Stating a Precise Rule 340
    The Question Determined by Prize Courts 341
    Field's Rule 341
    Rule of the Supreme Court of the United States 342
Application of the Rules 343
    Destination of Ships and Goods 345
    Destination, how Determined 345
    Case of the Springbok 346
    Case of the Peterhoff 349
The Doctrine of Continuous Voyages 351
    Difference between the Old and New Rule 352
Penalty for Contraband Trade 353
    Rule as to Innocent Cargo 354
    Release of Neutral Ship on Surrender of the Contraband
        Cargo 355
Neutral Conveyance of Enemy's Troops and Despatches . . . 356
    Definitions of the Terms 356
    The Destination Important 357
    Cases of the Friendship and Greta 357
    Presumption in the Case of Hostile Despatches 358
    Despatches of a Belligerent to its Ministers and Consuls in
        Neutral State 358
    Conveyance of Mails in the Ordinary Course of Business . 359
    Case of the Trent 360
Occasional Contraband 362
The Rule of Pre-emption 364
References 365

CHAPTER XIII.
BLOCKADE.

Blockade 366
    Definition of 366
    Right of Blockade, where Exercised 366
    Valid Blockade 367
    How Established and Notified 367
        (a) By Proclamation 368
        (b) By Notification or Endorsement 368
        (c) By Proclamation and Notification 368
    What Constitutes a Breach of 369
    Penalty for Breach of 370
    Cases of Innocent Entrance to Blockaded Ports . . . 370
    Duration of the Penalty 371
    Breach of Blockade by Egress 372
    Termination of Blockade 372
Pacific Blockade 373
References 373

CHAPTER XIV.
THE RIGHT OF SEARCH.

The Right of Search, a Belligerent Right 375
    When and Where Exercised 375
    Manner in which the Right is Exercised 376
    Duty of Boarding Party 377
The Right of Visitation 379
Impressment of Seamen 380
    Controversy between England and the United States . . 381
The Right of Convoy 383
    Views of England as to 384
    Views of the United States as to 385
    Not a Right According to International Law 386
Searches Authorized in Time of Peace 386
    (a) To Execute Revenue Laws 387
    (b) On Suspicion of Piracy 387
    (c) Search of Merchant Vessels by War Vessels of the
        Same State 387
    (d) Right of Approach to Verify Nationality 387
Case of the Virginius 388
References 392

B

APPENDIX A. Instructions for the Government of Armies in the Field. By Dr. Francis Lieber 395
" B. The Geneva Convention of 1864 and 1868 . . 429
" C. The Declaration of Paris of 1856 437
" D. The Declaration of St. Petersburg of 1868 . . 440
" E. The Rules of War on Land, Recommended for Adoption by the Institute of International Law at its Oxford Session of 1880. 442

INDEX 461

LIST OF AUTHORITIES
CITED IN THE PREPARATION OF THIS VOLUME.

Abdy. See Kent's Commentaries.
Amos, Sheldon. Political and Legal Remedies for War. New York, 1880.
    The Science of Law. New York, 1875.
Azuni. The Maritime Law of Europe. 2 vols. New York, 1806.

Bar, E. International Law (Private). Edinburgh, 1883.
Bernard, Mountague. The Neutrality of England during the American Civil War. London, 1870.
Bluntschli, J. C. Le Droit de Butin en Général et Spécialement du Droit de Prise Maritime. Brussels, 1877.
    Le Droit International Codifié. Paris, 1874.
    Das moderne Volkerrecht der civilisirten Staten als Reichsbuch dargestellt. Leipsic, 1877.
Boyd, A. C. See Wheaton.
Brenton, E. P. The Naval History of Great Britain, 1783–1836. 2 vols. London, 1837.
Bryce. The Holy Roman Empire. London.
Bynkershoek, Cornelius. Treatise on the Laws of War. American Edition. Philadelphia, 1810.

Calvo, Carlos. El Derecho Internacional. Paris, 1862.
    Le Droit International. Paris, 1862.
    Colleccion Completa de los Tratados de Todos los Estados de la América Latina. 6 vols. Paris, 1862.
Cooley, T. M. The General Principles of Constitutional Law in the United States of America. Boston, 1880.
    Constitutional Limitations. 5th Edition. Boston, 1883.
Creasy, E. S. First Platform of International Law. London, 1876.
Cushing, Caleb. The Treaty of Washington. New York, 1873.
Cussy, Ferdinand de. Dictionnaire ou Manuel Lexique du Diplomate et du Consul. Leipsic, 1846.

Dahlgren, Admiral J. A., U.S.N. International Law. Boston, 1877.
De Lolme. The Constitution of England. Chandos Edition. London and New York, n. d.
Dictionnaire Universel du XIXme Siècle. P. Larousse. 16 vols. Paris, 1866.
Diplomatic Correspondence of the United States. Various years. Washington, D.C.
Dumont, Jean. Corps Universel Diplomatique du Droit des Gens. 8 vols. Amsterdam and The Hague, 1726–31.

Elliot, Jonathan. The American Diplomatic Code. 2 vols. Washington, 1834.

Field, D. D. Draft Outlines of an International Code. 1 vol. New York, 1874.
Foreign Relations of the United States. Various years. Washington, D.C.

Garden. Histoire Général des Traités de Paix. 14 vols. Paris, 1853.
Geneva Arbitration. Foreign Relations of the United States. 1872, 1873. 4 vols. Washington, 1873.
Gessner, L. Les Droits des Neutres sur Mer. 2d Edition. Paris.
Grotius, Hugo. De Jure Belli et Pacis. 1 vol. Paris, 1625.
    Barbeyrac's French Edition. Various editions. Paris, 1724–1768.
    The Laws of War. First English Edition, 4to. London, 1738.
    "   " Whewell's English Edition. London, 1853.
(There are also translations in German, Dutch, Swedish, and Danish.)

Hall, W. E. International Law. Oxford, 1880.
Hallam, H. The Constitutional History of England. Chandos Edition. New York and London, n. d.
Halleck, H. W., Maj.-Gen. U.S.A. International Law, by Sir Shepstone Baker. 2 vols. London, 1878.
    International Law. 1. American Edition. 1 vol. San Francisco, 1861.
    International Law. 2. Students' Edition. Philadelphia, 1866.
Hautefeuille, J. B. Des Droits des Nations Neutres, etc. Paris, 1859.
Heffter, A. G. Le Droit International Public de l'Europe. Bergson's Edition. 1 vol. Paris, 1866.

LIST OF AUTHORITIES. xxi

Henshaw, J. S. A Manual for United States Consuls. New York, 1849.
Hertslet, Lewis. Complete Collection of Treaties and Conventions between Great Britain and Foreign Powers. London, 1827-35.
Map of Europe by Treaty since the Peace of 1814. 3 vols. London, 1875.
Hildreth, R. History of the United States. 6 vols. New York, 1849.
Holmes, O. W. See Kent.

Ihne, William. History of Rome. 5 vols. London, 1871.

Kent, James. Commentaries on American Law. Holmes's Edition. 2 vols. Boston, 1873.
Commentaries on American Law. Abdy's Edition. London, 1878.
Klüber, J. L. Droit des Gens Moderne de l'Europe. Ott's Edition. Paris, 1861.
Droit des Gens Moderne de l'Europe. 2d Edition. Paris, 1874.

Laveleye, E. de. Des Causes Actuelles de Guerre en Europe et de l'Arbitrage. Brussels and Paris, 1873.
Lawrence, W. B. A Study on Consular Jurisdiction (see Revue de Droit Int.). Brussels, 1878.
See Wheaton.
Lawrence, T. J. Essays on Modern International Law. 1 vol. London, 1884.
Laws. See Revised Statutes of the United States.
Lorimer, J. The Obligations of Neutrals. Edinburgh, 1873.
Institutes of the Law of Nations. Edinburgh, 1884.
The Final Problem of International Law (see Revue de Droit Int.). Brussels, 1877.

Maine, Sir H. S. Ancient Law. New York, 1864.
Lectures on the Early History of Institutions. New York, 1875.
Popular Government. New York, 1886.
International Law. London, 1888.
Manning, William Oke. Commentaries on the Law of Nations. Amos's Edition. London, 1875.
Martens, Ch. de. Recueil Manuel et Pratique des Traités, Conventions, etc., 1760-1857. Leipsic, 1857.
Causes Célèbres du Droit des Gens. Leipsic, 1827.
Nouvelles Causes Célèbres du Droit des Gens. G. F. de Martens's Edition. Leipsic, 1844.

Martens, G. F. de. Précis du Droit des Gens Moderne de l'Europe. Ch. Vergé's Edition. 2 vols. Paris, 1864.
Recueil des Traités. 8 vols., with Murrhard's Continuation. Paris, 1817-1844.
Recueil des Traités, with Samwer and Hoff's Continuation. Göttingen, 1876.
Cours Diplomatique. 3 vols. Berlin, 1801.
Mills, H. E. The Law of Eminent Domain. St. Louis, 1879.
Miltitz, A. de. Manuel des Consuls. London, 1843.
Mommsen. The History of Rome. 4 vols. New York, 1885.
Moore, John B. Moore on Extradition. 2 vols. Boston, 1891.
Morey, W. C. Outlines of Roman Law. New York, 1884.

Neumann, L. Handbuch des Consulatswesens mit besonderer Berücksichtigung des österreichischen Reichs. Vienna, 1854.
Nys, E. Les Origines de la Diplomatie et le Droit d'Ambassade Jusqu'à Grotius. Brussels, 1884.
La Guerre Maritime. Brussels, 1881.

Ortolan, E. Diplomatie de la Mer. 2 vols. Paris, 1856.

Phillimore, Sir R. International Law. 4 vols. 2d Edition. London, 1871.
Puffendorf. De Juræ Naturæ et Gentium. London, 1672.
French edition by Barbeyrac, 1706.

Ranke, L. von. History of the Popes. 2 vols. Philadelphia, 1841.
A History of England, principally in the 17th Century. 5 vols. Oxford, 1875.
Universal History. Vol. 1. New York, 1885.
Revised Regulations, United States Army. Washington, 1881.
Regulations, United States Navy. Washington, 1876.
Reports, American. Supreme Court.

Vols.	1-4,	Dallas.	Vols.	1-4,	1790-1800.
"	5-13,	Cranch.	"	1-9,	1800-1815.
"	14-25,	Wheaton.	"	1-12,	1816-1827.
"	26-41,	Peters.	"	1-16,	1827-1842.
"	42-65,	Howard.	"	1-17,	1843-1860.
"	66, 67,	Black.	"	1, 2,	1861, 1862.
"	68-90,	Wallace.	"	1-23,	1863-1874.
"	91-103,	Otto.	"	1-10,	1875-1880.

LIST OF AUTHORITIES. xxiii

Reports, English. Admiralty and Prize.
    Robinson's Admiralty Reports. 6 vols. Boston, 1861.
    Dodson's Admiralty Reports. Boston, 1861.
Revised Statutes of the United States. Washington, 1878.
Revue de Droit International. Vols. i.-xiv. (1869-1882). Brussels.
Rymer, Thomas. Fœdera, Conventiones, etc. Clarke's Edition. London, 1816.

Schuyler, Eugene. American Diplomacy and the Furtherance of Commerce. New York, 1886.
Spear, S. T. The Law of Extradition. New York, 1885.
Stephen, Sir J. F. History of the Criminal Law of England. 3 vols. London, 1883.
Story, Joseph. Commentaries on the Conflict of Laws. Boston, 1834.
    Commentaries on the Constitution of the United States. 2 vols. Cooley's Edition. Boston, 1873.

Thiers. A History of the French Revolution. Philadelphia, 1847.
    History of the Consulate and Empire. London, 1876.
Treaties of the United States. See Treaties and Conventions of the United States. Washington, 1871. A later edition, with valuable notes, was issued in 1889.
    See also United States Statutes at Large, 1875, pp. 819-902 for Analytical Index. Washington, 1875.
    United States Statutes at Large. Annual Volumes, 1875-91. Washington.

Upton, F. H. The Law of Nations Affecting Commerce during War. 1 vol. New York, 1863.

Vattel, E. de. Le Droit des Gens ou Principes de la Loi Naturelle Appliqués à la Conduite et aux Affaires des Nations et des Souverains. 2 vols. Leyden, 1758.
    The Law of Nations. Chitty's English Edition. London, 1797.
    Of the older works upon International Law, Vattel is cited more frequently than any other. This is the case not only in the works of text writers, but in the diplomatic correspondence of modern states.

Ward, Robert. An Enquiry into the History and Foundation of the Law of Nations in Europe. 2 vols. London, 1795.
Warden, D. B. On the Origin, Nature, Progress, and Influence of Consular Establishments. Philadelphia, 1813.
    The same. French Edition. Paris, 1815.

LIST OF AUTHORITIES.

Wharton, F. The Conflict of Laws (Edition of 1881). Boston, 1881.
    A Digest of the International Law of the United States. 3 vols. Washington, 1886.
Wheaton, Henry. The Elements of International Law. 3 vols. Philadelphia, 1836.
    W. B. Lawrence's Edition. Boston, 1863.
    R. H. Dana's Edition. Boston, 1866.
    A. C. Boyd's Edition. London, 1878.
    French Edition. 2 vols. Paris, 1841.
    "   "   " Leipsic, 1874.
    History of the Law of Nations in Europe and America. New York, 1845.
    Digest of the Law Maritime, Captures, and Prizes. New York, 1815.
Wildman, R. Institutes of International Law. 2 vols. London, 1849.
Woolsey, T. D. Introduction to the Study of International Law. 5th Edition. New York, 1878.

OUTLINES

OF

INTERNATIONAL LAW.

CHAPTER I.

DEFINITION AND HISTORY.

1. *Definition.*—In its most general acceptation the term *law* is applied to the rule or principle underlying and controlling a sequence of events. When used in a political sense, and with reference to the external and internal relations of states, it is divided into:

(*a.*) *Municipal Law*—comprising those rules of conduct which are sanctioned by a state and imposed by its sovereign power upon its citizens or subjects.[1]

---

[1] In their desire to discriminate between *law* and *morality* some English writers have given to the term law a narrower meaning than is usual in other languages. This tendency is seen in their frequent denial of the existence of a science of international law; a denial based upon a narrow and technical definition of the term *law* itself. From their point of view a law is not entitled to that name unless a superior authority be conceived to exist, powerful enough to compel obedience to its commands. If that which would be regarded as law by this restricted definition be closely examined, it will be seen that its right to the title is by no means clear. As most modern states are now organized no law can long endure, or be rigidly enforced, which does not commend itself to the great mass of citizens of a state. So soon as they cease to regard it as just, or even expedient, its enforcement becomes difficult and the law is repealed, or

(b.) *International Law*—comprising the aggregate of rules and limitations which sovereign states agree to observe in their intercourse and relations with each other. As it deals with the relations of states in their sovereign capacity, it is sometimes called *Public International Law*, to distinguish it from that branch of the science which has to do with the relations of states to the citizens or subjects of other states, which is called *Private International Law;* or, as it is in question whether the courts of a state shall apply their own municipal laws or those of another state in the determination of a given cause, this branch of the subject has sometimes been called the *Conflict of Laws*.

2. *International and Municipal Law Compared.*— The essential difference between the two systems of law will be found to consist in the extent and character of the binding force of each. The sovereign authority of a state sanctions its own municipal laws, and, within its territorial limits, enforces obedience to their provisions. As sovereign states acknowledge no common superior, it is obvious that there is no authority above or outside a state which can effectively coerce it into obedience to the provisions of International Law. An individual who suffers an injury, or whose personal or

---

becomes a dead letter. Municipal laws, therefore, no less than international, in the last resort, depend for their efficiency upon the consent of those whose conduct is to be regulated by them; and a law which all nations expressly agree to observe, or tacitly accept as an international usage, is as well entitled to consideration as is a provision of municipal law which is enacted and obeyed because a majority of citizens believe it to be just and necessary. It is not necessary to say that the view here discussed is not shared by the later school of English writers, of which Professor Sheldon Amos and Sir Henry Sumner Maine are the able representatives.

property rights are invaded, seeks and obtains redress in the courts of his country, which are authorized to hear and decide his case, and are given power to enforce their judgments and decrees. If a nation be injured or invaded by another, or have a cause of difference with a foreign state, it cannot appeal to an international tribunal of any kind to remedy its wrong or to adjust its difference, but must seek redress by remonstrance or negotiation, or, as a last resort, by war, when all peaceable methods of adjustment have failed.

History of the Science.

3. *The Oriental Monarchies.*—International law can hardly be said to have existed in ancient times. The absolute and crudely organized Eastern monarchies were intolerant of the very existence of neighboring nations, and lived in a state of constant warfare with them. Of distant nations they knew nothing, and as there must be communication or intercourse of some kind between states in order that the rules may be deduced which shall govern their relations with each other, it was impossible that a science resembling international law could have existed among them.

4. The Greeks acknowledged the independent existence of other states, both within and without the Hellenic peninsula. They had intercourse with them, and sent and received ambassadors and diplomatic agents. The pressure of circumstances obliged them, at times, to enter into offensive and defensive alliances with each other, and some of their later confederacies were highly organized and possessed many elements of permanency. All foreigners, however, were known to them as barbarians; their customs in war were extremely cruel, and

breaches of faith were too common to favor the growth of a science which depends to a higher degree than any other upon the sacred observance of agreements and promises.

5. The Romans differed from the Greeks in that their intercourse with foreign nations was so great in amount, and so diversified in character, as to enable their jurists to deduce from their international experience a crude set of rules by which they conceived that their reciprocal intercourse with other states was governed. This was known among them as the *Jus Feciale*. It differs radically from the modern science of international law, which is founded upon the *consent* of nations and presupposes the existence of many independent states, and rather expresses the imperfect and one-sided views of international obligation which were held by the most powerful state of the ancient world.

6. From the downfall of the Western Roman Empire until the close of the dark ages a slow but gradual development of the science can be traced, chiefly in the history of the Mediterranean cities, which maintained more or less intimate commercial relations with each other during this period. Some of these cities had survived the wreck of the empire, and had maintained their corporate existence during the inroads of the Teutonic invaders. Others had been founded from time to time, especially during the period of revival of civilization. All had been able to endure the evil effects of the feudal system only with extreme difficulty, and it was not until those effects had in some degree passed away that the elements of civilization, which had been preserved among them, began to increase, and to exercise an influence upon the rude society by which they

were surrounded. The first signs of a revival began to appear toward the close of the dark ages, and were manifested in the marked interest shown in the revival of manufactures, and the establishment and extension of commercial intercourse.

7. *Effect of the Revival of Commerce.*—Commerce, and especially maritime commerce, cannot long be carried on without its participants agreeing upon some rules for its protection and regulation. All ships engaged in it are exposed alike to the depredations of pirates and the perils of the sea. The necessity of policing harbors, of lighting dangerous coasts, and of maintaining adequate port facilities must also have received early attention. As the cities were themselves independent, or were situated in different states and acknowledged no common superior, such rules, to have been regarded as obligatory, must have commended themselves to those engaged in commercial pursuits, must have existed with their tacit or expressed consent, and their binding force could have continued only so long as they were generally regarded as just and equitable.

8. *Early Codes of Maritime Law.*—Primitive codes of maritime law, fulfilling most of these conditions, and so possessing some of the characteristics of international law, are found to exist in the early sea-laws of the commercial cities of southern and western Europe. The most important of these were:

(*a.*) "*The Jugements of Oleron.*"—This was a body of regulations governing the navigation of the western seas, and is believed to have been drawn up in the eleventh century.[1] · Its authority was long recognized

---

[1] Azuni, "Maritime Law," vol. i., p. 379.

in most of the Atlantic ports of France, and for this reason portions of it were incorporated in the Maritime Ordinances of Louis XIV.

(*b.*) "*The Consolato del Mare ;*" or, "Customs of the Sea," was a more extensive collection of rules applicable to the decision of questions arising in commerce and navigation, both in peace and war. It also contained rules defining the rights of belligerents and neutrals, as they were then sanctioned and understood. It was probably drawn up in the twelfth century, the earliest authentic copy having been published in Barcelona in 1474. Its authors are unknown, but their work exhibits a thorough knowledge of the Roman maritime law, of the early maritime customs of the commercial cities of the Mediterranean, and of the principles of contract, as applied to trade and navigation. Great weight was attributed to the work by the commission to whom Louis XIV. intrusted the preparation of his celebrated Maritime Ordinances. Grotius speaks of the "Consolato del Mare" as containing the constitutions of France, Spain, Syria, Cyprus, the Balearic Isles, Venice, and Genoa.[1] Its provisions on the subject of "prize law, besides the concurrence of the states above named, coincided with all the treaties relating to their provisions made during several succeeding centuries,"[2] and "they agree at present with the maritime code of Europe, notwithstanding many attempts to revise their regulations."[3]

(*c.*) "*The Guidon de la Mar*" is a work of more comprehensive character than the "Consolato del Mare," and is of considerably later date. It was drawn

---

[1] Manning's "Law of Nations," p. 15.
[2] *Ibid.*   [3] *Ibid.*

up toward the close of the sixteenth century, at the supposed instance of the merchants of Rouen. It treats principally of the law of maritime insurance, the laws of prize, and contains a code of regulations governing the issue of letters of marque and reprisal.

Other Codes of Maritime Law.—The "Maritime Law of Wisbuy," the "Customs of Amsterdam," the "Laws of Antwerp," and the "Constitutions of the Hanseatic League" are names applied to bodies of sea-laws similar to those already described, which were recognized in the cities of northwestern Europe on the North and Baltic seas.

These early systems had some elements in common. The authorship of none of them is fully known. The best opinion is that they were drawn up by commissions of merchants or lawyers representing different cities, thus giving them in some degree the character of commercial treaties. All of them contain provisions extracted from the earliest-known maritime code, the Rhodian Laws, which were incorporated at an early date into the general body of Roman Law, and were recognized and sanctioned by the emperors Tiberius and Hadrian. In some of them the subjects of neutrality and neutral rights are so broadly and liberally treated as to leave but little room for improvement in the codes of more recent times. All of them evince, on the part of their authors, a familiarity with the Civil Law, and each in turn exercised a decided influence in the preparation of those which followed it.

These sea-laws, however, applied to but one phase of international relations—maritime commerce—and some of them had been in existence several centuries before the intercourse of states on land had become sufficiently general to make it possible to deduce any of its underlying principles, or even to formulate the common usages of states in peace or war. The nations of Europe during the period between the fifth and fifteenth centuries were in formative, transition state, of which little detailed history remains. General causes were at work, however, some of which tended to favor, and some to retard, the growth of international law. Some of these were:

9. (a.) *The Feudal System.*—As a system of land-tenure this institution is of great antiquity; as a system of government in Europe it dates back to the migrations of the Teutonic tribes into western and southwestern Europe, which were in progress during the period between the third and sixth centuries.

"The German nations who passed the Rhine to conquer Gaul were in a great degree independent; their princes had no other title to their power but their valor and the free election of the people; and as the latter had acquired, in their forests, but contracted notions of sovereign authority, they followed a chief less in quality of subjects than as companions in conquest. Besides, this conquest was not the irruption of a foreign army, which only takes possession of fortified towns; it was the general invasion of a whole people in search of new habitations; and, as the number of the conquerors bore a great proportion to that of the conquered, who were at the same time enervated by long peace, the expedition was no sooner completed than all danger was at an end, and of course their union also. After dividing among themselves what lands they thought proper to occupy, they separated, and, though their tenure was at first only precarious, yet in this particular they depended, not on the king, but on the general assembly of the nation.

"Under the kings of the *first race* the fiefs, by the mutual connivance of the leaders, at first became annual; afterwards they were held for life. Under the descendants of Charlemagne they became hereditary. And when, at length, Hugh Capet effected his own election, to the prejudice of Charles of Lorraine, intending to render the crown, which, in fact, was a fief, hereditary in his own family, he established the hereditaryship of fiefs as a general principle; and from this epoch authors date the complete establishment of the feudal system in France.

"On the other hand, the lords who gave their suffrages to Hugh Capet forgot not the interest of their own ambition. They completed the breach of those feeble ties which subjected them to the royal authority, and became everywhere independent. They left the king no jurisdiction, either over themselves or their vassals; they reserved the right of waging war with each other; they even assumed the same privilege, in certain cases, with regard to the king himself; so that if Hugh Capet, by rendering the crown hereditary, laid the foundation of the greatness of his family, and of the crown itself, yet he added little to his own authority, and acquired scarcely anything more than a nominal superiority over the number of sovereigns who then swarmed in France."[1] This system of government, which seems to have been the only one of which the Teutonic mind could conceive, was carried by the same methods into

---

[1] De Lolme, "The Constitution of England," book i., chap. i., pp. 148, 149.

Italy and Spain, and was suddenly introduced into England at the period of the Norman Conquest.

The system culminated when the modern states of Europe began to assume something of their present form. The great monarchies could only grow in size and strength at the expense of the power and possessions of the feudal nobles, and so soon as the former were securely established the power of the latter began to decline. While the system lasted its effects were, on the whole, unfavorable to the growth of international law. Europe was divided into a large number of small states, or groups of states, ruled by dukes and barons, each in a condition of constant hostility with his neighbors. Intercourse was always difficult, and at times impossible. Commerce by land could not exist, and the growth of towns was hampered and restricted. War was the rule, and peace the exception. The rules of war were cruel and harsh in the extreme. Quarter was rarely given; the garrisons of besieged towns were put to the sword; prisoners of war were reduced to slavery; and so great was the mutual distrust of sovereigns that they maintained but little intercourse with each other, and obtained such information as they desired by questionable means—through agents or spies.

10. (*b.*) *The Institution of Chivalry.*—This came into existence during the feudal period, and was in great part an outgrowth of the Crusades. It contributed powerfully to ameliorate some phases of the laws of war. Its code applied at first only to the conduct of knights towards each other; but, in so far as it recognized and practised, to some extent, the principles of Christianity, its effects were soon felt in the milder

treatment of captives and slaves, and in the different and stricter views which began to prevail in the matter of keeping faith with enemies and strangers.¹

11. (c.) *The Roman Church.* — Unquestionably the most powerful influence that was exerted upon the science of international law during its formative period was that of the Roman Church. As the political power of the Western Empire decayed, and finally disappeared, the Church, an organization having at once a religious and a secular aspect, became for a time the most powerful organ of civilization in that portion of Western Europe which had formerly acknowledged the sway of the Roman emperors. Its authority was generally acknowledged and respected, and its ministers and bishops, in addition to their sacred functions, frequently found themselves called upon to perform duties entirely secular in character. Out of this state of affairs grew the *Canon Law*, a code based, to a great extent, upon the Roman Law, but adapted to the peculiar exigencies of the Church and times. While intended primarily as a constitution for the government of the Church and the administration of its vast interests, its provisions were found to be applicable to the decision of a great variety of controversies, ranging in importance from the disputes of private individuals to the adjustment of difficulties of serious international concern.

It is a tribute to the profound influence of the Roman Empire upon the minds of men that the theory of universal sovereignty should have so long survived its

---

¹ For an account of the usages of war in the Middle Ages see Ward's "Inquiry into the Law of Nations before Grotius;" vol. i., chap. vi.-ix.

downfall, and that it should have been deemed necessary, in the Middle Ages, to find a substitute for it in existing institutions. Such a substitute was found in the empire founded by Charlemagne, but with an important modification. The *temporal* head of Christendom was the German emperor; its *spiritual* head was the Roman pontiff; but, as the line of division was not sharply drawn, these personages often came into conflict, and "the international law of the Middle Ages was influenced enormously by the conflicting claims of the pope and the emperor."[1] As the imperial power, at any time, depended largely upon the personal influence and character of the emperor, and as no line of political policy was long adhered to by them, the papacy, having a determined and well-settled policy, in time began to acquire a preponderance even in temporal affairs.

"The idea of a common superior still lingered among the nations, and greatly assisted the Roman pontiffs in their efforts to obtain a suzerainty over all temporal sovereigns. For as the empire founded by Charlemagne gradually decreased in extent till it scarcely extended beyond the limits of Germany, more and more difficulty was felt in ascribing to it universal dominion. Yet no one dreamed of asserting boldly that independent states had no earthly superior; and therefore, when the papacy came forward with its claims, men's minds were predisposed to accept them. As an arbitrator between states the pope often exercised great influence for good. In an age of force he introduced into the settlement of international disputes principles of hu-

---

[1] Lawrence, "Essays on Modern International Law," p. 149.

manity and justice, and had the Roman Curia always acted upon the principles which it invariably professed, its existence as a great court of international appeal would have been an unmixed benefit." [1]

Œcumenical Councils.—" The assembly of deputed representatives from the different Christian states gave to the Œcumenical Councils the composition of a sort of European congress. Besides the settlement of articles of faith, and the deposition or excommunication of princes, determined in these councils, there are distinct examples in which the pope was made referee in questions of international controversy. At the Council of Lyons, convened by Gregory X., in 1274, the inhabitants of Ancona having contested the right of the Venetians to levy tolls, and exercise other rights of exclusive dominion in the Adriatic, the question was referred to the pope and was discussed. Judgment was given that the inhabitants of Ancona had no grounds for their complaints, and that the Venetians were possessed of the sovereignty of the Adriatic. None of the ambassadors or princes present at the council objected to the decision, and the judgment passed without any protest respecting its validity. Decisions on questions were given by the pope individually, unassisted by such councils; as, for instance, when the Spaniards were pushing their discoveries in the West, and the Portuguese in the East, these nations referred to the pope for limits, in case their exploring parties should claim the same territories, and Alexander VI. accordingly gave them, in his well-known bull, a line of demarcation." " The advantage that might

---

[1] Lawrence, "Essays on Modern International Law," p. 149.

have been derived from the papal interference would have been very great had it been an authority exercised for justice, instead of abused for ambition."[1]

12. *Rise of the European Monarchies.*—During the period between the fourteenth and sixteenth centuries, and as a consequence of the decline of the feudal nobility, the great monarchies of Europe began to acquire strength and consistency, and to assume something of their present territorial form. These governments were absolute in character, and although some of them were at times administered with considerable liberality, in none were popular rights recognized, and none were limited by representative institutions. Not only were they absolute in form, but in most of them the idea of sovereignty had become associated with the person of the sovereign. He was the head of the state; the title to its territory and property was vested in him, and he was held to be able to dispose of it at will. Such restraints as were established upon the royal power had chiefly to do with internal affairs, and rarely extended to his foreign relations. Such being the case, diplomatic relations soon became common, alliances were entered into, agents were established at foreign capitals, through whom information was obtained as to the schemes and intentions of foreign powers. Embassies were sent and received, ambassadors maintained, and great wars were undertaken. Conquests were made, and territory changed hands; sometimes as a result of war, sometimes after the manner of a transfer of property among private individuals.

---

[1] Manning, pp. 12 and 13, citing Selden, "De Dominio Maris," i., c. xvi.

Such intricate and important international relations could not long exist without furnishing precedents of sufficient value to be cited in negotiation, or without some practices and usages acquiring, by frequent repetition, or common consent, the binding force of international customs. The sea-laws furnished a basis upon which to erect a code of maritime law; their recent experience in war and negotiation furnished abundant materials for the preparation of a code of international usages, and the Roman Law furnished a stock of legal maxims and principles with which to bind the whole fabric together.

13. *The Influence of Grotius.*—At the close of this period, and at a most opportune moment in the history of the science, there appeared the first authoritative treatise upon the Law of Nations, as that term is now understood. It was prepared by Hugo Grotius, a native of Delft, in Holland. He was a man of great learning, of considerable experience in public affairs, and a profound student of the Roman Law; and his treatise, which was published early in the seventeenth century,[1] is, in substance, an application of its principles to the external relations of states. It was at once perceived to be a work of standard and permanent value, of the first authority upon the subject of which it treats. General Halleck justly observes with reference to it that it "has been translated into all languages, and has elicited the admiration of all nations and of all succeeding ages. Its author is universally regarded as the great master-builder of the science of International Jurisprudence."[2]

---

[1] 1625.   [2] Halleck, vol. i., p. 12.

Great as were the inherent merits of Grotius's work, it could never have exercised so decisive an influence upon state affairs as it did, had it not appeared at a time when the existing political conditions were especially favorable for its reception. The Thirty Years' War, then drawing to a close, had been marked during its entire course by a refinement of barbarous cruelty, and by acts of atrocity perpetrated upon the unarmed and unoffending inhabitants of the valley of the Rhine which stand without a parallel in the history of ancient or modern war. Many of the military operations had been undertaken rather with a view to the chance of pillage than from a desire to injure or defeat the enemy. Population had diminished, great tracts of territory had been laid waste, and commerce and manufactures had well-nigh disappeared. With an experience of the horrors of war so bitter and long continued as that which Europe was even then undergoing, it is not remarkable that men should have been willing to listen to any scheme which promised to mitigate the severity of war, or to lighten, in any degree, its terrible burdens. But, great as the losses had been in men and material wealth, it may be doubted whether a desire to ameliorate the existing usages of war would have been, of itself, an agency sufficiently potent to bring about a reform of International Law, had not another and a more powerful factor contributed directly to the same end.

During the continuance of the Thirty Years' War the composition of the belligerent states and the purposes for which the war was carried on had undergone a complete change. The contest had originated in an attempt of the Protestant princes to achieve their political and religious independence. In its later stages it had been transformed into a struggle for preponderance between France and Austria, and it had terminated, in 1648, to the complete advantage of the former power. In the course of the war the old idea of papal and imperial supremacy had finally disappeared. The ancient standard of international obligation had ceased to exist, and a newer and more enduring standard had to be erected in its place. As the idea of a common earthly superior was no longer recognized, it became necessary to invent a theory which, while conforming to existing political conditions, should furnish a safe and practicable rule for the conduct of interstate relations.

Such a scheme was that proposed by Grotius. "His International Law had two sources—the Law of Nature and the consent of all or most nations; but the latter is only supplementary to the former, and cannot ordain anything contrary to it."[1] The Law of Nature, which is but another name for the *Jus Gentium* of the Roman Law, furnished the legal basis for Grotius's work, and from it he derived his fundamental idea of the equality and independence of sovereign states. States, like men, were, from his point of view, controlled in their actions and relations by the operation of a law of nature as ancient as the universe itself. This law could be added to, but not modified. He believed it to constitute a standard by which the conduct of states and the actions of individuals could be finally judged; and he imagined that the Roman Law afforded an historical example of its successful application in international affairs.

We now know that Grotius's theory of international

---

[1] Lawrence, "Essays on Modern International Law," p. 179.

obligation was in the main correct, however erroneous may have been his conception of its origin and sanction; and it is a remarkable tribute to the intrinsic excellence of his work that it has endured so successfully, for more than two centuries and a half, the assaults of destructive criticism and the crucial test of practical experience. None of the many ingenious theories which have been advanced in opposition to his have received even transient recognition, and upon the foundations so deeply and solidly laid by its immortal founder the fabric of the science securely rests.

14. THE SOURCES OF INTERNATIONAL LAW.

(*a.*) *Treaties and Conventions.*—As International Law derives its binding force from the consent of nations, and as treaties are compacts, freely entered into, describing the conditions and defining the limitations which nations agree to observe in their intercourse with each other, it follows that they are of the highest authority in determining what that law is upon any point covered by their stipulations. For example, many naturalization treaties stipulate for a period of residence, usually five years in length, as a condition preliminary to naturalization. This warrants the inference that a period of residence is a necessary preliminary to a change of national allegiance. Other treaties provide that consuls may, under certain circumstances, perform judicial acts in foreign ports. This warrants the inference that no such exercise of consular jurisdiction is legal unless authorized by treaty stipulations.

(*b.*) *The Judgments of International Courts, or Boards of Arbitration.*—These tribunals are created for the express purpose of adjusting international disputes and differences. Their judgments, therefore, should constitute precedents as binding upon sovereign states as are the decisions of municipal courts upon individuals who carry their difficulties to them for adjustment.

(*c.*) *The Diplomatic Correspondence of States, and other State Papers, upon Subjects Connected with Foreign Relations.*—This is a valuable source of information upon all questions connected with the law and usages of nations. The opinions of law officers and attorneys-general to their respective governments, the correspondence of a state with foreign powers, and the reports of commissions created for the purpose of obtaining and digesting information upon special subjects, are examples of this class. Unfortunately much correspondence between governments is still regarded as confidential, and so is not easily accessible. England and the United States, however, publish at intervals the greater part of their correspondence with foreign powers.

(*d.*) *The Roman Law.*—This is the earliest, as it is in many respects the most complete and elaborate code of law that has ever existed. Most of the codes of municipal law now in force among the Continental states of Europe are either directly based upon it, or derive from it the greater part of the legal principles which they contain. As it was the only system of law with which the earlier writers on International Law were familiar, and as its principles seemed to be sufficiently general, in character and scope, to apply to the reciprocal relations of states, its authority was frequently invoked by them in the preparation of their treatises.

The earliest form of the Roman Law, of which we have any authentic knowledge, is that contained in the Code of the Twelve Tables. Like all ancient legal systems, it was a development of the governmental experience of the Roman people, to whom its provisions exclusively applied. Such aliens and strangers as were resident in the city were, at first, without legal rights or privileges, and so long as Roman citizenship maintained its peculiar character of exclusiveness the sanctions and penalties of the Civil Law were held to be binding upon Roman citizens alone.

As the alien class increased in numbers, as well as in wealth and importance, it became necessary to give to its members a definite legal status, and to secure to them some measure of protection in their persons and property. "The expedient to which they resorted was that of selecting the rules of law common to Rome and to the different Italian commonwealths in which the immigrants were born. In other words, they set themselves to form a system answering to the primitive and literal meaning of *Jus Gentium*, that is, *law common to all nations*. The Jus Gentium was, in fact, the sum of the common ingredients in the customs of the old Italian tribes, for they were *all the nations* whom the Romans had any means of observing, and who sent successive swarms of immigrants to Roman soil. Whenever a particular usage was seen to be practised by a large number of separate races in common, it was set down as part of the *law common to all nations*, or Jus Gentium."[1]

"It is almost unnecessary to add that the confusion

---

[1] Maine, "Ancient Law," p. 47.

between *Jus Gentium*, or law *common* to all nations, and *International Law*, is entirely modern. The classical expression for *International Law* is *Jus Feciale*, or the law of negotiation and diplomacy."[1] "No passage," says Sir Henry Maine, in his "Ancient Law," "has ever been adduced from the remains of Roman Law which, in my judgment, proves the jurisconsults to have believed Natural Law to have obligatory force between independent commonwealths; and we cannot but see that to the citizens of the Roman Empire, who regarded their sovereign's dominions as conterminous with civilization, the equal subjection of states to the Law of Nature, if contemplated at all, must have seemed at most an extreme result of curious speculation. The early modern interpreters of the Jurisprudence of Rome, misconceiving the meaning of the *Jus Gentium*, assumed without hesitation that the Romans had bequeathed to them a system of rules for the adjustment of international transactions."[2] It is not necessary to suppose, however, that Grotius was mistaken, either in his view of the Roman Law, or in his application of its principles to states in their international relations. That system was the outgrowth of long experience, and its methods of dealing with the legal relations of individuals were elaborated with great care. From the standpoint of the Civil Law the Roman landowner was regarded as an independent proprietor within the boundaries of his landed estate. It provided elaborate and adequate remedies, which were applied whenever his personal or property rights were trespassed upon or invaded, and it regarded all

---

[1] Maine, "Ancient Law," p. 47. [2] *Ibid.* p. 50; Morey, p. 207.

citizens as equal before the law. Grotius, in his great work, but applied these principles to sovereign states. Each state, according to his view, was independent within its territorial limits, and all states were equal in dignity and in the number of sovereign rights which they enjoyed, however unequal they may have been in power and influence.

These principles lie at the foundation of modern International Law, and such of its doctrines as have received general sanction are based directly upon them. It was thus easy for Grotius and his successors to deduce from the Roman Law by far the greater part of the system of International Law as it exists to-day. In its fundamental principles it has changed but little since Grotius's day. In its detailed rules it is undergoing a slow but constant modification; the tendency being toward greater liberality of view in the treatment of new questions as they arise, and in the modification or amendment of old practices, to adapt them to the conditions imposed by modern civilization. Like Municipal Law, it keeps pace with the development of the human race; it is affected by that development, and, in turn, reacts upon it, influencing the current of human events to a remarkable degree.

(*e.*) *The Works of Text Writers.*—The writings of those who have made the history and development of international usages a subject of special study will always constitute our chief source of knowledge upon the subject. The earlier writers were roughly grouped into two schools. One, made up chiefly of Continental authors, whose works were largely based upon the Roman Law, and by whom great authority was attached to the views of text writers. The other, composed of

English and American writers, whose works, strongly influenced by the Common Law of England, attach the greatest weight to the decisions of competent courts and to the precedents established by the usages of nations and recognized by them as binding in their intercourse with each other. The present tendency is to obliterate this distinction. The history of both the Roman and Common Law has been exhaustively studied, and is now generally known, and the historical method of treatment is found to be as successful in its application to International as to Municipal Law.

A decided unanimity of opinion among authors as to the reason or justice of a particular usage is strong evidence of its general acceptance as a rule of International Law. "Writers on International Law, however, cannot make the law. To be binding, the law must have received the assent of the nations who are to be bound by it."[1]

The Decisions of Municipal Courts upon Questions of International Law.—Although the courts of a state have chiefly to do with the decision of questions arising under its own municipal law, they are sometimes called upon to recognize and apply the rules of International Law in the decision of particular cases. This is found to be necessary when the national character of an individual is drawn in question, or his capacity to perform certain acts; as to make contracts or to hold or transfer property. In the decision of what are called Prize cases, which is usually an incident of the jurisdiction of Admiralty Courts, the law administered is almost exclusively international. The decisions upon

---

[1] Justice Cockburn, in R. *vs.* Keyn; Stephens, "History of the Criminal Law," vol. ii., p. 41.

questions of International Law which have been rendered by Marshall and Story in the United States, and by Lord Stowell, Sir Robert Phillimore, and Dr. Lushington in England, are of the highest authority, and have been repeatedly cited as precedents in negotiation.

(*f.*) *The Municipal Law of States.*—Much information may be derived from this source upon questions having at once a municipal and an international phase. Such is the case with the subjects of citizenship and naturalization; of neutrality, extradition, and piracy. The army and navy regulations of different states, and the rules adopted by them for the guidance of their diplomatic and consular representatives, throw light upon many questions of international usage.

(*g.*) *General Histories, the Histories of Important Epochs, and the Biographies of Eminent Statesmen.*— From this source much information may be obtained as to the history of the wars, negotiations, and treaties which have exercised a great, and sometimes decisive, influence upon the mutual relations of states and upon the development of the science of International Law, and, finally,

(*h.*) *The Divine Law.*—The highest standard of ethics and morals, and the surest guide of conduct in the affairs of individuals and states.

15. *Divisions of International Law.*—The rules of International Law are susceptible of reference to one or both of two sources:

(*a.*) Those deduced from relations based upon ethical or moral principles. To this class belong good faith, humanity, and comity, the faithful observance of treaties and agreements.

(*b.*) Those deduced from usage or agreement, and so based upon the consent of nations.

Hence International Law is divided into:

(1.) *The Natural Law of Nations.*—As men living together in communities are guided in their actions and relations by well-known moral laws, so nations, which are but societies, or aggregates, of men, and the individuals who control and represent them, are guided in their actions by the same moral rules. From this body of ethical principles, governing alike individuals and nations, is deduced the *natural law of nations*.

The code of Christian ethics contained in the New Testament serves at once as a rule of conduct in international relations, and as a standard by which that conduct can be judged, and its inherent rightfulness or wrongfulness determined.

(2.) *The Positive Law of Nations.*—"As between nation and nation there are no laws properly so called, though there are certain established usages of which the evidence is to be found in the writings of persons who give the relations which have prevailed between nation and nation."[1] That body of usages which is deduced from the history of international relations is called the *Positive Law of Nations*. This branch of the subject is sometimes divided into—

(*a.*) The *Customary Law of Nations*, including those rules which are deduced from usage and precedent.

(*b.*) The *Conventional Law of Nations*, including those rules which are based upon, or deduced from, the con-

---

[1] Stephens, "History of the Criminal Law of England," vol. i., pp. 33, 34.

sent of states as expressed in the treaties and conventions entered into by them.

16. *Parties to International Law.*—The parties to International Law are sovereign states. In the fullest acceptation of the term it prevails only among the Christian states of Europe and those originally colonized by them in America and elsewhere. This is due to the fact that these states have had a common historical development, and recognize the same, or nearly the same, standards of law and morals. The area over which it operates, however, is slowly extending. Turkey became a party to it in 1856, and it is steadily gaining recognition in China, Japan, and other Asiatic states, though its acceptance in those countries can never be so complete as in the western nations of Europe and America.

References.—The history of the science of International Law has been made the subject of treatment by many writers, both English and Continental. The earliest English work upon this subject is that of Ward, whose "Enquiry into the Foundation and History of the Law of Nations in Europe" appeared in 1795. Wheaton's "History of the Law of Nations" is the fullest, and in many respects the most satisfactory, work of the kind in the English language. To a certain extent Ward and Wheaton supplement each other. The legal and historical works of Hallam, Freeman, Stephens, Amos, and Maine in English, and of Mommsen, Ranke, and Ihne in German, have contributed to throw much light upon the history of society and institutions, and it is impossible to understand the development of International Law without some knowledge of the historical development of the states and societies of whose relations with each other International Law is but the record. Most works upon the Law of Nations contain, in their introductory chapters, more or less full accounts of the history of the science. Among them may be mentioned those contained in Halleck, chaps. 1, 2; G. F. De Martens, §§ 1-15; Phillimore, Introduction and chaps. 3-9; Heffter, §§ 1-13; Hall, Introduction and p. 2, note; and Laurent, " Études sur l'Histoire de l'Humanité," liv. ii., chaps. 1-3; liv. iii., chaps. 1-4; liv. iv., chaps. 1, 2. The profound influence exerted by the Roman Law upon the development of the science is now fully appreciated. For a discussion of the question, see Maine, "Ancient Law," pp. 92-108; Amos, "Science of Law," pp. 332-341; Morey, " Outlines of Roman Law," pp. 207-214.

General Bibliography of the Subject of International Law.—For a full bibliography of the subject of International Law, see G. F. De Martens, "Précis du Droit de Gens," pp. 357-441; Klüber, "Droit de Gens," pp. 419-468. For a similar work in English, see Woolsey's "International Law," appendix I, pp. 413-429.

CHAPTER II.

STATES AND THEIR ESSENTIAL ATTRIBUTES.

1. *A state* is a society of persons having a permanent political organization, and exercising within a certain territory the usual functions of government.

The terms *state* and *nation* are by no means synonymous. The latter involves the idea of a community of race, the former is applied to a society of men organized under some form of government and occupying a fixed territory. A nation may furnish a contingent of population to several states. There is a Polish population in Austria, Russia, and Prussia; a German population in Prussia and Austria; on the other hand, the Russian and Ottoman empires include several distinct nationalities. As applied to societies of men, the term state represents an artificial, the term nation a natural, division. In recent times the tendency to reorganize states upon a national basis has been very marked. The movements within the present century which have resulted in quite a large measure of national unity in Germany and Italy are illustrations of this tendency.

2. *Sovereignty of a State.*—The *sovereignty of a state* is its inherent right to exercise jurisdiction over all questions arising within its territorial limits, and to control and regulate the actions and relations of all its citizens or subjects.

3. *Government of a State.*—The *government of a*

state is the organ through which its sovereign powers are exercised, and through which it maintains intercourse with other states. A constitutional government is one in which the powers of sovereignty are defined and limited in accordance with the principles of a fundamental law called a constitution. None of the modern Christian states that acknowledge the sanctions of International Law can be said to be absolutely without a constitution of some sort. There may be no substantial guarantees of individual right or of personal freedom; indeed, such rights may not exist, or may be restricted within very narrow limits. It may be a formal written instrument, as in the United States; it may be in great part unwritten, as is the case of the British constitution; or, as in many Continental states of Europe, it may be embodied in the municipal law, from which those principles which are of a fundamental character may be deduced and determined. In some form it must exist. Without such a body of fundamental principles no modern government could be carried on.

4. *Classification of Governments.*—Governments are classified according to the source of sovereign power, or the manner in which it is exercised in each.

A *monarchy* is a government in which the sovereign powers are concentrated in a single person. An absolute monarchy is one in which the concentration of sovereign powers is real. A limited monarchy is one in which the royal authority is restricted in its exercise, usually by representative institutions of some kind. These restrictions may be so extensive in character as to reduce the sovereign to the condition of an hereditary executive. This is the case in England.

An *Aristocracy* is a government in which the sovereign powers are held to reside in a class. If the ruling class constitutes a small proportion of the population the resulting government is called an oligarchy.

A *Democracy* is a government in which the sovereign powers are held to reside in all the people, and are exercised by them directly.

A *Republic*, or, as it is sometimes called, a *Democratic Republic*, is a government in which the sovereign power resides in the people, but is exercised by representatives elected by them for that purpose.

Classification of the Sovereign Powers.—The powers of sovereignty are susceptible of classification, and are usually arranged under three heads—executive, legislative, and judicial. The amount of influence and the degree of independence possessed by each department depends, in any particular case, upon the constitution of the state. It can only be said that the distribution of powers varies greatly in different states, no two exactly resembling each other in this respect.[1]

5. Governments are again classified, according to the opinion or belief of the person using the term, into governments *de facto* and *de jure*. A *de facto* government is one actually existing in a state, and for the time possessing sufficient strength to exercise sovereign powers. Thus the *de facto* government in France, in 1792, was that carried on by the National Convention. A *de jure* government is one which the person using

---

[1] The most successful modern experiments in government, however, have been those in which these departments exist, and are constituted in such a manner that each acts as a check upon the power and jurisdiction of the others.

the term believes to be the rightful government of the state. It may or may not be in enjoyment of the power of sovereignty. Thus, in 1792, Austria regarded the government of Louis XVI. as the *de jure* government of France. From the standpoint of International Law the term government is usually applied to the *de facto* government of a state, and such governments are generally recognized in fact, if not in name.

6. *The Essential Attributes of Sovereignty.*—The attributes which are essential to the conception of a sovereign state are three in number—*Sovereignty, Independence,* and *Equality.*

The term *Sovereignty* has already been defined. It is the inherent right of a state to exercise jurisdiction over all questions arising within its territorial limits, and to control and regulate the actions and relations of all its citizens or subjects.

The conception of *Independence* is included in that of sovereignty. It involves an immunity from all interference in the internal affairs of a state, and a corresponding obligation to abstain from interfering in the internal concerns of other sovereign states.

It has been seen that a state possesses a certain number of sovereign rights and powers. These rights are possessed in precisely the same number and to the same degree by every sovereign state. This is called the *Equality of States.* It is not to be inferred from this definition that all states are equal in dignity, importance, or power. It is only asserted that each state possesses the same number of sovereign rights and powers, and each to the same degree that they are possessed by every other state. For example: England

and Portugal have the same right to borrow money, to send ambassadors, and to make treaties of alliance. But whether one can borrow money at a lower rate of interest than the other, whether the ambassadors of both powers at Berlin have the same influence, and whether an alliance with one will be as advantageous as with the other, are questions that depend upon the financial resources, political influence, and military power of each state, which are all of them very unequal.

A *Sovereign State* is one which retains and exercises all of its essential attributes of sovereignty, which has parted with none of them, but retains them all unimpaired. Russia, France, England, China, and Japan are sovereign states.

A *Dependent, or Semi-sovereign State*, is one which has lost or surrendered some of its essential attributes of sovereignty, or which was not endowed with perfect sovereign rights when it was constituted a state. The Ionian Islands, placed by the Treaty of Paris under the protection of Great Britain, are cited by Klüber as a perfect example of a semi-sovereign state.[1]

7. A *Confederation* is an artificial state, resulting from the more or less complete union of two or more states. This involves the temporary or permanent surrender of some sovereign rights on the part of each of the confederated states to the artificial state created by the treaty of union, or constitution of the confederacy. The number and importance of the sovereign rights surrendered by the component states will determine the character and strength of the confederacy.

---

[1] Phillimore, vol. i., p. 100.

The United States, under the Articles of Confederation, the Holy Roman Empire, the Zollverein, and the German Confederation, as reorganized in 1815, are examples of loose confederations. The present German Empire is a stronger confederation. The Swiss Confederation, the union of England and Scotland, the United States under the present Constitution, are examples of close political union.

Rule for Determining the Strength of a Confederation or Union.—Between these extremes there may exist many kinds of confederacies. To determine the political strength of any particular confederation its constitution must be examined, and an accurate account taken of the powers surrendered and retained by each component state. If the power of making political treaties, of sending and receiving ambassadors, and of separate peace or war are vested in the central government, the confederacy is said to be close or strong. If a considerable number of these powers are retained by the component states the confederation is said to be loose or weak.

8. *Right of a State to Change its Constitution and Form of Government.*—As an incident of its sovereignty and independence, a state has a perfect right to make such changes in its constitution, government, and laws as it may deem expedient or desirable. These changes may be so radical in character as to effect a complete change in its form of government. The position of such a state in International Law is in no way affected by such changes, so long as they are strictly internal in character. The new government succeeds to the powers and privileges, and becomes responsible for the obligations, of the government which has been

displaced. None of these can be abrogated or in any way impaired. This follows from the principle that a state is a continuing body, capable of enjoying rights, of exercising sovereign powers, of incurring obligations and of performing duties. Of this body the government is the life, or moving force. A change of government, therefore, is but a change in the character of this moving force. It gives the state no new powers or rights, it absolves it from none of its duties or obligations. These ever remain unchanged.

9. *Acquisition of Sovereignty.*—Of the states now acknowledged as sovereign, in the civilized world, some were in existence when International Law began to assume importance as a separate science. Others have since been added to the family of states. A new state may come into being in one of two ways.

(*a*.) By separation from an existing state or states; and this may be brought about: (1) By peaceful methods, with the consent of the parent state, or with the mutual consent of the states from which the new state derives its territory and population; (2) By violent or hostile means, as by revolution or conquest.

(*b*.) By the combination of two or more states into a permanent union, the component states abandoning their identity completely, or surrendering permanently most of their sovereign powers.

10. A state may lose a part or the whole of its sovereign character. It may lose its identity completely, by absorption in another state; by peaceful methods of confederation or union, or by the hostile methods of conquest or subjugation. Sovereign rights and obligations, however, can never be destroyed. If they cease to be exercised by one state they pass with the popu-

lation and territory into the corporate existence of another, which assumes them, and, while enjoying the rights, must recognize and be bound by the obligations.

11. *Territory.*—It has already been seen that a state exercises its sovereign powers within a certain territory. From the definition of a sovereign state it is seen that the only possible line of demarcation that can exist between sovereign states is a territorial line. Where the sovereignty of one state begins that of another ends.

The territory of a state is that portion of the earth's surface over which a state exercises sovereign jurisdiction, and within which that jurisdiction is supreme. The boundaries of a state may be natural, consisting of mountains, rivers, or the coasts of oceans, seas, gulfs, or bays; or artificial, consisting of parallels of latitude or longitude, or lines described in treaties by their direction and length between terminal points. They are usually established by accurate surveys, and marked in position by permanent monuments.

Rivers as Boundaries.—When a river forms the boundary between two states the line of demarcation follows the mid-channel. If the channel changes, there is some difference of opinion as to whether the boundary changes with it, or remains in the ancient bed. In most cases that have arisen the rules of the Roman Law have prevailed in the settlement of the disputed question of boundary. Should the change be important the question would probably be adjusted by agreement among the interested states. Where rivers separate and traverse the territory of a number of states the question of boundary is necessarily affected by considerations of greater intricacy and difficulty having to do with their improvement and navigation.[1] In recent times the tendency has been to remove all restrictions upon the navigation of such rivers, and to throw them open to general commerce. These changes have been effected by treaties, to which the states interested in the navigation of particular rivers have been parties. In accordance with their stipulations uniform rates of toll have been established, unnecessary and burdensome charges have been abolished or modified, and the expenses of maintenance and improvement have been equitably assessed upon the riparian powers. To defray these expenses various expedients have been resorted to. In some of the earlier treaties the revenues derived from tolls were appropriated to the purpose. Later treaties provide for an apportionment of the expense of improvement among the riparian powers, and for the removal of *all* restrictions in the way of tolls and dues from the navigation of the river. In this way most of the navigable rivers of Europe, that are not entirely included within the territory of a single state, have been thrown open to general commercial use.

What Constitutes the Territory of a State.—All bodies of water, all inland seas, gulfs, lakes, and rivers lying entirely within the external boundaries of a state, are portions of its territory, and are subject to its jurisdiction. All littoral islands belong to the state to which they are adjacent. All gulfs and bays, river mouths

---

[1] In this respect an important difference was made in the Roman Law between rivers and the sea. The former were regarded as a portion of the *public* property of the state; the navigation of the latter was held to be the *common* right of all. Phillimore, vol. i., p. 189.

and estuaries included, or almost included, by the land, are also regarded as a part of the territory of a state. If the headlands be remote, the rule of possession is not yet fully determined, for the reason that no international understanding has as yet been reached as to the distance between headlands which shall determine ownership and jurisdiction in all cases. As claims are advanced to jurisdiction over particular bodies of water they are usually adjusted by the states locally interested, and their decision, if just and equitable, is acquiesced in by other nations.[1]

Jurisdiction over Closed Seas.—The question of jurisdiction over many such partly included bodies of water, sometimes called *closed seas*, has already been decided. The Chesapeake and Delaware bays are recognized as parts of the territory of the United States, Hudson's Bay and the Irish Sea as British territory; the Caspian Sea belongs to Russia, Lake Michigan to the United States. The Black Sea, before Russia obtained a foothold upon it, formed part of the territories of the Ottoman Porte; it is now subject to the joint jurisdiction of Turkey and Russia. The Baltic is acknowledged to have the character of a closed sea (and to be subject to the control of the powers surrounding it), certainly to the extent of guaranteeing it against acts of belligerency, when the powers within whose territory it lies are at peace.

Rights of Ownership and Jurisdiction in the Case of Straits.—The rights of possession and jurisdiction in the case of narrow straits and passes depend upon the ownership of the territory separated by them. The

---

[1] Halleck, vol. i., p. 140.

right of navigating them depends upon the character of the bodies of water which they connect. If the connected seas are open to general commercial navigation, the right extends to, and includes, the use of the strait as a necessary means of communication. This is sometimes called the right of innocent passage. The Strait of Gibraltar is free, because the Atlantic Ocean and Mediterranean Sea are open to the commerce of all nations. A similar rule applies to the Bosphorus, the Sea of Marmora, and the Dardanelles, connecting the Black and Mediterranean seas, subject to the restrictions upon the passage of war vessels which are contained in the treaties of 1856 and 1871.

The Danish Sound Dues.—The peculiar claim of Denmark to jurisdiction over the strait connecting the North and Baltic seas was long a fruitful source of complaint to all commercial nations. These claims were exercised in the form of a toll, or tax, called *Sound Dues,* levied upon all shipping which passed the strait in either direction. They were based, in part, upon immemorial prescription, and in part upon the expense incurred by Denmark in the maintenance of lights and buoys in the narrow and dangerous passage.

The question of the sound dues was settled in 1857 by a treaty entered into between Denmark and the great European powers. "The right of Denmark to levy these dues was not distinctly recognized, but compensation was made to her by the payment of a capital sum, on the ground of indemnity for maintaining lights and buoys, which Denmark stipulated to maintain, and levy no further duties."[1] As the treaty of 1857 dealt

---

[1] Phillimore, vol. i., p. 217.

with other questions, of strictly European concern, and to which the United States was unwilling to become a party, a separate treaty was entered into between that power and Denmark by which, in consideration of the payment of a lump sum, the shipping of the United States was to be exempted from similar levies in the future.[1]

If the territory separated by the waters of a narrow strait belongs to a single state, the right of jurisdiction over the separating strait is conceded to belong to the owner of the territory. The Strait of Messina, separating the island of Sicily from the Italian mainland, belongs to Italy, the Bosphorus and Dardanelles to Turkey, the Great and Little Belt and the Sound to Denmark. If the territory separated by the waters of the strait belongs to different states the strait belongs in part to each power. The line of territorial demarcation is determined as in the case of boundary rivers, and the jurisdiction of the adjacent states is separated in the same manner.

Ship Canals. — Artificial ways of communication, like ship canals, however important their construction may prove to be in its effects upon commerce, can acquire interest from the point of view of International Law only when they have been made the subject of treaty stipulation. No existing rules apply to them, or can be made to apply, by any process of construction. They are not arms of the sea, nor straits, nor rivers. Nor are they natural channels of trade or commerce over which all nations have the right of innocent passage. Their neutrality in war is the most se-

---

[1] "Treaties and Conventions of the United States," p. 213.

rious question that can arise with respect to them, and this can only be secured by a guarantee of the great powers, or by a sufficient number of them to secure the observance of such guarantee. The neutrality of the proposed Nicaragua Canal is guaranteed by Great Britain and the United States,[1] that of the Panama Canal by the latter power only.[2] The neutrality of the Suez Canal may be made the subject of a similar guarantee; at present, however, its neutrality is not secured—a situation which may lead to serious complications in the future.

Jurisdiction over a Portion of Coast Sea.—Although the strict territorial jurisdiction of a state ends at the low-water mark, where the high seas begin, its claim to exercise jurisdiction over a strip of sea three miles in width has long been generally recognized. Over this belt of coast sea, called the *Marine League*, a state is acknowledged to have complete jurisdiction as against other states. Whether its courts can assume jurisdiction over it or not, will depend upon its municipal laws. This peculiar jurisdiction is acknowledged to guarantee immunity from acts of belligerency between ships of nations other than that to which the coast sea belongs; to enable a state to carry into effect its maritime laws and customs regulations; to secure protection to the inhabitants of the coast—especially to those engaged in coast fisheries, and to provide for an adequate system of coast defence. As one of the chief reasons for recognizing jurisdiction over the three-mile limit has to do with questions of sea-coast defence, it

---

[1] "Treaties and Conventions of the United States," p. 378.
[2] *Ibid.*, p. 187.

seems proper that the width of this zone should increase, as the range of modern artillery increases.[1] A ship entering or passing through this strip of coast sea, in the prosecution of a voyage, is not regarded as having entered the territory of the adjacent state; nor is it subject to the rules of navigation which are sanctioned by that state, and enforced against its own shipping.

The municipal laws of many states also assume a limited jurisdiction over a wider zone of coast sea in defining offences against their revenue laws. This right has never been generally recognized, however, and is only assumed, or authorized,[2] for fiscal and defensive purposes.

Case of the Franconia.—Considerable light has been thrown upon the exact character and extent of the jurisdiction of a state over the sea included within the three-mile limit by the case of the Franconia.[3] The Franconia was a German steamer, commanded by Keyn, a foreigner, which, in the prosecution of a foreign voyage, passed within three miles of the English coast. While within the three-mile limit the Franconia collided with an English vessel and sunk her, causing the death of one of her passengers. Some time later Captain Keyn came within English jurisdiction, and was arrested and tried for manslaughter. He was convicted of that offence in the Central Criminal Court, but his case was carried up, on a question of jurisdiction, to the Court of Appeals.

---

[1] Ortolan, in his "Diplomatie de la Mer," liv. ii., chap. 8, and Halleck, chap. iv., § 13, advocate this view. For an opposite opinion, see Boyd's Wheaton, p. 239.

[2] Halleck, vol. i., pp. 137, 138.

[3] Regina *vs.* Keyn, 2 Exch. Div., pp. 202–205.

It was there held by a majority of the judges that, in so far as the court that had tried Keyn was concerned, the crime had been committed upon a foreign ship, on the high seas, and in the prosecution of a foreign voyage. The Central Criminal Court, therefore had no jurisdiction in the case. The view of the majority was, that in so far as other states were concerned, England had jurisdiction, for all purposes, over that portion of the high seas included within the three-mile limit; but, as the law of England stood at that time, jurisdiction over crimes committed within that limit had not been bestowed by Parliament upon any of the courts of the kingdom. Their criminal jurisdiction ended at the low-water mark, and crimes beyond that limit were therefore committed out of their jurisdiction.[1]

The High Seas.—This term is applied to the general ocean surface of the globe. It begins at the low-water mark, where, by legal presumption, the land is held to end. Upon the high seas all nations have equal rights. The privilege of sailing over them or of fishing in them belongs equally to all. No state can include them with-

---

[1] Soon after this decision was announced, Parliament, by the Territorial Waters Jurisdiction Act (40 and 41 Vic., chap. 73) assumed jurisdiction over the coast sea to the distance of a marine league, and bestowed it upon the Courts of Admiralty. This was done with a proviso that "no proceeding should be had in any case under the act unless with the consent of one of Her Majesty's secretaries of state, and on his certificate that the institution of the proceedings is, in his opinion, necessary." This reservation was doubtless intended to prevent a conflict between the executive and judicial departments of the government in the event of a case arising under the act of such a nature as to involve considerations of an international character.

in its territory, or extend its dominion over the whole or any part of the high seas.

The doctrine of the absolute freedom of the high seas is of relatively recent growth. In former times claims were made to exclusive jurisdiction over large portions of the sea, but none of them are now maintained.

Claims to Exclusive Dominion.—In the early part of the sixteenth century extravagant claims to dominion were advanced by Spain and Portugal, based upon their maritime discoveries. As these claims were of the most conflicting character, a controversy arose, which was submitted to Pope Alexander VI. for decision. He decreed that all those parts of the world which were not then in secure possession of any Christian prince should be divided between Spain and Portugal. A meridian line was established through a point one hundred leagues west of the Azores, as a boundary between the possessions of the two powers; all the territory to the west of the line was decreed to Spain, and all to the east of the same line to Portugal. Under this authority, which seems to have had international recognition, Portugal forbade all commerce with the East Indies and the west coast of Africa; Spain, claiming the Pacific Ocean and the Caribbean Sea as Spanish territory, forbade all commerce with Mexico, the west coast of North and South America, and the islands of the Pacific.

England at one time claimed that its jurisdiction over the narrow seas ended at the coasts of France and the Netherlands. This claim was resisted, especially by the Dutch, and so successfully that it was largely reduced in importance, and at the close of the seventeenth century finally abandoned. Russia, in 1822, laid claim to exclusive jurisdiction over that part of the Pacific Ocean lying north of the fifty-first degree of north latitude, on the ground that it possessed the shores of that sea, on both continents, beyond that limit, and so had the right to restrict commerce with the coast inhabitants. England and the United States entered vigorous protests against the right claimed by Russia, as contrary to the principles of International Law, and it was formally withdrawn in 1824.

12. *Rights of River Navigation.*—The liberal methods now so generally applied to the solution of questions having to do with the treatment of navigable rivers date from the Congress and Treaty of Vienna, in 1815. On the few previous occasions in which such questions had been made the subject of treaty stipulation the right of joint or public navigation, if recognized at all, had been hampered with needless and burdensome restrictions, originating in the mutual jealousy of the interested parties, and but little calculated to favor the development of interstate commerce. The Treaty of Vienna, however, inaugurated a marked change in this respect. The 16th *annexe* of that instrument contains a body of fundamental principles, in accordance with which detailed rules were to be prepared, by the states locally interested, for the regulation of navigation of six important European rivers—the Rhine, Main, Moselle, Neckar, Meuse, and Scheldt. The 109th article declares that these streams are thrown open to the commerce of all nations from the points where they become navigable to the sea. At different times between 1815 and 1856 arrangements, conceived in the same liberal spirit, were en-

tered into with reference to the Elbe, Vistula, Weser, and Po; and, in 1835, by a treaty between Spain and Portugal, the navigation of the Douro was declared common to the subjects of both powers.

Case of the Danube.—As Turkey was not a party to International Law at the time of the negotiation of the Treaty of Vienna, the provisions of that instrument were not extended to the Danube. The first attempt to regulate the navigation of that river is found in the Treaty of Bucharest, entered into between Turkey and Russia in 1812. By the fourth article of that treaty it was agreed that the boundary line between the two states should follow the left bank of the Danube from its junction with the Pruth to its mouth at Kilia, on the Black Sea; and the navigation of both rivers was declared to be free to the subjects of the signatory powers. The Danube enters the Black Sea through three principal channels. The most northern of these, which is known as the Kilian mouth, carries by far the greater part of its waters to the sea, and is the one best adapted to purposes of navigation. The central, or Sulina channel, discharges but a small part of the volume of the stream. The southern, or St. George's channel, carrying about one third of the volume of the river, reaches the sea, through several mouths, at a point about twenty English miles to the south of the Sulina channel. By the Treaty of Adrianople, in 1815, to which Turkey and Russia were the contracting parties, the Sulina mouth, which had been left in the possession of Turkey by the former treaty, was acquired by Russia, that power binding itself to maintain its channel at a sufficient depth to admit vessels at all times. This stipulation does not seem to have been rigidly observed by Russia, and its failure to maintain a navigable channel was made the subject of remonstrance, at different times, by several European powers. No change was made in the existing treaties, however, and the question remained in this condition until the close of the Crimean war.

By the Treaty of Paris, in 1856, to which instrument Turkey was a signatory party, the Danube was placed upon the same footing as the other great rivers of Europe. A commission was created for the purpose of erecting and maintaining such engineering works at the mouth of the river as were, or might become, necessary in the interest of navigation. The commission began its labors in 1857. The Sulina mouth was chosen as the one most susceptible of improvement, and suitable works were undertaken for its betterment. The funds for this purpose were supplied by Turkey during the years between 1857 and 1860; from 1860 onward they were obtained by a tax levied upon all vessels entering the river. The Treaty of March 13, 1871, extended the operations of the Danubian Commission for a further period of twelve years; and a new and significant step was taken by an agreement of the powers to a declaration guaranteeing the permanent neutrality of the works of improvement at the mouth of the river.

The cases of the Mississippi and St. Lawrence rivers, in the United States, gave rise to much controversial discussion.

Case of the Mississippi.—The Peace of Paris, in 1763, brought to a close the long series of wars for dominion between England and France, to which Spain had become a party, as an ally of France, in 1761.

By the Treaty of Paris the Mississippi River had been recognized as the boundary between the possessions of England and France in America, from its source to its junction with the Iberville, an eastern tributary, connecting it with the lake system of its lower basin. From that point the boundary line followed the course of the Iberville, through lakes Pontchartrain and Maurepas, to the Gulf of Mexico. The line of the Iberville separated Florida and Louisiana, which were ceded by the treaty, the former to England and the latter to Spain, and the right of navigating the Mississippi was secured to the subjects of Great Britain from its source to the sea.

The treaty of peace between England and the United States, which terminated the war of the Revolution, was signed on Sept. 3, 1783. On the same day a treaty was negotiated between England and Spain, by which the provinces of East and West Florida were retroceded to Spain. France ceded to Spain a portion of the province of Louisiana, thus giving to the latter power undisputed control over the lower waters of the river, from its mouth to its intersection by the thirty-first parallel of north latitude, the course of the river north of that point forming the boundary between the United States and the French possessions in North America. This state of affairs gave rise to a controversy between Spain and the United States, as to the right of citizens of the latter power to navigate that part of the river lying wholly within Spanish territory.

On the part of the United States it was claimed that the Treaty of 1763, between England and Spain, had given to the subjects of Great Britain the right to navigate the river from its source to the sea. This treaty had, in fact, created a territorial servitude, which had not been extinguished or repudiated by either of the treaties of 1763 or 1783. It was fair to presume, therefore, that it still existed, and that the subsequent transfer of territory on the east bank of the river had been made subject to the right of navigation which was then enjoyed by the inhabitants of its upper waters. A provision of the Roman Law was cited in behalf of the United States, by which all navigable rivers were held to be "so far public property that a free passage over them was open to everybody, and the use of their banks for the anchorage of vessels, lading and unlading cargo, and acts of the like kind, was regarded as incapable of restriction by any right of private domain."[1] It was also claimed, on the part of the United States, that the Mississippi River furnished the only practicable outlet to the sea for all the products of the upper valley. The claim, based upon this fact, was held by the American negotiators to be of sufficient importance to constitute a perfect right at International Law. These claims were rejected by Spain, whose right to control the navigation of the lower courses of the river was based upon the fact of its territorial jurisdiction. The position assumed by the United States was not regarded as a sound one in accordance with the provisions of International Law as then understood, and the controversy was brought to an end by the Treaty of Oct. 20, 1795, between the United States and Spain. By the terms of that treaty the navigation of the Mississippi was to be free to both

---

[1] Phillimore, vol. i., p. 189.

parties throughout its entire extent. The Americans were to enjoy a right of deposit at New Orleans for three years, at the end of which period either that privilege was to be continued, or an equivalent establishment was to be assigned them at some other convenient point on the banks of the Lower Mississippi.[1] The question of navigating this important stream was finally settled by the purchase of Louisiana, in 1803, and of Florida in 1819, which placed the river for its entire length within the territorial jurisdiction of the United States.

Case of the St. Lawrence.—The case of the St. Lawrence presents many considerations similar in character to those discussed in the case of the Mississippi. Its navigation was a matter of great importance to the United States for the reason that it furnished, at that time, the only outlet to the sea for commerce originating in the great lake system of North America. These lakes, with the exception of Lake Michigan, which lies wholly within the territory of the United States, lie upon, and form a part of, the boundary between the United States and the British possessions in North America. From the head of Lake Superior to the source of the St. Lawrence in Lake Ontario, and along the course of that river to its intersection by the northern boundary of the United States, the right of navigation was determined, beyond question, by the universally accepted rules of International Law, and belonged jointly to the two powers. The lower course of the river, from its intersection by the forty-fifth parallel of north latitude to its mouth in the Gulf of St.

---

[1] Hildreth, "History of the United States," vol. iv., p. 569.

4

Lawrence, lay entirely within the British territory. The question between the two governments, therefore, had exclusively to do with the right of navigation of the British, or lower, section of the river.

On the part of the United States it was contended, as in the case of the Mississippi, that, as the lower course of the river formed the only outlet for commerce arising in a large portion of the territory of the United States which lay upon the upper lakes, its navigation became a perfect right at International Law, and could be claimed, as a matter of necessity, by the state whose territory lay upon its upper waters. The right of navigating the Mississippi, stipulated for by England in a precisely similar case, was cited by the United States government in support of its view, as was the action of the Congress of Vienna, to which England had been a party, in throwing open a number of European rivers to general navigation in cases similar to those of the St. Lawrence and Mississippi. It was also contended, in behalf of the United States, that, on account of the character and importance of the bodies of water connected by it, the St. Lawrence should be regarded as a strait, rather than as a river, and that the question of its navigation should be determined, as in the case of straits, rather by the right to navigate the bodies of water connected by it than by the ownership of the banks along its lower course.

On the part of Great Britain the validity of the first of the positions assumed by the United States was denied, as not warranted by International Law. The contention was also made that, wherever such concessions had been granted, they had been based upon treaty stipulations. The liberal arrangements in regard to the joint or general right of river navigation made by the Congress of Vienna, and recognized in subsequent treaties, were based upon the *conventional* law of nations, and could be withdrawn or modified at any time. To the second claim, that the river should be regarded as a strait, it was replied that the application of such a rule must be general and international, and not local and particular. If it applied to the case of the St. Lawrence, it applied with equal force to the Hudson and Mississippi, and to the artificial channels in New York and Ohio which formed a part of the line of water communication between the great lakes and the sea. Unless, therefore, the United States was prepared to open these artificial channels to general navigation, the British government must decline to so regard that portion of the St. Lawrence which lay entirely within its territorial jurisdiction. The discussion, though ably conducted on both sides, led to no results of immediate or practical importance. The question of navigation was settled by the Reciprocity Treaty of 1854; by which, in consideration of certain concessions to British subjects in the matter of navigating Lake Michigan, the right of navigation of the St. Lawrence and the Canadian canals, forming a part of the system of communication between the great lakes and the sea, was conceded to citizens of the United States.[1]

In this connection it is well to observe that the con-

---

[1] Many of the navigable rivers of South America have been thrown open to general navigation (Phillimore, vol. i., p. 209; Lawrence's Wheaton, pp. 362–365). For a full discussion of the controversy between England and the United States on the subject of the St. Lawrence, see Phillimore, vol. i., pp. 204–209; Boyd's Wheaton, pp. 266–270; Lawrence's Wheaton, pp. 356–362; Halleck, vol. i., pp. 150–152.

cessions thus far obtained in the matter of throwing open rivers to general navigation, however liberal they may have been, are all of them based upon treaty stipulations. In none of these treaties is the question treated as one of amending or modifying the existing rules of International Law upon the subject of river navigation. Such boundary rivers, therefore, as have not thus far been made the subject of treaty stipulation, are subject, in all questions affecting their ownership and navigation, to the rules of International Law as they existed in 1815. No claim can be advanced to their navigation based upon the treaties above referred to, as none of them have changed or amended the existing rules of International Law.[1]

SERVITUDES.

13. *Origin and Application of the Term.*—The term *servitude* is borrowed from the Roman Law, and is applied in the international relations of states to express an obligation upon the part of one state to permit a thing to be done or a right to be enjoyed by another state within or upon its territory. The thing done, or the right enjoyed, however, must not be sufficient in amount or importance to constitute a restriction upon the sovereignty or independence of the servient or subordinate state.[2] The state enjoying the benefit or priv-

---

[1] "La Liberté de la Navigation Fluviale." E. Englehardt, "Revue de Droit International," tome xi. (1872), p. 363.

[2] Under the name of easements the principle of servitudes is recognized by the common law, with this difference, however, that whereas a servitude could have been imposed upon an individual or his property by the sovereign authority of the state, an easement must, according to the common law, originate in an agreement between the interested parties.

ilege of the servitude is called the *dominant state*. The state lying under the obligation involved is called the *servient state*. The existence of a servitude is not inconsistent with entire sovereignty and independence on the part of the servient state. The following examples are illustrations of servitudes: Suppose two states, A and B, to be separated by a river; A may lie under a servitude to B not to construct works of improvement upon the boundary river which shall injure the opposite bank. Suppose two states, C and D, to be situated, one above the other, upon the course of a navigable river, the mouth and lower waters being situated in the territory of C; C may lie under a servitude to D of allowing its citizens the privilege of navigating the river to the sea; D may lie under a servitude to C not to use the banks of the river within the territory of C for the purpose of loading and unloading cargoes.

How Created and Terminated.—Servitudes may exist by immemorial prescription, such existence being tacitly or expressly recognized by other states. Such, in great part, was the case of the Danish Sound Dues. They may also be created by treaty, and may be amended, increased, or modified in the same manner. They may be extinguished by treaty, by non-user, and in some cases by forcible denial of the obligation. They must consist in an obligation to allow a thing to be done, or a right to be exercised, or in refraining from doing a thing; they can never consist in an obligation to do a thing.[1] They are further classified into *positive* and *negative*. *Positive servitudes* consist in

---

[1] Phillimore, vol. i., p. 236; Morey, "Outlines of Roman Law," pp. 288-292.

allowing a thing to be done, or a right exercised upon the territory of the servient state. *Negative servitudes* consist in refraining from the exercise of rights by a servient state.

Examples of Servitudes.—The following examples of servitudes created by treaty are cited by Phillimore:[1]

(1.) In the Treaty of Utrecht, of 1713, between England and France, it was agreed on the part of France that the Stuart pretenders should not be permitted to reside in French territory.

(2.) In the Treaty of Utrecht, between Spain and England, the possession of Gibraltar by the latter power was confirmed by Spain on condition that Moors and Jews should not be permitted to reside there.

(3.) The Treaty of Paris, of 1814, provided that Antwerp was to be an exclusively commercial port.

(4.) By the Treaty of 1831 certain Belgian fortresses were to be demolished by Dec. 1, 1833.

THE RIGHT OF JURISDICTION.

14. *Right of Territorial Jurisdiction.*—From the definition of a sovereign state it follows that "the jurisdiction of a nation within its own territory is necessarily exclusive and absolute. It is susceptible of no limitation not imposed by itself. Any restriction upon it deriving validity from any external source would imply a diminution of its sovereignty to the extent of the restriction, and an investment of that sovereignty to the same extent in that power which could impose such restriction."[2]

Classification of Jurisdictional Powers.—This juris-

---
[1] Phillimore, vol. i., p. 236.
[2] Case of The Exchange, 7 Cranch, 116.

diction extends to all subjects and over all persons within its territorial limits, it matters not whether those persons be native born, or naturalized citizens, or aliens. It involves the right of maintaining any form of government, of administering that government in accordance with its own views and methods, and of changing it, whenever such a change seems necessary or desirable. It implies the right of classifying the sovereign powers, and of distributing them among several departments, or of concentrating all of them in the hands of a single ruler or sovereign. It involves an immunity from interference, from external sources, in the enjoyment and exercise of its sovereign powers, and a corresponding obligation to abstain from similar interference in the internal affairs of other states.

Right of Jurisdiction, in whom Vested.—The right of jurisdiction is inherent in the artificial body politic which we call the state. It is exercised, like other sovereign powers, through the government of the state, and the various rights of jurisdiction are usually classified and distributed among the different departments of government. The jurisdictional powers of a state are usually divided into:

(a.) *The Power to Make, Alter, and Repeal Laws.*— This is called the *legislative department.* In states which recognize the people as the ultimate source of sovereignty this department stands first in power and importance. It expresses, more directly than any other, the sovereign will upon any question coming within its jurisdiction. It determines the policy of the state upon all matters internal and external, and can change that policy at will. At the other extreme lie states in which the sovereign authority is held to reside in the person of a single ruler or sovereign. Here the legislative department does not exist, and the powers usually exercised by it are vested in the hands of the sovereign or executive.

(*b.*) *The Power to Enforce and Execute the Laws.*—This is called the *executive department*. In states which recognize the principle of popular sovereignty the executive himself represents the people in the exercise of that class of governmental powers which has to do with carrying the laws into effect. He is responsible to them for the manner in which he performs his duty, and either directly or through his subordinates represents them in all intercourse with foreign powers. In the exercise of the powers which are peculiar to his office he is independent of the other departments of the government. He also represents in the highest degree the dignity and majesty of the state; an insult to him is an insult to the state, and attacks directed against his person or authority are usually given the character of treason.

(*c.*) *The Power to Apply the Laws in the Decision of Cases Arising under them.*—This is called the *judicial power*. The jurisdiction of the courts of a state is further classified into *civil* and *criminal*. The former extends to the decision of all suits or controversies arising between individuals out of contracts, claims, and services, as well as from torts and injuries. The latter includes the power to try and punish all offences against the state or its sovereign representative, or against society or the individuals who compose it.

Exclusive Jurisdiction, where Exercised.—This right of jurisdiction is exclusive in all cases arising within the territorial limits of a state, or upon its public or private vessels on the high seas. It is of the most comprehensive character, and, within the territorial limits as above described, no offence can be committed, no act be done, no occasion arise for governmental interference of any kind that will not fall within the jurisdiction of some branch or department of the government of the state, or over which that jurisdiction will not be final and exclusive.

Extra-territorial Jurisdiction of a State.—Under certain circumstances a state may exercise jurisdiction over its subjects beyond its strict territorial limits. This extension of jurisdiction is sanctioned in the following cases:

(*a.*) Over the officers and crews of its ships of war, wherever they may be. They are a part of the public armed force of the state, and are governed by a special code of laws and regulations.

(*b.*) Over its merchant vessels on the high seas. The crews of these vessels are subject to the admiralty jurisdiction of the state whose register they carry. This extends to all cases of a civil or criminal character occurring on the high seas or beyond the jurisdiction of any civilized state. Merchant vessels on the high seas are, for purposes of jurisdiction, acknowledged to be a part of the territory of the state to which they belong, and under whose flag they sail. From this principle it follows that, in time of peace, these ships are exempt from visitation and search by foreign vessels of war,[1] except in strict accordance with treaty stipulations. They are subject to such visitation and examination at sea by public armed vessels of their own nation

---

[1] See case of the Laconia, "United States Foreign Relations," 1879, pp. 415, 432.

as is authorized by the municipal law of the state to which they belong. The right of search in time of war is a belligerent right, and will be discussed hereafter.

So soon, however, as a merchant ship enters a foreign port, it is subject in every respect to the municipal laws, and especially to the criminal jurisdiction of the country in which the port is situated. "For any unlawful acts done by her while thus lying in the port of a foreign state, and for all contracts entered into while there, by her master or owners, she is made answerable to the laws of the place. Nor, if her master or crew, while on board in such port, break the peace of the community by the commission of crimes, can exemption from the local laws be claimed for them. But the comity and practice of nations have established the rule of International Law that such vessel, so situated, is, for the general purpose of governing and regulating the rights, duties, and obligations of those on board, to be considered as a part of the territory of the nation to which she belongs. It therefore follows, that, with respect to facts happening on board which do not concern the tranquillity of the port, or persons foreign to the crew, or acts committed on board while such vessel was on the high seas, are not amenable to the territorial justice. All such matters are justiciable only by the courts of the country to which the vessel belongs."[1] The practice of France in this respect differs from that of most modern nations. She declines to allow her courts to take jurisdiction over crimes committed by one member of the crew upon an-

---

[1] Halleck, vol. i., pp. 190, 191; Massé, "Droit Commercial," tome ii., §§ 31–44.

other, on board a foreign merchant vessel in her harbors. If a French subject be the injured party, however, the French courts will take jurisdiction of the case.

(*c.*) Over its armies in the field, when beyond the limits of its territorial jurisdiction. The officers and enlisted men of the army, like the corresponding persons in the navy, are a part of the public armed force, and are governed at home and abroad by a special code of laws and regulations.

(*d.*) Over crimes committed by its subjects in territory occupied by savages, or unoccupied, and not claimed by any civilized power. If this jurisdiction were not assumed such crimes as kidnapping, engaging in the slave trade, etc., would go unpunished. For this reason most states, in their municipal laws, provide for their trial and punishment.

(*e.*) Over the crime of piracy, by whomsoever committed, on the high seas, or on land without the jurisdiction of any civilized state.

The Principle of Exterritoriality.

15. *Definition and Origin.*—In a limited number of cases states permit the jurisdiction of other states to be exercised within their territory. This is called the principle of *exterritoriality*. It is a fiction of law, invented to explain certain immunities and exemptions from the local law, which are recognized by all nations in their dealings with each other. It does not explain all of the circumstances that may arise in any of the cases to which it is applied, but it accounts for many, or most of them, more satisfactorily than does any other method of treatment that has been proposed.

From the definition of a sovereign state it is seen that such an exercise of jurisdiction can only be possible with the tacit or express consent of the state within whose territory it is exercised. It is therefore based upon comity, and is held to apply in the following cases:

(1.) *To Ships of War in Foreign Ports.*—It has been shown that the war vessels of a state, while on the high seas, are, like those of its merchant marine, subject only to the law of the state under whose flag they sail. By the general consent of nations this immunity from local jurisdiction is extended, in the case of public armed vessels, to cover the period of their sojourn in the ports or other territorial waters of a foreign state. There has been considerable discussion as to whether the exemption accorded to ships of war can be claimed, as a matter of strict right, or is based upon the comity of nations. The latter view is now generally accepted. The Board of Arbitration in the Geneva case ruled that "the privilege of exterritoriality accorded to vessels of war has been admitted into the Law of Nations; not as an absolute right, but solely as a proceeding founded on the principles of courtesy and mutual deference between different nations."[1] In this view Phillimore and Story agree.[2]

"If for reasons of state the ports of a nation generally, or any particular ports, be closed against vessels of war generally, or the vessels of war of any particular nation, notice is usually given of such determination. If there is no such prohibition the ports of a friendly nation are considered as open to

---

[1] "Decision Geneva Board," p. 184.
[2] The "Santissima Trinidad," 7 Wheaton, 283.

the public ships of war of all powers with whom it is at peace." [1]

War vessels are subject to the jurisdiction of the port in matters of quarantine, and are required to obey the local revenue laws and the port regulations on the subject of anchorage, lights, and harbor police.[2] They may be compelled, by force if need be, to observe such regulations as may be deemed necessary, by the state in whose ports they may be, for the maintenance of its neutrality.

The privilege of exterritoriality does not apply to members of the ship's company on shore. The local laws apply to them, under such circumstances, as fully and strictly as to any citizen of the state, or to any foreign sojourner. Crimes committed by officers of a public armed vessel or by members of its crew on shore, therefore, may not only be judicially noticed by the local tribunals, but may be made the subject of complaint in the diplomatic way.[3]

In this connection a question arises as to the duty of the captain of a public armed vessel in the matter of surrendering a criminal who has taken refuge on board his ship in a foreign port. The present rule is that, upon proper application by the local authority, it shall be the duty of the commanding officer to surrender such criminal. The privilege of exterritoriality rests upon comity, and a nation may, for good reason, de-

---

[1] Cranch's Reports, vol. vii., p. 141.
[2] Halleck, vol. i., pp. 188, 189.
[3] Bluntschli, "Le Droit International Codifié," liv. iv., § 321; Pinheiro Ferreira, "Cours de Droit Public," tit. ii. art. xviii., § 50; Hautefeuille, "Droit des Nations Neutres," tome ii., art. vi.; Halleck, vol. i., p. 190.

cline to extend it to foreign vessels of war visiting its harbors. If it may decline to extend it at all, it may grant it subject to restrictions imposed by itself, such restrictions being reasonable in character and generally known. "The essence of the privilege of ships of war in foreign territorial waters is, that the commanding officer is permitted to exercise freely, and without interference, on board his ship the authority which, by the law of his own country, he has over the ship's company. This permission is tacitly given by the very fact that the ship of war is allowed to enter foreign territorial waters. It implies an undertaking on the part of the local sovereign to abstain from all interference between the commanding officer and the ship's company brought by him into the territorial waters; for, if there were no such understanding, the privilege might be rendered illusory by the institution of inquiries, on the result of which the commanding officer's authority over the ship's company would depend."[1] Such being the origin and extent of the privilege, "no state can be supposed, by permitting a foreign ship of war to enter its harbors, to have consented that its own subjects should be able to free themselves from its own laws by going on board the ship. It may, perhaps, be inferred from such a permission, that the state which gave it meant, in certain cases, to rely for the due observance of its laws upon the assistance and good offices of the officers of the ship; but that is quite a different matter from giving up the laws themselves."[2] In the corresponding case of a criminal seeking asylum in the hotel of an ambassador, his surrender may be demanded, and

---

[1] Stephens, "History of the Criminal Law of England," vol. ii., p. 4b. [2] *Ibid.* p. 48.

if the demand be not complied with he may be extracted by force. It has never been claimed that the principle of exterritoriality applied with more or greater force to a ship of war than to the hotel of an ambassador. Indeed, the contrary is the case.¹ Should the surrender of a criminal be demanded and refused, the weight of opinion is that force may not be used to gain possession of the offender. Resort must be had to diplomatic means, to reprisals, or, in the last resort, to war.²

(2.) *To the Passage of Troops through the Territory of a Foreign State.*—This practice was much more frequent in former times than it is at present. The increasing strictness with which the rules of neutrality are now observed has rendered the practice obsolete in war, and the generally cherished desire to avoid international complications, by removing one of the most fruitful causes of international misunderstanding, has contributed powerfully to diminish its frequency in time of peace. Permission for such movements is now rarely accorded, save in very exceptional cases—as to an ally in war, or as an act of courtesy or humanity in time of peace. In the few instances in which it is permitted, the conditions of the movement are arranged, with great minuteness of detail, in a preliminary treaty.

---

¹ Kent holds that the writ of *habeas corpus* may be served on board a foreign vessel of war in the territorial waters of the United States. Abdy's Kent, p. 396. The Attorney-general of the United States held, in 1794, that civil and criminal processes could be served on board such ships. "Opinions Attorneys-general of the United States," vol. i., pp. 25, 27, 55, 56.

² Stephens, "History of the Criminal Law of England," vol. ii., pp. 48, 54–56.

The practice is disfavored, but not absolutely forbidden, by international law. The outbreak of war, therefore, or the existence of an emergency, may make it necessary to resort to it at any time. Should such a case occur, the principle of exterritoriality would apply to a movement of troops through foreign territory in the same way, and to the same extent, that it is applied in the admission of a ship-of-war to a foreign port. Its application would be attended with greater difficulty, however, arising in part out of the character of the act itself, and in part from the occurrence of circumstances, during the passage, which could not be provided for in advance. This would be especially true if the movement were effected by marching, and not by railway or steamer.

The moving force is governed, in transit, by the military laws and army regulations of its own government, with such additional restrictions as may be stipulated to be observed in the treaty or agreement authorizing the passage. Offences committed along the line of march are tried by courts-martial, or are punished summarily, when the offending and injured persons belong to the moving force. If the parties injured be citizens of the district traversed, the trial and punishment of the offenders would be arranged for by treaty. As such offences have a peculiarly aggravated character, they should be more severely dealt with than if committed at home. Questions of purchasing supplies in the country passed through are strictly regulated by treaty, as are similar questions arising as to the quartering of troops, the passage of ferries and bridges, and the use of wells or other sources of water supply. When such movements are made, as it is impossible to foresee and provide for all cases of injury and damage that may occur, it is proper to provide, in the preliminary treaty, for the indemnification of injured parties, by permitting their claims to be submitted in the diplomatic way, or by arranging for the organization of a commission having power to investigate such claims, and to determine the amount of damage sustained, with a view to its being liquidated by the government through whose agents it was inflicted.

(3.) *To the Person of a Sovereign, his Retinue and Attendants, while Passing through or Sojourning in Foreign Territory.*—There are numerous instances of such royal visits, and the practice of making them bids fair to continue in existence, if, indeed, it does not become more frequent than formerly. At the present time such visits are not attended by the political significance which formerly attached to them. They are either made with great formality—as when a visit of ceremony is made or returned, or a conference of sovereigns is arranged, with a view to an exchange of opinions upon some matter of serious international concern—or they may have an entirely private and informal character, the visiting sovereign waiving many of the honors and privileges to which he is entitled in his sovereign character.

If the consent of the sovereign whose territory is visited has been formally given, such consent is held to confer the privilege of exterritoriality. The visiting sovereign is permitted to exercise his functions as if he were still in his own dominions; and he may do any act which he is authorized to do by the laws of his own state, and which is not so repugnant to the law of the territory in which he is as to be forbidden to be exercised by its sovereign. Such acts, however, are presumed to have effect only within his own territory, and upon his own subjects. His control over his suite is not impaired, and their responsibility to him is in no way affected, by the fact of absence. Whatever articles of personal or movable property are carried with him enter the foreign state without inspection or payment of duty, and are exempt from taxation and imposts of all kinds during his sojourn there. In all other respects the privilege of exterritoriality applies to a sovereign, and to his retinue and train, in precisely the same manner, and to the same extent, that it does to an ambassador and his retinue.

Should a person of sovereign rank enter the territory of a foreign state without the permission of its sovereign or executive authority, he is conceded most of the immunities that are extended to him when such consent has been obtained. The circumstances under which such visits are made may be, and frequently are, so peculiar and exceptional as to make it impossible to lay down any definite rules on the subject. If the presence of such a person is dangerous to the safety of a state, or involves its neutral obligations in any way, or is offensive to, or threatens its relations with, friendly powers, asylum may be refused, and the visiting sovereign may be forbidden to exercise any of his functions, or to maintain a correspondence with persons in his own state, and he may even be compelled to quit the territory. If no such consequences ensue, or are likely to ensue, the visit differs in no important respect, in so far as the application of the principle of exterritoriality is concerned, from one made with the consent of the sovereign of the visited territory.

(4.) *To Ambassadors and Public Ministers.*—To the efficient and successful performance of an ambassador's duties, it is necessary that his person should be held inviolate, and that he should be entirely free from responsibility to the government to which he is accredited. Without such freedom of movement and action it would be impossible for him to adequately represent his own government, or effectively interfere in behalf of his fellow-subjects. This principle of inviolability and immunity has been recognized by all Christian states since permanent legations were first established in Europe, in the fourteenth century. It is now so universally conceded as not to admit of question or discussion.

"Whatever may be the principle upon which this immunity is established, whether we consider 'the ambassador' as in the place of the sovereign he represents, or, by a political fiction, suppose him to be extraterritorial, and therefore, in point of law, not within the jurisdiction of the sovereign at whose court he resides, still the immunity itself is granted by the governing power of the nation to which the minister is deputed. This fiction of exterritoriality could not be erected and supported against the will of the sovereign of the territory. He is supposed to assent to it."[1]

The subject will be more fully discussed in the chapter devoted to the privileges and immunities of ambassadors.

(5.) *To Consuls and to Foreign Residents in Certain Eastern Countries.*—From the beginning of intercourse with the Mohammedan nations inhabiting the south-

---

[1] Case of the Exchange, 7 Cranch, pp. 116, 138.

ern and eastern coasts of the Mediterranean Sea it has been found necessary, by reason of the radical difference between their legal and religious systems and those prevailing among the Christian nations of Europe, to withdraw from the operation of the local laws such subjects of the latter powers as were obliged, on account of their business or official character, to reside in the Levantine ports and commercial cities. These exemptions have been obtained in every case by treaty stipulations or concessions, and they are enlarged and modified, from time to time, in the same manner. When intercourse became general with China and Japan similar concessions were obtained in behalf of the subjects of the principal commercial nations of Europe and America. The subject will be treated at length under the head of *Consular Jurisdiction*.

References.—The theory of state sovereignty and jurisdiction is derived directly from the Roman Law. Upon the application of that theory to the mutual relations of states is based the claim of Grotius to the honor of being the founder of the modern science. The first edition of his work, "De Jure Belli et Pacis," was published in Paris in 1625. It has been translated into almost all of the modern languages of Europe. The last French edition appeared in 1864. An English translation appeared in 1738. The usual English edition, however, is that of Dr. Whewell, which was published in 1853. The classification of the powers of government is of quite recent origin, and can be studied to advantage in the constitutions of modern states. See Cooley's "Constitutional Law," Cooley's edition of "Story's Commentaries," and Holmes's edition of Kent for the United States. For England, see Stubbs's "Constitutional History," Bagehot's "English Constitution," and the works of Hallam, Amos, and Maine. The rules regarding territory and territorial jurisdiction are largely adopted from the Civil Law. The principle of servitudes is of similar origin, although in the doctrine of easements a modified form of the principle is known to the Common Law. For an account of the Law of Servitudes, see Morey, "Outlines of the Roman Law," pp. 289–292; Phillimore, vol. i., pp. 330–332. For the subject of the High Seas and the freedom of the sea, see Grotius, "Mare Liberum," written in reply to Selden's "Mare Clausum." See, also, Azuni, vol. i., chaps. i.–iii.; Phillimore, vol. i., pp. 209–224; Vattel, chap. xxiii., §§ 279–294; Heffter, pp. 146–148; Martens, G. F. De, § 43; and § 18 of Wheaton's "History of the Law of Nations." The fiction of exterritoriality is fully discussed in Halleck, chap. vii., §§ 24, 25; Boyd's Wheaton, pp. 139, 140; Heffter, pp. 86–90; Creasy, pp. 176–190, and p. 686.

CHAPTER III.

PERFECT AND IMPERFECT RIGHTS.

1. *Perfect Rights.*—The essential attributes of a state have been defined to be those of sovereignty, independence, and equality. Any state right fairly deducible from any one of these, or from all of them, is a perfect right. The denial of a perfect right, therefore, constitutes an invasion of the sovereignty of the offended state, justifying, if not atoned for, forcible measures of redress. If the sovereign rights of a state can be denied, trespassed upon, or invaded in one respect, they can in all respects, and its sovereignty and independence would be abridged, and finally lost, by such repeated invasions or denials. For these reasons the rule has received universal sanction that the perfect rights of a state can be drawn in question or denied only at the risk of war.

The perfect rights of a state are susceptible of classification under one of two heads.

First. The right of a state to a free and independent existence within its territorial limits.

Second. The right to be respected as a sovereign state in its intercourse with other states.[1]

Some of the more essential of the perfect rights and duties of states are:

(*a.*) *The Right of Self-preservation.*—This is called

---

[1] Heffter, pp. 47, 48.

into being whenever the corporate existence of a state is menaced. It corresponds to the individual right of self-defence. The danger may be internal, as in the case of insurrection or rebellion, or external, as in the case of invasion, either real or threatened. "The right of self-preservation is the first law of nations, as it is of individuals. A society which is not in condition to repel aggression from without is wanting in its principal duty to the members of which it is composed, and to the chief end of its institution. All means which do not affect the independence of other nations are lawful to this end. No nation has a right to prescribe to another what these means shall be, or to require any account of her conduct in this respect."[1]

In the exercise of this right a state organizes its land and naval forces in time of peace or war, maintains them at such strength as it may deem adequate to the national defence, and protects its coasts, harbors, and land frontiers by such works of defence as it may deem necessary to secure them from attack. The military establishment that is maintained by any particular state is determined by its institutions, its military policy, the character of its foreign relations, and, to some extent, by its financial resources. Any limitation upon such establishments must be strictly internal in character. External dictation in such matters is ordinarily not permissible. "Armaments suddenly increased to an extraordinary amount," however, "are calculated to alarm other nations, whose liberty they appear to menace. It has been usual, therefore, to require and receive amicable explanations of such warlike prepara-

---

[1] Phillimore, vol. i., p. 252.

tions; the answer will, of course, much depend upon the tone and spirit of the requisition."[1]

The assertion of the right of self-preservation on the part of a state involves the duty of recognizing the same right in other states. If a state resents invasion of its sovereign rights, it is bound to respect the territory and rights of other states. It cannot invade them itself, nor can it permit its subjects, or others within its jurisdiction, to use its territory as a base of hostile operations against a state with which it is at peace. Its power and responsibility are equal, and it cannot plead its weakness, or the insufficiency of its municipal laws, whenever such hostile attempts originate within its jurisdiction.

(*b.*) *The Duty of a State to Protect its Citizens or Subjects.*—It is a fundamental maxim of government that every citizen owes a duty of defence to his country in time of public danger. In return, the citizen is entitled to the protection of his government, in person or property, against insult and aggression of every sort. This protection surrounds him at home, and follows him wherever he may travel or reside.

Such injuries may be committed: 1. When a state, through its officers or duly authorized agents, acts directly against the subject of a foreign state, in violation of international law. 2. When a state acts indirectly, by failing to secure adequate remedies to strangers who have been injured by individuals within its jurisdiction.[2] In either case it is the right and duty of the offended state to protect its subjects in foreign parts by every means authorized by International Law.

---

[1] Phillimore, vol. i., p. 253.   [2] Heffter, p. 120.

It does not follow that every case of aggression of this kind must of necessity result in war. If an individual subject have a cause of complaint against a foreign state he makes proper representations to his own government. The case is investigated, and, if the complaint is found to be well grounded, redress is demanded in the diplomatic way. It is only when the cause of complaint is unusually serious, or when redress has been refused or needlessly delayed, that recourse is had to hostile methods in order to obtain justice.

Citizens of one country travelling or resident in another are not only subject to the local laws, they are bound to observe them in good faith and in every detail. They are not entitled to the protection of their own government when their conduct has been such as to amount to a violation of such local laws. "It is a perfectly well-understood principle of law that no citizen of a foreign nation—excepting, perhaps, in certain cases, a representative clothed with diplomatic privileges—is free from the obligation of conforming himself to the laws of the country in which he is residing."[1]

(c.) *The Right of Reputation.*—This right presents itself in two aspects. 1st. A state is entitled to respect as to its internal affairs. This includes the recognition of its government and institutions, of the methods and agencies by which that government is maintained and administered, and of the officers who compose it, each in his proper function, from highest to lowest. 2d. A state is entitled to respect as an independent body politic, and as a member of the great

---

[1] Mr. Adams's Statement in the Geneva Case. Creasy, p. 157.

family of states in which all nations have equal rights. From this point of view a state may be regarded as a moral being, capable of acquiring and enjoying a good reputation; entitled, by right, to immunity from insult or injury to such reputation, and liable to the obligation of respecting the reputation of other states. It is, therefore, its duty to resent insults offered to its moral dignity, to its flag, which is the visible symbol of its majesty and power, and to the ministers or public officials who represent it abroad.

(*d.*) *The Duty of Non-interference.* — As states are entitled to a complete immunity from interference in their internal concerns, a corresponding duty devolves upon them to refrain from interfering in the internal affairs of other states. This is called the *duty of non-interference*. No occasion less urgent than self-preservation, or the infringement of treaty stipulations, can justify such acts of interference.

(*e.*) *The Enforcement of Treaty Stipulations.*—Treaties are voluntary engagements entered into by sovereign states, by which mutual duties and obligations are created or defined. They convert *imperfect* into *perfect* rights, and so the violation of a treaty stipulation may afford just cause for war.

(*f.*) *The Right of Interference.*—In international affairs *non-interference* is the rule, *interference* the exception. This follows from the definition of state sovereignty and independence. The recognition of any other rule would strike at the very foundation of International Law, and would render the maintenance of general peace impossible. For this reason the right of interference is denied save in certain extremely exceptional cases, in which the circumstances must be of such a character as not only to justify that course, but to render the adoption of any other impossible.

The instances of such interference, in history, are but too frequent. In a vast majority of cases they have not been justified by existing facts, and have led to results in every way more deplorable than those which they were intended to prevent. "The list includes the invasion of Holland by the Prussians in 1787, to restore to his old prerogatives as stadtholder the Prince of Orange, who was brother-in-law to the Prussian king. It includes the infamous and pernicious attacks on Poland by Austria, Prussia, and Russia, the invasion of France in behalf of Louis XVI. by the Prussians and Austrians in 1791, and the interference of the Holy Alliance with the popularized governments of Spain, Naples, Sicily, and Piedmont, in 1820 and the three following years. The historical student of these transactions will be fully qualified to form a judgment as to whether such proceedings are calculated to promote or to impair the general benefit of the community of nations."[1]

If the right of interference exists, therefore, as a perfect right at International Law, it can be accepted and sanctioned only with important reservations, and can be exercised only in accordance with, and subject to, limitations of the severest character. It may be said to exist in the following cases:

(*a.*) *To Assist a State in Suppressing an Insurrection or Rebellion.*—International Law is essentially conservative in character. It recognizes an existing state of affairs, and opposes, and is slow to recognize, changes

---

[1] Creasy, p. 289.

effected by violent and revolutionary methods. Interference in favor of insurgents is never sanctioned, and when undertaken by a state is equivalent to a declaration of war against the state within whose territory the rebellion exists. Not only is armed interference in behalf of insurgents not justifiable, but the furnishing of any assistance, direct or indirect, or even a failure to strictly observe neutral obligations, is a just cause of offence. In cases of interference in behalf of a central government, the initiative cannot be taken by the interfering state. Assistance may only be furnished on the request of the belligerent government, and then only in accordance with the terms of the invitation.

(*b.*) *In Accordance with Treaty Stipulations.*—It will be seen that certain questions of strictly internal concern may properly be made the subject of treaty guarantee. Such are the maintenance of a particular government or constitution, the permanent neutrality of a state, or its existence within certain territorial limits. When the particular state of affairs which has been made the subject of guarantee is menaced with change, or when its existence is threatened in any way, by force applied from without, or originating within the guaranteed territory, it becomes the duty of the guarantor to interfere, and to carry into effect the stipulations of the treaty. Interference under such circumstances is both just and legal. It is limited in character and amount by the terms of the treaty which authorizes it, and it becomes unlawful, and must cease, when the cause of danger is removed and the internal affairs of the state have been restored to their normal condition.[1]

---

[1] The United States, in its treaty of 1846 with New Granada,

(c.) *In Self-defence.*—A state is not only independent within its own territory, but is entitled to an absolute immunity from external interference, and from acts of hostility or annoyance originating beyond its boundaries, but carried into effect within its territory. An insurrectionary movement within its jurisdiction may be largely supported and maintained by persons residing beyond its borders, and the offending state may be unable or unwilling to lend its aid toward their prevention. In such an event a state is authorized, in the exercise of the right of self-defence, to invade the territory of the offending state, and secure redress for the injury it has received. To justify such a course, however, the cause of offence must be clear, redress must have been demanded and plainly denied, and the wrong must be of such a character as to render necessary a resort to forcible measures of redress.

(d.) *Interference in Behalf of the Balance of Power.*— The term *Balance of Power* is applied to a rude equilibrium of political forces which was established at an early date among the different states of Europe, and the preservation of which is sanctioned by their general consent. It originated in an instinctive exercise of the right of self-defence, and its continued existence is rather a matter of policy and expediency than of strict right. It is justified, apart from the considera-

---

guaranteed the sovereignty of the latter state. In 1885 it was obliged to interfere to assist in the repression of disturbance. England and the United States, by the treaty of 1850, agree to interfere in certain cases in Nicaragua. The United States, by its treaty of 1867, with Nicaragua, is also obliged to interfere when the case exists which is contemplated by the sixteenth article of that instrument.

tions of self-preservation that are involved, by the fact that, at different times, it has powerfully contributed to preserve the general peace of Europe on numerous occasions when that peace has been threatened by the selfish schemes of ambitious states.

Its right to exist cannot be deduced from any principle of International Law, unless the state system of Europe be regarded as a kind of alliance or confederation, having for its purpose the maintenance of peace and the prevention of useless and unnecessary wars. It came into being, largely as a matter of necessity, so soon as the great states of Europe began to assume something of their present territorial form, and was developed out of repeated instances of the exercise of the right of self-preservation by those states as they found themselves obliged, from time to time, to impose checks upon the power of ambitious neighbors. The first wars waged in its behalf were those carried on by Francis I. of France, in the first half of the sixteenth century, to resist the dangerous and increasing power of the Emperor Charles V., whose control of the almost unlimited resources of Spain, Germany, and the Netherlands was a constant menace, not only to the peace of Europe, but to the sovereignty and independence of the other European states. From that epoch until 1815, a period of more than two hundred and fifty years, wars were of such frequent occurrence, and were so long continued, as to cause a state of permanent peace to be regarded as a very desirable, but extremely unlikely, contingency. Whether the greater number of these wars were due to attempts to overthrow or to defend the principle, and whether wars would have been more or less frequent had the principle never been asserted, need not be discussed here.

For the forty years succeeding the Congress of Vienna, in 1815, the peace of Europe was certainly due to a constant and successful observance of the principle—a result in every way memorable as the first instance in which peace had been maintained on the continent of Europe for so long a time since the beginning of modern history. It is as obvious, however, that most of the great wars that have occurred since the Peace of Paris, in 1856, have been due to the non-observance or abuse of the principle.

The maintenance of peace in Europe during the greater part of the first half of the present century was not obtained without corresponding sacrifices. The principle of the balance of power during this period was not simply recognized or passively acquiesced in as a desirable fact; on the contrary, it was vigorously asserted, and to a great extent maintained, by an alliance or concert of action on the part of the great powers. This organization was conservative in character, and seems to have originated in an agreement of the crowned heads at Paris, in September, 1815, which has become known in history as the Holy Alliance. The concert thus established was maintained and perpetuated by the various congresses which were held during the decade next ensuing. These alliances were intended not only to maintain the equilibrium as established at the Congress of Vienna, but to discountenance revolutionary movements, and, by a resort to measures of a repressive and reactionary character, to prevent the general adoption of even desirable constitutional reforms.

At present, owing to the great increase in military strength which has taken place in some of the more powerful states of Europe, and to a corresponding diminution in the importance of other states which were formerly powerful, the existence of the equilibrium is in constant danger, its permanent guarantee is impossible, and the balance is maintained from day to day with great and ever-increasing difficulty.

De Marten's Statement of the Principle of the Balance of Power.—"Every state has a natural right to augment its power, not only by the improvement of its internal constitution and the development of its resources, but also by external aggrandizement, provided that the means employed are lawful; that is, that they do not violate the rights of another. Nevertheless, it may so happen that the aggrandizement of a state already powerful, and the preponderance resulting from it, may, sooner or later, endanger the safety and liberty of the neighboring states. In such case there arises a collision of rights which authorizes the latter to oppose by alliances, and even by force of arms, so dangerous an aggrandizement, without the least regard to its lawfulness. This right is still more essential to states which form a general society than to such as are situated at a great distance from each other; and this is the reason why the powers of Europe make it an essential principle of their political system to watch over the balance of power in Europe. It is clear, also, that it is not always the extent of the acquisition that ought to determine the danger. Everything here depends on circumstances. The annihilation of a state, which at present serves as a counterpoise, may become as dangerous to the general safety of the neighboring states as the immediate aggrandizement of another state."[1]

The subjoined rules are based upon the exhaustive discussion of the subject by Vattel:

(1.) "The mere fact that a state has acquired, and is acquiring, power greatly preponderant over its neighbors, does not *of itself* justify other states in making war upon it for the purpose of reducing its power.

(2.) "Under such circumstances other states are justified in watching the preponderant state with cautious vigilance, and in forming leagues with each other for mutual defence from it.

(3.) "If the preponderant state commits acts of injury against its neighbors, or any of them, or, by the arrogance of its pretensions, the tone of its public despatches and manifestoes, or by any other course of conduct, beyond the mere increase of its strength, it clearly threatens to attack or oppress its neighbors, then other states are justified in combining together and in making war upon it, so as to prevent it from committing disturbance of the general security of the commonwealth of civilized nations, or of the security and independence of any of them."[2]

These are to be accepted, however, with certain limitations:

(1.) The internal development of the resources of a country has never been considered a pretext for such an intervention, nor has its acquisition of colonies or dependencies at a distance from Europe. It seems to be held, with respect to the latter, that distant colo-

---

[1] Creasy, "First Platform of International Law," pp. 279, 280, citing De Martens, §§ 122–124.
[2] Creasy, p. 285; Vattel, book iii., chap. iii., §§ 42–50.

nies and dependencies weaken, and always render more vulnerable, the metropolitan state.

(2.) Although the increase of the wealth and population of a country is the most effectual means by which its power can be augmented, such an augmentation is too gradual to excite alarm.

(3.) The injustice and mischief of admitting that nations have a right to use force for the express purpose of retarding the civilization and diminishing the prosperity of their inoffensive neighbors are too revolting to allow such a right to be inserted even in the lax code of International Law.

(4.) Finally, therefore, interferences to preserve the balance of power have been confined to attempts to prevent a sovereign already powerful from incorporating conquered provinces into his territory, or increasing his territory by marriage or inheritance, or exercising a dictatorial influence over the councils of an independent state.[1]

(*e.*) *Intervention in Behalf of an Oppressed Population and Against the Government of a State.*—From the definition of a state it is clear that any interference between a state and its subjects is opposed to the fundamental principle of International Law. It should be an event of the rarest occurrence, and would be justified only in cases of the greatest emergency. As a matter of fact, it has occurred but too frequently, and has rarely been justified by existing circumstances. A rule deduced from the experience of nations would, therefore, express the conditions under which the law

---

[1] Essay by N. W. Senior, on "Interference to Support the Balance of Power," in No. 77 of the *Edinburgh Review*, cited by Creasy, pp. 285, 286.

of nations had been disregarded, and set at defiance, or evaded, rather than obeyed. It is possible, however, for a case to exist in which a part of the people of a state may be so oppressed or persecuted as to warrant other states in interfering upon grounds of humanity. Such a case would be likely to occur when a part of the population of a state was of a different race or religion from the great majority of their fellow-subjects, the acts of oppression originating in race or religious prejudice. The mere fact that a people belonging to a particular race, or professing a particular religious belief, were placed at some disadvantage by the law or policy of a state, would constitute no valid ground for remonstrance, still less for interference. To justify acts of positive interference one or more of the following conditions must be fulfilled:

(1.) A remedy for the wrongs complained of must first be sought in the way of protest or remonstrance.

(2.) The oppression or persecution must be so serious in character and so great in amount as to incur the condemnation of the civilized world, and the act of interference must be participated in, or sanctioned by, all the states of Christendom.

(3.) The interference must be limited to the application of a remedy to the wrong complained of, and should cease so soon as substantial guarantees are furnished that the wrongful acts will not be repeated.[1]

2. *Duty of Mutual Respect.*—A state, in its capacity as a body corporate, has not only a right of reputation, but is entitled to certain external and visible tokens of respect in recognition of its dignity and im-

---

[1] Heffter, pp. 97–99.

portance as a member of the great commonwealth of nations. This consideration is also extended to those persons who represent a state in an official capacity. Within its territorial limits the honors to be paid to its officers are determined largely by custom and tradition; to a certain extent, also, they are recognized and sanctioned in its municipal laws. Without its territorial jurisdiction the question is regulated by the usage of nations, and certain honors which have been received and paid during long periods of time are, by such long-continued usage, recognized as obligatory at International Law. "These are matters of, perhaps, trivial importance in themselves, but their due observance facilitates the amicable intercourse of nations, and their neglect frequently leads to international differences, discussions, and enmities, which have sometimes terminated in long and bloody wars."[1]

The practice originated in the honors shown to sovereigns in early times, when they represented, to a greater degree than is now the case, the majesty and sovereignty of the states which they ruled by hereditary right, and whose territory they regarded as their own. This early view culminated toward the close of the seventeenth century, when Louis XIV. was at the height of his power, and before the principle of popular sovereignty had begun to make itself felt as a political force in state affairs. During this period there was no surer cause for war than a failure in respect toward a great sovereign or his representative, and not a few of the many wars waged were caused or prolonged by no better reasons than this. From that

---

[1] Halleck, vol. i., p. 107.

time onward the practice began to decline in importance, and merely regal honors began to be less strongly insisted upon. The power and dignity *of the state itself*, rather than that of its *ruler*, began to be regarded as the real object of honor and respect. Within the last century the general tendency of treaties and usage has been to diminish the number and variety of these ceremonial observances, and to simplify and regulate those which have been retained, or whose continued observance is deemed necessary or desirable.

At the present time all states are regarded as being equal in right and dignity, and the honors now observed are regarded as due:

(1.) To the state itself, in its sovereign capacity. These consist in certain honors paid to its flag, to its sovereign or chief executive, as the representative of its sovereignty, to its ships of war in foreign ports or on the high seas, and to organized detachments of its land forces when in foreign territory.

(2.) To those persons who represent it abroad in an official capacity. Under this head fall certain honors and marks of respect shown to its ambassadors and consuls in their different grades, and to persons in its civil or military service whose duties are performed in foreign territory, or who appear in such territory in an official character.

The observance of these forms is now held to be obligatory:

(1.) In the forms of mutual courtesy. This is shown chiefly in the recognition of an existing form of government, including its sovereign, or executive, and other administrative officials, whose functions are provided for by its constitution and laws. In former times none but monarchies were recognized as having the first rank, and an order of precedence was established among them, based largely upon the rank and titles of their respective sovereigns. Republics were, to some extent, disfavored, and in matters of honor and precedence were relegated to a place of secondary or minor importance. This is no longer the case, however, and all sovereign states are now placed upon a footing of perfect equality in all matters of ceremonial.

A state, as an incident of its sovereignty, may regulate the honors to be paid within its jurisdiction to its own flag and officials, and to those of foreign states. It may also prescribe the conduct of its representatives abroad, subject to the limitation that its instructions cannot be carried into effect if they are opposed to, or inconsistent with, the usages or policy of the state within whose jurisdiction it is attempted to exercise them. In accordance with this principle every state prescribes, in its laws or regulations, the forms of respect to be shown to its flag, or to the person in whom its sovereignty is vested, and no greater honors may be shown to a foreign sovereign than are thus prescribed to be paid to its own sovereign or chief executive.

(2.) In naval and military ceremonials observed on the high seas, or in the territorial waters of a state, between ships or fleets, between ships in port, and between ships and forts or fortified places.

(3.) In similar observances, on land, between armies, forts, military and naval officers, and in certain military honors shown sovereigns, or to the higher grades of civil officers in the administrative or diplomatic service of a state.

(4.) In the formality and ceremonial observed in diplomatic intercourse and interstate correspondence.

Maritime Ceremonial.—The subject of maritime ceremonial is regulated by usage, and, to a perceptibly increasing extent, at the present time, by treaty and agreement of the maritime powers. Ships of war visiting foreign ports have a peculiarly representative character. They are required to pay certain honors to the territorial sovereign and his representatives, and may expect in return that special respect shall be shown to the flag under which they sail, and to the state whose commission they bear.

The forms of maritime ceremonial consist in the firing of salutes, manning the yards, dressing the ship, and in hoisting the flag of the state or person saluted. It is also customary, in firing salutes in port, to furl the sails; and a similar practice prevails of hoisting a particular sail in saluting or returning the salutes of war ships or fleets at sea. The national flag of a public armed vessel, however, should never be lowered as a token of respect to any foreign state or individual. As an expression of grief it may be lowered to half-mast; it may be dipped in returning a similar salute rendered by a foreign vessel, but in every other case it should be carried in its proper situation during those hours of the day in which its display is required by regulations.

Ceremonial on the High Seas.—"When two ships of war meet upon the high seas, courtesy requires that the commanding officer lowest in rank shall salute first." "The same rule holds with respect to the flag-ships of squadrons; but a single ship, no matter what its rank, meeting a squadron, salutes first."¹ "These are returned gun for gun. Vessels carrying sovereigns, members of royal families, rulers of states, and ambassadors are to be saluted first."²

Merchant vessels of the same or different nations, meeting or passing upon the high seas, usually hoist their national colors, but otherwise do not, as a general rule, salute each other. It is customary, however, for them to ascertain, by hailing or the use of signals, the name, origin, destination, and cargo of passing vessels. This information is noted in the ship's log, and, as a matter of commercial news, is sometimes reported to the port of origin of the vessel hailed.

Ceremonial in Foreign Ports.—The first duty of a ship of war upon its arrival in a foreign port is to salute the flag of the state within whose jurisdiction it has come. If public vessels of other nations are in port, their flags are saluted in a similar manner. "This salute is a compliment to the flag, and consequently is considered international rather than personal. The same rule holds with respect to the interchange of compliments and visits with the authorities on shore; the compliment or visit being first made from the vessel, without regard to relative rank, even if it were possible to fix any relative rank for officers so different in their nature and character. The rule making such compliments international avoids any necessity of attempting such assimilation."³

---

¹ Halleck, vol. i., p. 114. ² *Ibid.*

³ This rule is a very general statement of the international obligation, and applies to ceremonial visits in which, from the nature of the case, it is impossible to establish a standard of relative rank by which to determine the official precedence of the persons by whom the visits are received and returned. Where such a scale of relative

"An apparent exception is made to this rule in the case of vessels carrying persons of sovereign rank, members of the royal family, or ambassadors representing sovereigns or sovereign states. In such cases the forts, batteries, and garrisons always salute first. But such salutes are intended for the persons carried, and not for the vessel carrying them, and, consequently, the vessel does not return the salute. It is customary, however, for such vessel, if foreign, to afterward salute the fort or garrison in the usual manner; which salute is, of course, to be returned gun for gun. Ambassadors visiting foreign ports, not the capital or seat of the court of a sovereign or a sovereign state, first receive the visits and compliments of the local authorities. This rule of courtesy results from their supposed representative character. Where vessels of war, in foreign ports, land or receive on board their own sovereigns, or officers of their own government, the salutes to be given and ceremonies to be observed are to be determined by their own laws and regulations. The same remark applies to the compliments to be paid on such occasions by other ships in port, and by the military establishments on shore, each being governed by their own laws and regulations."[1]

Maritime Honors to be Paid to Ambassadors and Consuls.—The duty of interstate respect having been performed, such salutes and formal visits as are provided for by the navy regulations of its own state are

---

rank has been agreed upon or is generally recognized, as is the case with the military or naval officers of different states, the present tendency is to require the first visit to be paid by the junior in grade.

[1] Halleck, vol. i., p. 115.

paid to its diplomatic and consular representatives who are resident or present in the visited port.

International Agreement as to Salutes.—A proposition originating with the British government has received such general approval and sanction from other maritime powers as to entitle it to acceptance as an international usage. In accordance with its terms the following classification is made of salutes:

"I. Salutes not to be returned:

"(1.) To royal personages, the chief of a state, and to members of royal families, whether on arrival at or departure from any port, or upon visiting a ship of war.

"(2.) To diplomatic, naval, military, or consular authorities, or to a governor, when visiting a ship of war.

"(3.) Salutes upon occasions of national festivals.

"II. Salutes which are not considered as personal, and should therefore be returned gun for gun.

"(1.) To the national flag on arriving at a port.

"(2.) To flag-officers when met with at sea or in port."[1]

Observance of National Anniversaries.— "Vessels of war in foreign ports celebrate their own *fêtes* according to the regulation of their own government. Courtesy also requires them to take part in the national *fêtes* of the place, by joining in public demonstrations of joy or grief. The same mark of respect is shown to vessels of a third power which celebrates *fêtes* in foreign ports. But if such celebrations are of a character to offend or wound the feelings of their own countrymen, or the nation in whose waters they are anchored—as public rejoicings for a victory gained

---

[1] Adopted by the United States August 18, 1875. "Foreign Relations of the United States," pt. ii., pp. 656, 657.

—ships of war will remain as silent spectators or leave the ports, according to the circumstances of the case. In public ceremonies upon land the commandants of vessels or fleets usually land with the officers of their staff, and receive a place of honor according to the hierarchy of rank, precedence being determined by grade, and, if equal, by date of arrival. In case of disputes as to rank, it is proper for the contestants to withdraw, and become mere spectators of the ceremonies."[1]

Visits of Ceremony.—When a public armed vessel arrives at a foreign port it is customary for the proper naval authority of the port to send an officer on board the arriving ship to tender the courtesies of the port to the commanding officer; the same usage is obligatory upon the commanders of fleets or vessels of other nations who happen to be in port at the time. These offers are at once acknowledged by the commanding officer of the arriving fleet or vessel. Within twenty-four hours after the arrival of the foreign vessel a formal visit is paid to the same persons by the commander of the arriving vessel, if of equal or junior grade, and these visits are returned within the same limits of time. In accordance with the present usage, however, if the commanding officer of the arriving vessel be the senior in grade the first visit will be paid by the inferior.[2]

Ceremonial on Land.—A similar ceremonial is observed on land, between armies, forts, and military or naval officers representing different states, who come into official or personal contact in the performance of

---

[1] Halleck, vol. i, pp. 116, 117.
[2] "British Navy Regulations," art 57, p. 15; "French Navy Regulations," art. 851, p. 243; Circular No. 3, "United States Navy Department," April 28, 1877.

their official duties. Suitable military honors are paid to foreign sovereigns and ambassadors, and to the higher grades of officials of the civil or military service of a foreign state.

The Formalities of Diplomatic Intercourse. — The privileges and immunities of public ministers, and the usages which are observed in diplomatic intercourse, will be discussed in the chapter on ambassadors and consuls.

3. *Imperfect Rights.* — There is another class of state rights or duties to which attention will now be drawn. It has been seen that a state, in its capacity as a body politic, possesses many of the attributes of a moral person. It may express sympathy, it may perform acts of charity, humanity, or courtesy, and may be held morally responsible for their non-performance. The performance of such acts is incumbent upon a state for the same reason and to the same extent that it is incumbent upon an individual. Its failure to perform them, like a similar failure on the part of an individual, violates no perfect right, and is therefore not punishable, or a proper subject for redress. As a nation is actuated to the performance of these duties by considerations of *courtesy* or *good-will*, and as a failure to observe them does not constitute a sufficient cause for war, they are called *imperfect rights;* or, since they are founded upon considerations of moral obligation, they are sometimes called *moral claims.*[1]

The following are some of the more important of these imperfect rights or duties:

---

[1] Dr. Woolsey was, I think, the first to use this term. It explains the obligation more fully than does the other, which is the more generally used.

(*a.*) *The Duty of Humanity.*—A state, in the performance of this duty, has chiefly to do with individuals who are obliged to seek shelter in its territory from acts of hostility or from the perils of the sea. The cases of the crews of wrecked vessels, or those of ships of war or merchant vessels seeking refuge from a superior force of the enemy, and of bodies of defenceless troops fleeing across a neutral frontier to escape capture, are illustrations of the performance of this duty.

The duty of humanity, however, is not of exclusive application to individuals. "If a nation is suffering under a famine, all others having a quantity of provisions are bound to relieve its distress, yet without thereby exposing themselves to want."[1] "The like assistance is due whatever be the calamity by which a nation is afflicted. Whole sections of countries are sometimes devastated by floods, and cities and towns destroyed by fires and earthquakes, leaving vast numbers of people destitute of the means of shelter and subsistence. It is, first, the duty of their own government to provide for these wants; but not infrequently the calamity is so great that the government is unable to give its aid to the extent and within the time required to render its aid efficacious. In such cases the laws of humanity would impose a duty on others. In many instances of this kind, however, the active charity of individuals and communities renders any action on the part of the governments of other states unnecessary. But a government may always stimulate and assist such charity, and by thus reflecting and giving effect

---

[1] Halleck, vol. i., p. 406.

to the general feelings of its people manifest its sympathy and generosity. Of such a character was the assistance rendered by the government of the United States in transporting to Ireland the contributions of provisions spontaneously offered by the American people."[1]

(*b.*) *The Duty of Comity.*—"There is a set of courteous and convenient observances, usually followed in the conduct of states toward each other, too definite, and often too minute and conventional, to make it proper to call them moral principles. The violation or neglect of these is not considered sufficient in itself to justify war, though one state is, by such violation or neglect, often placed in an attitude of avowed ill-will and suspicion toward another state. These observations of courtesy and convenience are said to depend on what jurists and statesmen style the *comity of nations.*"[2] The practice of extradition, the recognition of the principles of Private International Law, the privileges of exterritoriality extended to foreign sovereigns and ambassadors, to armies in transit, and to public armed vessels, are all based upon the comity of nations.

(*c.*) *The Duty of Intercourse.*—In the discussion of this duty it is necessary to regard it from two points of view, and to consider, 1st. The duty of a state to enter into relations of intercourse with other states, to send and receive ambassadors, to permit consuls to reside and to perform their duties in its commercial cities, to negotiate treaties, and to permit aliens to travel or reside in its territory. 2d. The duty of com-

---

[1] Halleck, vol. i., p. 407.   [2] Creasy, p. 36.

mercial intercourse, which consists in permitting foreigners to engage in commerce with its subjects, and to exchange its products for those of other nations.

In the former case a nation, by establishing a rule of strict non-intercourse, shuts itself out from being a party to International Law. It declines to be bound by its sanctions, and it cannot of right expect other states to observe them in such casual and irregular intercourse as they may have with it. Aliens who enter its territory do so at their peril; and, as its own citizens in foreign parts cannot look to their own government for protection, many of their wrongs must go unredressed. It is not necessary to discuss the subject further, for the reason that no state now assumes, or has ever assumed, such an attitude of complete isolation. It is only necessary to observe, in this connection, that, in proportion as a nation withdraws itself from intercourse with other states, or hampers its international relations with needless and burdensome restrictions, in the same proportion it withdraws itself from the benefits and privileges of International Law. If it ceases to sanction, or formally withdraws, privileges which have been granted to other states, or to aliens resident within its territory, or which they have enjoyed with its tacit consent, it is guilty of a violation of comity which will gain for it the ill-will of nations, and, if such a policy be persisted in, may in the end result in measures of retaliation.

In respect to the duty of commercial intercourse, it has been contended by some writers that the right to such intercourse is a perfect right, and that a refusal to enter into commercial relations is a just cause for war. Others claim that such intercourse is a perfect right only when an article of commerce is produced by one state which is absolutely necessary to the existence of another. Neither of these views is fairly deducible from the fundamental principles of International Law. In the first place, while many articles of trade are highly desirable, none have thus far been shown to be so absolutely necessary and indispensable as to justify a resort to forcible methods to obtain them. Such a view is not to be inferred from the theory of state sovereignty and independence, and a refusal to enter into such relations would certainly not justify acts of hostile interference. "Vattel lays down the general rule that every nation, in virtue of its natural liberty, has a right to trade with those which shall be willing to correspond with such intentions, and to molest it in the exercise of its right is an injury."[1] "The obligation of trading with a foreign state is imperfect in itself, and gives them only an imperfect right, so that, in cases where the commerce would be detrimental, it is entirely void."[2] "China and Japan for a long time declined all commercial intercourse with other nations, and even now permit only a very restricted trade, in particular articles and at particular places. The question was at one time discussed whether these people could not be compelled to open their ports to foreigners, and engage in trade and general intercourse with the rest of the world. But, as a question of international jurisprudence, it scarcely merits consideration. No doubt on this point could arise in the mind of any person except those who contend that the rules

---

[1] Halleck, vol. i., p. 402.
[2] *Ibid.*, p. 404; Vattel, "Droit de Gens," liv. ii., chap. ii., § 24-48.

of International Law adopted by Christian nations are wholly inapplicable to the countries of Asia. But this opinion, although at one time supported by writers of unquestionable ability, is now almost universally rejected by publicists."[1]

References. — For a discussion of the fundamental, or perfect, rights of states, the student is referred to the following authorities: Hall, "International Law," pp. 37-50; Creasy, "First Platform of International Law," chap. viii.; G. F. De Martens, "Précis du Droit des Gens," liv. iii., chaps. 1-3; liv. iv., chaps. 1-4; Halleck, vol. i., chaps. iv.-vii., and chap. xiii.; Vattel, chap. iii., §§ 35-48; Woolsey, §§ 36-52. For the rules and forms of international ceremonial, diplomatic, naval, and military, see Halleck, chap. v., §§ 15-29; Ortolan, "Diplomatie de la Mer;" G. F. De Martens, liv. v., §§ 175-184; Heffter, liv. iii., chaps. 1 and 2; Vattel, chap. iii., and the naval and military regulations of various states. The subject of "Imperfect Rights" is treated by Creasy, pp. 15-23; Phillimore, vol. i., pp. 181-183; Halleck, vol. i., chap. xiii., §§ 1-25; G. F. De Martens, liv. v., §§ 164-184; Vattel, bk. ii., chaps. i. and ii. Under the head of duties, or moral claims, this subject is quite fully treated by Dr. Woolsey, "International Law," §§ 22-25.

---

[1] Halleck, vol. i., p. 405.

CHAPTER IV.

NATIONAL CHARACTER.

1. *National Character of an Individual, how Determined?* — The national character of an individual is determined by his citizenship.

2. *Definition of the Term Citizen.* — A citizen or subject of a state is an individual member of the body politic, owing it allegiance and entitled to its protection in person and property. The terms citizen and subject, as used in International Law, have precisely the same meaning. They apply to all the inhabitants of a state, of both sexes, and of all ages and conditions. The term citizen is usually applied in states having republican forms of government; the term subject in those having monarchical institutions. It is not an essential condition of citizenship that an individual subject or citizen should have any share in the government of a state. His position at International Law is the same in either case. The right of suffrage is strictly municipal in character, and is a privilege granted, or withheld, by a state in accordance with its constitution and laws. In some states it does not exist, in others it is greatly restricted, in none does it extend to all who have the rights and privileges of citizenship.[1]

---

[1] In the United States it is possible, however, for an alien to acquire the right to vote, in many states, without becoming a citizen of the United States. But such persons would not be citizens of

3. *Classification of Citizens.* — *Citizens* or *subjects* may be either *native born* or *naturalized*. The first is a natural, the second an artificial, state of allegiance. A native-born citizen is one born within the territory of a state, and subject to its jurisdiction. This condition of allegiance is called the citizenship of birth, or nativity. It adheres through life, unless terminated by expatriation, or by process of law. When the nationality of an individual is drawn in question, his citizenship by birth is always presumed, and it is incumbent upon him to prove any subsequent change of allegiance. If, however, he has acquired another national character, by undergoing the process of naturalization elsewhere, with the consent of his native state as expressed in its laws and treaties, he is as fully a citizen of the latter state as if he were there native born, and is as fully entitled to its protection.[1]

---

the United States, and would not be entitled to its protection abroad. They are not citizens according to the rule of International Law.

[1] The term native-born citizen is extremely difficult of definition, for the reason that it is impossible to deduce a uniform rule upon the subject which is observed by all nations. Most modern states, however, follow one of two rules, and determine the nationality of a child, 1. By the nationality of its parents; 2. By the place of its birth. Until the close of the last century the former rule prevailed among most civilized states. Since the beginning of the present century, and by reason of the greater and more frequent movement of individuals from one state to another, and especially to newly-settled countries, the second rule has acquired great prevalence. England and the United States claim all persons born within their territory as native born citizens, whatever may have been the nationality of their parents. Denmark, Portugal, Holland, and Italy follow substantially the same rule, as, with some exceptions, do France, Belgium, Baden, Greece, and Spain. The other states of Europe regard a child as having the citizenship of its parents. The definition stated in the text applies more generally than any other.

A *naturalized citizen* is one who has relinquished his citizenship of nativity, and has acquired a new allegiance in a state other than that of his birth.

The citizenship of a dependent person is that of his principal or superior. Hence the citizenship of a child is that of his father, if legitimate, of his mother, if illegitimate; of a ward that of his guardian; of a wife that of her husband. Hence children born on the high seas, or while passing through foreign countries, have the legal nationality of their parents. Citizenship in a state may be renounced by an individual with a view to undergoing the process of naturalization elsewhere. It may also be terminated by process of law, as by sentence of death or exile, which in most states has the effect of destroying civil rights. It may be forfeited by emigration, or by long-continued absence. Once forfeited it may be resumed with the consent of the native state, by a compliance with the formalities of its municipal law.

4. *Naturalization* is that process of municipal law by which an individual effects a change in his national character.

Most states that recognize the sanctions of International Law claim and exercise the right of admitting foreigners to their allegiance, and of bestowing upon them the privileges and responsibilities of citizenship. Nearly all of them recognize the right, on the part of their subjects, of renouncing their native allegiance and of acquiring a new citizenship in a foreign state. The process of naturalization consists of two essential parts: 1st. A renunciation of the old allegiance. In some states this is expressly required, in others it is presumed by the act of naturalization.

From the nature of allegiance it is obvious that an individual can maintain the relation to but one state at a time. 2d. A formal assumption of the duties and obligations of citizenship in the new state. This is usually effected by an oath of allegiance. A period of residence is also required as a condition precedent to naturalization.

Conditions of Naturalization.—The following conditions of naturalization are now generally sanctioned by the usage of nations.

(*a.*) The result of the process of naturalization is to effect an entire change in the national character of an individual. He is as fully invested with the rights of citizenship in the new state as if he were there a native-born citizen, and is entitled to the same extra-territorial protection. Such protection can be extended to him in the state of his nativity only as the result of treaty stipulation.

(*b.*) A state, by exercising its right of naturalization in favor of an individual, cannot absolve him from any legal obligations due to his former sovereignty at the time of his emigration; and he is liable to be held to the performance of such obligations should he return at any time to the jurisdiction of his native state.

(*c.*) An individual, after having been naturalized in a state, may renounce such citizenship, and may renew his native allegiance, or may form a new tie of citizenship elsewhere. Should he return to his native state and settle there, with the intention of remaining, he is usually regarded as having forfeited his acquired allegiance, and his citizenship of nativity is resumed.

(*d.*) The municipal laws of every state enumerate and define the rights and privileges which may be acquired by its naturalized citizens. In no case do such persons acquire all the privileges of native-born citizens. The most usual restrictions apply to the holding of political and military office, the highest grades of which, in every state, can only be filled by native-born citizens. In the United States, whose policy of naturalization is extremely liberal, the offices of President and Vice-President can only be held by native-born citizens.

(e.) A naturalized citizen who returns to his native country and takes up his residence there with the intention of remaining, is presumed to have renounced his acquired citizenship. His adopted country, in such an event, is justified in declining to extend its protection to a person who has ceased to perform the duties of citizenship, and who declines to be bound by its obligations.

These rules are illustrated by several cases arising in the foreign relations of the United States.

(1.) *Heinrich's Case.*—This occurred in 1872. Heinrich was born in the city of New York, in 1850, of Austrian parents who were temporarily resident there. They were never naturalized in the United States, and so, in accordance with the naturalization treaty with Austria, were never citizens of the United States. In 1852 Heinrich returned with his parents to Austria, where for the next twenty years he remained, performing none of the duties of an American citizen, but, on the contrary, enjoying some of the rights and privileges of Austrian citizenship. In 1872 he was notified that he would be held to the performance of his military duties in Austria. To this he demurred, claiming the interposition of the American minister in his behalf, upon the ground that he was an American citizen. According to the several municipal laws of the interested states he was a native-born citizen—of the United States because born in its territory; of Austria because of his Austrian parentage. After some correspondence the United States government declined to interfere in his behalf on the ground that he had expatriated himself: 1st. By his long residence in Austria, by which he created the presumption that he intended to reside there permanently; 2d. By his having signified his willingness to become an Austrian subject, by obtaining passports and travelling under them in that character.

Case of Martin Koszta.—Koszta was a Hungarian, and so a native-born citizen of Austria. He was concerned in the revolutionary outbreak of 1848, and at the unsuccessful termination of that movement effected his escape to Turkey, where he was arrested and imprisoned, but finally released on condition that he should quit Turkish territory. He went to the United States, took up a residence there, and at the proper time made a declaration in due form of his intention to become an American citizen. In 1853, and so before the naturalization process had been completed in his case, he went to Smyrna on business, and was there granted a travelling pass by the United States consul. This paper conferred upon him, to a certain extent, the national character of an American, and stated that he was entitled to American protection. Not long after his arrival in Smyrna his presence was made known to the Austrian consul, and, on June 21, 1853, Koszta was seized by certain persons in the pay of the Austrian consulate, and taken out into the harbor in a boat. At some distance from the shore he was thrown into the water, and was picked up by boats from the Austrian man-of-war Hussar. He was taken on board that ship and was there confined with a view to his ultimate conveyance within Austrian jurisdiction.[1]

The United States consul at Smyrna protested against this arbitrary action, but without avail, and, as a last resort, reported the circumstance to the American Legation at Constantinople. The St. Louis, a public armed vessel of the United States, commanded by Captain Ingraham, happened to be lying in the harbor of Constantinople at the time, and Captain Ingraham was requested by the *Chargé d'Affaires* to proceed to Smyrna and demand Koszta's release, if necessary by a resort to force. In compliance with these instructions Captain Ingraham went to Smyrna and demanded the surrender of Koszta, stating that unless he were delivered up he should take him by force of arms. As such a conflict, aside from its international consequences, would have led to the certain destruction of much of the shipping in the harbor, and to the possible destruction of the town itself, the French consul offered his mediation, and Koszta was delivered into his custody pending the result of the negotiations in his case. As a result Koszta was conveyed back to the United States, the Austrian government reserving the right to proceed against him should he ever return to Turkish territory.

This case has been frequently cited as illustrating many phases of the question of citizenship and allegiance. The following are the more important considerations involved:

---

[1] "Foreign Relations of the United States," 1873, part 2, p. 1298.

(*a.*) The papers in Koszta's possession gave him the character of an American citizen in so far as the Turkish government was concerned, and entitled him to its protection. If he were not entitled to those papers, the question resulting was one for decision between Turkey and the United States.

(*b.*) The action of the Austrian consul was a gross violation of the sovereignty of Turkey, and a serious infraction of the rules of International Law.

(*c.*) The use of force by Captain Ingraham to secure the release of Koszta was also without warrant of International Law. It differed from that of the Austrian officials only in that its effects were to vindicate the sovereignty of Turkey. Upon this ground it was defended at the time, and generally justified.

(*d.*) Koszta was not an American citizen. His declaration of intention to become one, however, *to that extent* entitled him to a qualified amount of protection on the part of the United States; especially in a state where he had the character of an alien, pure and simple, and where the question of his partially acquired allegiance was not complicated by considerations arising out of his allegiance of nativity.

(*e.*) Had his case been drawn in question by any disinterested power, Koszta would have been regarded as an Austrian subject. This would have resulted from the application of the rule of nativity to his case.

(*f.*) If a formal decree or sentence of exile was had against Koszta in Austria, that power could have retained jurisdiction over him to the extent of giving perpetual effect to its decree of banishment, by preventing his return to Austrian territory.

Largomarsini's Case.—Largomarsini was born in

Italy, of Italian parents, and when two years of age was brought by them to the United States. Upon reaching the proper age, and having fulfilled the usual conditions of residence and intention, he was naturalized in San Francisco, a place which he had chosen as his durable abode. He resided there and elsewhere in California until 1875, when he visited Italy for a temporary purpose, and with the intention of returning to the United States and of resuming his residence there at the end of a year. A few days after his arrival in Italy he was notified that he had been drafted into the military service. Claiming to be a citizen of the United States, he refused to obey the summons, and upon this refusal he was arrested as a deserter from the Italian military service. His case was appealed to the highest military tribunal, where the charge of desertion was not sustained, but he was held to the performance of his military service. Intervention was made in his behalf by the United States minister, but without avail, the refusal to release him being based upon the ground that he was an Italian subject, and that his naturalization in the United States had no effect upon his individual status when he returned to Italy.

Case of Ungar.—Leopold Ungar was born in Bavaria, but emigrated to the United States, where he completed the naturalization process in 1856. In 1857 he obtained a passport from the Department of State and returned to Europe, passing and repassing several times between the two countries. The last *visé* of his passport bore the date of 1861. In 1873 he arrived in Egypt from Italy, under an assumed name, and was arrested at the instance of the Prussian consul in Alexdria, with a view to his extradition for a crime committed in Cologne. He claimed to be an American citizen, but protection was denied him. 1. Because he had expatriated himself; this was proven by long absence from the United States with no intention of returning. 2. Because he had voluntarily subjected himself to Prussian jurisdiction by committing a crime within Prussian territory. His flight to Egypt in no way affected the question of his national character, as he was subject to the extradition process in Egypt, on the demand of Prussia, in accordance with the terms of an existing treaty of extradition between the two countries.

It is thus seen that to make perfect and complete the change of national character, in the case of an individual, the existence of a treaty is necessary. Many such treaties have been negotiated in recent times.

The United States has thus far negotiated twelve naturalization treaties, the first of them with Prussia, in 1868. All of them, except that with Great Britain, stipulate for a five years' period of residence as a condition essential to naturalization. All except two[1] expressly provide that a naturalized citizen returning to his native country shall be held liable to trial for all actions punishable by the laws of his native state, committed prior to his emigration. Nine of them contain the provision that an individual returning to his native country shall, after a residence of two years, be presumed to have renounced his acquired citizenship. The naturalization treaties of the United States have thus far successfully endured the test of practical applica-

---

[1] Great Britain and Denmark.

tion. They have been administered in a liberal spirit, and but few cases have arisen under them for which they have not afforded an adequate remedy.

5. *Expatriation.*—The term *expatriation* is applied to the process by which the allegiance of an individual to a particular state is terminated. It may be voluntary, the act originating with the individual; or it may result from the operation of law; in the latter case it is called exile, or banishment. The act of voluntary expatriation is, in strictness, an essential incident of the naturalization process; for an individual rarely puts off his citizenship unless with the intention of changing his national character, and this change can only be effected by undergoing the process of naturalization.

The doctrine of indelible allegiance is now either tacitly or expressly abandoned by nearly all states that are parties to International Law, and there is very general agreement among them as to the following fundamental principles:

(*a.*) From birth, to the date of emigration, the jurisdiction of the country of nativity is complete. It may therefore determine the conditions to be fulfilled by its subjects before emigration, as an incident of its municipal jurisdiction.

(*b.*) The act of emigration cancels no obligation incurred prior to its date.

(*c.*) A citizen, or subject of a state, by undergoing the process of naturalization in a foreign state, is not released from any obligation to the state of his nativity incurred previous to his emigration.[1]

(*d.*) The acceptance by an individual of political or

---

[1] See case of Largomarsini, p. 106.

military office in the service of a foreign state, without the consent of his own government, is equivalent to expatriation. Whether this shall be permanent or not will depend on the municipal law of the individual's state.

While the restrictions which are placed upon emigration by the municipal laws of different states vary considerably, it is still possible to assign each of them to one of two groups. In most of the Continental states of Europe where a system of military conscription prevails, the act of emigration, without permission, involves a forfeiture of civil rights. "Each country hampers expatriation with such restrictions as it thinks fit, and this must probably continue to be the case so long as the present conscription laws are retained."[1] In England and the United States a more liberal policy prevails. In England the subject of expatriation is regulated by the Naturalization Act of 1870, which concedes the right of voluntary expatriation, and regards British subjects as expatriate so soon as they have completed the process of naturalization in a foreign state. In the United States a difference of view existed, for a long time, among the different departments of the Federal government. The view of the judiciary has been that citizenship was a compact between a state and each of its subjects, and that this compact could not be dissolved by the latter without the consent of the former, as expressed in its municipal laws. This view is in substance that maintained by the English courts on the same subject. The view of

---

[1] Opinion of Mr. Abbot to English Naturalization Commission, "United States Foreign Relations," 1873, p. 1248.

the political departments of the government has always been that the right of expatriation was an individual right, existing at all times, and capable of being exercised at will. This view they have constantly endeavored to incorporate into the conventional law of the United States. In 1868 an Act of Congress was passed declaring that "the right of expatriation is a natural and inherent right of all people, indispensable to the enjoyment of the rights of life, liberty, and the pursuit of happiness." This act, which is declaratory in character, has never received judicial interpretation.

6. *Aliens and Domicile.*—The peculiar view of allegiance which prevailed during the feudal period survived the downfall of the system in which it had originated, and, in the form of the doctrine of indelible allegiance, became part of the internal political policy of most European states. An individual, born a subject, always retained that character. Such personal and property rights as he was permitted to enjoy grew out of the fact of his allegiance to his native sovereign, and were not recognized beyond that sovereign's territories. The result was to make the lot of an alien a particularly hard one in early times. So soon as he passed the frontiers, and entered the territory of another state, he was regarded as being without rights. Such privileges of residence and occupation as he enjoyed were held upon sufferance only, and could be withdrawn or cancelled at the pleasure of the sovereign in whose territory he was resident. If he died in a foreign country his property, both real and personal, was forfeited to the sovereign in accordance with the *droit d'aubaine;* or, at a later period, when more humane usages had begun to prevail, was heavily taxed

when withdrawn from the territory, in accordance with the *droit de détraction*.

As civilization increased, and as commerce and interstate intercourse became general, these harsh provisions were gradually relaxed, though they did not finally disappear until the beginning of the present century. Other restrictions remained, however, notably a disability in the matter of holding land, and "it is only of late years that the right of holding lands on the same conditions as subjects has been conceded to foreigners by most countries."[1] In the matter of holding and

---

[1] Boyd's Wheaton, p. 112: "In Belgium this was effected by the law of the 27th of April, 1865.[a] Russia conceded the privilege in 1860.[b] Some of the Swiss cantons do not even now permit foreigners to hold real property without the express sanction of the cantonal government unless there be a treaty to that effect.[c] Austria,[d] the Netherlands,[e] and Sweden,[f] only accord the right on condition of reciprocity in the foreigner's country. The constitution of the German empire provides that every person belonging to one of the confederated states is to be treated in every other as a born native, and to be permitted to acquire real estate.[g] But, as regards other countries, the laws of Bavaria, Prussia, Saxony, and Würtemberg exact for their own subjects, when abroad, the same rights they extend to foreigners in their own dominions.[h] In Italy, Denmark, and Greece[i] aliens are under no disabilities in this respect. The ownership of land in the United States is regulated by the laws of the individual states of the Union. Some states impose no restrictions on foreigners; others require residence and an oath of allegiance; in others a declaration of an intention to become a naturalized citizen of the United States is necessary."[j]

---

[a] "Report of (English) Naturalization Commission, 1869," p. 115.
[b] *Ibid.*, p. 128. [c] *Ibid.*, p. 131. [d] "Civil Code of Austria," § 33.
[e] "Civil Code of the Netherlands," §§ 884-957. [f] "Swedish Statute of Inheritance," chap. xv., § 2. [g] Hertslet, "Map of Europe by Treaty," art. iii., vol. iii., p. 1931. [h] "Report of (English) Naturalization Commission, 1869," pp. 114, 124, 129, 138. [i] *Ibid.*, p. 116; Italian Civil Code," art. iii.; "Civil Code of Greece," art. v. [j] "Report of (English) Naturalization Commission, 1869," p. 131.

transferring personal property, the practice of nations has been much more liberal. This difference of view in regard to the two kinds of property was due in part to the fact that, in early times, only land and immovables were recognized as having the quality of property, and in part to the fact that personal property, especially in the form of money and valuables, could be easily concealed and withdrawn from the operation of the law. The result was that personal property began to be made the subject of legal regulation at a much later date, and when more enlightened views had begun to prevail upon the subject of ownership and property regulation.[1]

The term *alien* is applied to any person within the territory of a state, at any time, who is not a citizen or subject of that state, either by birth or naturalization. These foreigners or strangers are susceptible of classification into,

(*a.*) *Aliens*, or *Aliens Proper*, including all those persons who are sojourning temporarily within a state, or who are passing through its territory.

(*b.*) *Domiciled Strangers*, including all those persons who have acquired a legal domicile at some place within its territorial jurisdiction.

From the principle that all persons within the terri-

"Feudal principles were maintained so long in England that, until the year 1870, an alien was incapable of holding land for more than twenty-one years; that is, he could not purchase a freehold. This, however, was remedied by the Naturalization Act of 1870,[a] which relieved aliens of most of their disabilities, and, as regards land, placed them on the same footing as subjects."—Boyd's Wheaton, p. 113.

[1] Amos, "Science of Law," p. 164.

[a] 33 and 34 Victoria, chap. xiv., § 2.

tory of a state, at any time, are subject to, and are protected by, its municipal laws, it follows that aliens, so long as they obey those laws, will be as fully protected by them as are the citizens of the state in which they are resident. They are subject to some restrictions, however, from which citizens are exempt; and, on the other hand, are not held to the performance of certain duties to which citizens are liable from the fact of their allegiance. The most important of these is an exemption from personal imposts[1] and from obligatory military service—a duty, from its nature, incumbent upon citizens alone. "During the American civil war the protection of England was frequently demanded by British subjects against conscription in the United States army. Lord Lyons was instructed that there is no rule or principle of International Law which prohibits the government of any country from requiring aliens resident within its territories to serve in the *militia* or *police* of the country, or to contribute to the support of such establishments.[2] But Her Majesty's government would not consent to British subjects being compelled to serve in the armies of either party where, besides the ordinary incidents of battle, they would be exposed to be treated as rebels or traitors in a quarrel in which, as aliens, they had no concern, and on their return to England would incur the penalties imposed on British subjects for having taken part in the war.[3]

---

[1] The term *impost*, as here used, refers to impositions of personal service, as for jury duty, etc., and to impositions of money in the way of poll-taxes, or other levies upon citizens alone.

[2] Despatch to Lord Lyons, No. 76, April 4, 1861.

[3] *Ibid.*, No. 349, Oct. 7, 1861; "Parliamentary Papers, North America," 1864, No. 13, p. 34.

All who could prove their British nationality were, accordingly, exempted from military service.[1] But if a British subject had become naturalized in America, England refused to protect him so long as he remained there.[2] Individuals who had declared their intention of becoming naturalized, but had not completed the necessary formalities, were also treated as aliens, and exempted;[3] but Her Majesty's government declined to interfere in their behalf if they had voted at elections, or in any way exercised any of the exclusive privileges of a citizen.[4] In 1863 an Act of Congress was passed specially including 'intended' citizens in a further enrollment of the militia;[5] and a proclamation of the President allowed sixty-five days to such persons to leave the country, or become liable to be enrolled by remaining. To this Great Britain acquiesced, the period allowed for departure being deemed sufficient.[6] It was regarded as an established principle that a government might, by an *ex post facto* law, include in its conscription any persons permanently resident in its territory, provided it allowed them reasonable time and facilities for departure on the promulgation of such a law."[7][8]

In states where a military establishment is maintained by a system of voluntary enlistments, few re-

---

[1] Despatch to Lord Lyons, No. 379, July 29, 1861.
[2] *Ibid.*, No. 259, June 7, 1862.
[3] Mr. Seward to Mr. Stuart, Aug. 20, 1862.
[4] Consular Circular from Mr. Stuart, No. 99, July 25, 1862.
[5] "United States Statutes at Large," vol. xii., p. 731.
[6] Despatch to Lord Lyons, No. 485, Aug. 31, 1863.
[7] "Parliamentary Papers, North America," 1863, No. 13, p. 34; Despatch to Lord Lyons, No. 293, Nov. 27, 1862.
[8] Boyd's Wheaton, pp. 209, 210.

strictions are placed upon the admission of aliens to the military or naval service. By such an act, however, and during the period of such service, an alien forfeits the protection of his own government, and must look for protection to the state under whose flag he serves. In nearly all states aliens are debarred from holding public office of a political character, and are denied the right of suffrage, when that right exists. Some states still place them under special disabilities in the matter of holding land, or engaging in business, or following certain trades or professions; others make this conditional upon reciprocity.[1] In nearly all the Continental states of Europe aliens are placed at some disadvantage as regards subjects in instituting or maintaining suits at law, and in testifying in certain cases. They also require a register of aliens to be kept, and, in many instances, claim and exercise the right of expelling them from their territories for cause. Many of these restrictions are reasonable, and, if they are generally known, furnish no ground of complaint to other states whose citizens are subjected to them. In some cases, notably in certain Mohammedan and pagan countries, whose systems of government and law are radically different from those of Christendom, the separate treatment of aliens has been made the subject of treaty stipulation.

---

[1] In the courts of the United States alien friends are entitled to the same protection in their rights as citizens. Nor are their suits barred by proof that the remedy is not reciprocal. Tayler *vs.* Carpenter, Story, vol. iii., p. 458. Aliens in the United States are not liable to militia duty. For treatment of alien enemies by the United States, see §§ 4067–4070 of the "Revised Statutes of the United States."

Interference by a Government in Behalf of its Citizens Abroad.—If the government of a state has reason to believe that its citizens are being subjected to restrictions which are unjust, excessive, or unreasonable, it is usual to represent the case to the offending government in the diplomatic way, and to request their modification or removal. Should these means fail to secure the desired result, and should the restrictions be of such character as to amount to a denial of justice, a state would be justified in resorting to retaliatory measures, and could impose similar or equivalent restrictions upon the subjects of the offending state who might be found within its jurisdiction.

7. *Domicile.*—Of all the persons residing in a state at any given time two classes have elsewhere been described—aliens and citizens. Between these extremes is found a large class of persons who are not temporary sojourners, neither have they the quality of citizenship. Their residence is not transient, as is that of aliens proper, and they are not members of the body politic, owing it the allegiance of defence, and enjoying the rights and political privileges of citizens. These persons are called *domiciled strangers*. While their residence is to some extent permanent, they are unwilling, for reasons of their own, to give up their citizenship of nativity; and it is not inconsistent with their peculiar relation that they should cherish a remote intention of returning to their native countries should it ever become desirable to do so.

Definition of Domicile.—Domicile may, therefore, be defined as the place which an individual has freely chosen as the centre of his domestic and jural relations, and a *domiciled stranger* is an alien who, for purposes of residence or business, has selected a certain place as his durable abode, with no present intention of removing therefrom.

There has been some confusion expressed in the works of writers upon the subject as to the precise meaning of the terms *citizenship* and *domicile*. From the definition given it will be seen that they are not synonymous; indeed, in strictness, they have no possible connection with each other. The *citizen* is a creature of the municipal law of a state, with which other states ordinarily have no concern. The *rules of domicile* determine the status of an individual from the standpoint of International Law, and have no necessary connection with citizenship. *Domicile* is a fact, and, when the domicile of an individual is drawn in question, is proved, like other facts, by evidence as to residence or intention. *Citizenship* results from birth, or the operation of law, and is acquired by undergoing a legal process, the various steps of which are regulated by the municipal law of a state. It is, moreover, a matter of legal record, and, when the citizenship of an individual is questioned, it is established by the production of a duly authenticated certificate of origin, or naturalization.

In one state citizenship may be acquired with but little effort; in another with extreme difficulty, or not at all. This is a matter of strictly municipal concern, which every state regulates for itself as an incident of its sovereignty. A state may make such rules on the subjects of naturalization and expatriation as it deems just, or suited to its policy, the only limitation being that such laws must not project themselves into the jurisdiction of another state, and give rise there to a conflict of allegiance.

The rules of domicile, in so far as they are recognized and sanctioned by International Law, must, like all its rules, be based upon the general consent of nations. A state may, by its municipal laws, grant certain privileges to domiciled strangers, but those privileges are local in character, not international, and can have no effect beyond the territorial jurisdiction of the state granting them. In a similar way several states may arrange, by treaty, to secure for their subjects special privileges as to domicile in each other's territories, or may obtain for them special exemptions from the operation of certain municipal laws. These privileges and exemptions, however, are restricted in their operation to the territorial limits of the states that participate in the treaty. An individual may also have a domicile in several places at the same time; indeed, a strict application of the international rules of domicile may cause the prize courts of a state to regard a fellow-citizen as an alien enemy. The opposite rule prevails as to citizenship, and an individual, in his character as a citizen or subject, can owe allegiance to but one state at the same time.

Conditions of Domicile.—(*a.*) To constitute domicile there must be actual residence, with the intention of remaining. This intention is inferred from the acts of an individual. If he hires or purchases a place of residence, enters into business relations, makes contracts which will require considerable time for their execution, or does any acts of a similar character which are susceptible of being proved by evidence, a court will deduce from such acts that intention of remaining which constitutes domicile.

(*b.*) Domicile must be freely chosen. Constrained

residence does not give domicile. By constrained residence is meant any residence not the result of free choice on the part of an individual otherwise capable of free action. The residence of an officer in the military or naval service is of this character, as is that of ambassadors, their secretaries, and the *attachés* of a legation. The domicile of these persons is the same as their citizenship, native or acquired. They undergo no change of domicile, no matter how long they may be absent from home or resident abroad, provided such residence has an official character, and is in obedience to military orders, or is in the exercise of diplomatic functions. The domicile of a person undergoing a sentence of imprisonment, exile, or banishment, is not changed by such constrained absence, unless the exile or banishment be in the execution of a life-sentence. As consuls do not enjoy the privileges of exterritoriality, they become domiciled, for most purposes, at the place where they reside in a consular capacity. It is difficult, however, to state a rule of domicile which will be of general application as regards this class of public officers. They are subject to the law of the place where they reside, and the legality of their private acts is determined by the local law. If, in addition, they are subjects of the state in which they are resident consuls, they differ in no respect, as to citizenship or domicile, from other citizens. If, on the contrary, they are citizens of the state which they represent in the consular capacity, their residence is constrained, and their domicile is unchanged.[1]

---

[1] Halleck, vol. i., p. 368; Phillimore, vol. ii., pp. 310, 311; Case of The Indian Chief, Robinson, "Admiralty Reports," vol. iii., p. 26; The Josephine, Robinson, vol. iv., p. 26; The President, Robinson, vol. v., p. 277; The Falcon, Robinson, vol. vi., p. 197.

(*c.*) The domicile of an inferior or subordinate person is that of the legal superior. Hence the domicile of the wife is that of the husband; of a child, that of the father, if legitimate, or of the mother, if illegitimate; of a ward, that of the guardian; of a slave, that of the master. A change in the domicile of the superior produces a similar change in the domicile of the inferior or dependent person.

(*d.*) Domicile is always presumed.[1] When once the essential conditions of residence have been fulfilled by an individual, and when the facts of such residence have been established by competent testimony, a court is bound to draw the inference that the intention is to acquire domicile. This rule is of the first importance; indeed, no other rule upon this subject would be susceptible of legal enforcement. The validity of a person's acts must be determined by one of two systems of law—(1) that of his nationality, or (2) that of his domicile. There can be no middle ground; one or the other must be chosen; otherwise the greatest confusion would result. Such being the case, less hardship will ensue from the adoption of the rule that the law of a person's domicile, rather than that of his nationality, shall determine the validity of his acts; for it is easier, as it is certainly more just and convenient, that the local law should regulate his legal and business relations, than that they should be made to depend upon the law of a distant country. Indeed, the latter course would be obviously impossible.

(*e.*) As domicile may be freely chosen, so may it be relinquished or changed at the will of the individual.

---

[1] Halleck, vol. i., pp. 367, 368.

To effect such a change it is only necessary for him to fulfil, in another state, the legal conditions of domicile as to residence or intention. Domicile follows the changed conditions, and is established as a fact whenever its essential conditions are perfected or complied with in any place.

The rules of domicile are of importance because they largely determine the status of an individual at International Law. They are applied, by the courts of all civilized states, in the decision of cases arising in Private International Law; and they become specially important in time of war, since by them the character of an individual as an enemy or neutral is fixed and determined.

References.—The international view of citizenship has changed so radically in recent times as to render obsolete most of the literature, upon the subject of national character, which antedates the present century. For an account of the origin and development of the principle of popular sovereignty, to which the changed view of allegiance is largely due, see Maine, "Popular Institutions;" Cooley, "Constitutional Law," pp. 25, 26; Amos, "Science of Law," pp. 13-27. For the old view of allegiance, see Grotius, bk. i., chap. i., par. v., note, 28–32; chap. iii., par. ix.; bk. ii., chap. iii., par. viii.; and Vattel, chaps. v. and viii. For the modern view, see Halleck, vol. ii., chap. xii.; Heffter, chap. i., § ii. Considerable interest in the subject of allegiance and national character was manifested by many nations between the years 1860 and 1880. During this period a number of naturalization treaties were negotiated. For information upon the subject of Naturalization, Expatriation, and Domicile, the student is referred to existing naturalization treaties, to reports of commissions upon those subjects, and to the new works, or new editions of old works, which have appeared since 1870. In this connection see Hall, appendix iv., pp. 677–685; Halleck, vol. i., chap. xii.; Heffter, chap. i., § ii. See, also, the "Report of the English Naturalization Commission of 1868" ("Diplomatic Correspondence of the United States, 1873," part ii., pp. 1232–1424), and the naturalization treaties of the United States; "Treaties and Conventions of the United States, 1776–1870." The rules of domicile are very fully discussed in Wharton and Story; Halleck, vol. i., chap. xii.; Heffter, chap. i., § iii.; Phillimore, vol. iii., chaps. iii.–xxviii.; Hall, pp. 202 and 428 *et seq.*; Boyd's Wheaton, pp. 115–393; Bar, "International Law," pp. 84–109, 149, 150, 186–188, 322–326, 365–380, 653–672.

CHAPTER V.

EXTRADITION.

1. *The Right of Criminal Jurisdiction.*—The right of a state to try and punish crimes committed within its territorial limits is indisputable. It is an essential incident of its sovereignty. It matters not by whom such crimes are committed, for all persons, whether aliens, citizens, or domiciled strangers, are alike subject to the law of the state in which they may be at any time. They are presumed to know those laws, and a plea of ignorance as to the law will not shield them from the consequences of disobedience. Nor can an individual claim the protection of his own government in any course of action which is opposed to the law of the state in which he is sojourning. He can demand such protection, as a matter of strict right, only when his behavior has been correct, and his conduct in all respects legal.

Duty of a State as to Crimes Committed Abroad.—The duty of a state to assist other states in the execution of their criminal laws is less generally conceded. Some writers have maintained that it is incumbent upon every state to refuse asylum to, and upon proper application to deliver up, all persons charged with crimes of excessive atrocity, or which affect the peace and security of society. Chancellor Kent advocates this view, and after citing authorities in its support, gives it as his opinion that it is based upon the plainest principles of justice.¹ The contrary view, that extradition is a matter of comity, or treaty stipulation, has been as ably maintained, and is now more generally accepted by text writers of authority,² and sanctioned by the usage of nations.

Extradition by Comity and Treaty.—The practice of refusing asylum to foreign criminals, and of surrendering them through comity, prevails to a considerable extent on the continent of Europe. In England and the United States the almost invariable practice has been to surrender criminals only in accordance with treaty stipulations. While no positive rule can be laid down upon this subject, it may, perhaps, be said that extradition by comity is more common among states having strongly centralized governments, than in those in which representative institutions are so firmly established as to constitute an efficient check upon the executive branch of the government, and where restrictions upon personal liberty are not readily tolerated.

Difference of View as to Criminal Jurisdiction.— The views as to criminal jurisdiction which prevail in different states vary considerably, and depend, in any particular state, partly upon its constitution and partly upon the source from which it derives its system of law. In England and the United States, where the Common Law prevails, criminal jurisdiction is regarded as strictly territorial. Crimes are tried and punished at the place of their commission, and criminal courts have no jurisdiction over offences committed beyond, or outside of, certain territorial limits, which are ex-

---

¹ Kent, vol. i., p. 37.
² Hall, pp. 48, 49; Bar, p. 17, and pp. 623–625, 685–686, 708–737.

actly defined in the laws which create them. These states, therefore, are willing to surrender criminals who have taken refuge within their borders, even when they are subjects of the surrendering state. They object to such surrender only when the offence is of a political character, when the definitions of crime in the demanding state are much stricter than their own, or when the forms of trial are such as to be regarded as unjust, or unfair, when judged by their own standards of criminal procedure. Among the Continental states of Europe, and in those of Central and South America, whose criminal codes are largely based upon the Roman Law, a different view of jurisdiction prevails. The law of the state is presumed to follow a subject wherever he may go, and to control and regulate his actions and conduct to the same extent abroad as at home. Their criminal courts, therefore, have power to try the *case* if the *person* of the offender is subject to their jurisdiction, and so can punish a subject after his return home, for a crime committed abroad. These states, therefore, while they will surrender *foreign* criminals who have escaped to their territory, hesitate, and often decline, to surrender *their own subjects* for crimes committed abroad.

As a result of increased international intercourse, and with the rapid extension of commerce which has taken place in recent times, each group of nations has found it necessary to modify, to some extent, its peculiar view of criminal jurisdiction. All modern nations punish the crime of piracy, wherever committed; and most of them punish their own subjects for engaging in the slave trade. England and the United States punish many crimes committed by their subjects beyond their territorial jurisdiction, especially on the high seas. On the other hand, many Continental states find it no longer necessary to assert so extensive a jurisdiction, in criminal matters, as is warranted by their legal systems. Jurisdiction over many offences of small importance, amounting to misdemeanors at common law, is now generally abandoned by them, and crimes of a more serious character are triable only on complaint of the injured party, when both have come within their territorial jurisdiction. Most states, however, punish crimes against the state, such as treason, counterfeiting, etc., wherever committed, when the person of the criminal is found within their jurisdiction.

2. *Definition.*—The term *extradition* is applied to that legal process by which one sovereign state surrenders to another state, for trial, the person of a criminal who has sought refuge within its territory.

Methods of Extradition.—Extradition may be effected in three ways: 1st. By treaty; 2d. In accordance with the authority of municipal law; 3d. By comity.

Few extradition treaties were in existence at the beginning of this century, and most of those now in force have been negotiated within the last thirty years. Their number is steadily increasing, and the present tendency is to regulate the surrendry of criminals exclusively in accordance with their stipulations. These treaties are usually construed with great strictness; the list of criminal offences contained in the body of the treaty is rigidly adhered to, and requests for extradition of persons charged with crimes not mentioned in such lists are almost invariably refused.

Extraditable Offences.—The crimes for which extradition may be requested are those as to which there is a concurrence of opinion among all civilized states as to definition and punishment, and also as to the amount of evidence necessary to secure a conviction. Wherever that course seems necessary they are accurately defined in treaties. Those common to most extradition treaties are, arson, assaults of an aggravated character, burglary, counterfeiting, embezzlement—(a) of public funds by a public officer, (b) by any persons, hired or salaried, and to the detriment of their employers—forgery, murder, piracy, rape, and robbery.

Request for Extradition, by whom Made.—In general the request for extradition, and the consequent surrender, are acts of high sovereign authority, and are made in the formal diplomatic way. In the extradition treaty between the United States and Mexico, however, requests for extradition may be made by the governors, or other civil authorities, of the frontier states, or, in case the civil authority is suspended, then through the chief military officer in command of such state or territory.

3. *Conditions of Extradition.*—The following provisions are included in most treaties and statutes on the subject of extradition:

(*a.*) The more serious crimes only, amounting to felony at common law, are extraditable.

(*b.*) Those crimes only are extraditable as to which there is a general agreement, among civilized states, in the matter of definition, proof, and punishment.

(*c.*) The sufficiency of evidence as to the crime for which extradition is asked is determined by the law of the state in which the criminal has taken refuge.

(*d.*) A state, before giving effect to a request for extradition, will punish the criminal for any offence which he may have committed against its own municipal laws.

(*e.*) Most states will surrender a criminal only with the understanding that he is to be tried for the crime mentioned in the request for extradition, and for no other.

(*f.*) Many states, for a reason already given, decline to surrender their own citizens, or subjects, whose extradition is asked by a foreign state.[1]

(*g.*) Most states refuse to surrender persons charged with political crimes.

(*h.*) Due regard being had to differences between codes of criminal law and procedure, crimes can best be tried and punished at the place where they were committed.

4. *Extradition Treaties of the United States.*—The United States has thus far negotiated thirty-four extradition treaties. The first was entered into in 1794, and is comprised in Article 27 of Jay's Treaty with England. It included the crimes of murder and forgery only, and contained no stipulation as to the manner in which persons, charged with either of these crimes, were to be extradited. No legislation was had by Congress for the purpose of carrying that part of the treaty into effect, and, as it was not self-executing, it was held to be legally inoperative, and expired by limitation in 1806. I can find but a single instance in which it was attempted to surrender a criminal in accordance with the extradition clause of this treaty. One Jonathan Robbins, who had participated in an

---

[1] Boyd's Wheaton, pp. 165, 166.

act of mutiny on board the British ship Hermione, in 1791, was arrested in Charleston in 1799. Judge Bee, of the United States District Court, was notified by the Secretary of State that a demand had been made for his delivery as a fugitive criminal; and that the President advised, in the event of the evidence being deemed sufficient to sustain the charge, that the prisoner be delivered to the British consul. Robbins was soon after brought before the District Court on a writ of habeas corpus. A hearing was had and the privilege of the writ was denied, the prisoner being surrendered to the British consul. Such a surrender was clearly illegal and created great popular excitement.

Of the extradition treaties now in force, thirty-three in number, twenty contain the provision that political offences are not extraditable, though none of them contain a definition of the term. Nineteen contain a provision that citizens of the state upon which the demand is made are not to be surrendered; as citizens are not excepted in the other treaties, the presumption is that they would be surrendered upon due application. Twenty-two of them contain a clause authorizing the surrendering state to try and punish offences against its own laws before giving effect to the extradition process. In all of them it is expressly stipulated that the sufficiency of evidence as to the commission of the crime for which extradition is demanded shall be determined by the laws of the state in which the criminal has taken refuge.

5. *Interstate Extradition.*—The subject of interstate extradition in the United States is regulated by the Federal Constitution, which provides that "a person charged in any State with treason, felony, or other

crime, who shall flee from justice, and be found in another state, shall, on demand of the executive authority of the state from which he fled, be delivered up, to be removed to the state having jurisdiction of the crime."[1] This provision covers only cases arising within the territorial limits of the United States. The power to surrender fugitives, who, having committed offences within the jurisdiction of a *foreign* state, have fled to one of the United States for shelter, belongs, under the Constitution, exclusively to the United States.[2] The practice of extradition between the states of the Federal Union is carried on with nearly as much strictness as is that between foreign nations, and in accordance with similar rules. It has been decided, however, by the Supreme Court of the United States that the term "other crime," as used in the extradition clause of the Federal Constitution, refers to the definition of the offense according to the law of the state in which the crime was committed. In this respect the rule of interstate extradition is opposed to the international rule on the same subject. This should be the case, as the systems of criminal law, of proof, procedure, and punishment, in the several states of the Union, are so nearly the same as to make the observance of the international rule unnecessary.

The same tribunal holds that "where demand is made in due form, it is the duty of the executive on whom the demand is made to respond to it, and he has no moral right to refuse. Nevertheless, if he does refuse, no power has been conferred on the Federal courts to compel obedience, and the governors of states

---

[1] Constitution of the United States, § 2, art. 4.
[2] Holmes *vs.* Jennison, Peters, vol. xiv., p. 540.

have often refused compliance with the demand, when, in their opinion, substantial justice did not require it.[1]

References.—For the latest and most valuable discussion of the important subject of Extradition, both international and interstate, see "Moore on Extradition," by J. B. Moore, formerly of the Department of State, but now professor of International Law in Columbia College; see also Spear's "Law of Extradition;" Hall, "International Law," p. 48; Halleck, vol. i., chap. vii., §§ 28-35; Boyd's Wheaton, pp. 156-162, and pp. 645-650; Amos, "Science of Law," p. 263; Klüber, §§ 60-66; G. F. De Martens, § 99-102; Heffter, §§ 63, 63a; Bar, p. 17, and pp. 623-737, and Teichmann, "Les Délits Politiques, le Régicide et l'Extradition," in vol. xi. of the "Revue de Droit International," pp. 475-524.

---

[1] Cooley, "Constitutional Law," p. 191; Kentucky *vs.* Dennison, Howard, vol. xxiv., p. 66.

CHAPTER VI.

PRIVATE INTERNATIONAL LAW.

1. *Relations of States and Individuals at International Law.*—It has been seen that "the relations of states to one another are twofold in character. Either the governments of the different states have relations to each other, or the individual citizens of the different states have relations to each other. The first class of relations give occasion to what is called Public International Law, and the latter to what is sometimes called, with less precision, Private International Law."[1]

2. *Definition.*—That branch of International Law which treats of the relations of states with the citizens or subjects of other states is called *Private International Law;* or, as it is a question of determining whether the courts of a state are to apply their own municipal law, or that of another state, in the decision of a given cause, it is sometimes called the *Conflict of Laws.*

The Practice Based upon Comity or Consent.—From the definition of sovereignty it has been seen that "the jurisdiction of a nation within its own territory is necessarily exclusive and absolute. It is susceptible of no limitations not imposed by itself. Any restriction upon it deriving validity from any external source would imply a diminution of the sovereignty

---

[1] Amos, "Science of Law," p. 25.

to the extent of the restriction, and an investment of that sovereignty to the same extent in that power which could impose such restriction."[1] The extent, therefore, to which the courts of one state may apply the laws of another in the decision of cases, as it is based upon comity or consent, must be determined by the municipal law of the state in which the court sits. It may be prohibited altogether, or may be permitted subject to such restrictions as that state may see fit to impose in accordance with its views of justice or expediency.

Origin of the Practice.—The rules of Private International Law "come into being through the moral claim that is presented either by persons who, not being citizens of a given country, come into the courts of justice of that country while sojourning there to have rights recognized and protected which they have acquired in their own country; or, by those who, being citizens of one country, but having acquired rights while sojourning in other countries, come into the courts of their own country to have those rights recognized and protected.

"On every occasion for inventing rules applicable to these cases the question is presented whether the courts of justice of a country shall recognize rights acquired, either by their own citizens or by foreigners, in other countries; or, in other words, whether the laws of other countries, giving validity to those rights, shall or shall not be held to be effectual in the courts of justice which are invited to interfere. The cases are generally further complicated by the nature of the processes and

---

[1] Case of the Exchange, Cranch, vol. vii., p. 116.

transactions out of which the asserted rights spring. Part of the transactions may have taken place in one country and part in another, and the remedy may be sought for in a third. Or, the person seeking the remedy, or against whom the remedy is sought, may be the citizen of one country, have his permanent residence or domicile in another country, and be temporarily sojourning in the country in which the remedy is sought.

"It is obvious, from a mere enumeration and description of the cases which give rise to rules, that the purpose of the existence of these rules is always the facilitation of intercourse between the citizens of different states, and the prevention of practical injustice. These objects must be served in the highest degree, if the greatest possible uniformity of principle obtain, in the courts of all nations, in creating and applying the rules. In this way reasonable expectations are likely to be best satisfied, and fraudulent invasions of the law of any particular country are likely to be most effectually prevented. It happens, however, that, owing to the political jealousies that have hitherto kept apart the most considerable nations of Europe, and to the foolish prejudice with which individual nations have fostered principles of law familiar in their own courts, however alien to the practice of all other countries, there have hitherto been made only very imperfect attempts at uniformity, either of principle or practice, in this respect. It is probable that an increasingly clear apprehension of the logical relations of the different branches of law touching ownership, contract, family life, or crime, will produce the effect of assimilating the substance, as well as the form, of the rules of law forming the so-called Private International Law of different countries."[1]

As the practice of Private International Law is based upon the comity of nations, it is obvious that the modern science cannot, in its origin, antedate the recognition of comity as a general international obligation. The remote origin of the practice, however, is much more ancient, and can unquestionably be traced to the *Jus Gentium* of the Romans, which was, in substance, a formal recognition of the principles involved in Private International Law by the greatest state that has ever existed. The Roman Civil Law applied to Roman citizens alone; the *Jus Gentium*, or Law of Nations, was made up of those principles of law which were common to all the nations of which they had any authentic knowledge. This system was administered by the Roman courts during the existence of the empire, and was revived, by Grotius, more than a thousand years after the downfall of the state in which it had originated, for the purpose of furnishing a logical and legal basis for the new science of International Law.

The rules of domicile, which lie at the base of the subject, were the first to receive attention, and to be made the subject of judicial decision. This was especially true of their application by prize-courts in ascertaining the domicile of owners of captured vessels, with a view to determining the nationality, and so the liability to capture and condemnation, of their property. Aside from this, however, but little attention was paid to the subject, as a matter of public law, until after the

---

[1] Amos, "Science of Law," pp. 26, 27.

middle of the seventeenth century, when the rules regarding the treatment of aliens began to be relaxed in severity, and the alien class began to demand protection in their personal and property rights. Its progress has not been rapid at any time, though an increased interest in it has been manifested since the beginning of the present century, and all states that are parties to International Law now recognize its rules, and, to a greater or less extent, permit their courts to apply them in the decision of cases arising within their jurisdiction. Their practice is far from uniform, however, some states being slow to recognize their binding force, while others constantly seek to extend their field of operation, at times going so far as to negotiate treaties for that purpose. The *tendency* of all modern states is in the same direction, though some move more rapidly than others.

3. *Subjects Treated of in Private International Law.*—The rules of Private International Law have chiefly to do—

(1.) With the legal status of aliens, and with their capacity to do certain acts in a state, *not* in accordance with *its* municipal law, but in accordance with the municipal law of another state.

(2.) With questions arising as to the validity of foreign marriages or divorces.

(3.) With similar questions arising as to the validity or binding force of contracts or agreements.

(4.) With questions connected with the ownership, or transfer, of land and goods.

(5.) With foreign judgments and bankruptcies.[1]

---

[1] Amos, "Science of Law," p. 319.

Limitations upon the Practice of Private International Law.—The courts of a state, in applying the rules of Private International Law in any one of the foregoing cases, cannot give effect to, or apply, a foreign law which is 'repugnant to the municipal law, or moral standards, or public policy of their own state. In accordance with this principle the following exceptions are stated by Wharton, in his "Conflict of Laws:"[1]

(1.) Distinctions of rank, or caste, have no extraterritorial effect.

(2.) Laws destructive of capacity are disfavored internationally; those protective of capacity are favored. To the former class would belong laws recognizing slavery, or imposing disabilities on account of religious belief.

(3.) Property, whether real or personal, is subject to the *lex rei sitæ*.

(4.) In all matters relating to a decedent's estate, except as to realty, the law of the last domicile of the decedent is to prevail.

(5.) Contracts, as a general rule, are to be governed by the law of the place of performance.[2]

(6.) Process, as a general rule, is to be governed by the *lex fori*.

(7.) Persons are, in general, subject to the law of their domicile; "but, when visiting other lands, they can only claim to be invested with the law of such domicile to the extent which is consistent with the common law of Christendom, which is the foundation of Private International Law." Hence "a polygamous or incestuous marriage, even though sanctioned

---

[1] Wharton, "Conflict of Laws," § 19.   [2] *Ibid.*

by a foreign state, and contracted within its borders, has no exterritorial force. Foreign judgments of divorce, to be respected, must be rendered by courts having jurisdiction according to the judgments of Private International Law. Foreign incapacity, arising from minority or subjection to tutelage, will only be recognized when there is something in the person so subjected to put persons dealing with him on inquiry."[1]

Effect of Foreign Judgments.—A *foreign judgment* is one obtained in the courts of a foreign state, the recognition and enforcement of which is asked in the courts of the state in which the defendant is resident, or subject to legal process. The great majority of states give effect to a foreign judgment in all cases in which the following conditions have been fulfilled:

(1.) The tribunal which pronounced the judgment must have been competent, according to the law of the state to which it belonged, to decide upon the matter adjudicated upon.

(2.) The jurisdiction must have been complete both as to subject-matter and over the parties to the suit.

(3.) The foreigner who was a party must have been fairly heard before the tribunal, according to the laws of the state, and on an equality, in every respect, including the right of appeal, with a native subject.

(4.) The tribunal must have decided upon the very subject-matter which it is attempted to litigate upon, and the decision must have been final, or made by the court of last resort.

Condition of Reciprocity. — To these conditions some nations add another, that of reciprocity. If these

---

[1] Wharton, "Conflict of Laws," § 19.

conditions are fulfilled they will constitute a valid ground upon which to base a plea in bar of a second litigation, and, if properly authenticated, the foreign judgment will be executed by them as if it were their own.[1]

Foreign Judgments, why Produced before the Courts of a State.—Whenever a foreign judgment is brought to the judicial notice of the courts of a state it is with a view of obtaining one of two results:

(1.) "It may be pleaded in bar.

(2.) "It may be given effect to, and executed in the same manner as a domestic judgment."[2]

Conditions under which they are Given Effect.—In accordance with the practice of most states of Christendom, foreign judgments are permitted to have effect only in the following cases:

(1.) With the consent of the state in which execution is desired.

(2.) By the authority and order of its tribunals.

(3.) When it contains no provisions or order contrary to the public morals or policy of the state in which execution of it is sought.[3]

Practice of States in the Matter of Foreign Judgments.—Although there is considerable variance in the policy of states as to the effect given in each to foreign judgments, most of them are susceptible of classification under one of three heads:

(1.) "Those which recognize the rule of reciprocity.

(2.) "Those which refuse to recognize foreign judgments.

---

[1] Phillimore, vol. iv., pp. 729, 730.
[2] *Ibid.*, p. 729; De Martens, liv. iii., § 94.
[3] Phillimore, vol. iv., p. 728.

(3.) "Those, like England and the United States, which recognize them even without reciprocity."[1]

References.—The admirable treatises of Wharton and Story upon the subject of "Private International Law," or the "Conflict of Laws," both works of the highest authority, practically exhaust the subject in all its departments. Bar's "International Law" is a standard German work upon the subject, and may now be obtained in an English translation. Fœlix, "Traité de Droit International Privé" is a French work of high authority. The fourth volume of Phillimore is devoted to the subject of Domicile and Private International Law. For briefer and less elaborate accounts, see Boyd's Wheaton, §§ 78–92; Halleck, vol. i., chap. vii.; and Brocher's "Théorie du Droit International Privé," in vols. iv., v., of the *Revue de Droit International*.

---

[1] Phillimore, vol. iv., pp. 731, 732.

CHAPTER VII.

THE RIGHT OF LEGATION.

1. *Origin of the Right.*—The right of legation is one of the oldest, as it is one of the most generally sanctioned of international usages. It has existed from the earliest times, and among all peoples of whom we have any authentic knowledge. It is recognized and practiced to some extent even by barbarous nations in their occasional intercourse with each other.

As nations cannot treat directly with each other, it follows that intercourse between them must be carried on by means of agents or intermediaries; these agents are called ambassadors.

The practice of maintaining public ambassadors at foreign courts, though recognized to some extent in Europe at an earlier date, did not become general until about the middle of the seventeenth century. The treaty of Westphalia, which was concluded in 1648, marked an important epoch in European history. As an immediate result of its execution the influence of the Roman Church in secular matters was largely reduced in importance, and the principle of balance of power was, for the first time, generally sanctioned and specially guaranteed. As a consequence the foreign relations of the different European states rapidly increased in volume and intricacy, and the necessity of establishing permanent legations was generally recognized and acted upon. The profession of diplomacy soon became the most important one in which an individual could engage, and the departments of foreign affairs were regarded as the most important branches of governmental service, demanding in their administration ministers of the highest ability and the widest experience. The position assumed by the profession has been constantly maintained, and the states of Europe and America now deem it a matter of the first consequence to be ably represented, not only near the courts of the Christian states, but also at the capitals of those Eastern nations which, as yet, but imperfectly recognize the sanctions of International Law.

The Right of Legation.—The *right* of sending and receiving ambassadors is one of the essential attributes of a sovereign state. The *obligation* to do so is less strong, and is not generally regarded as a matter of strict right. A nation, however, which refuses, without good reason, to receive a minister from a foreign power exposes itself to retorsion; and a state would run counter to the tendencies of modern civilization which rejected, or refused to receive, communications from a state with which it was at peace.[1]

The power of sending and receiving ambassadors belongs also to dependent states, unless its exercise is expressly forbidden by the states upon which they are dependent. In the case of confederacies the right belongs to each of the component states, unless it has been expressly surrendered by them in the treaty of confederation.

A state, though willing to receive an ambassador from another, may, for good reason, decline to receive

---

[1] Heffter, p. 377.

a particular person in that capacity. It may thus decline to receive one of its own subjects, or a former subject who had been exiled or who had gone into voluntary exile, or a person of doubtful or immoral character, or one who had been engaged in a conspiracy or agitation directed against the government to which he is accredited as an ambassador. "A state may also decline to receive ministers whose powers are incompatible with its constitution or public policy. For this reason no state is obliged to receive as minister the legates or nuncios of the pope. Their powers are conferred, either expressly or tacitly, by ecclesiastical laws, and an attempt to enforce them may bring the papal representative into collision with the sovereign authority of the state upon some question of a religious character."[1]

It has already been explained that the government of a state is the organ through which it communicates with other powers. In such intercourse with other states a government may communicate directly, through its ministry of foreign affairs, or through ambassadors selected by the proper governmental authority in accordance with its constitution and laws.

2. *Classification of Diplomatic Agents.* — Heffter makes the following classification of these agents of intercourse.

(*a.*) Public ministers. These are clothed with a public and official character, and are sent by the sovereign authority of a state to a foreign government, as its general diplomatic representatives, or to undertake

---

[1] Heffter, p. 377.

special negotiations. They may have either a permanent or temporary character.

(*b.*) Diplomatic agents, charged with similar duties, but without public or official character.

(*c.*) Commissioners, appointed for special purposes, as to locate and mark boundaries, to adjust international differences, or to carry into effect special clauses of treaties. The members of this class do not communicate directly either with a foreign sovereign or with his ministers.[1]

3. *Rank of Ambassadors.*—The absence of a well-defined rule by which to determine questions arising as to the powers and dignities of the different classes of diplomatic agents gave rise to great confusion, especially at the beginning of the present century. To remedy this the representatives of the European powers assembled in Congress at Vienna, in 1815, agreed upon a classification of public ministers, and recommended the preparation and adoption, in each state, of rules to regulate their precedence. The arrangement proposed at Vienna,[2] as modified by the action of the Congress of Aix-la-Chapelle,[3] in 1818, has received such general sanction as to entitle it to consideration as a rule of International Law. In accordance with its provisions diplomatic agents are now arranged into four classes:

(*a.*) Ambassadors, ordinary and extraordinary, legates and nuncios.

(*b.*) Envoys, ministers, or other diplomatic agents accredited to sovereigns.

(*c.*) Ministers resident, accredited to sovereigns.

---

[1] Heffter, p. 378.   [2] *Ibid.*   [3] *Ibid.*

(*d.*) *Chargés d'Affaires*, and other diplomatic agents accredited to ministers of foreign affairs (whether bearing the title of minister or not), and consuls charged with diplomatic duties.[1]

Ambassadors of the first class are alone clothed with the representative character; they have special prerogatives, and are entitled to special honors, as they represent the sovereign in his *personal* character. Members of the other classes represent his affairs only. In general the immunities to which ministers are entitled depend upon their letters of credence. Those accredited to sovereigns are entitled to the immunities of ambassadors, those accredited to ministers of foreign affairs are not.

4. *Titles of Ambassadors.*— The titles of ambassadors are regulated by the municipal laws of the states which they represent. The terms *ordinary* and *extraordinary* at first determined the character of the diplomatic employment of the ministers to whom they were applied. They have now no special meaning. Legates and nuncios are the representatives of the pope at foreign courts. Legates have the rank of cardinal, and represent, to a certain extent, his spiritual as well as his temporal authority. Nuncios represent him in the latter capacity only. In determining the rank and titles of ministers sent to foreign courts, the principle of reciprocity prevails, and a state sends to another a representative of the same class that it receives. Several ministers may be maintained at the same court, and a single person may represent a state at several courts.

---

[1] Heffter, p. 388.

5. *Manner of Sending and Receiving Ambassadors.* —To enable a minister to be received in that character, he is provided by the sovereign or other chief executive authority of his own state with two important papers, called his *Letter of Credence* and *Full Power.* The Letter of Credence is addressed to the sovereign to whom he is accredited. It contains his name and title, confers upon him the diplomatic character, and serves to identify him as a public minister, but does not authorize him to enter upon any particular negotiation. The Full Power authorizes him to act as the general diplomatic representative of his government at the court to which he is accredited. It describes the limits of his authority to negotiate, if such there be, and upon it the validity of his acts as a minister largely depends. Ambassadors who represent states at Congresses and Conferences, or as members of International Courts, or Boards of Arbitration, are not usually provided with Letters of Credence. They bear Full Powers, under the authority of which they act, and copies of them are exchanged among the different members of the board or conference.[1]

Reception of Ambassadors.—An ambassador or minister accredited to a sovereign, upon arriving at his station, forwards a copy of his Letter of Credence to the Minister of Foreign Affairs, and requests an audience with the sovereign. At this audience, which may be either public or private, his Letter of Credence is presented, and complimentary speeches are usually exchanged. He may then enter upon the performance of his duties.

---

[1] De Martens, vol. i., pp. 84, 86.

6. *Duties of Ambassadors.*—The duties of a public minister are not susceptible of exact description. Some of them are regulated by International Law, and some by the municipal law of the ambassador's state. They depend upon the importance of the power to which he is accredited, upon the amount of intercourse, commercial and otherwise, existing between it and the state which he represents, and, to some extent, upon the difference in their systems of government. He is expected to keep his government informed upon all questions of general interest, and to advise it of any change in the government, constitution, or state policy of the country in which he is resident. It is also his duty to make proper representations in behalf of subjects of his own state who may stand in need of protection, to secure a remedy for injuries which they may have received, or, in case they exceed his jurisdiction, to inform his government fully of the facts in each case in order that proper measures of redress may be taken. In general he represents the interests of his state, and those of its individual subjects, in the country to which he is accredited. That he may do so effectively at all times, and under all circumstances, he is bound by every consideration of honor and duty to scrupulously abstain from all interference in the internal affairs of the state to which he is accredited.

7. *Diplomatic Language.*—Every state has a right to employ its own language in its communications to other powers, and must recognize a corresponding right, on the part of other states, to a similar use in all communications addressed to itself. Until the beginning of the eighteenth century Latin was in general

use as a convenient neutral language. The treaties of Nimeguen, Ryswick, and Utrecht, and the Quadruple Alliance, concluded at London in 1788,[1] were drawn up in Latin. The official acts of the Holy See are still written in that language. French, however, has gradually displaced Latin as the diplomatic language, and, to a great extent, still retains that character. The treaties of Vienna, in 1815, those of 1833, concerning the separation of Belgium from Holland, and the treaty of Paris, in 1856, were drawn up in French.

8. *The Functions of Ambassadors, how Suspended and Terminated.*— The functions of an ambassador, and consequently his official character, may be suspended, and may, or may not, be terminated—

(*a.*) As a result of some difference or misunderstanding between the two powers, not resulting in war.

(*b.*) Upon the occurrence of important political events, which render the continuance of his mission improbable; as a sudden or violent change in the constitution or form of government, in either state. Such a suspension continues until it is removed, by proper authority, in the state in which it originated.

A mission may be terminated—

(*a.*) By the death, or by the voluntary or constrained abdication of one or both sovereigns. This, however, only in case the ambassador represents the sovereign in his personal capacity.[2]

(*b.*) By the withdrawal, or cancellation, of his Letters of Credence and Full Power.

(*c.*) By his recall at the outbreak of war; or upon the completion of the duty which he was appointed to

---

[1] Heffter, p. 433.   [2] Ibid., p. 414.

perform, the expiration of his term of office, or upon his promotion or removal to another sphere of duty.

(*d.*) By his removal, which may be voluntary, or forced by the government to which he is sent.

(*e.*) By death.[1]

When the functions of an ambassador cease for any cause his departure is attended by formalities similar to those observed at his reception. He requests an audience with the sovereign, at which he presents his letters of recall. If normal relations exist between the two governments, formal expressions of regret are exchanged at this interview. In strictness his functions and privileges cease when his letter of recall has been presented. Through courtesy, however, the immunities which he has enjoyed during his period of residence are extended to him until he passes the frontier of the state on his homeward journey.

9. *The Privileges and Immunities of Ambassadors.* —To the successful and efficient performance of an ambassador's duties the most complete personal independence and freedom of action are necessary. This immunity lies at the foundation of the system, and has been most jealously guarded and preserved since the beginning of modern diplomacy. It was recognized by the nations of antiquity, and is insisted upon as a necessary preliminary to intercourse with those Eastern countries whose standards of civilization differ so widely from our own. It is illustrated by the swiftness with which nations have always resented offences against the persons of their ministers and diplomatic agents.

---

[1] De Martens, vol. ii., p. 160.

10. *The Principle or Fiction of Exterritoriality.*—From the *fact* of the inviolability of an ambassador's person, the *fiction of exterritoriality* has been deduced to account for and explain the various exemptions which public ministers enjoy in foreign countries. This principle has been defined, and its limitations have been pointed out, elsewhere.

This immunity is both personal and territorial. Personal in that it involves an exemption of his person from the civil and criminal jurisdiction of the state in which he is resident; territorial in that his residence or hotel is presumed to be a part of the territory of the state which he represents. In strictness his privileges and immunities become effective when he enters upon the performance of his diplomatic duties. It is usual, however, to recognize them as existing so soon as he enters the territory of the state to which he is accredited. The exemption which an ambassador enjoys extends to his family, to the secretaries and other *attachés* and employees of the legation, and to his domestic servants. Some question has arisen as to the precise extent of this immunity in the case of servants, especially when they are natives of the country in which the minister is resident. Unquestionably any privilege which a servant may have "is not the privilege of the servant himself, but of the ambassador, and is based on the ground that the arrest of the servant might interfere with the comfort or state of the ambassador."[1]

Immunity from Criminal Jurisdiction.—As respects criminal jurisdiction, an ambassador is exempt from

---

[1] Phillimore, vol. ii., p. 145.

criminal prosecution, of every sort, during the entire period of his residence at a foreign court. A crime committed against the person of an ambassador, except in the way of self-defence, is given an aggravated character, and is punished with exceptional severity by the municipal laws of every state. The only exception to the immunity which a minister enjoys in this respect would arise from his own misconduct. For any minor violation of propriety the government to which he is accredited may signify its displeasure, either privately to the minister himself, or to his government in the diplomatic way. For a more serious offence, amounting to crime, his recall may be demanded. If the request be not acceded to, he may be summarily dismissed, or notified to quit the territory of the offended state. For crime of an aggravated sort, amounting to treason, or a treasonable conspiracy against the government, he is deemed to have forfeited his immunity, and may be forcibly expelled; but he may never be subjected to criminal prosecution in the state in which he resides in the character of ambassador.

Immunity from Civil Jurisdiction.—A similar immunity from civil jurisdiction is sanctioned by the general usage of nations. An ambassador, in his public character, is exempt from the service of process, and suits against him can only be brought in the courts of his own country. His furniture, and other movable property, are exempt from taxation, and from seizure in execution of judgment. This immunity, however, only attaches to him in his diplomatic capacity. It does not extend to any other interests he may have in the state in which he is resident; and, as a merchant, trustee, or executor, his property is subject to the local law. If he waives his diplomatic privilege, and submits himself to the jurisdiction of the local courts by appearing in them as a party to a cause, he must abide by their decision. It has been held, however, that a judgment against him can only be satisfied out of property held by him in his private capacity.

Immunity of an Ambassador's Hotel.—If the principle of exterritoriality were of invariable application, it would follow that, since his house and premises are held to be part of the territory of the state which he represents, his jurisdiction over them would be complete and exclusive as regards the authority of the government to which he is accredited. This is not the case, however. If a crime be committed by a person of his suite against a foreigner, the offender may be arrested or detained by the minister, and held subject to the extradition process, or sent home for trial; or, with the consent of the minister's government, he may be surrendered for trial in the local courts. A crime committed by one person of his suite against another is justiciable only in the courts of the minister's country. Nor can an ambassador's house be made an asylum for criminals. The surrender of an offender who takes refuge there may be demanded, and if denied he may be forcibly removed. The privilege of an ambassador is thus seen to be, to a certain extent, negative in character. The law of nations secures to him such personal immunity as is necessary to the proper and adequate performance of his duties. It also guarantees to him such honors and privileges as befit the representative of a sovereign state. But no such privilege or immunity attaches to him when committing a crime or doing a wrongful act, and he may be restrained, if need be by force, if he attempts to commit a crime against the person or property of another. In the exercise of the right of self-defence he may be resisted, and wounded, or even killed, by the person whom he has assaulted, and this without giving cause of complaint to the government which employs him.

While the immunities accorded to public ministers are of the most extensive and important character, amounting, in fact, to an almost complete exemption from the operation of the local laws, it does not follow that they are exempt from all legal responsibility, or that there are no courts which have jurisdiction over them. They are in all respects amenable to the jurisdiction of the courts of their own country, and before those courts they may be required to appear as parties defendant in causes of a civil or criminal character.

Privilege of Religious Worship.—The privilege of religious worship according to a prohibited form, or one different from that prevailing in the country to which an ambassador is accredited, is now generally accorded, subject to certain restrictions as to publicity. Increasing tolerance, however, in all matters of religious opinion has detracted somewhat from the advantage of the concession, as it has deprived the restrictions of much of their former significance and force. A certain jurisdiction is also conceded to ministers in the performance of certain legal acts in behalf of their fellow-subjects, such as formalizing and registering marriages, births, and deaths, and other acts of like character.

Exemption from Customs Dues, etc.—Foreign ministers are usually exempted from the payment of customs duties upon articles imported by them, and intended for their personal use. Such articles are subject to the usual inspection, and precautions calculated to prevent an abuse of the privilege are justifiable. To avoid such abuses some states permit a certain amount to be imported free of duty, and collect the usual dues upon articles imported in excess of the authorized amount or value. The privilege of an ambassador does not exempt him from the observance of the police and sanitary regulations of the city in which his official residence is situated. For a violation of such ordinances, however, he can only be proceeded against in the diplomatic way. Nor does his privilege exempt him from the payment of tolls, or of postage upon such of his correspondence as may be intrusted to the ordinary mails for delivery.

11. *Consuls.*—Consuls are persons appointed by the government of a state to represent its commercial interests, and those of its subjects, in the principal ports of other nations.

The practice of maintaining consular representatives in foreign ports and commercial cities dates back to the very beginning of modern commerce. It was developed among the commercial cities of the Mediterranean, and grew out of the exigencies and necessities of their intercourse with the Levantine cities, whose forms of government and law were radically different from their own. "The ships of foreign merchants were held to be navigated under the jurisdiction of the nation whose flag they carried; and the general practice was for vessels engaged in long sea voyages, some of which occupied a period of not less than three years, to have on board a magistrate, whose duty it was to administer the law of the country of the flag among all on board, not merely while the vessel was on the high seas, but while she was in a foreign port, loading or unloading cargo. This magistrate was termed the *alderman* in the ports of the North and Baltic seas, while in the Mediterranean ports he was designated by the familiar name of *consul*, and was the precursor of the resident commercial consul, who continues in the present day to exercise within merchant ships of his own nationality, notwithstanding they are within the territorial jurisdiction of another state, a portion of the personal jurisdiction formerly exercised by the ship's consul. The exercise of this consular jurisdiction requires no fiction of exterritoriality to support it. Its limits are either regulated by commercial treaties, or, where it has originated in charter privileges, it is now held to rest upon custom."[1]

The institution had become fully established, in much the same form as it now exists, by the end of the twelfth century, at which time Venice was represented in the East by consuls at Constantinople, Aleppo, Jerusalem, and Alexandria. The Eastern Empire maintained a consul at Marseilles, and foreign consulates had long been established and recognized at the port of Barcelona, in Spain. These early consuls performed many of the duties of modern ambassadors, and had something of their inviolable character. As a result of the general establishment of permanent missions in Europe in the seventeenth century, an important change was made in the consular function in all the states of the West. The diplomatic duties were transferred to the class of public ministers, to whom the character of inviolability was attached; and there remained to the consuls a class of duties of a commercial character,

---

[1] Article by Sir Travers Twiss, (English) *Law Magazine*, Feb. 1876.

closely resembling those which they now perform. In the Levant, however, where no permanent missions were established, consuls continued to enjoy their old powers and privileges. These, to a great extent, they still retain.

The Duties of Consuls.—It is their duty to watch over the commercial interests of their nation, to supervise the execution of commercial treaties, and to assist, by interference and counsel, such of their fellow-citizens as may be sojourning, either permanently or temporarily, at the place of their official residence. They are authorized to adjust disputes arising on board vessels of their own nation, to hear and act upon complaints of members of their crews, to issue and countersign passports to their fellow-citizens, to authenticate the judgments of foreign courts by their consular seal, and, if the local laws permit, to act as administrators upon the estates of decedents of their own nationality. They are also authorized to register births, marriages, and deaths, and may solemnize marriages when the contracting parties are of the same nationality as themselves, unless forbidden to do so by the municipal law of their own states, or that of the state in which they officially reside. They are permitted to exercise a certain voluntary jurisdiction over their fellow-citizens in cases with which the local law has no concern; "but no contentious jurisdiction can be exercised over their fellow-countrymen without the express permission of the state in which they reside, and no Christian state has, as yet, permitted the criminal jurisdiction of foreign consuls."[1] They are presumed to be entitled to all the powers and privileges that their predecessors

---

[1] Phillimore, vol. ii., p. 170.

have enjoyed, and may properly claim any right exercised by a consul of another nation, unless such right is based upon treaty stipulations.

12. *Classification of Consuls, and Method of Appointment.*—They are usually classified into consuls-general, consuls, vice-consuls, and consular agents, and each state, by its municipal law, determines the manner of appointment, the tenure of office, and the special duties of its consular representatives in foreign ports. In this way a state may confer upon its consuls such power and jurisdiction as it wishes them to exercise, provided such exercise of jurisdiction is sanctioned by the usage of nations, or has been conceded by treaty. In the Christian states of Europe and America consuls have none of the privileges and immunities of ambassadors. In the Levant, however, in many Asiatic and African ports, and in the islands of the sea, they perform the duties and are entitled to the exemptions of public ministers.

13. *Privileges of Consuls.*—Consuls enjoy certain privileges which are sanctioned by International Law. They are exempt from personal imposts and the performance of personal services, from the quartering of troops, and, in general, from such restrictions as are calculated to interfere with the efficient performance of their consular duties. They are usually permitted to place their national flags and coats-of-arms over their offices, and in most states their archives are regarded as inviolable.

They may engage in business, if the municipal law of their own country permits them to do so, and may be prohibited from so doing by the same authority. They are in all respects amenable to the civil and criminal jurisdiction of the state in which they are resident. They may sue and be sued in its courts; they are in every way subject to process, and judgments against them may be satisfied out of their property. Halleck holds that they may be punished for their criminal offences by the laws of the state in which they reside, or sent back to their own country for trial, at the discretion of the government which they have offended. A distinction is made, however, between personal offences and official acts done under the authority, or by the direction, of their own governments. The latter are matters for diplomatic arrangement between the respective states, and are not justiciable by the local courts.[1] Consuls are subject to taxation and to the payment of customs dues. Their place of residence is regarded as their domicile to the extent that, in time of war, their goods on the high seas are subject to seizure if their domicile gives them the hostile character.

14. *By whom Appointed.*—Consuls are appointed by the sovereign, or chief executive authority of the state which they represent, subject to such restrictions in the matter of citizenship, character, and qualifications as are determined by its municipal laws. They are provided with commissions, or letters of appointment, which are submitted, through their ministers, to the Department of Foreign Affairs of the state in which they are to perform consular duty. If that government consents to recognize them in the capacity of consuls, an *exequatur* is issued, upon the receipt of which they are authorized to enter upon the perform-

---

[1] Halleck, vol. i., p. 313.

ance of their duties. For misconduct or crime, or for excess of jurisdiction, the exequatur may be withdrawn or revoked at any time; and if this action be taken for just and sufficient cause, the government of the state to which the consul belongs will have no reasonable ground of complaint. This procedure is by no means uncommon. In October, 1793, the exequatur of the French consul at Boston was withdrawn for having taken part in an attempt to rescue a vessel out of the hands of the United States marshal, which had been brought in as a French prize, but upon which process had been served at the suit of the British consul, who claimed that she had been illegally captured in the neutral waters of the United States.[1] Another and more remarkable case occurred in 1861. In order to protect British commerce, Her Majesty's Government was desirous that the Confederates should observe the last three articles of the Declaration of Paris, and accordingly Mr. Bunch, the British consul at Charleston, S. C., was instructed to communicate this desire to the Confederate authorities. The United States thereupon demanded that Mr. Bunch should be removed from his office, on the ground that the law of the United States forbade any person, not specially appointed, from counselling, advising, or interfering in any political correspondence with the government of any foreign state in relation to any disputes or controversies with the United States, and that Mr. Bunch ought to have known of this law, and to have communicated it to his government before obeying their instructions. It was also urged that the proper agents to make known

---

[1] Hildreth, "History of the United States," vol. iv., p. 437.

the wishes of a foreign government were its diplomatic, and not its consular, officers. On these grounds Mr. Bunch's exequatur was withdrawn.[1]

15. *Manner of Appointment in the United States.*— The members of the United States Consular Establishment are arranged into three principal classes—consuls-general, consuls, and commercial agents.[2] They are appointed by the President with the consent of the Senate. They receive fixed salaries, augmented in certain cases by fees, and those whose salaries exceed one thousand dollars per annum are forbidden to engage in trade. Consular positions of the highest class can only be filled by citizens of the United States. Their general duties are ascertained and fixed by law. They are required to act in behalf of owners of stranded vessels,[3] to receive from the masters of American vessels, upon their arrival in port, their registers, sea letters, and Mediterranean passports, and to return them when a proper clearance has been obtained, by such masters, from the port authorities.[4] They are required to make reclamation of deserters from merchant vessels, and, when treaty stipulations authorize it, to demand from the local authorities such assistance as they may need to effect their capture and return.[5] They are also required to certify invoices of merchandise which it is proposed to import into the United States, and to re-

---

[1] Boyd's Wheaton, p. 305; "United States Diplomatic Correspondence," 1862, p. 1.

[2] Halleck, vol. i., pp. 315, 316, gives a full list of the legal and acting titles of United States consuls. For fuller information as to their powers and duties, see the official "Regulations Prescribed for the Consular Service of the United States," Washington, Oct. 1, 1870.

[3] "Revised Statutes of the United States," § 4238.

[4] *Ibid.*, §§ 4559, 4586.   [5] *Ibid.*, §§ 4598–4600.

quire satisfactory evidence, by oath if need be, of their correctness.[1] They are to keep lists of seamen shipped and discharged by them, and of vessels arrived and cleared, with an account of the nature and value of their cargoes.[2] They are to care for destitute seamen, and to cause the same to be transported to the United States,[3] and are to procure and transmit to the State Department such authentic commercial information respecting the country in which they reside as may be required by the head of that department.[4] They are authorized to solemnize marriages between persons who would be permitted by law to marry if resident in the District of Columbia,[5] and may take possession, in certain cases, of the personal estates of any citizen of the United States who may die within their consular jurisdiction leaving no legal representatives. They may sell such of this property as is of a perishable nature to pay debts due from the estate, transmitting the residue to the treasury of the United States.[6] The President is empowered to define the territorial limits of the different consulates, and to make all needful regulations for the consular service.

16. *Consular Jurisdiction.*—In certain Eastern countries, whose standards of law and morals differ materially from our own, an extensive jurisdiction, both civil and criminal, is exercised by the consuls of the principal Western powers. It was obtained in the first instance by treaty stipulation, and by later treaties has been modified and extended, from time to time, as the exigencies of commercial intercourse made such changes

---

[1] "Revised Statutes of the United States," § 2862. [2] *Ibid.*, § 1708.
[3] *Ibid.*, § 4577. [4] *Ibid.*, § 1711. [5] *Ibid.*, § 4082. [6] *Ibid.*, § 1709.

either necessary or desirable. The effect has been to withdraw foreigners almost completely from the operation of the local laws, and to subject them to the jurisdiction of the consuls of their respective states. The extent of this jurisdiction is defined by treaties with the Christian powers. These treaties are carried into effect by the municipal laws of the signatory states, which determine, within the limits of the treaty concession, the extent and character of the consular jurisdiction. "This jurisdiction is subject, in civil cases, to an appeal to the superior tribunals of their own country. The criminal jurisdiction is usually limited to the infliction of pecuniary penalties, and, in offences of a higher grade, the consular functions are similar to those of a police magistrate, or *juge d'instruction*. He collects the documentary and other proofs, and sends them, together with the prisoner, home to his own country for trial."[1] Such jurisdiction was obtained for consuls of the United States by treaties made at different times with Turkey, China, and Japan, and with Siam and Madagascar. Suitable laws have been passed by Congress to give effect to their provisions. By the Act of July 1, 1870, the operation of the statute was extended "to any country of like character with which the United States may hereafter enter into treaty relations."[2] The jurisdiction conferred upon United States ministers and consuls by the Act of June 22, 1860, is both civil and criminal, but is re-

---

[1] Boyd's Wheaton, p. 152; Boyd, "The Merchant Shipping Laws," index, title, "Consular Offices;" Pardessus, "Droit Commercial," pt. vi., tit. 6, chap. ii., § 2; chap. iv., §§ 1, 2, 3; De Steck, "Essai sur les Consuls," § 7, par. 30–40.

[2] Act of July 1, 1870, extending Act of June 22, 1860.

stricted in its exercise to citizens of the United States. Consuls are authorized to hear, and finally decide, civil causes in which the amount involved, exclusive of costs, does not exceed five hundred dollars. When the amount exceeds that sum, or in his opinion the case involves legal perplexities, the consul is authorized to summon not less than two, nor more than three, citizens of the United States, who are to be selected, by lot, from a list previously submitted to the minister and approved by him. If the consul and his advisers concur in opinion, their decision is final. If they fail to agree, or if the amount at issue exceeds five hundred dollars, either party may appeal to the minister. In China and Japan the decision of the minister is final in all suits when the amount at issue does not exceed two thousand five hundred dollars. Cases involving a greater amount may be appealed to the United States Circuit Court for the district of California, whose decision in the case is final.

Consuls are also authorized to hear and decide criminal cases, and, in the event of conviction, to impose penalties of not more than ninety days' imprisonment, or a fine not exceeding five hundred dollars. In cases not involving a higher penalty than one hundred dollars' fine, or sixty days' imprisonment, their decision is final. Whenever the consul is of opinion that an important question of law is involved in the decision of a case, or deems a greater punishment necessary than he is authorized to inflict, he may summon as advisers, in cases not capital, not less than one, nor more than four, American citizens to assist him in his decision. In cases involving capital punishment not less than four such assistants must be summoned. In the event of disagreement the case, with evidence and opinions, is forwarded to the minister for decision. His decision is final, except in cases arising in China and Japan, from which an appeal may be taken, as in civil cases, to the United States Circuit Court in California. The jurisdiction of the minister is appellate, except in capital cases, or when the consul is a party; and, finally, ministers and consuls are enjoined to exert all their official influence to induce litigant parties to adjust their differences by arbitration.[1]

A somewhat similar jurisdiction is exercised by the British consuls in the East.

References.—Most existing works upon the subject of diplomacy are of foreign origin. Many of them either appeared originally in French, or are accessible in French translations. The most important of these are, for the period before Grotius, Nys, "Origines de la Diplomatie," and, for its later history and practice, Ch. de Martens, "Le Guide Diplomatique," and "Causes Célèbres du Droit des Gens" (1827), and the "Nouvelles Causes Célèbres," published by the same author in 1844. See also the "Traité Complet de Diplomatie," par un Ancien Ministre; Schuyler, "American Diplomacy;" and the "Rights and Duties of Diplomatic Agents," by E. C. Grenville-Murray. The following works upon the functions and duties of consuls may be consulted with advantage: "Dictionnaire ou Manuel Lexique du Diplomate et du Consul," by Baron F. de Cussy; Miltitz, "Manuel des Consuls;" Neumann, "Handbuch des Consulatswesens;" and Henshaw's and Warden's works on the duties of consuls. As the exercise of consular jurisdiction is based upon treaty stipulations, it is necessary, in conducting inquiries upon this subject, to consult the treaties themselves. For this purpose, see the collections referred to at the end of chap. viii. For a very full account of the diplomatic and consular policy of the United States, see Schuyler, "American Diplomacy and the Furtherance of Commerce."

---

[1] "Revised Statutes of the United States," §§ 4083-4148.

CHAPTER VIII.

TREATIES AND CONVENTIONS.

1. TREATIES are compacts or agreements entered into by sovereign states for the purpose of increasing, modifying, or defining their mutual duties and obligations.

Purpose of Treaties.—To secure the observance of the generally accepted rules of International Law, treaties are not necessary, certainly among Christian states. They become so only when states find it either necessary or expedient to amend or modify their existing obligations, to define usages that are not clear, to secure concerted action looking to the abandonment of unjust or oppressive practices, or to obtain general sanction in behalf of improved methods, or the general acceptance of desirable reforms.

The Right of Making Treaties.—The right of making treaties is one of the essential attributes of sovereignty, and there can be no surer test of a semi-sovereign or dependent state than is deduced from the fact that its ability to enter into treaty relations has been abridged or destroyed. Dependent states, however, may retain the right, to a greater or less degree, depending upon the number and character of the sovereign rights which they have yielded, or of which they have been deprived. They frequently retain the right of making treaties of commerce and extradition, postal and customs conventions, and, in some cases, treaties of alliance and naturalization. The existence of such powers, however, would be inconsistent with any considerable degree of dependence on the part of the semi-sovereign state. In the German Confederation, as reorganized in 1815, a considerable degree of treaty-making power was reserved to the component states. The present German empire is a closer confederation, the imperial government having sole power to conclude treaties of peace or alliance, or treaties of any kind for political objects, commercial treaties, conventions regulating questions of domicile, emigration, and postal affairs, protection of copyright, and consular matters, extradition treaties, and other conventions connected with the administration of civil or criminal law.[1] The states of the American Union are forbidden to enter into treaties with foreign states; or to make agreements with other states of the Union, except with the consent of Congress.

Contracts and Agreements with Individuals.—As sovereign states have many of the essential characteristics of corporations, they have the power of entering into contracts or agreements with individuals. These instruments are not treaties, however, nor are they, in all respects, the same as contracts between private persons or corporations. This for the reason that, where a sovereign state is a party to a contract, it cannot be coerced into specific performance of its agreement except by reprisals or war; nor, without its consent, can it be sued for a failure to fulfil its obligation to an individual.

2. *The Treaty-making Power.*—That authority in

---

[1] Hall, p. 22; Hertslet, "Map of Europe by Treaty," p. 1931.

the government of a state which is intrusted with the duty of entering into treaty relations is called the *treaty-making power*. In states having a monarchical form of government the treaty-making power is one of the prerogatives of the crown; in states having republican institutions it is exercised by the executive, either directly, or subject to the approval of some branch of the legislative department of the government. The constitution and laws of every state define the treaty-making power, and determine what restrictions, if any, are placed upon its exercise; and any agreements undertaken in excess of these limitations are unauthorized and void.

3. *Conditions Essential to the Validity of Treaties.*— To the validity of a treaty it is essential: 1st. That the contracting parties should possess the power to enter into treaty engagements. 2d. The formal consent of the parties must be given, and this consent must be mutual, reciprocal, and free. 3d. The subject of stipulation must not be opposed to morality and justice.

(*a.*) *The Power of Contracting Parties.*—States which are parties to a proposed agreement must possess full treaty-making power as to its subject-matter. Dependent states cannot enter into agreements which are not authorized by their dependent condition; and states which are members of a confederation cannot treat upon subjects which are reserved to the central government by the constitution of the confederacy. In the same manner the agents who are empowered to negotiate treaties may not exceed the limits laid down in their instructions or full powers. Any agreements entered into by them in excess of their authority are void, and ratification of them may be refused.

Such unauthorized agreements have been made at different times, usually by military commanders. They are called *sponsions*, and are invalid unless approved by the sponsor's government.

(*b.*) *The Consent of the Contracting Parties.*—The consent of the participating states must be expressly and freely given. It must also be reciprocal; and one state, by its ratification or approval of a treaty, cannot constrain another to ratify it, or to regard its provisions as binding. In contracts between individuals, if either party act under constraint, the resulting contract is void. In the preparation of certain treaties, however, especially in treaties of peace and in cartels and capitulations, one of the contracting parties acts under constraint of the most oppressive and humiliating kind; but this does not have the effect of invalidating the treaty. "Private contracts may be set aside on the ground of the influence of fraud and unfair dealing, arising from their manifest injustice and want of mutual advantage. But no inequality of advantage, no *lesion*, can invalidate a treaty."[1]

(*c.*) *It must be Possible of Execution.*—The conduct of states, like that of individuals, is regulated by well-known moral standards, from which they are bound not to depart. They are, therefore, prevented from making that a subject of treaty stipulation the execution of which is physically or morally impossible. Heffter holds those conditions to be morally impossible which are repugnant to moral order, or are opposed to the free development of nations.[2] Such would be stipulations tending to the destruction of a sovereign

---

[1] Phillimore, vol. ii., p 72. [2] Heffter, § 83.

state, or the establishment of slavery. The same may be said of provisions which are opposed to previous treaties with other powers, or which are prejudicial to the sovereign rights or powers of a third state.

4. *Binding Force of Treaties.* — Treaties entered into in conformity to these conditions are binding upon all the signatory parties, and they continue in force, whatever changes may take place in the internal affairs of the participant states. Changes of government affect in no way their binding force, and they cease to be obligatory only when a state ceases to exist. Their inviolability, even when not especially guaranteed, is the first law of nations. Obligations created by treaty are of the most sacred character, and their violation, if persisted in, or not atoned for, is universally regarded as a just cause for war.

5. *Manner of Negotiating Treaties.* — In former times treaties were frequently negotiated by sovereigns in person;[1] at present they are usually entered into by ministers or plenipotentiaries, selected for the purpose by the proper municipal authority, and furnished with special full powers to act in behalf of their respective governments in the preparation and signature of the treaty. Preliminary negotiations are usually necessary, to determine the place and time of meeting and the conditions of representation. In the preparation of treaties of peace, or of agreements preliminary to such treaties, the neutrality of the place is secured by proper guarantees, and the personal security of the ambassadors is carefully provided for, not

---

[1] The Holy Alliance of Sept. 14 (26), 1815, was signed by the emperors of Austria and Russia and the king of Prussia.

only at the sessions of the conference, but in their journeyings to and from the place of meeting. If the proposed agreement be one of general interest, the questions to be discussed are submitted to the powers in advance, the limits of discussion are to some extent defined, and the number and character of representatives from each state is determined upon.

At the time appointed the representatives assemble and exchange their credentials and full powers. If several states are represented the conference is usually presided over by the principal minister of foreign affairs of the state in whose territory its sessions are held, or by the representative of the government with which the project originated. If need be, rules of procedure are agreed to at a preliminary session. Each power represented has a right to be heard, at length, upon all projects submitted for discussion which in any way affect its interests. The proceedings of each session are reduced to writing, and are properly authenticated, and the negotiation continues until an agreement has been reached, or until the impossibility of reaching such an agreement has become apparent. If questions are submitted to vote, nothing short of unanimous consent is sufficient to carry a measure of prime importance. After an essential article or stipulation has been adopted, the majority rule may prevail in the decision of questions of detail, or in accessory stipulations of minor importance.

Language Used in the Preparation of Treaties.— The language used in the preparation of treaties is subject to no fixed rule. Each party may, of right, insist upon the use of its own in the preparation of treaties, as in every other public act, or a neutral language may be adopted. In the former case there would be as many original copies as there were participant states. This would be true in form only, and not in fact, since one of these originals would furnish a model upon which the translation of the others would be based. Latin was formerly used, as a convenient and generally understood neutral language. It is still the official language of the Holy See. Toward the close of the seventeenth century it was replaced by the French, which became the general diplomatic language of Europe and America. It still retains that character to a higher degree than any other. Since the beginning of this century the greater part of the treaties which have been negotiated in Europe have been drawn up and signed in French. When France is one of the signatory parties, however, a clause is usually inserted to the effect that the use of that language is not to be regarded as constituting a precedent. Treaties to which England or the United States are parties are usually drawn up in both languages, in parallel columns. Treaties with the Ottoman Porte are drawn up in Arabic and French.

Form and Signature.—No rigorous form is necessary to be followed in the preparation of these instruments so long as the conditions of the agreement are clearly expressed, and assented to, by the signatory parties. Those entered into by Christian states begin with a solemn invocation to the Deity, though this is frequently omitted in treaties of a commercial character. The first paragraph contains the name and designation of the contracting parties, followed by a clause stating, in general terms, the object of the treaty or convention, and by the names and titles of the ministers who have been empowered to represent the interested states in the negotiation. Next follows the body of the treaty, which is made up of stipulations mutually agreed to. It is divided into articles and clauses, the last of which fixes the terms of ratification and the date of signature. As many copies are prepared as there are contracting parties; and, in affixing the signatures and seals, the representative of each state signs first the copy intended for his own government. The order of the other signatures is determined by lot, or alphabetically, the initial letter of each state determining the order of signature.

Ratification of Treaties.—On account of the magnitude and importance of the interests involved, treaties acquire binding force only when they have been ratified by the sovereign authority of the states which are parties to their operation, and all modern treaties contain provisions stipulating for such an exchange of ratifications. Ratification by one party does not constrain the others to a similar course; but the act of ratification, when completed by all parties, is retroactive in its operation, and gives effect to the treaty from the date of signature, unless the contrary is expressly stipulated. There has been considerable discussion as to whether ratification could be withheld, without lack of good faith, in treaties containing no such provision. Some Continental writers, following the rule of the Roman Law, have held that states are bound by the acts of their plenipotentiaries, when they have not exceeded their full powers and confidential instructions; as principals are bound by the acts of their duly authorized agents. Others justly make a distinction, in this respect, between treaties and contracts. Treaties are compacts between sovereign states, involving interests of the greatest magnitude, and often of the most intricate character, far transcending in importance the agreements of individuals, which, however complicated, are relatively simple in comparison. However full and minute the powers and instructions of ministers may be, they are still liable to errors of judgment or mistakes of policy, which can only be discovered and remedied by a careful and disinterested examination of their work, and a full criticism of its provisions from all points of view.

Treaties sometimes contain provisions for the accession of third parties to their operation. The Declaration of Paris is an example. Such accession is had by a formal act on the part of the state desiring participation, by which it assumes, and agrees to be bound by, the obligations of the treaty. This is especially the case in treaties having in view some modification or amendment of the rules of International Law. The provisions of the Declaration of Paris, in 1856, have been acceded to by many states in Europe and America. England and the United States, in the Treaty of Washington, of 1871, agreed to use their influence to induce other nations to accept the principles of maritime law laid down in that instrument.

6. *Classification of Treaties.*—Treaties are susceptible of classification, according to their subject-matter, into:

(*a.*) Treaties, properly so called.
(*b.*) Cartels.
(*c.*) Capitulations.
(*d.*) Suspensions of Arms, or Truces.

Those of the first class, or treaties proper, are again subdivided into:

(1.) *Transitory Agreements or Conventions.* — These are treaties the immediate execution of which is essential, and which expire when the stipulated act has been performed. Their effects only are permanent. Such are boundary conventions, treaties of cession, etc., corresponding to executed contracts at Common Law.

(2.) *Permanent Treaties.* — These have continuing effect, and regulate the future relations and actions of the contracting parties. Treaties of friendship and commerce, of neutrality, extradition, and naturalization, and postal and customs conventions are examples of this class. These treaties may be of perpetual or limited duration. They may go into effect at a fixed date in the future, and may expire at a certain date, at the expiration of a certain period, or may be terminated at the will of either party, upon due notification. Their existence may be terminated by war, or they may come into effect only during hostilities between the interested parties.

Cartels are agreements entered into in time of war, for the exchange of prisoners. They are made by the commanders-in-chief of the belligerent forces, with the express or presumed consent of their governments. They may be transitory in character, or for the period of the war. In some European states this term is applied to an agreement entered into in time of peace for the extradition of deserters from the military service.

Capitulations are agreements entered into, in time of war, by the commanders of hostile fleets or armies, for the surrender of a fortified place or fleet, or of a defeated army. The proposition may originate with the commander of the place, fleet, or army, or may be in the nature of a demand made upon him by the opposite, or successful, party. Upon either of these, as a basis, the capitulation is drawn up, the terms being modified, and the conditions of surrender determined, by the relative strength and resources of the belligerent parties. Every general commanding a besieged place or separate army is presumed to have authority to enter into arrangements of this kind, though his power may be restricted in some way by the sovereign authority of his own state. In such an event his action would be subject to the approval of his government, and he should notify his opponent that such is the case. Cartels and capitulations are drawn up in the same form as treaties. The latter are signed first by the successful party.

7. *Objects of Treaties.*—The purpose or object of a treaty is, in most cases, sufficiently determined by its title. There are some, however, which require additional explanation.

Treaties of Alliance.—These are agreements undertaken by two or more states with a view to secure concerted action for a certain purpose. They may be either temporary or permanent in character, and are entered into by states which are menaced by a common danger, or whose mutual interests are threatened. They are based upon treaty stipulations, and, however slight the concert of action may be, the resulting alliance possesses some of the essential features of a league or confederation. The terms of the treaty of alliance determine the conditions of the union. Alliances may be equal or unequal, offensive or defensive, or both. Allied states may guarantee the continuance of a certain state of affairs in a third state, or in one of the states of the alliance. They are *defensive* when their object is to defend a common interest against aggression. Such alliances are conservative in character, and, by aggregating the influence and resources of a number, aim to secure respect for the sovereign rights of each of the component states. *Offensive* alliances are formed for the purpose of attacking a state, or league of states, either directly, or upon the occurrence of certain conditions. From their nature they are a constant menace to the peace of nations. The leagues organized to resist the schemes of Louis XIV. and Napoleon, though *offensive* in form, were really *defensive* in character, and tended to preserve the principle of balance of power. If alliances of this class be excepted, it will be found that the offensive combinations of which history has preserved the records, whatever may have been the real or assumed necessity of their organization, and however wisely they may have been administered, have rarely secured the prevalence of justice, or contributed to the advancement of any righteous cause.

Equal Alliances stipulate for the same or similar contributions of force or resources, or for a proportionate contribution based upon the resources of each ally.

Unequal Alliances are those in which the contributions stipulated for are unequal in character or amount, or in which the allied powers enjoy different degrees of consideration or influence. Each party to a treaty of alliance is the sole judge as to when the case contemplated by the treaty exists, or the action or intervention of an ally is required.

Treaties of Guarantee.—These compacts are accessory in character, and are entered into for the purpose of securing the observance of a treaty already existing, or the permanence of an existing state of affairs. If the guarantee covers the violation of any and every right, the treaty of guarantee creates an alliance. The term guarantee, in its most general sense, includes all treaties the purpose of which is to secure the observance and execution of other treaties, or the maintenance of certain existing conditions for a limited or unlimited period of time. The conditions of the guarantee are stated, in detail, in the body of the treaty. The guarantor state decides when the case exists which was contemplated in its guarantee. It is required to fulfil the conditions stated in the guarantee, and no more. Any change in the guaranteed treaty, without the consent of the guarantor, annuls the obligation. If the duty or aid stipulated is inadequate to the end proposed in the guarantee no additional duty or aid can be required.

The following conditions have been made the subjects of guarantee:

(a.) The political existence of a state, its sovereignty, or independence, or its existence within certain territorial limits.[1]

(b.) The permanent neutrality of a state,[2] or its neutrality under certain conditions.[3]

(c.) The free navigation of certain rivers,[4] and the

---

[1] The sovereignty and independence of Greece was guaranteed by France, Great Britain, and Russia, in a treaty negotiated at London, in 1832. The Treaty of Paris, of 1856, contained a somewhat similar provision respecting the Ottoman empire.

[2] The case of Switzerland is an example of this.

[3] The perpetual neutralization of Belgium was guaranteed by the great powers in the treaty of April 19, 1839.

[4] Klüber, p. 204.

permanent neutrality of works of improvement upon them.

(*d.*) The payment of loans.[1] In this case the guaranteeing powers usually become sureties, and are obliged to make good any default of their principals in their stipulated payments of principal or interest.

Reciprocity Treaties.—These are compacts containing stipulations requiring the mutual or reciprocal observance of certain duties or obligations. Most treaties, to a certain extent, involve reciprocal action, or the recognition of mutual rights and duties. It is only when a treaty involves a considerable number of such obligations that it receives this name. Extradition and naturalization treaties are reciprocal, but only on the subject from which each is named. Most reciprocity treaties, properly so called, are of a commercial character, and stipulate for specially favorable terms of commercial intercourse, for consular privileges, for the admission of certain products of each state into the ports of the other at special rates of duty, or without the payment of duty. They are usually entered into for a limited period of time, at the end of which they expire, or, at the will of the interested states, are revised and extended for a further period. The component states of a union or confederacy are frequently obliged, by the constitution or treaty of union, to grant many reciprocal privileges to each other. This was the case in the Zollverein, and is so in the existing German confederation. According to the Constitution of the United States, the states of the

---

[1] In the Treaty of London, in 1832, France, Great Britain, and Russia guaranteed a loan of Otho, the Bavarian prince who had been created by them King of Greece.

Federal Union are obliged to extradite criminals on the demand of other states, to accord the privileges of citizenship to citizens of other states, and to give full faith to the properly authenticated records and judgments of courts in the other states of the Union.

8. *Termination of Treaties.*—Treaties cease to be binding—

(*a.*) At the end of a stipulated period, or at a date mutually agreed upon by the signatory parties.

(*b.*) When the act stipulated for has been performed.

(*c.*) With the mutual consent of the contracting parties, or when either party retains the right, according to the terms of the agreement, to terminate it upon due notice; then at the expiration of the notice.

(*d.*) When either party wilfully violates his promises, or ceases to be bound by them, or fails to act in good faith according to their stipulations. This will be the case if but a single article has been violated, for the agreement was to observe the treaty in its entirety. In this event the other party is released from his obligations, and the instrument becomes void; or he may insist upon a compliance with the stipulations of the treaty, and may demand indemnities for any injury that has resulted from such failure, on the part of the defaulting state, to observe its agreement. As treaties convert *imperfect* into *perfect* obligations, the injured party may resort to force to obtain redress for the injury which he has sustained.

Treaties are suspended, and by some authorities are cancelled, by the occurrence of war between the contracting parties. They remain suspended during the period of the war, from the outbreak of hostilities until the negotiation of a treaty of peace. The least effect of war is to interrupt peaceful relations. It therefore suspends the operations of all treaties not permanent in character, or which do not contemplate a state of war. The belligerent states resume friendly relations by the execution of a treaty of peace, and that treaty should determine to what extent treaty relations between them shall be resumed.

The following treaties, however, are not suspended by the outbreak of war between the contracting parties:

(1.) Treaties of a permanent character, executed with full knowledge that war may occur, but given a permanent character by special stipulation.

(2.) Treaties entered into with a view of modifying or amending the rules of International Law.

(3.) Treaties which contemplate the occurrence of war, and which come into effect only at the outbreak of hostilities.

9. *Rules for the Interpretation of Treaties.*—Treaties, like laws, are drawn in general terms, and in their preparation the effort is made to frame their provisions in such terms as will include all cases that may fairly arise under them. This is a task of extreme difficulty. As the parties to such agreements, more frequently than not, speak different languages, and represent different, and sometimes opposing, legal and political systems, it is not at all remarkable that causes of difference should arise more frequently in the execution of treaties than in the operation of municipal laws. The *rules* of interpretation in both cases are the same; the *task* of interpretation, however, is vastly more difficult, in the case of treaties, than in the case of contracts and municipal laws. The attempt to

frame rules for this purpose has been frequently made; not always, however, with entirely satisfactory results. The English rules of Rutherforth are based upon the Common Law rules of interpretation as applied to contracts. Those of Vattel and Domat are based upon the rules of the Roman Law. To these authors the student is referred for a general discussion of the subject.

The following rules are now generally sanctioned:

(1.) Interpretation must be mutual. Neither party to a treaty can apply his own rule without impairing, or destroying, the binding force of the instrument.

(2.) A clause can have but one true meaning.

(3.) The words of a treaty are presumed to have been used in their usual sense and acceptation at the time the treaty was made, unless such interpretation involves an absurdity.

(4.) Terms technical to an art are used in the sense or meaning applied to them in that art.

(5.) Clauses inserted at the instance, or for the benefit, of one party, are strictly construed against the party in whose favor they were inserted. It is his fault if he has not expressed himself clearly.

(6.) Favorable clauses are to be interpreted liberally. Odious clauses are to be interpreted strictly. Favorable clauses are those granting privileges to individuals or states, or doing away with, or modifying, restrictions upon rights. Harsh clauses are those depriving individuals, or classes of persons, of rights already existing, or abridging such rights or privileges, or rendering them ineffective.

(7.) An interpretation which renders a treaty inoperative is to be rejected. Treaties are entered into for the purpose of accomplishing an end, or of attaining an object. Any interpretation, therefore, which renders a treaty wholly or in part inoperative, is absurd.

(8.) Special clauses are to be preferred to general. Prohibitory clauses to permissive; and, in general, that which is expressed in great detail is to be preferred to that which is stated in general terms, or in less particular detail. General clauses are declaratory of a principle. If exceptions exist, they are accurately defined and stated in the modifying clauses which follow the principal clause. The broad terms of a general clause, or title, cannot be appealed to as authority against the precise limitation or exemption of the special clause.

(9.) In the interpretation of a treaty the instrument must be regarded as an organic whole, and every part must be considered with reference to every other part. Hence earlier clauses are explained by later clauses in the same treaty, or by clauses on the same subject in later treaties. Obscure clauses by clearer and more precisely stated clauses of later date. As regards any particular subject of stipulation, the whole treaty policy of two states on that subject is to be considered. Later treaties explain and modify earlier treaties on the same subject.

Strict, or Restrictive Interpretation, consists in the precise application of the terms of an instrument to a particular case arising under it. It involves the exclusion of all cases not covered by a literal rendering of its terms.

Liberal, or Extensive Interpretation, consists in an attempt to so construe the provisions of a treaty as to include within its operations cases similar in principle to those specifically provided for. It is, in substance, a broad and comprehensive rendering of the clauses of a treaty, regard being had to the *spirit* rather than the *letter* of the instrument.

In connection with the subject of interpretation the following definitions are given of terms frequently occurring in treaties:

Protocol.—This is a word of Byzantine origin, and was at first applied to the first, or outer, sheet of a roll of manuscript, upon which was written or impressed the writer's name, the date of the instrument, and the title of the minister from whose office it issued. As a diplomatic term it is applied to the rough draft of a public act, and also to the formally authenticated minutes of the proceedings of a congress or conference. In a similar sense it is applied to the preliminary acts and agreements entered into by ambassadors in the preparation of a treaty.

Recez.—This term is applied to the act of a diet, or congress, in reducing to writing the result of its deliberations upon a particular subject, before final adjournment.

Separate Articles.—These are clauses added to a treaty after it has been formally signed and ratified. They are contained in a separate instrument, and are duly authenticated, but are construed in connection with the treaty to which they refer, and of which they form a part.

The most Favored Nation Clause.—The use of this clause is becoming constantly more frequent in treaties, especially in those of a commercial character. It commends itself by its convenience. Its effect is to extend its scope and operation to cover any concessions of privileges, of a similar character to those stipulated for, which may be granted in the future, by either party, to other states, or to their citizens or subjects. The clauses of later treaties granting such concessions in this way become an integral part of the earlier treaty. The following clause, extracted from a recent treaty of the United States, illustrates the principle involved: "If either party shall hereafter grant to any other nation, its citizens or subjects, any particular favor, in navigation or commerce, it shall immediately become common to the other party, freely, when freely granted to such other nation, or on yielding the same compensation when the grant is conditional.'

References.—The most valuable collection of treaties in the English language is that of Hertslet, vols. i.–iv. This work should be used in connection with "The Map of Europe by Treaty," by the same author. For the treaties of the United States, see "Treaties and Conventions of the United States," etc., 1776–1889, and "The United States Statutes at Large" (annual vols.), 1889–1891. The Spanish work of Calvo, in six volumes, contains all treaties negotiated by the Latin states of America prior to 1862. There are many valuable collections of treaties to which the Continental states of Europe have been parties. None of them are complete, however. Jenkinson's collection contains most English treaties between 1648 and 1785. See, also, G. F. De Martens, "Esquisse d'une Histoire Diplomatique des Traités," etc.; "Recueil des Principaux Traités," etc., 1761–1818, by G. F. De Martens, with Murrhard's continuation, bringing the work to 1860; and the "Corps Universel Diplomatique" of J. Dumont, which, with its additions, etc., covers, with more or less fulness, the period between 315 and

---

[1] "United States Statutes at Large," 43d Congress, 1873–1875, p. 68.

1738 A.D. Rymer's "Fœdera," etc., contains a collection of treaties, between England and other powers, between the years 1101 and 1654. A supplement to this work, in fifty-seven volumes, is preserved in the British Museum. For a full bibliography of this subject, see Klüber, pp. 424-437.

CHAPTER IX.

THE CONFLICT OF INTERNATIONAL RIGHTS.

1. *Causes of Conflict.*—When a conflict of international rights arises, as is the case whenever one state has a cause of difference with another, it is customary for the state whose rights have been denied, or trespassed upon, to make known its cause of complaint to the offending state, and to demand that justice be done for the wrong that has been committed. The urgency of this demand is always proportional to the gravity and importance of the injury sustained. The motive of some violations of perfect or sovereign rights may be so obvious and unmistakable that no explanations are asked for by the offended state, and resort is at once had to forcible measures of redress. On the other hand, the offence may consist in the violation of some minor rule of comity of so little importance that a mere exchange of diplomatic notes is deemed a sufficient remedy. Between these two extremes lie the various methods of settling international disputes.

2. *Methods of Adjusting International Differences.*—Those most frequently resorted to are—

(*a*.) An amicable adjustment of the difference by the interested states.

(*b*.) Mediation.

(*c*.) Arbitration.

(1.) *The Amicable Adjustment of Disputes.*—Whenever a state has occasion to complain of the action of another toward itself, or toward one of its subjects, a statement of the particular act complained of is prepared in the Foreign Office of the offended state. This statement is based upon all the ascertainable facts of the case, which should be so carefully sifted and verified, by those charged with their investigation, as to make it impossible to question their substantial accuracy. This is necessary because it is impossible, in international affairs, to produce evidence in the ordinary legal acceptation of the term. The facts thus ascertained and verified are next examined with a view to ascertaining whether they do, or do not, constitute a violation of International Law. If they do a case is prepared, and a formal demand for redress is made and forwarded, through the proper diplomatic channels, to the government by whom the injury was committed. In support of this case reference is made to the works of standard text-writers, to the provisions of treaties, if the case be covered by them, and to precedents in international intercourse, especially to those established by the offending state in its international relations. In conclusion, such explanation, disavowal, or reparation is demanded as is warranted by the circumstances of the case.

If that government be clearly in the wrong it acknowledges its error, or disavows the act of its subordinate officials; and offers reparation, accompanied by such explanation and apology as the occasion seems to demand. In cases where such a remedy is suitable, money indemnities are agreed upon and paid to injured parties. It rarely happens, however, that either state, in a particular controversy, is either entirely right, or entirely wrong; and the same facts are, in general, differently regarded by each of two interested states. This leads to controversial discussion, each state advancing arguments and citing authorities in support of that view of the case which it believes to be most nearly in accordance with justice. A correspondence of this kind may continue through a period of years, and rarely leads to results of direct or immediate importance. It is resorted to when two states cherish different views as to the justice of a practice maintained or advocated by one and denied by the other. Such was the long controversy between England and the United States upon the right of search, which extended over a period of more than fifty years. When a nation complains of a clear and decided violation of International Law, however, and no dispute exists as to the facts in the case, reparation on the part of the offending state is usually made with the greatest promptness.[1]

---

[1] The following cases are cited in illustration of this principle:

Case of the Laconia.—In December, 1878, the American whaling-ship Laconia, while in the port of Zanzibar, Africa, was boarded by an officer of the British ship of war Leader, Captain Earl. The boarding party took from the Laconia three Africans, claiming that they were slaves, Captain Earl justifying his act under the treaty of 1862, between England and the United States, for the suppression of the slave trade. The matter was represented to the British government, by whom the action of Captain Earl was promptly disapproved, and the regrets of Her Majesty's government at the occurrence were conveyed, through the British minister, to the government at Washington ("Foreign Relations of the United States," 1879, pp. 415–432).

Case of the James Bliss.—In 1872 the American schooner James Bliss was seized, in British territorial waters, by the Canadian police cutter Stella Maris, for an alleged violation of the fishery laws. Soon after her arrival in the port of Gaspé Basin the commanding officer of the police cutter caused the Dominion flag to be hoisted

Duty of Moderation.—In this method of adjustment, much depends upon the tact and moderation shown by the diplomatic representatives of the interested states in dealing with the question of difference. "It not infrequently happens that what is at first looked upon as an injury or an insult is found, upon a more deliberate examination, to be a mistake rather than an act of malice, or one designed to give offence. Moreover, the injury may result from the acts of inferior persons, which may not receive the approbation of their own governments. A little moderation and delay, in such cases, may bring to the offended party a just satisfaction, whereas rash and precipitate measures may often lead to the shedding of much innocent blood. The moderation of the government of the United States in the case of the burning of the American steamboat Caroline, in 1837, by a British officer, led to an amicable adjustment of the difficulties arising from a violation of neutral territory, and saved both countries from the disasters of a bloody war."[1] The cases of the Creole and of what is known as the Tahiti affair are illustrations of the same principle. In the former case "the feeling in the southern states of the Union was strong

---

above the American, at the mast-head. The act was repeated on the following day, in both instances against the protest of the American consul. The facts were then reported to the Department of State in Washington, by whom they were brought to the attention of the Governor-general of Canada in the diplomatic way. Action was at once taken in the matter. Lord Dufferin, the governor-general, disavowing, in the amplest manner, any intention of showing disrespect to the American flag. He also announced that he had given most particular instructions directing the discontinuance of the practice ("Foreign Relations of the United States," 1872, pp. 200–208).

[1] Halleck, vol. i., pp. 413, 414.

in favor of war, and in all human probability would have caused it, had it not been for the friendly and courteous spirit in which the American and British governments carried on their communications on the subject with each other." In the latter case, " the menacing effects of popular indignation at a supposed gross national insult were averted by the fairness and temperance with which one government made its claim for redress, and by the readiness on the other side to enter into a calm investigation of all the circumstances of the case, and to listen to reason and justice rather than to give way to national vanity. Here we have three occasions in which, by the self-action of the parties concerned, by a cool and candid examination of the subject in dispute, and by a gentle method of terminating differences, three of the greatest countries in the world set examples of forbearance that deserve to be recorded as precedents worthy of imitation."[1]

Mediation.—Of all the methods hitherto proposed for preventing international strife this has been by far the most effective and successful in its practical working. It consists, in substance, of a reference of the cause of difference to a disinterested power, who suggests a remedy, or, more frequently, proposes an adjustment based upon such mutual concessions as will remove the cause of difference or irritation. Mediation may be asked by the interested states, or a third power may tender its good offices, with a view to the maintenance of peace. In the latter case the friendly

---

[1] Sir Edward Creasy, "First Platform of International Law," pp. 391, 392; Abdy's Kent, p. 72.

powers tender their good offices, which may be accepted, or not, by the interested states. This method of adjusting international differences was frequently resorted to during the Middle Ages, especially by the pope, and there are numerous instances of his successful mediatory interference to be found in the history of Europe during that period. In modern times the tendency to mediation has greatly increased in force, and but few cases of conflict of international right have arisen, in recent times, in which the good offices of friendly powers have not been tendered to the litigant states. Although these offers have not always, or even usually, been accepted, their effect has been beneficial, inasmuch as they have furnished new grounds, or reasons, for the settlement of existing difficulties, and have suggested methods of adjustment which had not occurred to the interested parties.

Arbitration.—*Private arbitration* consists in the reference of an international difference or dispute to a tribunal composed of one or several persons. To this tribunal the question of difference is submitted, and its decision, when rendered, is binding upon the interested parties. This method of adjustment does not afford so prompt a remedy as can be obtained through mediation, and is applicable to a somewhat different class of cases. It possesses an advantage over that form of adjustment, however, in that its decisions have greater binding force, since, if rendered in good faith, they cannot be rejected by litigant parties as can offers of mediation.

The composition of the tribunal, the method of selecting its members, the time and place of meeting, its rules of procedure, and the precise question to be referred to it for decision, are always made the subject of a preliminary treaty. This instrument also contains a solemn agreement, on the part of the interested states, to abide by the decision of the board of arbitration. If a person of sovereign rank is selected to act as an arbitrator, the case on each side is submitted to him, through his minister of foreign affairs, and his decision is rendered through the same channel. If the tribunal is composed of several members, the cases are submitted by counsel, whose arguments are heard. The provisions of the Roman Law on the subject of arbitration may, with the consent of the interested parties, be made obligatory upon the tribunal. A more liberal code of procedure is frequently provided, or the rules of the Roman Law are somewhat modified in their application to a particular case.

In reaching a decision the majority rule prevails, unless otherwise precisely stipulated in the preliminary treaty, and the decision of the tribunal binds the litigant states, unless its validity can be contested upon any one of the following grounds:

(1.) If one of the members of the tribunal has not acted in good faith; or if its decision be tainted with fraud.

(2.) If any of the conditions of the preliminary treaty, as to method of procedure, time and place of meeting, have not been complied with; or if the decision has not been rendered within the time therein stated.

(3.) If the tribunal has exceeded its jurisdiction; or if its decision goes outside the case submitted to it for adjudication.

3. *Mediation and Arbitration Compared.*—If the cases be compared in which these methods of adjust-

ing international disputes have been successfully applied, it will be seen that mediation has been found most useful when it has been resorted to to prevent threatened hostilities, especially in cases involving national reputation, or when considerable national feeling has been aroused. It has also been found a successful method of terminating an existing war, especially when a disinterested state has chosen a fitting opportunity, during an interval of hostile operations, to tender its good offices to the belligerent powers. Arbitration, on the contrary, "implies a belief on the part of both that either a legal or quasi-legal question is involved, and that each is, in his own opinion, right; or, in other words, that, when the state of facts is carefully examined, and the law or equitable principle accurately expounded, each hopes and thinks the result will be in his own favor. A *bona fide* belief in the justice of one's own cause is an essential element in a successful arbitration. If such a belief is absent, there can be no readiness to obey the award, and the same causes of acrimony exist after the award as before it."[1] "Arbitration is an expedient of the highest value for terminating international controversies; but it is not applicable to all cases or under all circumstances, and the cases and circumstances to which it is not applicable do not admit of precise definition. Arbitration, therefore, must of necessity be voluntary; and though it may sometimes be a moral duty to resort to it, cannot be commanded, in any form, by what is called the positive law of nations."[2]

4. *Measures of Redress, Involving the Use of Force,*

---

[1] Amos, "Science of Law," p. 348.
[2] Sir Montague Bernard, Letter to *London Times*, Oct. 18, 1873.

but Falling Short of War.—Between the peaceable methods of adjusting international disputes, which have already been described, and an actual resort to force, lie certain measures of redress of a more serious character. These methods presume the existence of a cause of difference between two states, justifying a departure from the normal relations existing between the nations in time of peace, and the measures adopted at times involve the use of violence or force; but, even when exercised to an extreme degree, they fall far short of open or public war. They are resorted to only when redress has been asked for and denied, and are justifiable only when the offending nation acts with full knowledge, and persists in doing injustice after its attention has been repeatedly drawn to its wrongful acts.

The measures of redress involving the use of forcible or hostile methods are susceptible of classification under one of two heads—retorsion and reprisals.

Retorsion consists in an application of the same rule of conduct in our relations with another state as is applied, by that state, in its relations with us. It is an application of the law of retaliation in international affairs. If a state imposes unjust restrictions upon aliens residing within its territories, the state whose subjects they are is justified in imposing the same, or equivalent, restrictions upon the subjects of the offending state who are resident within its borders. If it refuse privileges usually granted by states to ambassadors and consuls, the offended states are justified in a similar refusal of privileges to its consuls and diplomatic representatives.

The field within which the principle of retorsion may be applied, already very extensive, is constantly increasing. This state of affairs is due to the fact that the commercial relations of states are increasing in intricacy in direct proportion as they increase in extent and amount, giving rise to frequent conflicts between the business, or internal, policy of particular states, and their external, or international, policy. Illustrations of this tendency are to be found in the experience of states which derive a large portion of their public revenue from customs duties. If some article of native production falls in price on account of foreign competition, an attempt is made to remedy the difficulty by increasing the duty upon the corresponding foreign article. This is felt at once in the state in which the particular article is produced, or manufactured, and retaliatory measures are resorted to with a view of compelling the removal of the trade restriction.

Acts of retorsion must be confined to the class of imperfect rights, except when resorted to by way of retaliation for similar or identical acts on the part of a foreign state. The denial of a *perfect* right amounts to a just cause for war.

Reprisals.—*Reprisals* consist in the forcible seizure or detention of property belonging to an offending state, or to its citizens, which may be found within the territory of the offended state, or on the high seas. The things seized are held subject to the termination of the controversy. If it be settled amicably, the property is restored, and reparation is sometimes made for the delay and damage that have resulted from the seizure. If the dispute results in war, the property seized is condemned as prize.

Reprisals differ from retorsion not only in kind but in degree. Retorsion is resorted to when imperfect rights have been trespassed upon, or when there has been a failure to observe the rules of comity. *Reprisals* are resorted to when perfect rights have been drawn in question, or denied, or when there has been an absolute refusal of justice. They are acts of violence, and may be regarded by the state toward which they are directed as amounting to a declaration of war. They are justifiable only when there has been an absolute denial of justice, so deliberate and intentional on the part of the offending state as to constitute a sufficient cause for war. If war does not result, it is because the offended state, appreciating the hardship and suffering that are involved in a resort to actual hostilities, chooses to regard the offence as technical, by undertaking to redress its wrong by similar, though less violent, measures. In recent times they have been less frequently resorted to than formerly, especially by the more powerful states of Europe and America in their occasional controversies with each other. The present tendency is to resort to them only when the injured state is considerably more powerful than its adversary, and generally with the effect of obtaining the desired redress without recourse to war. "Much of what appears in the older and even in some modern books upon the subject of reprisals has become antiquated. Special reprisals, or reprisals in which letters of marque are issued to the persons who have suffered at the hands of a foreign state, are no longer made; all the reprisals that are now made may be said to be general reprisals, carried out through the ordinary authorized agents of the state, letters of marque being no longer issued."[1]

---

[1] Hall, p. 312, note.

References.—Three methods of adjusting international disputes have been discussed in this chapter—1. Amicable adjustment; 2. mediation; 3. arbitration. Under the head of amicable adjustment, the following references are suggested: Hall, p. 306; Halleck, vol. i., chap. xiv., §§ 1–3; Heffter, liv. ii., chap. i., §§ 106–108; Vattel, book ii., chap. xviii., §§ 324–326; Creasy, pp. 390, 391; Phillimore, vol. iii., chap. i., pp. 2–5. For mediation, see Boyd's Wheaton, pp. 97–99, and pp. 345, 706; Halleck, vol. i., chap. xiv., §§ 5–6; Heffter, liv. ii., chap. i., § 107; Creasy, pp. 390–392; Klüber, chap. iii., §§ 318–321; Vattel, book ii., chap. xviii., § 328. Under the head of arbitration see Hall, p. 306; Manning, pp. 499–504; Halleck, vol. i., chap. xiv., §§ 7, 8; Boyd's Wheaton, § 288; Vattel, book ii., chap. xviii., §§ 329–334; Wildman, vol. i., p. 186; Heffter, § 109; Klüber, § 318; Creasy, p. 83, and pp. 394–397, 698; Phillimore, vol. iii., pp. 2–15; G. F. De Martens, vol. ii., § 176. For the schemes which have been suggested for the peaceable settlement of international differences, see Manning, chap. xiv.; Amos, "Science of Law," pp. 345–359; Amos, "Political and Legal Remedies for War;" Bernard, "Neutrality of England," pp. 494–506; Wheaton, "History of the Law of Nations," pp. 750–758; Laveleye, "La Guerre en Europe et Arbitrage;" Abbot, "Essays on Modern International Law," essay v., "The Primacy of the Great Powers;" essay vi., "The Evolution of Peace."

CHAPTER X.

WAR.

"The choler and manhood that you have, score it, in God's name, upon the fronts of your enemies, but stain not the honor of a soldier by outraging unarmed innocence. Live upon your means like soldiers, and not by pilfering and spoiling like highway robbers. This if you do not you shall ever be infamous, and I with such help shall never be victorious."[1]—GUSTAVUS ADOLPHUS.

1. *The Right of Redress.*—As there is no superior authority to which a state can appeal for redress when any of its sovereign rights have been trespassed upon, denied, or impeded in their exercise, it is compelled, as a last resort, to redress its own injury, or wrong. This it does by a suspension of all friendly relations with the offending state, and by a resort to such acts of hostility as are authorized by the laws of war. Again, in the performance of its duty of protecting its citizens and their property from acts of domestic violence, a government sometimes finds its ordinary legal machinery inadequate to the purpose, and is compelled to make use of the public armed force in order to compel obedience to the law, to quell insurrection and rebellion, or to enforce respect for its neutral obligations. In one case the state uses force against another state; in the other its force is directed against a portion of its own population.

2. *Definition and Purpose of War.*—War may there-

---

[1] Abbot, "Essays on Modern International Law," p. 162.

fore be defined as an armed contest between states or parts of states. It is undertaken by one state against another, for the purpose of compelling an offending state to fulfil its obligations as a party to International Law. It is undertaken against persons within its territory for the purpose of compelling obedience to its municipal laws. When its object is attained, in either case, war itself becomes unlawful and must cease.

3. *Rightfulness of War.*—With the inherent rightfulness of war International Law has nothing to do. War exists as a fact of international relations, and, as such, it is accepted and discussed. In defining the laws of war, at any time, the attempt is made to formulate its rules and practices, and to secure the general consent of nations to such modifications of its usages as will tend toward greater humanity, or will shorten its duration, restrict its operations, and hasten the return of peace and the restoration of the belligerent states to their normal relations.

4. *Classification of Wars.*—Wars are classified according to the point of view from which they are examined or discussed. They are classified according to their causes into *wars of opinion, religious wars, wars of independence, of conquest, or subjugation.* In a military sense they are either *offensive* or *defensive.* In a political sense they are classified into *external* and *internal* wars. *Internal* wars are further subdivided into, 1st. *Civil wars,* in which the belligerent parties are distributed over a large part of the territory of a state; the object being to secure a change of government or laws, but not at the expense of national unity. 2d. *Rebellions* or *insurrections,* in which a portion of the population of a state rises against the central gov-

ernment, sometimes with the design of securing a separation from it, sometimes with a view to resist the execution of harsh or oppressive laws, or measures of administration.

5. *The Belligerent Parties.*—The parties to a war are called *belligerents*. Their operations must be carried on in accordance with certain accepted usages, which are sanctioned by all nations under the name of the *Laws of War*.

Whenever a state occupies the position of a belligerent, it is vested with all the rights, and charged with all the obligations, incident to a state of war. The parties to an internal war are also called belligerents. They acquire belligerent rights so soon as the central government decides to resort to warlike methods in order to quell the insurrection. The recognition of such rights by the central government, or by foreign powers, in no way involves the recognition of the rebellious government as a separate political organization. It only implies that the laws of war are to prevail in the military operations undertaken for the purpose of suppressing the rebellion, enforcing the laws, and restoring the supremacy of the national government. In wars with savages, and, to a certain extent, in wars with nations which do not acknowledge the sanctions of International Law, it is impossible for a state to be guided in all respects by the laws of war. This is so because one of the belligerents, having a different standard of morals, or being without such a standard, declines to recognize the rules of civilized warfare. This does not absolve a civilized state from its obligation to observe those laws; it rather strengthens it, and it will be justified in resorting to retaliatory measures only when such measures are rendered absolutely necessary by the barbarous or inhuman conduct of its enemy.

6. *Right of Declaring War, in whom Vested?*— The right of declaring war is an essential attribute of sovereignty. It is the act of the supreme governmental authority of a state, and is limited in its exercise, if at all, only by its constitution or fundamental law. In former times this power was delegated to colonial governments, and even to commercial companies; at present, however, such delegation of authority is no longer recognized, and the positive power of declaring war is held to be lodged exclusively in the sovereign authority of a state. This does not prevent distant dependencies from recognizing the fact of war, if declared by another power; and they may resist invasion, or even carry the war into an enemy's country.

7. *Causes of War.*— Although it falls within the province of International Law to determine how war between civilized states shall be carried on, and with what formalities it shall begin and end, it is impossible to deduce from the history of international relations any precise rule for determining what fact, or facts, shall constitute a just cause for war. It has been said that a sovereign right of a state can be invaded, or denied, only at the risk of war, and, in so far as International Law is concerned, a state is legally justified in regarding the denial of such a right as a sufficient cause for war. The question of determining whether a particular cause of offence is, or is not, sufficient to justify war, is strictly internal in character, and concerns the offended state alone. With the government of that state rests the entire legal and moral responsi-

bility of decision. The efficient check upon a nation in this respect must be found in international public opinion rather than in International Law.

Responsibility for a Resort to War.—While it is technically true that a violation or denial of a perfect right is regarded as a just cause for war, it is true only because no other remedy is provided for the violation, by a state, of a rule of International Law. As there is no authority above a sovereign state to which it can appeal, it is of necessity compelled to redress, by its own means, any injuries that it may receive from another state. Not every denial of a perfect right results in war, even when justice has been demanded and refused. Those in whose hands the government is must consider whether the injury that has been received is sufficient, in amount or importance, to counterbalance the evils that are involved in a resort to war. The chance of success must be considered, as well as the ability of the state to bear the burden of long-continued hostilities.

Moral Considerations Involved.—Certain moral considerations are also involved in the decision, the responsibility for which no government can evade. "If reparation can otherwise be obtained, a nation has no necessary, and therefore no just, cause for war: if there be no probability of obtaining it by arms, a government cannot, with justice to their own nation, embark it in war; and if the evils of resistance should appear, on the whole, greater than those of submission, wise rulers will consider an abstinence from a pernicious exercise of right as a sacred duty to their own subjects, and a debt which every people owes to the great commonwealth of mankind, of which they and their enemies are alike members. A war is just against a wrongdoer when reparation for wrong cannot otherwise be obtained; but it is then only conformable to all the principles of morality when it is not likely to expose the nation by whom it is levied to greater evils than it professes to avert, and when it does not inflict, on the nation which has done the wrong, sufferings altogether disproportioned to the extent of the injury. When the rulers of a nation are required to determine a question of peace or war, the bare justice of their case against the wrongdoer never can be the sole, and is not always the chief, matter on which they are morally bound to exercise a conscientious deliberation. Prudence in conducting the affairs of their subjects is in them a part of justice."[1]

8. *Declaration of War, Ancient and Modern Rule.*— In former times war was declared with great formalities. This is no longer the case, the formal declaration having ceased when the necessity for its existence had passed away. When the relations of two states become strained the fact is at once known throughout the civilized world, and the subjects of the unfriendly powers have sufficient time to arrange their business affairs, and to accommodate their legal relations to the changed conditions. When all attempts at peaceable adjustment have failed, diplomatic intercourse ceases, ministers are withdrawn, and the military and naval forces of the belligerents are mobilized and placed upon a war footing. So far as the opposing nations are concerned, no further declaration is now necessary.

---

[1] Mackintosh's Collected Works, p. 430, cited by Creasy, "First Platform of International Law," pp. 362, 363.

Official Notification of an Intended Resort to War.—Although the practice of making formal declarations no longer obtains, a state which assumes a belligerent attitude toward another is obliged to give public notice of its intention in each of the following cases: 1st. To its own subjects; 2d. To neutrals. This notice is frequently given by proclamations, which contain a statement of the cause of the war, and of the purposes, or motives, for which it is undertaken. They also contain the date after which a state of hostility will legally exist. This is a matter of great importance, in that it enables neutral powers to give effect to their neutrality laws, to issue proclamations of neutrality, and to fix the date upon which their neutral obligations become binding. No declaration, or notice, is required from the state which acts on the defensive.

9. *Effect of War upon Treaties of Alliance, Guarantee, and Subsidy.*—Treaties of alliance, of subsidy, and of guarantee, made in anticipation of war, come into effect the moment war is declared by, or against, one of the allied states. Each state which is a party to a treaty of alliance must decide for itself whether the case contemplated by the treaty exists or not. If its decision be affirmative, its obligations as an ally go into effect immediately. If it decides in the negative, its action cannot be constrained by any method short of reprisals or war. The other allies, however, may look upon its failure as a violation of treaty stipulation, which they may regard as a just cause for war. A treaty of subsidy obliges a state to grant such aid in troops, supplies, or money as it may have stipulated to furnish, either on formal notification, or when a particular state of affairs exists which was contemplated

by the treaty. In this case, as in that of an alliance, each contracting party decides for itself whether the case exists which is contemplated by the treaty, and each is fully responsible for its decision. The aid agreed upon is furnished strictly in accordance with the provisions of the treaty of subsidy, and the obligation incurred is fulfilled when the stipulated duty has been performed. If the assistance proves inadequate to the purpose, or if it be impossible of fulfilment, no obligation rests upon the subsidizing state to render other or further service of the same kind.

Treaties of guarantee, in so far as they relate to war, usually consist in an obligation, assumed by one or more states, to enforce respect for the neutrality of a third state, or to assure the existence of such a state within certain territorial limits. They become effective when the neutrality of the protected state is threatened from any quarter, or when the guaranteed territory is invaded, or menaced with invasion. Subsidiary treaties may also exist, providing in detail for interference in either of these cases. If such treaties exist, they must be strictly observed in making good the guarantee.

The effect of war upon treaties generally has already been discussed.[1]

10. *Effects of a State of War.*—The direct effects of a state of war are: 1st. To place both the belligerent states and their subjects in a condition of non-intercourse with each other. 2d. Each citizen of one state becomes the legal enemy of every citizen of the other. This state is *legal*, not *actual*, for no subject of either state can take the life of his enemy, or make captures

---

[1] Ante, pp. 179, 180.

on land or sea, or do any hostile act, without the express authority of his government. Commercial intercourse between subjects of the belligerent states becomes illegal. Contracts and other legal obligations are suspended during the continuance of hostilities, and a similar rule is applied to partnerships and other business arrangements. Shares in the public stocks of either state, which are held in the territory of the other, are not confiscated or forfeited. Interest ceases to be paid at the outbreak of hostilities, but is resumed at the peace, the interest accrued during the war becoming payable at its close.

Citizens of one belligerent power in the territory of the other at the declaration of war may be required to depart, or may be permitted to remain, at the discretion of the state in whose territory they are resident.[1] The latter course has been pursued in most recent wars, and is the one most in accordance with the dictates of humanity. This question has frequently been made the subject of treaty stipulation. It is now generally recognized, however, that such persons are not to be made prisoners of war, and, if ordered to depart, they are to be given a reasonable time for removal with their property and effects. Subjects of the enemy who are permitted to remain in a belligerent state may be subjected to such special police regulation and supervision as may be deemed necessary by the government for its security. For reasonable cause they may be required to depart, or may be forcibly expelled. If they give aid or information to the enemy, or to their own government, they become subject to the laws of

---

[1] Boyd's Wheaton, p. 366, note.

war, and may be treated, according to the nature of their offence, as prisoners of war, or as traitors or spies, and may be punished accordingly.

The Property of Enemy's Subjects.—The property of enemy's subjects found within the territory of a state at the outbreak of war is not confiscable. Debts due an enemy's subject are suspended during the war, but resume their obligatory character at its termination. "The right of the original creditor to sue for the recovery of his debt is not extinguished by the war, and revives in full force on the restoration of peace."[1] "The debts due by American citizens to British subjects before the war of the Revolution, and not actually confiscated, were judicially considered as revived, together with the right to sue for their recovery, on the restoration of peace between the two countries. The commercial treaty of 1794 also contained an express declaration that it was unjust and impolitic that private contracts should be impaired by national differences; with a mutual stipulation that neither the debts due from individuals of the one nation to individuals of the other, nor shares, nor moneys which they may have in the public funds, or in public or private banks, shall ever, in any event of war or national differences, be sequestered or confiscated."[2]

"Some writers have drawn a distinction between debts due from a subject of one belligerent to a subject of the other, and debts due from a belligerent state to subjects of the other. It is said that there exists a right to confiscate the former, while the latter are to be

---

[1] Boyd's Wheaton, p. 366.
[2] *Ibid.*, p. 367; Dallas, vol. iii., pp. 4, 5, 199–285.

exempt. The Confederate States acted upon this distinction, and confiscated all property and all rights, credits, and interests held within the confederacy by or for any alien enemy, except public stocks and securities. Lord Russell strongly protested against this, as being an act as unusual as it was unjust."[1]

"But this is the only instance in recent times of such measures having been adopted, and it is an example that seems unlikely to be imitated. The confiscation of private debts of any sort, besides exposing the state doing so to retaliation, only cripples the enemy in a very indirect way. It has no effect at all on the military or naval operations of the war, and cannot, therefore, be justified on any principle."[2]

THE LAWS OF WAR.

11. *Character and Tendency of the Laws of War.*— That department of International Law which treats of the manner in which war shall be carried on by belligerents, on land and sea, is called the *Laws of War*. These laws are constantly changing, to adapt them to the ever-changing conditions of modern warfare. The tendency of these changes is, and always has been, in the direction of greater humanity and liberality. Harsh usages are modified, cruel practices become obsolete, or are abandoned by treaty or general consent, and new methods are constantly suggested for diminishing the inevitable hardships of war. This improvement is observable in all departments; it is most remarkable, however, in the treatment of individuals,

---

[1] "Parliamentary Papers," 1862, "Correspondence Relating to Civil War," p. 108.   [2] Boyd's Wheaton, p. 3C9, note.

combatant and non-combatant, and in the greater consideration shown to the wounded and to prisoners of war. There has been the least progress in the rules relating to private property on land and sea. The Declaration of Paris restrains the states who were parties to it from capturing private property at sea, except enemy goods in enemy ships and contraband of war. The practice of privateering has declined, probably never to be revived. In war on land pillage is sternly forbidden, but private property may still be taken by way of requisition. Contributions are still recognized, and certain kinds of property may be captured and destroyed, or regarded as booty. There are no indications, at present, that belligerents will voluntarily surrender any of the rights which they now exercise over private property on land. In the few instances in which such property has been exempted from capture or requisition its immunity has been due to the fact that, in those instances, rapidity of movement was an essential condition of success, which could not have been attained had the force employed, in the particular undertakings, been compelled to depend for its subsistence upon the slow and uncertain methods of requisitioning supplies from an unwilling or hostile population. The recommendations of the conferences at Brussels and St. Petersburg illustrate these tendencies. The declarations on the subject of combatants and non-combatants, the treatment of wounded men and of prisoners of war, are plain and positive in character, and commend themselves to all nations. Those on the subject of private property are brief, obscure, and unsatisfactory, reflecting but too clearly the opinions upon that subject of those who framed them.

14

12. *Subjects Treated of in the Laws of War.*—The Laws of War have chiefly to do with the following subjects:

(*a.*) The forces that may be employed in war, on land and sea.

(*b.*) The methods of carrying on war.

(*c.*) The instruments that may be employed.

(*d.*) The rules regulating captures on land and sea.

(*e.*) The treatment of the public and private property of the enemy.

(*f.*) The treatment of non-combatants in the theatre of war.

(*g.*) The treatment of captured persons, or prisoners of war.

(*h.*) The government of occupied territory.

(*i.*) The intercourse of belligerents in war.

13. *The Amount and Kind of Force that may be Used in War.*—International Law recognizes the fact of war, and sanctions a resort to hostile methods to obtain redress for an international wrong. It does not sanction or approve acts of indiscriminate violence, however, nor the use of force in excess of the precise amount needed to redress the injury, or its continued use after the legitimate purpose of the war has been accomplished.

Legal Effects of a State of War upon the Subjects of the Belligerent States.—It has already been seen that the existence of a state of war makes each subject of one belligerent the legal enemy of every subject of the other. An individual domiciled in a belligerent state becomes an enemy, his property becomes enemy property, and, as an enemy, he ceases to have a legal status in the courts of the hostile state. This is a consequence of the relation of the belligerent states to each other. The states are at war, and so the individual units who compose them must share the same hostile relation. This state of individual hostility, however, is *legal*, not *actual*, and does not of itself justify a subject of either state in taking the life of an enemy, in making captures, or in doing any act of hostility whatsoever. Upon this point the international usage is plain. No individual is permitted to commit any hostile act, save in self-defence, without the positive, express authorization of his government. Whoever undertakes an act of hostility without such authorization does so at his peril, and if captured is not entitled to the protection of the laws of war.

Who may Lawfully Carry on War.—In general war is carried on by the regular armed force of each belligerent power. The character of that force, and its composition, are internal questions, to be determined by the municipal law of every state. In addition to its regular armed force a state may call into its service, for the period of the war, or for a shorter term, such additional forces as it may deem necessary to prosecute the war successfully. This force may consist of conscripts, of volunteers, or of such militia or reserve forces as are, or may be, provided for by its constitution and laws. This force must, in general, be organized and disciplined, commanded by responsible officers, and should either be uniformed, or required to wear some distinguishing mark or badge by which its members may be recognized and known.

"*Partisans* are soldiers, armed, and wearing the uniform of their army, but belonging to a corps which acts detached from the main body, for the purpose of making inroads into the territory occupied by the enemy. If captured they are entitled to all the privileges of the prisoner of war."[1]

A *Levée en Masse* is a general rising of the population of a state to resist an invader. Such risings usually take place with the consent, and by the direction, of the government of the invaded state, and there may or may not be time for the movement to be organized and regulated by the government. In such cases the question arises: Are the individual members of such a body entitled, if captured, to be treated as prisoners of war? The weight of opinion is that they are, so long as they observe the laws of civilized war in conducting their operations. Two views have been entertained upon this subject. One, maintained by states having large standing armies, and whose military operations are more likely to be offensive than defensive, holds that such risings are unauthorized. This view is largely influenced by self-interest. The other, held by states maintaining small military establishments, and so more concerned with *defensive* than *offensive* operations, justifies them on the grounds of necessity and self-defence. The latter view is now held by the greater number of states. Of those which maintain the former opinion the two most important, Prussia and Russia, have each, at different times, authorized such risings during invasions of their territories.[2]

At the Brussels conference, in 1874, a proposition

---

[1] General Orders No. 100 of the U. S. War Department, Series of 1863.
[2] Prussia in 1807, during the Napoleonic wars. Russia in 1700, and again in 1812. On the former occasion to resist Charles XII., and on the latter to resist Napoleon.

was submitted requiring such general levies to conform to certain conditions, in order to secure for them the protection of the laws of war. These conditions were:

"Art. IX. 1. That they have at their head a person responsible for his subordinates.

"2. That they wear some distinctive badge recognizable at a distance.

"3. That they carry arms openly; and,

"4. That, in their operations, they conform to the laws and customs of war. In those countries where the militia form the whole or a part of the army they shall be included under the denomination of army.

"Art. X. The population of a *non-occupied* territory, who, on the approach of the enemy, of their own accord take up arms to resist the invading troops, without having had time to organize themselves in conformity with article IX., shall be considered as belligerents, if they respect the laws and customs of war."[1]

The effect of these rules is made to depend upon the meaning attached to the term "occupied territory," as used in a previous article. It is defined in article I. to be "territory actually placed under the authority of the hostile army. And the occupation is declared to extend to those territories where this authority is established and can be exercised."[2] The construction of the term is left to the belligerent invader, and, so long as the views held upon the subject of occupation are so divergent as they are at present,

---

[1] "Proceedings of Brussels Conference," 1874, articles ix. and x.
[2] *Ibid.*, article i.

it is extremely unlikely that the rules of the conference, humane as they are in many respects, will receive general international sanction.

The term *guerilla* is applied to persons who, acting singly or joined in bands, carry on operations in the vicinity of an army in the field in violation of the laws of war. They wear no uniform, they act without the orders of their government, and their operations consist chiefly in the killing of picket guards and sentinels, in the assassination of isolated individuals or detachments, and in robbery and other predatory acts. As they are not controlled in their undertakings by the laws of war, they are not entitled to their protection. If captured, they are treated with great severity, the punishment in any case being proportioned to the offence committed. Their operations have no effect upon the general issue of the war, and only tend to aggravate its severity. Life taken by them is uselessly sacrificed, and with no corresponding advantage.[1]

14. *Forces that may not be Used in War.*—In carrying on military operations against a belligerent, a state may not use, as a part of its armed force, any persons or corps that are not, or cannot be, subjected to military discipline, or who cannot be restrained from committing acts of cruelty in violation of the laws of war. This restriction prohibits the use of bodies of troops composed of individuals of savage or semi-civilized races, whose cruel instincts lead to the perpetration of all sorts of barbarities. A general who finds the force of his enemy composed of such elements is justified in

---

[1] Halleck, vol. ii., p. 7; also p. 8, note.

resorting to retaliatory methods to compel its discontinuance.[1]

15. *Wars with Savages.*—Civilized states, in carrying on necessary wars with barbarous races, or against nations which are partly civilized, but who do not understand, and so fail to observe, the laws of war, have peculiar duties and responsibilities toward such opponents. Their irregular and barbarous usages should be carefully studied, and the operations undertaken against them should be so planned and arranged as to render it impossible for serious violation of the laws of war to occur. The task is not one of serious or particular difficulty. Barbarous nations yield only to superior force or superior cunning. They violate the rules of civilized warfare chiefly in their cruel treatment of wounded and unwounded prisoners, and in their tendency to indiscriminate slaughter, pillage, and destruction while passing through inhabited districts. To remedy this, the forces employed against them should be sufficient in amount to accomplish the legitimate purpose of the war as expeditiously as possible. Forces inferior in strength to the enemy should never be employed. Wounded men should not be permitted to fall into their hands; straggling should be rigidly prohibited; small, isolated parties should not be employed beyond the lines of the army, and the tactical units of the invading force, in all marches and military operations, should be required to keep within supporting distance of each other.

16. *Forces Employed at Sea.*—In conducting naval

---

[1] To this class belong the Bashi-Bazouks, employed by Turkey and some of the Cossack mounted forces in the service of Russia.

operations and in effecting captures at sea, a state makes use of its public armed vessels, manned by the officers and men of its regular naval establishment. Its naval force may be increased, both in ships and men, by methods similar to those resorted to to increase its military strength. It may also make use of privateers.

Privateers are armed vessels, commanded by private persons, who receive a commission from a belligerent government authorizing them to make captures of enemy ships and goods on the high seas. These commissions are called *Letters of Marque*.

Letters of Marque and Reprisal are commissions of a somewhat similar character, which were formerly issued to private persons, authorizing them to make captures by way of reprisal, and in satisfaction for some injury done them by an offending state. The practice is now obsolete.

Although the practice of privateering is still sanctioned by International Law, it seems hardly probable that it will be extensively resorted to in future wars. Its defence has been that it enabled a state which, from policy or want of means, maintained a small standing navy, to make a great and sudden increase in its naval force at the outbreak of war. This increase, however, was attended with serious disadvantages. The force of privateers could only be used to effect captures of unarmed merchant ships. It was never available for general naval operations, and the damage done to the enemy, however great, was at best but indirect, and did not have the effect of weakening his military power. The belligerent employer of privateers incurred the same responsibility for captures made by these cruisers as it did for those made by its public armed vessels, while its control over their officers and crews was, at best, but feeble and indirect. It had but little security against their aggressions upon neutral rights, while it was absolutely responsible for acts done by them in their exercise of the right of search upon neutral vessels. As neutral rights steadily increase, and are more and more strongly insisted upon by neutral nations, the exercise of belligerent rights against them becomes constantly more difficult, involving a knowledge of International Law which is rarely possessed by the commanding officers of private armed vessels, and presenting questions of the greatest intricacy and difficulty, which require in their decision the fullest knowledge of the rights and responsibilities of belligerents and neutrals. For these reasons the practice of privateering, which had always been regarded with disfavor, has within the last half century been much less frequently resorted to than formerly. Those states whose policy it is to maintain small naval establishments in time of peace find it possible to increase them, at the outbreak of war, by a resort to methods similar to those made use of in increasing their land forces. Ships are purchased or chartered by the government, and the vessels thus acquired are placed under the command of regular naval officers. Over this force the control of the government is absolute and complete. It possesses the advantage that it can be used in all sorts of maritime undertakings, and is not restricted in its operations to the capture of unarmed merchant vessels.

The practice of privateering has been very much restricted by the operation of the rules of the Declaration of Paris, which will be discussed under the head of maritime capture.

17. *Effect of Modern Inventions, and of Improved Methods of Attack and Defence.*—The discovery of new methods of attack and defence, and the improvements which have been made in the range and efficiency of artillery and small arms since the middle of this century, have served to mark an epoch in the history of modern war. Standing armies and navies are now maintained at a point in numbers, training, and efficiency never before reached, or even attempted, and at an expense which absorbs no inconsiderable portion of the revenues of most modern states. These causes combined have so increased the cost and destructiveness of war as to render its occurrence less frequent, and to materially shorten its duration, while, by reducing the time during which operations are carried on, and territory occupied by invading armies, they have contributed powerfully to restrict its most injurious effects.

18. *Methods of Carrying on War.*—With the strategical and tactical methods resorted to by trained and disciplined armies in their operations against each other, International Law has but little to do. Such operations must be carried on in accordance with the principle that no forcible measures against an enemy which involve the loss of human life are justifiable which do not bear directly upon the object for which the war is undertaken, and which do not materially contribute to bring it to an end. International public opinion severely judges useless and unnecessary operations, and sharply criticises mistakes and blunders which might have been avoided by a reasonable exer-

cise of foresight and skill, and fixes the responsibility of error, in just proportions, upon the governments which authorize such measures and the generals who execute them.

19. *Rule of Good Faith; Use of Deceit.*—No measures can be resorted to against an enemy in war which involve a breach of good faith. An attack cannot be condemned, or complained of, because it partakes of the character of a surprise, because it is the duty of a belligerent to exercise such due vigilance as will render such measures abortive. Deceit, in the form of circulating false information in order that it may fall into the hands of the enemy, is justifiable, because it is the enemy's duty to weigh carefully the sources from which he receives intelligence. The services of traitors and deserters may be accepted, and the employment of spies for the purpose of obtaining information is legitimate, but no person can be compelled to act as a spy. The poisoning of wells and springs is prohibited, as it ever has been since the laws of war came into existence. The food and water supply of a besieged place may be shut off, however, with a view to hasten its surrender.

20. *The Attack of Places.*—In the attack of places a distinction is made between forts or fortified places, and what are called open, or undefended towns. The latter, if they offer no resistance, cannot be attacked. On the contrary, it is the first duty of the commanding general of the force occupying them to prevent pillage, and to insure public order and the protection of private property. Fortified places may be taken by open assault, or may be reduced by regular siege operations. If an open assault be attempted, no notice is

given, as surprise in such an operation is an essential condition of success. The very fact of war is a sufficient notice to the non-combatant inhabitants of such places that an attack is at least a probable contingency. If they continue their residence it is presumed that they do so with full knowledge that the place may become the centre of active military operations.

It should be remembered in this connection, however, that peace is the normal state of mankind, and that other than military conditions now prevail in the location, growth, and development of cities and towns. This fact must be recognized by belligerent states, and by their generals commanding in the field. There is scarcely a fortified place now in existence which does not contain a large contingent of non-combatant population, composed, in great part, of persons whose circumstances are such as not to permit them to change their residence at will. This fact is now considered, in the fortification of important centres, by placing the defensive works beyond the range of siege artillery. The claims of these defenceless persons should constantly be borne in mind by all those who have to do with siege operations, the duty of consideration falling with equal force upon besiegers and besieged. No measures directed against a besieged place are justifiable which are calculated to increase, unnecessarily, the hardships of their already distressing condition. The improved methods of conducting siege operations make it possible to neutralize fortified places by close investment, and to reduce them by restricting the attack to the defensive works alone. Commanding officers of such places are not justified in persisting in the defence when the burden of such defence begins to bear with deadly effect upon their non-combatant population.

Duty of a Commanding Officer of a Besieged Place in the Matter of Surrender.—The questions of defence in the case of a garrisoned fort and a fortified town are by no means the same. Duty may require a commander in the former case to resist to the last; in the latter considerations of humanity enter into the problem of defence, and great weight must be attached to them when the question of surrender is presented to him for decision.

In former times there were instances in which the commanding officer of a besieged place incurred some penalty by protracting his defence beyond the time when such defence could be maintained with any reasonable chance of success. This is no longer the case. The defence of a place is a question over which a besieger has no control. The commanding officer of the besieged place may therefore protract his defence so long as any military advantage accrues to his own government by so doing. When no such considerations are involved, however, and the question of defence is limited to the place itself, a commander is justified in continuing it so long as any hope of success remains. When, in his opinion, it can no longer be hopefully maintained, any further sacrifice of life is unwarranted, and it becomes his duty to surrender. This is a duty which he owes to his country, and to the men under his command, and not to the enemy. If his force is sufficient to justify him in such an undertaking, it is proper for him to make the attempt to cut his way out. Whenever he surrenders he is entitled to demand, for himself and for his command, the rights of prisoners of war, and his enemy is not justified in refusing to grant him such rights, still less in threatening to deny quarter to himself or his garrison. On the other hand, should he blindly refuse to surrender when defence is no longer possible, and so compel his enemy to take the place by assault, he cannot complain of any loss of life that may legitimately ensue, nor can he expect his antagonist, in the heat of an attack, to recognize his tender of surrender, when the time for such tender has passed away.[1]

21. *Use of the Enemy's Uniform and Flag.*—It is forbidden in war on land to make use of the enemy's flag for purposes of deceit. It is also forbidden to use the enemy's uniform except with some distinguishing mark, sufficiently striking in character to attract attention at a distance. On the sea the national flag of a public armed vessel must be displayed before an engagement begins, or a capture is made. These rules are based on the fact that flags and uniforms are used for the purpose of determining the national character of troops in the field. A violation of these rules indicates a want of good faith, a quality equally obligatory in peace and war.

22. *Giving and Receiving Quarter, and Treatment of Individuals of the Enemy; Forbidden Practices.*—A belligerent cannot refuse to give quarter, nor can he announce his intention to give no quarter, except

---

[1] The Duke of Wellington, in a despatch to Mr. Canning bearing date of Feb. 3, 1820, maintained the view that the garrison of a besieged place that refused to surrender could be put to the sword. It is to be said to his credit, however, that he never applied the rule in practice.—" Wellington Despatches," vol. i., p. 80, cited by Creasy, p. 452.

in case of some conduct of the enemy in gross violation of the laws of war, and then only in the way of retaliation for similar acts. The practice of firing upon outposts, picket-guards, and sentinels, except for the purpose of driving them in during a reconnoissance, or as a preliminary to a general advance, is strictly forbidden. These individuals of the enemy are particularly helpless. They take no part in operations of an aggressive character, and are always ordered not to attack. They are to resist only when themselves attacked, and yield ground only to a superior force of the enemy. The rules of war forbid the robbery of individuals of the enemy who fall into the hands of a belligerent. Their clothing and private property are as secure from violent appropriation as are those of non-combatant citizens; arms and articles of public property in their possession become the property of the captor's government—never the private property of an individual. The wounding of prisoners, or the infliction of additional injuries upon those already wounded and helpless, is discountenanced upon pain of death, as offensive alike to humanity and the rules of civilized warfare. The power of these persons to do harm has been destroyed by the fact of wounding, or capture, and their helpless and distressing condition entitles them to the most considerate treatment. A similar reason forbids the use of forcible measures against prisoners with a view to extort from them information as to the force, positions, or intentions of the enemy.

23. *Instruments of War.*—In no department of human endeavor has greater ingenuity been displayed, in recent times, than in the invention and improvement of arms, projectiles, and other instruments of

war. Their destructive power has kept pace with the increase in their range and efficiency, and with the rapidity with which their fire can be delivered. The result has been to make war so destructive as to shorten its duration, and so to materially diminish the losses incurred in proportion to the forces engaged on either side.

It is not an objection to a weapon or projectile that it is merely destructive. All instruments of war have that character, some of them to a remarkable degree. That one weapon or projectile is more destructive than another simply means that the belligerent adopting it has, to the extent of its superior destructive power, a legitimate advantage over his adversary. The decision as to whether a particular instrument may, or may not, be employed in war will depend upon the wound or injury caused by its use. If the wound produced by it causes unnecessary suffering, or needless injury, it is to be rejected, otherwise not. This rule is applicable to all instruments of whatever character, whether weapons or projectiles, which may be used in war. The application of this rule forbids the use of cutting or thrusting weapons which have been poisoned, or which are so constructed as to inflict a merely painful wound. To this class belong arrows with easily detached heads, etc. The recommendations of the St. Petersburg Conference upon the subject of explosive projectiles, forbidding the use of projectiles weighing less than four hundred *grammes* (twelve ounces avoirdupois), has received the general sanction of civilized nations. The adoption of this rule renders unlawful the use of explosive bullets in small arms.

The use of hot shot, and of chain and bar shot, has

been regarded as questionable by some authors, apparently because their purpose and use was not fully understood. *Hot shot* were used in engagements between forts and wooden ships with a view to set fire to the latter. Their use would still be authorized for the same purpose. *Chain shot* and *bar shot* were used in naval engagements for the purpose of cutting away standing rigging and spars. For these objects their continued use would be lawful. As it is impossible to use either form of projectile in modern rifled guns, and as they would be alike ineffective against modern ironclads, which have no standing rigging, they are now practically obsolete.

Torpedoes, as instruments of both offensive and defensive warfare, have come into general use within the last twenty-five years. That their use has received general sanction is shown by the energetic measures which have been taken by most modern states to equip their navies with them, and to adopt them as an important auxiliary in their systems of coast defence. Military mines, which greatly resemble them in purpose and destructive effect, have been regarded as an essential feature of all systems of permanent fortification since the days of Vauban, and the art of countermining in siege operations has kept pace with the development of military mining as a means of offensive warfare. This is likely to be the case with torpedoes. As new forms are devised, and new methods of applying them are invented, corresponding means of counteracting their effects will be discovered, with the result, it is hoped, of restricting within the narrowest limits their terribly destructive effects. On the other hand, if their offensive use should prove to be capable of indefinite development, and if the coasts and harbors of a state be so skilfully defended with torpedoes and submarine mines as to make it practically impossible for hostile fleets to approach, then the object of the state in defending its ports will have been completely attained, in securing to the inhabitants of its sea-coast towns a practical immunity from hostile attack.

23. *Usages of War at Sea.*—The usages of war at sea are the same in substance as those on land, although, from the circumstances of the case, they are much simpler of application. The same rules apply as to giving and receiving quarter, and as to the treatment of wounded and unwounded prisoners of war. The crews of captured merchant vessels of the enemy are made prisoners of war. When neutral vessels are seized for carrying contraband, or for attempting to violate a blockade, their crews, not being belligerents, are not subject to confinement as prisoners of war, unless by their conduct they render such restraint necessary.

24. *The Public and Private Property of the Enemy; Treatment of Property on Land.*—The property of an enemy on land may be classified into *public* and *private*. Public property is again classified into—1. Property of a military character, or susceptible of appropriation to military use. To this class belong forts, arsenals, dockyards, magazines, and military stores of all kinds. 2. Money and movables of all kinds belonging to the belligerent government as proprietor. 3. Property essentially civil, or non-military in character, and used for religious, charitable, scientific, or educational purposes. The two former may be captured and destroyed, or converted to the military use of the

enemy. The latter is now exempt from seizure, and should be protected by a belligerent if situated in, or near, the theatre of active operations.[1]

25. *Private property* is classified into *real* and *personal*. Real property, whether consisting of land or buildings, is exempt from seizure or destruction, except as a direct necessity of military operations. It may be occupied or used, and during such occupation should be protected from all needless injury and damage. *Personal property* is divided into—1. That which is susceptible of direct military use by a belligerent. To this class belong pack, saddle, and draft animals, means of transportation of all kinds, cattle, fuel, provisions and food products, medicines, forage, cloth, leather, and shoes; in general all articles of wear and supply for men and animals. 2. That which is not susceptible of direct military use; including money, works of art, furniture, valuables, clothing, and articles of general merchandise. The former may be captured, or taken by way of requisition; the latter is exempt from capture or confiscation. If such property be taken by way of pillage, the act is severely punished. The taking of private property within the limits here described is sanctioned by the law of nations. It is sometimes paid for, more frequently, perhaps, now than formerly, but when compensation is made, it is dictated rather by motives of policy than justice. Illiberal and unjust as the practice may be, it is universally recognized, and so receives the unwilling sanction of International Law. The army regulations of all nations provide specifically, and in great detail, for the maintenance of their

---

[1] Hall, pp. 139-141; Halleck, vol. ii., §§ 12, 13.

troops in the enemy's territory, by supporting them, wholly or in part, on the country, and prescribe the methods of quartering troops, and of collecting and distributing subsistence and forage.[1]

26. *Requisitions* are the formal and regular levies of supplies, made by an invading army for its support, in accordance with the municipal laws and army regulations of the state to which it belongs. These laws, regulations, and orders prescribe the methods in accordance with which the requisitions are to be made. The articles to be paid for, if there be any such, the tariffs, or rates of payment, and the cases in which receipts are to be given, are stated in such regulations and orders. They also contain provisions denouncing pillage, and prescribing punishments for that and other unauthorized taking of enemy property.

Receipts should always be given. They are of importance, as payments, whether made by the invaders' government or their own, are based upon them; and, if not taken up and paid, they may serve to mitigate the severity of future requisitions by the same invader. Requisitions may be made by commanding officers of any grade, but always in strict accordance with law and regulations. Unauthorized requisitions are usually regarded as acts of pillage, and are punished accordingly.[2] A question arises as to whether a belligerent can compel the personal services of individuals of the population of the invaded territory. Such services may be voluntary, either on the part of individuals or cor-

---

[1] Hall, pp. 139–141; Halleck, vol. ii., §§ 12, 13.

[2] Art. 18, Brussels Conference; Halleck, vol. ii., pp. 92, 114; Hall, pp. 361–363; Heffter, p. 237; Boyd's Wheaton, p. 411 note; "United States Instructions," § 44.

porations, and, if so, are paid for when rendered. With these International Law has nothing to do. The right of a belligerent to take means of transportation, by way of requisition, has always been asserted, and almost invariably acted upon. This involves the right to compel the services of drivers and teams, and also of railway, steamship, and telegraph companies, and of blacksmiths, carpenters, and other tradesmen. These services must be obtained by force, as the duty of a citizen to his own government forbids him to render voluntary service to the enemy. The question of payment is discretionary with the belligerent employer, and, as in the case of other requisitions, is rather a matter of policy, or expediency, than of strict justice.[1]

The policy of the United States in the matter of requisitions has been far from liberal. At the beginning of the campaign in Southern Mexico, General Scott was directed to subsist his troops in the enemy's country. Upon the urgent remonstrances of that officer as to the injustice and impolicy of such a course, the order was rescinded, and the regulation of the matter left to the discretion of the general commanding in the field. He therefore directed reasonable prices to be paid for such articles as were needed for the subsistence of his army, and experienced so little difficulty in obtaining them as to make a resort to requisitions unnecessary. During the war of the rebellion

---

[1] In January, 1871, the Germans, who were then in military occupation of Nancy, required the services of five hundred laborers upon a work of repairing the railway — of considerable importance to the success of their operations. Notice was given that if they were not forthcoming, at the time indicated, a certain number of the officers and employees would be seized and shot.—Hall, p. 364.

generals in the field were authorized to seize such articles of subsistence, or forage, as were needed by their commands. For the property thus taken receipts were to be given, payable at the end of the war, upon proof of loyalty. If such proof were not produced, no payments were to be made. This amounted, in fact, to the taking of enemy's property without compensation.

27. *Contributions.*—Contributions are levies of money or supplies, made by the authority of a belligerent government, through the commander-in-chief of its armies in the field. They are levied upon the property, or taxable resources, of a city or district of territory. They are usually assessed, collected, and paid by the local authorities, upon the formal demand of the invading general. If the amount of the contribution be not paid, or delivered, at the specified time, the invader takes such measures as he may deem necessary to enforce his decree. Unlike requisitions they are never refunded, or reimbursed, by the belligerent who levies them, though they may be deducted from the amount of an indemnity proposed to be levied by a conquering invader in the preparation of the treaty of peace.

28. *Captured Property on Land.*—Public property on land, and in some instances private property also, may be captured by a belligerent. Such captured property is called *booty*. It consists of all public property that is susceptible of capture in war, and of such private property as is susceptible of direct military use. In strictness all articles that may be obtained by way of requisition fall under the head of booty. Aside from the articles obtained by requisition, booty may consist of arms, ammunition, provisions, and military supplies of all kinds, and of all public and pri-

vate property captured in battle, or as a direct result of military operations.[1] As is the case with all property which may be captured in war, on land or sea, the title first vests in the captor's government. Such title is held to be complete after twenty-four hours of actual possession, upon the presumption that secure possession will be obtained within that time. The capturing government may make such disposition of this captured property as it deems best. It may convert it to its own use; it may cause it to be sold, and may appropriate the proceeds of the sale to governmental uses; or it may decree the whole, or a part, to the actual captors as a reward for their services. The British government, in certain cases, recognizes and rewards such services. The government of the United States has adopted the contrary rule, and appropriates to its own use all property captured by its armies on land.

The rules regarding booty, and those regarding the treatment of private property seem to be in conflict. They are not so in fact. Private property on land, however great in amount, is exempt from capture except it be susceptible of direct military use by a belligerent, or contributes directly to the support and maintenance of his armies. Arms, ammunition, equipments, and all sorts of military stores, clothing, or cloth suitable for uniforms, shoes, leather, blankets, medicines, and food and forage supplies of all kinds, are susceptible of such appropriation. Money, except by way of contribution, clothing and cloth not adapted

---

[1] For the latest authoritative discussion of this subject see the article, "The Right of Booty in General, and especially the Right of Maritime Capture," by Professor Bluntschli, in the *Revue de Droit International*, vol. ix. (1877), p. 508.

for use as uniforms, and all other products, manufactures, and commodities, are exempt from capture, and are entitled to protection by the laws of war.

29. *Treatment of Non-Combatants in the Theatre of War.*—It has been seen that the subjects of two belligerent states become enemies at the outbreak or declaration of war. They continue in this hostile relation during its continuance. This status does not authorize them to commit acts of hostility, however, which can only be undertaken by persons having the express authorization of the belligerent governments. The rest of the population of a belligerent territory are not only forbidden to take an active part in military operations, but are entitled to personal immunity and protection so long as they refrain, in good faith, from taking part in the war. A portion of their property may be taken, with or without compensation, their houses and lands may be occupied, and injured, or possibly destroyed, as a matter of military necessity; but their persons, and such of their property as is not confiscable by the laws of war, are, by the same laws, completely protected. Any offence committed against them, or their property, is an offence against the laws of war, and is promptly and severely punished. This exemption from the operations of war they continue to enjoy so long as they take no active part in hostile operations. If they act with the authority of their government, they become a part of its military force, and are treated accordingly. If they act without such authorization, and in violation of the usages of war, they are no longer protected, but are punished according to the nature and degree of their offence.

A *combatant* is a person who, with the special authorization of his government, takes part, either directly or indirectly, in the operations of war. The term includes, in addition to the troops of the line, all staff officers, surgeons and chaplains, officers and employees of the supply and transport service, all agents, contractors, and others who accompany the army in an official capacity, and who assist in its movement, equipment, or maintenance; and all retainers to the camp.

A *non-combatant* is a resident of a belligerent state who takes no part in the war. He is not subject to the laws of war, and is protected by them, in his person and property, so long as he refrains from participation in military operations.

30. *Prisoners of War.*—A *prisoner of war* is a combatant who, by capture or surrender, falls into the hands of an enemy. In strictness an enemy has the right to make prisoners of those persons only whom he may lawfully kill in war. In practice, however, the former class is much more numerous than the latter. This is because the right of making prisoners, as now exercised, inflicts no particular hardship upon the captured person; while his detention, as a prisoner, may serve to materially injure the enemy, by impeding him in his military operations, or by interfering with the efficient administration of his government. For this reason "he may capture all persons who are separated from the mass of non-combatants by their importance to the enemy's state, or by their usefulness to him in his war. Under the first of these heads fall the sovereign and the members of his family when non-combatants, the ministers and high officers of the government, diplomatic agents, and any

one who, for special reasons, may be of importance at a particular moment." [1]

Treatment of Prisoners.—So soon as an individual of the enemy ceases his armed resistance he becomes vested with all the rights of a prisoner of war. The right to injure him is, at that instant, changed into the duty of protecting him, and of preventing his escape. The public property and arms found in the possession of a prisoner, at the time of his capture, become the property of the capturing state. His private property is respected, and secured to him, by the usages of war. Were it not so protected every consideration of honor and humanity should deter his captor from any act of aggression toward one who, from his situation, is unable to defend himself.

Prisoners are usually sent to the captor's state, or are removed to points at a distance from the actual theatre of war, where they can be securely held. They are fed and clothed at the expense of the captor's government. They are entitled, in addition to proper food and clothing, to medical attendance, and to a reasonable allowance of fuel, quarters, bedding, and camp equipage. They are subject to such measures of restraint as are necessary to their safe keeping; and are held to the observance of such sanitary and police regulations as are made necessary by their confinement. The rules

---

[1] Hall, p. 341. The practice has become quite general of releasing surgeons and sometimes chaplains left with the wounded on the field of battle, so soon as their duties have been performed. This is done, or not, at the discretion of the captor, however, and cannot be claimed or demanded as a right. This subject is now regulated by the terms of the Geneva Convention, to which the principal states of Christendom are parties.

of war authorize a belligerent to require them to perform a certain amount of labor, as a reimbursement of the cost of their support. No labor may be required of them, however, that is calculated to assist the captor, directly, in his military operations. In recent times the practice has been to require no services of prisoners of war except such as have contributed directly to their comfort and welfare.

Prisoners of war are not guilty of a crime in having defended their country. Their confinement, therefore, cannot assume a penal character, but must consist in such measures of detention as will secure them against danger of escape. A prisoner of war, in attempting to escape, does not commit a crime. It is his duty to escape if a favorable opportunity presents itself. It is equally the duty of his captor to prevent his escape, and he is justified in resorting to any measures, not punitive in character, that will best secure that end. A prisoner of war may be killed in attempting to escape. If recaptured his confinement may be made more rigorous than before.

According to the present rule of International Law the status of a prisoner of war may be terminated— 1. By exchange; 2. By ransom; 3. By the treaty of peace at the end of the war.

Exchange of Prisoners.—The exchange of prisoners between belligerents is made in accordance with agreements, entered into for that purpose, called *cartels*. The making of such agreements is purely voluntary, and cannot be constrained by subjecting prisoners to special hardships. The time, place, and method of exchange are fully detailed in the cartels, the provisions of which are always strictly construed. The basis of exchange is usually that of strict equivalents, man for man, rank for rank, disability for disability. The exchangeable values of the different grades of officers and non-commissioned officers are established, and expressed in terms of private soldiers. Numbers are then computed for exchange upon the basis thus agreed upon. An excess on either side may constitute a credit, or may be extinguished by a payment of money. Prisoners of war who escape from confinement, or who are exchanged, are by such acts revésted with all the rights of belligerents. The binding force of cartels, like that of all other agreements between belligerents, rests upon the good faith of the contracting parties. If the terms of a cartel are violated by one belligerent they cease to be obligatory upon the other.

31. *Paroles.*—A parole is a promise, either verbal or written, made by an individual of the enemy, by which, in consideration of certain privileges or advantages, he pledges his honor to pursue, or refrain from pursuing, a particular course of conduct. Paroles are ordinarily received only from officers, and, when necessary, are given, by officers, for the enlisted men of their commands. They are accepted from enlisted men only in exceptional cases. Paroles are given by officers to secure greater freedom of movement, or to obtain special privileges, while held by the enemy as prisoners of war. These may, or may not, be in writing. They are also given to obtain a release from captivity, with permission to return home. Such paroles are accompanied by a pledge to refrain from taking part in an existing war until regularly exchanged. They are given in writing, usually in duplicate, one copy being retained by the captor, the other by the

officer giving the parole. These instruments are obligatory upon the government of the state to which the individual belongs only when accepted, or recognized, by its authority. That government may refuse to permit its officers to give their paroles, when held as prisoners of war, and may refuse to recognize them when given. In such an event, however; it is the duty of the paroled officer to return at once to captivity. As legal instruments paroles lose their binding force—
1. Upon the formal exchange of the paroled officer;
2. At the termination of the war.

A *breach of parole* is an offence against the laws of war. Its enormity consists in the breach of good faith that is involved in the commission of the offence. The punishment inflicted is in proportion to the importance of the parole given. The extreme penalty is death, which may be inflicted upon a paroled prisoner who is captured in arms before he has been regularly exchanged.

32. *Intercourse between Belligerents.*—Although the rule of non-intercourse between belligerent states prevails with great strictness during the existence of war between them, it would be impossible even for hostilities to be carried on, if all intercourse, irrespective of its character and purpose, were to be absolutely prohibited. International Law recognizes this necessity, and deduces from the usages of nations in war the rules governing such intercourse, the conditions upon which it is based, and the formalities with which it shall begin and end. Such intercourse, to be lawful, must have some direct connection with the existing state of war, or must be carried on with a view to the re-establishment of friendly relations.

Flags of Truce.—Communication between belligerents in the field is established by means of flags of truce. They are sent toward the enemy's lines habitually during an interval of active operations. In case of extreme urgency they may be sent during an engagement. Though each party has a right to send them, there is no corresponding obligation on the part of the enemy to receive them, though it is usual to do so save in very exceptional cases. After due notification has been given they may be warned away; and, after a reasonable time has been given to allow them to withdraw, they may be fired upon. An officer coming under a flag of truce has no *right* to enter the enemy's lines, nor can he demand that he be conducted into the presence of the commanding general. As a matter of strict right he cannot expect to pass the outposts of the hostile army. His message, if written, may there be transferred to the officer receiving him, or, if verbal, the belligerent may demand that it be reduced to writing, or that it be delivered orally to such person as the commanding general may designate to receive it. If permitted to pass the outposts he may be blindfolded, or resort may be had to such other means as will prevent him from obtaining information. While the officer accompanying a flag may see whatever the enemy permits him to see, while in that enemy's lines under a flag of truce, and the bearer of a *bona fide* message, the rules of war justly forbid the sending of flags of truce with a view of obtaining information, either directly or indirectly. The present rule of war regards the use of flags for the purpose of obtaining information as illegal and dishonorable, subjecting the bearer to punishment as a spy.

33. *Cartels and Capitulations.*—A *cartel* is an agreement entered into between the commanding generals of opposing armies, or fleets, for the purpose of effecting an exchange of prisoners. *Capitulations* are compacts entered into, between the same parties, to regulate the details of surrender of a fortified place, a vessel of war, or a defeated army in the field. They are drawn up in the same manner as treaties, though not with the same formalities, and are interpreted in accordance with the same rules. The general commanding an army in the field is presumed to have authority to make them, and to give effect to their provisions. If he lacks such authority, or if his powers in this respect be limited, it is his duty to so notify his enemy.

34. *Safe-conducts and Safeguards.*—A *safe-conduct* is a pass given to an enemy subject by the general commanding an army in the field. It authorizes the bearer to pass from one specified point to another, by a specified route, and within certain stated limits of time. If the authority granted be exceeded, the holder is liable to be regarded as a prisoner of war. If undue advantage be taken of a safe-conduct, to obtain information, the offender violates the laws of war, and may be punished accordingly. A *safeguard* is a written protection to persons, or property, or both, such persons being resident, or property situate, within the lines of the general issuing it. It is given upon the authority, and by, or in the name of, the general-in-chief, and is binding upon all persons under his command. "Sometimes they are delivered to the parties whose persons or property are to be protected; at others they are posted upon the property itself, as

upon a church, museum, library, public office, or private dwelling. They are particularly useful in the assault of a place, or after its capture, or after the termination of a battle, to protect the persons or property of friends from destruction by an excited soldiery."[1]

Violations of either safe-conducts or safeguards are punished with the greatest severity.

It is seen that safe-conducts and safeguards are binding upon the troops commanded by the general who issues or signs them. Whoever violates them, therefore, not only violates the laws of war, but is also guilty of the most serious of all military offences—disobedience of orders. For this reason escorts are usually furnished to enforce respect to these instruments, and severe penalties are imposed upon those who violate them. "Such escorts or guards are justified in resorting to the severest measures to punish any violation of their trust."[2]

35. *Licenses to Trade.*—Licenses to trade are written instruments authorizing their holders to engage in certain trade with the enemy. The rules in accordance with which the trade is to be conducted, the articles to be bought, sold, or exchanged, the amount of trade authorized, the vehicles, whether ships or wagons, etc., in which it is to be carried on, are all specifically laid down in the permit. A breach of any of its conditions involves the forfeiture of the goods, conveyances, and other implements engaged, as it constitutes an offence similar to breach of blockade.

Licenses are issued by a belligerent government, or

---

[1] Halleck, vol. ii., pp. 353, 354.   [2] *Ibid.*

by a general in the field, with the sanction of his government. Trade carried on under them becomes legal, and is so regarded by courts of the state by whom the license is granted.

36. *Crimes and Offences against the Laws of War.*— Certain acts done during a state of war are regarded by all nations as violations of the laws of war. They are crimes at International Law, and may be punished by the belligerent who suffers by their commission. Such an infliction of punishment by one belligerent furnishes the other with no ground of retaliation or complaint. All crimes against the laws of war lose their criminal character at the close of the war, and are then no longer punishable. They are crimes according to a code of law which ceases to exist when peace is declared; therefore all prisoners held by a belligerent, for violation of the laws of war, are entitled to be set at liberty at the date when the treaty of peace goes into effect.

Spies.—A spy is a person who enters the lines of an army in disguise, or under false pretences, for the purpose of securing information. An individual who, in the proper uniform of his army, penetrates within an enemy's lines, is not a spy, for it is the duty of the enemy to maintain his line of outposts at such strength and efficiency, in point of numbers, as will make it impossible for individuals to pass them. Concealment or disguise, and the employment of false pretences, are essential elements to the crime of being a spy. Those who undertake to gain information of the enemy's movements by means of balloons cannot be regarded as spies, for none of the essential conditions of the offence attend such operations. Spies are employed at rates of pay commensurate to the risks they undertake, and are presumed to be aware of the penalty incurred in the event of their being captured by the enemy. Service as a spy is voluntary, and cannot be compelled. A state cannot require an individual in its military service to act as a spy. If it permits or authorizes a person in its military or naval service to act in that capacity, the fact of his being in such service will not screen him from punishment, should he be apprehended by the enemy; nor will retaliation be justifiable on the part of the belligerent who so employs persons in his military service.

For being a spy the punishment is death. An individual charged with the crime cannot demand a trial; it is granted, if at all, by the municipal law of the captor's state.

Guerillas.—These are persons who lurk in the vicinity of an army, and commit acts of hostility without the authorization of their government, or who carry on their operations in violation of the laws of war. Small bands or organized parties, commissioned by their government and forming a part of its regular forces, are called *partisans*. Their operations, however annoying to an enemy, are perfectly lawful so long as they are carried on in accordance with the laws of war. The evil must be remedied by opposing such partisan forces by other forces of a similar character.

Guerillas, however, are not partisans, "their acts are unlawful, and when captured they are not treated as prisoners of war, but as criminals, subject to the punishment due to their crimes. . . . The perpetrators of such acts, under such circumstances, are not enemies, legitimately in arms, who can plead the laws of war in their justification, they are robbers and murderers, and, as such, may be punished."[1]

Pillaging consists in the forcible taking of property in an enemy's country, without authority, and in disobedience of orders. It has been seen that the laws of war prescribe a method in strict accordance with which certain kinds of property may be taken in war. If it be taken in any other way such taking constitutes pillage, and is punishable accordingly. There can be no higher test of discipline in a command than is shown by the manner in which the private property of an enemy is treated within its sphere of operations. If such property is respected, if acts of pillage are strictly repressed and severely punished, the discipline is good. If property and life are unsafe in its vicinity, if irregular seizures are permitted, if orchards and fields are devastated, discipline worthy of the name cannot be said to exist.

The punishment of pillage varies with the nature of the offence. The extreme penalty is death.

Crimes of Violence.—Certain crimes of violence, such as murder, robbery, mayhem, rape, burglary, assault and battery, and assaults with intent to commit crime, when committed by, or against, residents or individuals of the invading army, are punishable by military commissions, or other tribunals of like jurisdiction. The punishment inflicted is usually more severe than that awarded by the law of the place where the offence is committed. This course is made necessary

---

[1] Halleck, vol. ii., p. 7. General Halleck includes *guerillas* and *partisans* under the same designation. In this matter it is rather the service in which these persons are engaged, than their name, by which their status is regulated.

by the fact that, in the immediate theatre of war, all civil authority is suspended, the local courts being prevented, by the fact of war, from exercising their ordinary functions. If such crimes were not punished by the belligerent they would go unpunished, a most undesirable event from every point of view. Crimes, at such a time, are of more frequent occurrence, and are usually of greater enormity, than during a state of peace. The ordinary restraints of law are removed or suspended, and the criminal class soon asserts itself as it finds that opportunity, temptation, and apparent immunity go hand in hand. Instances have occurred in which prisons and jails have been emptied upon the approach of an invading army. The very presence of a hostile force upon the soil of a country seems to breed a special criminal class. This class is recruited by deserters from both armies, who, operating singly or in small bands, commit depredations of all kinds, accompanying their criminal acts with the most barbarous atrocities. It is to the suppression of this kind of brigandage that every belligerent finds himself obliged to devote considerable time and attention, and, not infrequently, a large amount of military force. No repressive measures are too severe which effect any reduction in this kind of crime. The criminals themselves are outlaws, beyond the protection of all law, civil or martial, and may be hunted down like wild beasts.

37. *Temporary Occupation.* — When an invading force has taken secure possession of a portion of the enemy's territory, such territory is said to be occupied, and the invader may exercise there all the rights of occupation. The former sovereignty has been dis-

placed by force. The allegiance of the inhabitants to their former sovereign, although suspended by war, has not been destroyed. Their allegiance to the invader is constrained and involuntary, and can be retained by him only so long as the occupying force is maintained at such strength as to compel obedience.

History of the Different Views of Occupation.—The theory of the Roman Law, upon the subject of occupation, was that territory, or other property, lost by a state as a result of war, became the property of him who was sufficiently powerful to occupy and retain it; and that, during such transient occupancy, all the rights and powers of sovereignty were vested in the invader. The allegiance of the inhabitants to their former sovereign was legally dissolved, and was, by the fact of hostile occupation, transferred to the new sovereign. This view was maintained, in practice, until after the middle of the eighteenth century. Toward the close of the last century, and as a consequence of the frequent cases of occupation during the wars that followed the French Revolution, a different view began to prevail. The doctrine of a complete transfer of allegiance and sovereignty was generally abandoned, and was replaced by a theory of temporary substitution of sovereignty, involving a temporary transfer of allegiance on the part of the inhabitants of the occupied territory. This view may be stated as follows: "The power to protect is the foundation of the duty of allegiance; when, therefore, a state ceases to be able to protect a portion of its subjects, it loses its claim upon their allegiance, and they either directly pass under a temporary or qualified allegiance to the conqueror, or, as it is also put, being able, in their state of freedom, to enter into a compact with the invader, they tacitly agree to acknowledge his sovereignty in consideration of the relinquishment by him of the extreme rights of war which he holds over their lives and property."[1]

Present View of Occupation.—The present view of occupation is that no permanent change ensues in the national character, or allegiance, of the population of an occupied territory as a result of the mere fact of occupation. The invader maintains himself in such territory by force. The relation existing, between the commanding general of the occupying force and the population, is not that of allegiance, but of constrained obedience; and it exists only so long as he is able to compel such obedience by force. The authority exercised by an invader is something entirely different from that exercised by the legitimate government, and rests upon an entirely different basis. In most respects it is greater and more extensive than the latter, and has no foundation in the consent of the governed. The legitimate government of the occupied territory is temporarily displaced and overthrown; the functions of its officers and agents are suspended, and the territory is ruled by martial law. If the ordinary laws of the country, or any of them, are permitted to exist, and if the courts are permitted to administer them, they do so at the pleasure of the commanding general. No guarantees, constitutional or otherwise, are effective against his will, and his consent to their existence, or execution, may be withdrawn at any time. The occupation is

---

[1] Hall, pp. 397, 398, citing Kluber, § 256; Halleck, vol. ii., chap. xxxiii., § 14; De Martens, § 280.

military, not *civil*, and the invader, in carrying on his government, is controlled by various considerations, among which, from the necessities of the case, those of a military character are likely to prevail.

Rights of Occupation.—The movable property of the displaced government vests in the belligerent invader by right of capture. He may make such use of the state property and lands as he sees fit, and the income from such property is payable to him during the period of his occupation. Taxes due, and payable, are collected by his authority, and are appropriated to his use. If he increases them, or imposes any other burdens or exactions upon persons or property, he does so in virtue of his right to levy contributions and requisitions.

The purpose of war is to obtain redress for an international wrong. To accomplish this purpose the use of force which is excessive, or which does not directly contribute to the end in view, is not lawful. An invader, therefore, is not justified, during his temporary occupancy, in making political or constitutional changes in the government of the occupied territory. The courts of the country should be kept open, the subordinate officers of the administration should be continued in their functions; supported and sustained, if need be, by the military force of the invader. The responsibility of maintaining public order, and of punishing crime, falls directly upon the commanding general of the occupying force. In the performance of this duty he may make use of the local criminal courts, wholly or in part; or he may resort to martial law.

Martial Law.—*Martial law*, or, to speak more correctly, *martial rule*, or the *state of siege*, is a term applied to the government of an occupied territory by the commanding general of the invading force. Martial law also prevails in the immediate theatre of operations of an army in the field. The reason in both cases is the same. The ordinary agencies of government, including the machinery provided for the prevention and punishment of crime, are suspended by the fact of war. This suspension takes place at a time when society is violently disturbed, when the usual restraints of law are at a minimum of efficiency, and when the need of such restraints is the greatest possible. This state of affairs is the direct result of the invasion, or occupation, of the disturbed territory by an enemy. The only organized power capable of restoring and maintaining order is that of the invading force, which is vested in its commanding general. Upon him, therefore, International Law places the responsibility of preserving order, punishing crime, and protecting life and property within the limits of his command. His power in the premises is equal to his responsibility. In cases of extreme urgency, such as arise after a great battle, or the capture of a besieged place or a defended town, he may suspend all law, and may punish crimes summarily, or by tribunals of his own constitution.

If his occupation be temporary, amounting to a mere passage through a portion of the enemy's territory, he may decline to interfere in local affairs, further than to make such transient dispositions as will protect non-combatants and their property along his line of march. If he occupies a district for a considerable period of time his responsibility becomes more general, and the performance of his duty more intricate and difficult.

To deduce a rule that shall control a general commanding in an enemy's country, his position and duty must be clearly understood. He appears in the occupied territory as an agent of his government, charged with conduct of certain military operations. His first responsibility is to his own government, for the successful conduct of the military operations with the direction of which he is charged. In carrying on those operations his government and himself are bound by the laws of war. The usages of war authorize him to employ certain forcible measures toward his enemy. They forbid indiscriminate violence, the use of excessive force, or the use of any force which does not contribute directly to the end for which the war is undertaken. His exercise of authority in the occupied territory must, therefore, be the least possible, consistent with these ends. He may suspend the constitution and municipal laws, but he cannot change them, because such changes in no way contribute to the prosecution of the war. He can impose no unusual or unauthorized burdens upon persons and property, because the laws of war require him to protect them.

If the territory is to be occupied for a considerable time, but without the intention, on the part of the invader, of permanently incorporating it in his own dominions, it is usual to permit the local laws to prevail, and to sanction their enforcement by the existing courts and other legal agencies. Crimes of special atrocity, offences against the laws of war, and crimes over which neither the local nor military courts have jurisdiction, are tried and punished by military commissions, or other special tribunals, constituted for the purpose by the commanding general. The existence of these tribunals is recognized by the laws of war as a necessity of martial rule.

Difference of Opinion as to the Meaning of the Term Occupation.—The precise meaning of the term *occupation* has given rise to much difference of opinion. A definition was attempted at the Brussels Conference, in 1874. In accordance with this definition, "A territory is considered as occupied when it is actually placed under the authority of the hostile army. The occupation only extends to those territories where this authority is established and can be exercised."[1]

Opposing Views.—Two views have been advanced as to what constitutes military occupation. One, maintained by England and the smaller European states, regards a portion of territory as occupied only when it is held by a force sufficient to maintain, at all points, the authority of the invader, and to suppress uprisings against such authority. The Swiss delegate to the Brussels Conference properly compared this view of military occupation to a valid blockade; both, to be binding, must be maintained in sufficient force to be effective. The other, and opposite view, is supported by some of the more powerful Continental states; they regard occupation as complete when actual armed resistance has ceased, and the authority of the legitimate government has been displaced or overthrown. Obedience then becomes the *duty* of the population, independently of the force by which such authority is maintained. Risings against the authority of an invader are by them viewed as *illegal;* subjecting persons, dis-

---

[1] "Article 1, Project of an International Declaration Concerning the Laws and Customs of War," Brussels, 1874.

tricts, and towns who favor them, or who take part in them, to severe punishments.

The operation of this rule would work to the advantage of states which maintain large standing armies, and would greatly facilitate aggressive warfare. They would operate with greatest force against states which maintain small permanent establishments, whose policy is rather defensive than offensive, and who would be obliged to rely, in time of war, upon the united resistance of their entire combatant population.

Of the two views which have been described, there can be no question that the former is more nearly in accordance with the present rule of International Law. Occupation is an act of force, the martial rule of the invader is maintained by force, the obedience of the population is compelled by force, and obedience exists only so long as the constraint continues. The right of revolution is now recognized to exist, even against the regular government of a state, which rests upon the presumed consent of the governed. Still more does the right of armed resistance exist against an authority, which not only has no basis in the consent of the governed, but which is enforced and maintained, against such consent, by superior military force.

Permanent Occupation.—The rules which have been discussed refer to cases of temporary occupation. When a conquest is to be made permanent, as when a province is recovered by the state to which it originally belonged, a belligerent is justified in making such permanent political changes as he may deem expedient or necessary.

38. *Retaliation.*—The laws of war are equally obligatory upon the belligerent states and their allies,

and upon the generals who control and direct their military operations in the field. The duty of observing these laws is reciprocal, and bears equally upon both belligerents. If either of them violates a rule of war, or fails to conduct his operations in strict accordance with them, he cannot complain of similar conduct on the part of his enemy. On the contrary, he must expect it. The power of compelling an enemy to observe the rules of war, or to refrain from violating any particular one of them, is called the *right of retaliation*. A general who suffers a wrong at the hands of an enemy, or who finds that his enemy has violated any of the accepted usages of war, addresses him a communication setting forth the facts which constitute his ground of complaint. If no explanation or apology is attempted, or if the enemy assumes the responsibility of the act, he is justified in resorting to measures of retaliation. In choosing a means of retaliation, revenge cannot enter into the consideration or decision of the question. His sole purpose must be to constrain his adversary to discontinue the irregular acts complained of. Unless the enemy's act be in gross violation of the dictates of humanity, he must retaliate by resorting to similar acts in his military operations. *States* which find themselves compelled to resort to retorsion, as a means of obtaining justice, are permitted to make use of *equivalent* wrongs. *Generals* who are obliged to have recourse to retaliatory measures, however, must confine themselves to the *same or similar* acts. This because of the difficulty of balancing wrongs, and because the enemy, not appreciating the justice of the remedy adopted, may feel himself justified in still further departing from the accepted usages, and may ultimately decline to be bound by any of the rules of civilized warfare.

The Termination of War.

39. *Truce and Peace.*—A *truce,* or *suspension of arms,* is a discontinuance of hostile operations over the whole, or a part, of the theatre of military operations. They are classified according to their purpose and duration, and according to the authority of the officers who may make them, into special and general truces. A *special truce* may be entered into by officers, of any grade, who command armies or separate detachments. They are always of a temporary character, and are made for the purpose of arranging the details of surrender of a defeated army, or besieged place; for burying the dead, or removing the wounded, after a battle or assault; or for conveying a message to the enemy, and receiving his reply, in some matter of necessary intercourse. These truces may be verbal or written. In general the agreement consists in the letter of one general proposing a truce for a certain purpose, and in the reply of his adversary accepting the proposed arrangement. The duration of the truce, in point of time, is precisely stated in the agreement; and the truce expires, without notice, at the hour fixed for its termination. Special truces are binding upon all persons under the command of the officers who make them.

What may be Done during a Special Truce.—During a truce the contracting parties are bound to refrain from all acts of hostility, and to desist from all military operations of a hostile character, and from all preparatory movements, or manœuvres, which could not have been performed during the continuance of hostilities, or which would have been performed under the fire of the enemy. This rule of conduct is deduced from the definition of a truce—a suspension of hostilities. The end of a truce should find both belligerents in precisely the same situation in which they were when it began. Whatever could have been done without regard to the enemy, during hostilities, may continue to be done during a truce. The movement of trains over a line of supply, the process of collecting forage and provisions, by requisition, in districts within the secure control of either party, may continue during a truce. It has also been contended that a closely invested place may stipulate for the privilege of receiving an amount of supplies equivalent to that consumed during the truce. In strict justice, perhaps, this claim should be admitted. The fall of such a place, however, is usually only a question of time; the besieger occupies a position of decided advantage, and the parties enter the truce upon very unequal terms. The besieger, therefore, may properly decline to yield the advantage which he has fairly earned, by permitting provisions to be introduced into the besieged place. To avoid difficulty and misunderstanding, it is always desirable to specify, in the agreement, what particular acts may or may not be done during its continuance.

A General Truce or Armistice is an entire suspension of arms over the whole theatre of military operations. They are made by the belligerent governments, or, with their authority, by the generals commanding in the field, and include within their scope all operations and forces of whatever character. They are usually entered into when the issue of the war has been settled decisively in favor of one of the belligerents, and with a view to negotiations for peace. These agreements are made with greater formality than is the case with special truces, and describe, in considerable detail, what may and may not be done during the existence of the armistice. They are binding upon all forces, both military and naval, engaged in the war on either side. They go into effect from the date of signature, and become binding upon individuals from the date of notification. In naval operations some time is necessary for such notification to reach vessels of war on distant stations, and special arrangements are made in such cases to regulate the disposition of captures made between the dates of negotiation and ratification.

In the preparation of general truces, or armistices, the possible resumption of hostilities is provided for by a clause terminating the truce at a certain date, or upon the expiration of a certain notice. On the date thus agreed upon the truce ceases to have obligatory force, and hostilities are resumed by both belligerents.

Treaties of Peace.

40. *Treaties of Peace* resemble ordinary treaties in form, in the detailed method of preparation, and in binding force. They differ from ordinary treaties, and from private contracts, in respect to the position of the contracting parties, who, from the necessities of the case, do not enter them upon equal terms. This in no respect detracts from their obligatory character, which cannot be too strongly insisted upon. "Agreements entered into by an individual while under duress are void, because it is for the welfare of society that they should be so. If they were binding, the timid would be constantly forced by threats or by violence into a

surrender of their rights, and even into secrecy, as to the oppression under which they were suffering. The [knowledge] that such engagements are void makes the attempt to extort them one of the rarest of human crimes. On the other hand, the welfare of society requires that the engagements entered into by a nation under duress should be binding; for, if they were not so, wars would terminate only by the utter subjugation and ruin of the weaker party."[1]

When either belligerent believes the object of the war to have been attained, or is convinced that it is impossible of attainment; or when the military operations of either power have been so successful as to determine the fortune of war decisively in its favor, a general truce is agreed upon, and negotiations are entered into with a view to the restoration of peace. There is no rule of positive obligation as to the manner in which such negotiations shall be established. The initiative may be taken by either belligerent, either directly with the hostile state, or indirectly through a neutral power. A neutral state may tender its good offices to either belligerent, at any time during the continuance of hostilities. The purpose of the preliminary negotiations is to arrange for a meeting of duly accredited representatives charged with the preparation of a treaty of peace. In choosing a place of meeting a point may be selected within the territory of either belligerent, or in that of a neutral state. If need be, a preliminary agreement is made, guarantee-

---

[1] Senior, in vol. lxxvii. of the *Edinburgh Review*, p. 307; cited by Creasy, pp. 41, 42. See also Halleck, vol. i., pp. 260-266; Phillimore, vol. i., pp. 151-154; Bluntschli, p. 398; Heffter, § 179. For an opposite view, see Mommsen, "History of Rome," vol. i., p. 403.

ing the neutrality of the place of meeting, and the personal immunity of the ambassadors.

The representatives of the belligerent states meet at the time and place agreed upon, and, after an exchange of full powers, enter upon the task of preparing the treaty of peace. When substantial agreement has been reached as to the general terms of peace, a preliminary draft or treaty is sometimes prepared, containing these provisions, and describing the questions that are to be deferred for final settlement in the permanent treaty. The preliminary treaty is signed and duly ratified by the contracting parties. If the war has been carried on by allies on either side, no one of them is justified, by any reason less strong than self-preservation, in making peace without the consent of the others, or in entering into a treaty prejudicial to the common interest of the allied powers.

Treaties of Peace, when Binding.—Treaties of peace become binding upon the signatory powers from the date of signature. They bind individuals from the date of notice. If the war has been carried on in distant dependencies, or on the sea, it is usual to stipulate in the treaty for the restoration of captures made between the dates of signature and notification.

Effects of Treaties of Peace.—The cause for which the war was undertaken is presumed to have been settled by the resort to arms, and by the amnesty contained in the treaty. This is the case whether the state which was the aggressor in the war has been successful, or not, in its resort to force to obtain redress. The subjects of the belligerent states, who were placed in a condition of non-intercourse, and of legal hostility, as a result of the declaration of war, are restored to their normal relations. Obligations which were suspended, by the fact of war, resume their force with the establishment of peace. The payment of public and private debts, and of interest upon public stocks, is resumed.

Treatment of Occupied Territory. — Questions connected with territory, occupied by either belligerent at the close of the war, are finally settled by the terms of the treaty. In doing this some *status* is assumed, and this may be that existing before the war, or at its close; or an intermediate status may be chosen that existed at some instant during the continuance of hostilities. The details of evacuation of occupied territory, fortresses, and ports are arranged with great precision. If the treaty contains no stipulations as to occupied territory, the rule of *uti possidetis* prevails, and each belligerent retains the territory occupied by him at the close of the war.

The rule as to the real property of the enemy is substantially the same as that applied to territory. Immovable property, belonging to either belligerent, shares the fate of the territory in which it is situated, unless otherwise stipulated in the treaty. Forts, arsenals, dock-yards, and naval ports, the surrender or evacuation of which is arranged for in the treaty, are transferred in the condition in which they were at the date of the treaty. They cannot be dismantled, disarmed, or destroyed, but no obligation exists to repair them after that date, even when such repairs are necessary. Movable property of the enemy in the hands of a belligerent, at the date of the treaty, becomes his by the fact of possession. Contributions levied, but not collected, become void when the treaty goes into effect; and no new contributions or requisitions can be levied by either party, without the express authorization of the treaty. The right to levy them is an incident of belligerency, and ceases at the termination of hostilities.

If a portion of territory be ceded by either party, no guarantee of the allegiance of the population of the ceded district is given or expected. The fact that allegiance is based upon consent is now so generally recognized in such transfers, as to permit individuals to dispose of their property and to withdraw to their native state, when the territory within which they reside has been ceded to an enemy as a result of war or conquest.

The Rules of Maritime Capture.

41. The rules of war regarding the treatment of private property on land have been characterized by a marked and constant improvement since the beginning of modern history. To appreciate this change it is only necessary to compare the laws of war on land, as they are now understood, with the barbarous practices that prevailed during the Thirty Years' War, or even with the corresponding usages during the Napoleonic wars at the beginning of this century. The tendency has been to give to war on land the character of an armed contest between belligerent governments, restricting its operations and effects to the armed forces engaged on either side, and exempting private persons and private property from its hardships wherever such exemption has been possible. There has been no such general improvement in the laws having to do with the treatment of private property at sea, and the rules regulating maritime capture have advanced but little since they were codified, more than eight hundred years.

ago, in the *Consolato del Mare*. As different states have, at different times, obtained undue preponderance at sea, their invariable tendency has been to shape the rules of maritime capture, rather in accordance with their views of temporary policy and self-interest, than in accordance with the demands of humanity and civilization. As a motive in making and authorizing such captures, the selfish desire for booty has been only too apparent; easily predominating over all of the more or less plausible reasons that have been alleged in favor of the practice. From time to time proposals have been made to exempt from capture at sea all private property not contraband of war. These propositions have never been favorably received, however, and there is no present prospect of the general discontinuance of a practice, as unjust in principle as it is inefficient, as a means of redressing an international wrong.

Forces that may be Employed in Maritime War.— The force that may be employed in naval operations has already been described; it may consist of the regular naval establishment of the state, supplemented by such volunteer forces as may be deemed necessary. It may also consist of privateers. In time of war no small part of the duty of the naval force of a belligerent power consists in the exercise of the right of search, in the maintenance of blockades, and in effecting the capture of enemy's ships and goods upon the high seas. No such captures are legal, or can be made, except with the direct authorization of the captor's state. The making of captures without such authorization constitutes the crime of piracy. Captures may be made upon the high seas, or within the territorial waters of either belligerent. Captures made in neutral waters are illegal, and must be restored, with suitable apology and reparation, to the neutral government whose sovereignty has been invaded.

Definition of Prize.—The term *prize* is applied to all captures of property made at sea. The term *booty* is applied to similar captures of property on land.

Title to Prize, in Whom Vested.—The title to the prize first vests in the captor's government, and the further disposal of all such captures is regulated by its municipal law. The capture is made by its authority, and upon its responsibility. It may therefore make such disposition of its prize as it may deem best. It may convert it to its own use, or cause it to be destroyed, or sold; and it may distribute the whole or a part of the proceeds of the sale among the captors, in accordance with the provisions of its municipal law.

There has been some difference of opinion as to the precise instant when the title to a prize passes from the original owner and vests in the captor's government. Three rules have been applied: 1. *The twenty-four-hour rule,* based upon twenty-four hours of secure possession on the part of the captor. 2. *The rule of pernoctation,* according to which the prize must have been in possession of the captor during the period between sun and sun. 3. *The rule of cessation of resistance,* by which the title is held to pass to the captor when armed resistance ceases, and the flag is struck, or a voluntary surrender is made. This rule is now the one most generally accepted.

Duty of Captor.—It is the first duty of a captor to convey his prize into a court of his own country for adjudication. In former times he was permitted to take his prize into a neutral port. This is still the rule of International Law; but the almost invariable practice of neutrals in recent wars has been to forbid such a use of their ports, except in cases of distress or emergency. The crews of enemy merchant vessels captured on the high seas become prisoners of war, and are entitled to the rights guaranteed to that class by the rules of war. The crews of captured neutral vessels cannot be regarded as prisoners of war. They are simply detained subject to the action of the prize court upon the ship, on board of which they are employed. They are not enemies, and are not subject to detention or punishment. No measures of severity toward them are justifiable except in cases of great emergency, and for such injuries, when shown to be unnecessary, prize courts may decree damages to the injured parties.

Vessels captured on the high seas are sent into port under charge of a prize-master, who, with an adequate prize-crew, is placed on board for that purpose. It is the duty of the prize-master to secure the ship and goods in his charge from spoliation or damage during the homeward passage, and to deliver his prize, immediately upon her arrival, into the legal possession of the court having jurisdiction over the case. The ship's papers, log-book, register, sea-letters, and bills of lading are sealed by the commanding officer of the capturing vessel, and they, with two or more members of the ship's company,[1] are conveyed into port by the prize-master, and are delivered with the prize into the custody of the court.

The practice of furnishing prize crews tends to deplete the fighting strength of the captor, and, if a

---

[1] One of whom should be an officer when practicable.

number of captures are made, a time must come when a commander, having a due regard to the safety and efficiency of his own ship, can no longer make such detachments from his crew. This emergency is recognized and provided for by the law of nations, and by the municipal law of most states, which authorize him in such an emergency to destroy his prize, or to accept a ransom.[1] As the present tendency of neutral states is to close their ports to maritime prizes, such disposition of prizes is more likely to increase than decrease in frequency. The practice of destroying prizes has been objected to, but rather on the ground of humanity than legality. If the right to capture enemy property at sea be admitted, the right to destroy it follows as a natural consequence. The title of the original owner has been forcibly divested by an act of war. If any injury has been inflicted upon the belligerent, that injury consists in the fact of capture, which amounts to a destruction of the property, in so far as the owner and his government are concerned. It can matter little to either what disposition is made of the property, after the owner's title has been extinguished.

The Ransom of Captured Vessels.—Ransom consists in an agreement entered into between a captor and the master of a captured vessel, acting in behalf of the owners, by which, in consideration of the latter bind-

---

[1] Abdy's Kent, p. 276. "If the prize is a neutral ship, no circumstances will justify her destruction before condemnation. The only proper reparation to the neutral, in such a case, is to pay him the full value of the property destroyed" (Twiss, "International Law During War," § 167, p. 331; The Felicity, Dodson's "Admiralty Reports," vol. ii., p. 386; Boyd's Wheaton, pp. 432, 433).

ing himself to pay a stipulated sum, he is permitted to continue his voyage, by a specified route, to a certain port of destination. The instrument containing this agreement is called a *Ransom Contract*, and when regularly made, its binding force is recognized by the law of nations.

The Ransom Contract is executed in duplicate, one copy being retained by the captor, and the other by the master of the captured vessel, to whom it serves as a safe-conduct during the rest of his voyage. The precise route to be pursued is stated in the contract, and if he departs from it he is liable to a second capture. In this case the ransom contract constitutes a prior lien upon the prize, and must be satisfied out of the proceeds of the sale, the remainder only being decreed to the second captor. The copy of the ransom contract which is furnished the enemy master is, in effect, a guarantee against capture, by another cruiser of the captor's state, while in prosecution of the voyage described in the agreement. He forfeits whatever protection the contract gives him if he is found out of the course therein prescribed, unless driven from it by stress of weather or other evident necessity. The contract usually specifies that, if the ship is wrecked on the high seas, or by the perils of the sea, the instrument is void. It is otherwise, however, in case the vessel be stranded, or wrecked intentionally by the master. "If the captor, after having ransomed an enemy's vessel, is himself taken by the enemy, together with the ransom bill of which he is the bearer, this ransom bill becomes a part of the capture made by the enemy; and the persons of the hostile nation who were debtors of the ransom, are thereby discharged from their obligation under the ransom bill."[1] If the Ransom Contract has been conveyed to the captor's state, or to a place of safety, prior to capture, it retains its obligatory character.

Ransom Contracts constitute one of the exceptions to the rule of non-intercourse between enemies in war, and a suit to recover, on such a contract, should not be barred because the plaintiff is an alien enemy. The intercourse which is implied by the negotiation of such an instrument is a recognized necessity of war, and, for the purpose of enforcing his legal right, an alien enemy should be recognized as having a legal standing in the courts of the debtor's state. Indeed, such is the course pursued by most modern states. England, alone, constitutes an exception to the rule. "The English courts have decided that the subject of an enemy is not permitted to sue in the British courts of justice, in his own proper person, for the payment of a ransom, on the technical objection of the want of a *persona standi in judicio*, but that the payment could be forced by an action brought by the imprisoned hostage in the courts of his own country for the recovery of his freedom. This technical objection is not based upon principle nor supported by reason, and the decision has not the sanction of general usage."[2]

Hostages.—It was the practice in former times to give hostages to the captor as additional security for the payment of ransom. They were conveyed to the captor's country, and were there detained as prisoners until the ransom was paid. They were not always

---

[1] Halleck, vol. ii., p. 360.
[2] Halleck, vol. ii., p. 361; Boyd's Wheaton, p. 476; case of the Hoop, Robinson's "Admiralty Reports," vol. i., pp. 169, 201.

treated as prisoners of war, however, but were at times subjected to special hardships and restrictions, imposed upon them with a view of constraining the payment of the ransom contract. If they died in captivity the ransom contract still remained binding, as they were only regarded as collateral security for its payment.

Recapture and Postliminy.—When a prize has been made at sea, it has been seen to be the duty of the captor to send it to a port of his own country, or that of an ally, for adjudication. In the prosecution of this voyage it is liable to recapture, and a question arises as to its ownership in such a case. The prize has been recaptured by an armed vessel of the same nationality as the original owner; but the recapture, in so far as the recaptor is concerned, was attended by the same risk and danger that would have been involved in an original capture of the same vessel from the enemy. The captor has acquired certain rights in the prize, and, at the same time, the title of the original owner to the property has been to a certain extent revested. The fiction of law which has been invented to adjust these conflicting claims is borrowed from the Roman Law, and is called the *rule of postliminy*. It was applied by the Romans to all captures of persons or property made by an enemy in war, and a similar rule applied to such portions of the public territory as passed into the hands of an enemy as the result of conquest. The title to captured property vested in the captor so long as it remained in his secure possession. As prisoners taken in war became the slaves of their captors, their status in Rome, as freemen, was suspended during captivity. If slaves were captured the rule of property applied. When *recaptured* from the enemy the title of the original owner was revived, and the property was restored to him on payment of salvage. A person who was recaptured became, according to the rule of war, the property of his recaptor; but the law permitted him to resume his freedom, or citizenship, upon the payment of a specified sum.

The modern rule of postliminy resembles in principle the rule of the Roman Law, although it is more just and humane in its application. Persons recaptured in war resume, at once, all their personal and property rights. Slavery and private ransom are alike discountenanced by International Law. Property recaptured from an enemy on land, if possible of identification, reverts to its owner without cost or payment. Property recaptured from an enemy, at sea, is restored to its original owner; but is charged with the payment of a reward to the recaptor, to reimburse him for the risk incurred and the service rendered. The reward paid to recaptors for the recovery of property captured at sea is called *salvage.* The amount of salvage to be paid, in any particular case of recapture, is determined by a prize court, in accordance with the municipal law of the recaptor's state. The amount of salvage awarded varies with the difficulty of recapture, and the value of the prize. It depends also upon the character of the vessel by which the recapture is made, the award being greater in the case of a privateer or merchant vessel than in that of a vessel of war; none being awarded for the recapture of one public armed vessel by another.[1] "In general no salvage is due for the

---

[1] For the law of the United States on this subject see § 4652, "Re-

recapture of neutral vessels and goods, upon the principle that the liberation of a *bona fide* neutral, from the hands of the enemy to the captor, is no beneficial service to the neutral, inasmuch as the same enemy would be compelled, by the tribunals of his own country, to make restitution of the property thus unjustly seized."[1]

As recapture is possible only between the place of original capture and the port to which it is sent by the captor, the right of postliminy exists between the same limits of time and place. The title of the original owner is finally extinguished by the action of the prize court in decreeing the condemnation and sale of the captured property; and the title acquired by the purchaser is good, even against the original owner or his government. If such property be recaptured after it has been regularly condemned and sold, it is not restored to the original owner, but is regarded as lawful prize, and is treated as such. England furnishes the only exception to this rule. According to the English law, property recaptured, during the continuance of a war, is restored to its owner upon payment of salvage, no matter how long it has been in the enemy's possession, nor through how many hands it may have passed in the way of purchase and sale. A treaty of peace is alone held to confirm and perfect the title to captures made during a war.

42. *Prize Courts and their Jurisdiction.*—Whenever a capture has been made at sea, it becomes the first

---

vised Statutes of the United States." For that of France, England, Spain, Portugal, Denmark, Sweden, Holland, see Boyd's Wheaton, pp. 442–450; Hall, p. 424.

[1] Boyd's Wheaton, p. 435.

duty of the captor to cause it to be conveyed to a port of his own country, or that of an ally, for adjudication. The municipal laws of all states provide special tribunals whose duty it is to determine questions of prize. These tribunals are called *Prize Courts*, and as the decision of such questions is an incident of admiralty jurisdiction, the admiralty courts of most states are given jurisdiction over cases of maritime capture. This power may be vested in these courts as a branch of their general admiralty jurisdiction, or jurisdiction may be conferred upon them by special commission during a particular war. The former practice prevails in the United States, the latter now prevails in England.[1]

Prize courts may sit in the ports or territory of a belligerent, or in those of an ally. They cannot sit in neutral ports, even with the consent of the neutral government,[2] and a belligerent would justly regard the granting of such permission as a violation of neutral obligation. This arises from the peculiar jurisdiction of these tribunals. Prize courts do not try criminal cases, or determine controversies arising between individuals. The question before them in any case is, whether, according to the law of nations, a ship and cargo were liable to capture, and, if so, whether the capture was lawfully made. If their decision be in the affirmative, the ship and cargo are condemned; if the decision be in the negative, they are released. In its investigation of the circumstances of the capture, and in reaching a decree of condemnation, the court,

---

[1] 3 and 4 Victoria, chap. 65, § 22.
[2] Boyd's Wheaton, pp. 455, 456; Halleck, vol. ii., pp. 422, 423.

to a certain extent, acts in behalf of the state under whose authority it sits, and its decree fixes upon that government, in the highest degree, the responsibility for the seizure and condemnation of the enemy's property, or contraband goods. Its action, therefore, to a much greater degree than is the case with ordinary judicial proceedings, constitutes an act of sovereignty, and for this reason it cannot perform such an act within the jurisdiction of another sovereign state.

The Law Applied by Prize Courts.—In deciding cases of maritime capture prize courts apply the rules of *international* rather than municipal law. For this reason decisions in similar cases, rendered by the prize courts of other states, are regarded by them as constituting precedents of a binding character. "Prize courts are in no way bound to regard local ordinances and municipal regulations, unless they are sanctioned by the law of nations. Indeed, if such ordinances and regulations are in contravention of the established rules of international jurisprudence, prize courts must either violate their duty, or entirely disregard them. They are not binding on the prize courts, even of the country by which they are issued. The stipulations of treaties, however, are obligatory upon the nations which have entered into them, and prize courts must observe them in adjudicating between subjects or citizens of the contracting parties."[1]

Procedure in Prize Cases.—The principles of prize, as at present applied to maritime captures, are almost identical with the provisions of the Roman Law on

---

[1] Halleck, vol. ii., p. 438; case of the Maria, Robinson's "Admiralty Reports," vol. i., p. 340; Phillimore, vol. iii., pp. 648, 649; Creasy, pp. 556, 557; Twiss, pp. 335-340; Manning, p. 472.

the same subject. "The allegations, proofs, and proceedings are, therefore, in general modelled upon the Civil Law, with such additions and alterations as the practice of nations and the rights of belligerents and neutrals unavoidably impose. . . . Not only the proceedings, but also the rules of evidence, are, in many respects, different from those of courts of common law; and prize courts not only decide upon the claims of captors, but also upon their conduct in making the capture, and subsequently, and not infrequently, declare a forfeiture of their rights with vindictive damages.

"In prize causes the evidence to convict or condemn must come, in the first instance, from the papers and crew of the captured ship. It is the duty of the captors to bring the ship's papers into the registry of the district court, verify them on oath, and to have the examinations of the principal officers and seamen of the captured ship taken on the standing interrogatories, and not *viva voce*. It is exclusively upon these papers and examinations that the cause is to be heard in the first instance. If, from this evidence, the property clearly appears to be hostile or neutral, condemnation or restitution immediately follows. If the property appears to be doubtful, or the case suspicious, further proof may be granted according to the rules which govern the legal discretion of the court, if the claimant has not forfeited his right to it by a breach of good faith. . . . Where the national character does not distinctly appear, or where the question of proprietary interest is left in doubt, further proof is usually ordered."[1]

---

[1] Halleck, vol. ii., pp. 435, 436.

The common-law doctrines, as to the competency of witnesses, are not applicable to prize proceedings. No person is incompetent in those courts merely on the ground of interest. His testimony is admissible, subject to all exceptions as to its credibility.¹ The rule that the testimony, for the condemnation of a prize, must be obtained, in the first instance, directly from documents or witnesses found on board the vessel at the time of her seizure, is always adhered to, unless satisfactory reasons are shown for departing from it in a particular instance.²

Right of Appeal in Prize Cases.—The right of appeal is invariably recognized in the laws creating prize courts and defining their jurisdiction; and, on account of the importance of the interests involved, special provision is frequently made to enable prize cases to be carried up, by way of appeal, to a court of last resort, in a much shorter time than is usual, and without passing through any of the courts intervening between those of original and final jurisdiction. The laws of the United States provide for this contingency by permitting an appeal to be taken directly to the Supreme Court, from the District Courts, which, in the United States, have original jurisdiction in all cases of maritime capture.

Rules for Determining the Nationality of Ships and Goods.—It has been seen that, in the determination of a question of prize, the decision will depend upon whether the property seized has, or has not, the enemy character. To determine questions thus arising, as to

---

[1] The Anne, Wheaton, vol. iii., p. 435.

[2] The Zavalla, Blatchford, "Prize Cases," p. 173; The Jane Campbell, Blatchford, "Prize Cases," p. 101.

the nationality of ships and goods, certain rules are recognized by the prize courts of all nations. The more important of them are—

(*a.*) The nationality of ships and goods is, in general, determined by the domicile of their owner. Those owned by one domiciled in a hostile country are enemy goods; those owned by one having a domicile in a neutral state are neutral goods.

(*b.*) The products of hostile soil, and articles manufactured in enemy's territory, are hostile, by whomsoever owned.

(*c.*) The share of a neutral partner, in a firm having a hostile domicile, is hostile.

(*d.*) If an owner of, or partner in, a business situated in a neutral state, has himself a hostile domicile, his share in the neutral house is regarded as enemy property.

(*e.*) A neutral sailing under the enemy flag, or carrying his register, or license to trade, is regarded as an enemy.

(*f.*) The nationality of goods is determined by their ownership at the instant of capture; a change made in ownership after that date is not recognized.

(*g.*) "Vessels of discovery, or of expeditions of exploration and survey, sent for the examination of unknown seas, islands, and coasts, are, by general consent, exempt from the contingencies of war, and are therefore not liable to capture. Like the sacred vessel which the Athenians sent with their annual offerings to the temple of Delos, they are respected by all nations, because their labors are intended for the benefit of all mankind. It has been the invariable practice of European powers to grant safe-conducts to ships sent to explore the Arctic regions, against being captured by ships of war on their return, in the event of war breaking out during such absence."¹

(*h.*) "Fishing-boats have also, as a general rule, been exempted from the effects of hostilities. As early as 1521, while war was raging between Charles V. and Francis I., ambassadors from these two sovereigns met at Calais, then English, and agreed that, whereas the herring fishery was about to commence, the subjects of both belligerents engaged in this pursuit should be safe and unmolested by the other party, and should have leave to fish as in time of peace. In the war of 1800 the British and French governments issued formal instructions exempting the fishing-boats of each other's subjects from seizure."²

References.—For the definition and causes of war, see Halleck, vol. i., chaps. xv. and xvi.; Heffter, §§ 105-113; Klüber, §§ 231-237; Creasy, pp. 360-394; G. F. De Martens, liv. viii., chap. iii., §§ 263-265; Vattel, book iii., chap. i., §§ 1-3; Phillimore, vol. iii., pp. 77-84. For the rules and usages of war, see Vattel, book iii., chap. ii., §§ 6-23; chap. viii., §§ 136-159; chap. ix., §§ 166-173; Heffter, §§ 123-129; Halleck, chaps. xviii.-xx.; Hall, chaps. ii. and vii.; "La Guerre Actuelle," by C. F. Rolin-Jacquemyn; *Revue de Droit International*, vol. ii. (1870), pp. 643-720 (series); Rivier, "Manuel des Lois de la Guerre;" Dr. Lieber "Instructions" (Halleck, vol. ii., pp. 36-51); "Rules of the Brussels Conference," Boyd's Wheaton, pp. 476-483. For the rules as to the treatment of property on land, see Vattel, book iii., chap. v., §§ 69-77; chap. ix., §§ 160-173; Heffter, §§ 127-140; Halleck, chap. xxi.; Hall, part iii., chap. iii.; Bluntschli, "Le Droit de Butin en Général et Spécialement du Droit de Prise Maritime;" *Revue de Droit International*, vol. ix., pp. 544-549. For the subject of temporary occupation, see Hall, part iii., chap. iv., §§ 153-161; Halleck,

---

¹ Halleck, vol. ii., pp. 149-151.   ² *Ibid.*, pp. 151, 152.

vol. ii., chaps. xxxiii. and xxxiv.; Heffter, § 185; Klüber, § 265; Boyd's Wheaton, § 346; Creasy, pp. 483-495, and pp. 502-516. See also "Report of the Brussels Conference," Boyd's Wheaton, p. 476, "Parliamentary Papers, Miscellaneous," 1875, No. 1; De Martens, § 282 b. For the subject of requisitions and contributions, see Creasy, p. 518-535; "Report of the Brussels Conference," "Parliamentary Papers, Miscellaneous," 1875, No. 1; G. F. De Martens, § 280; Halleck, vol. ii., chap. xvi., §§ 15-27; Hall, §§ 140-142; Vattel, book iii., chap. ix., §§ 160-166. For maritime capture, see Halleck, vol. ii., chap. xxii., §§ 1-24; chap. xxxi; Hall, part iv., chap. iii., §§ 143-152; chap. vi., §§ 167-175; Manning, chap. v.; Heffter, §§ 137-139; Nys, "La Guerre Maritime;" Dahlgren, "International Law;" Wheaton, "History of the Law of Nations;" Bluntschli, "Le Droit de Butin en Général et Spécialement du Droit de Prise Maritime;" Phillimore, vol. iii., pp. 559-647. For the procedure of prize courts, see Halleck, vol. ii., chaps. xxxi. and xxxii.; Manning, chap. xiii.; Phillimore, vol. iii., part xi., pp. 648-769; Bulmerincq, "Le Droit de Prises Maritime;" *Revue de Droit International*, vol. x. and xi.; Bluntschli, "Le Droit de Butin en Général et Spécialement du Droit de Prise Maritime;" *Revue de Droit International*, vol. ix. and x.; Nys, "La Guerre Maritime," chap. vii.

CHAPTER XI.

NEUTRALITY.—THE RIGHTS AND DUTIES OF NEUTRALS.

1. The term *neutrality* is applied to the relation existing between the states which are parties to a war and those which refrain from taking part in its operations, either as belligerents or allies.

A *neutral state* is one which wholly abstains from participation in an existing war, rendering no aid or service to either belligerent in his military operations.

Character of the Neutral Relation.—In strictness, the relations existing between two states, at any time, must be either those of peace or war. International Law recognizes no intermediate condition. When a state occupies the position of a neutral it simply undertakes to maintain, without interruption, its peaceful relations with both belligerents. The maintenance of such relations is, of course, more difficult in war than in time of profound peace; and to this end a neutral state finds itself obliged to take such precautions, within its territorial limits, as will guarantee the continuance of such friendly relations. For the same purpose it has recourse to such positive measures as will secure immunity from acts of belligerency within its territory, and compel respect for its sovereignty and independence.

2. *History of Neutrality.*—The rules of neutral obligation are of relatively recent growth, and, in their present form, are largely the result of a compromise be-

tween the conflicting rights and interests of belligerents and neutrals. In ancient times the very conception of neutrality was impossible. So long as one powerful state aspired to or claimed universal dominion, it was impossible for other and less powerful states to maintain that separate, independent existence which is essential to the recognition of state rights, and so to the development of a true theory of neutrality. War, among the ancients, was the normal state of mankind, in which all nations participated, either as principals or allies. Had any ancient state attempted to occupy a position remotely resembling that of neutrality, according to the modern acceptation of the term, and had it attempted to compel respect to its neutral rights, the belligerent against whom the attempt was made would have regarded it as an act of war, and would have governed itself accordingly. This state of affairs continued until the modern idea of state sovereignty and territorial independence began to be generally recognized toward the close of the Middle Ages.

The Origin and Development of the Neutral Theory.—The theory of neutrality is based upon, and deduced from, the conception of a number of sovereign states, or political communities, each enjoying a separate existence, and each recognizing the separate and independent existence of every other. Such conditions were fulfilled by the Mediterranean cities that participated in the revival of commerce, toward the close of the period of the Dark Ages; and it was among them that the modern theory of neutrality was developed. The first conception of neutral right to acquire general recognition among them seems to have consisted in the idea that, at the outbreak of war between any two cities, the commerce of the rest, who remained friendly to the belligerents, as it in no way concerned the hostile cities, should undergo the least possible interruption. Out of this immunity grew the idea of the exemption of neutral or friendly goods from capture in time of war.

These cities were either independent communities, or were situated in separate states, and commercial relations had become so firmly established among them by the close of the eleventh century, as to warrant the preparation of a code of Sea Laws containing their common maritime usages. The earliest of these codes, the *Consolato del Mare*, recognized the distinction between the property of friends and enemies in war, and declared that the former was exempt from capture and confiscation, even when found on an enemy's vessel. If such property were delivered at its destination, freight was due to the belligerent captor who effected the delivery. Similar provisions were contained in the later Sea Laws; indeed, so long as maritime commerce was controlled by the *cities* of southern and western Europe, the treatment of neutral property at sea was marked by extreme liberality.

The cities that were identified with the revival of commerce engaged in such pursuits for purely mercenary reasons. They were rivals in commerce only, and none of them aspired to territorial, as distinguished from commercial, dominion. Their commercial rivalry was keen, however, and some of them asserted claims to the exclusive control of certain waters for purposes of trade. Conflicts of interest thus arose, which, at times, resulted in war; but as their commercial interests were, on the whole, of the first importance, their relations were more generally peaceful than hostile. Upon the outbreak of war the greater number of cities found it to be to their interest to refrain from participation in its operations, and to continue their friendly relations with both belligerents. The relations of the non-belligerent, or neutral, cities with each other underwent no change. They were at peace, and simply maintained, without interruption, their ordinary commercial intercourse. As the greater number of these cities were usually at peace, it is easy to see that it was to the general interest that their commercial relations should suffer, during war, the least possible interruption. The necessity of combining to protect their merchant-vessels from the depredations of pirates must have suggested to them, at a relatively early date, the desirability of similar concerted action to secure a like immunity from acts of belligerency, and to compel respect for their neutral rights.

The Rule of the Consolato del Mare.—Out of this state of international relations grew the rule of the *Consolato del Mare*, that enemy goods were liable to capture, and neutral goods were exempt from capture, wherever found. This rule was generally accepted by the commercial cities, and, later, by the European powers. With occasional interruptions, due, in great part, to treaty stipulations, it continued to be the most generally-accepted rule upon the subject of the liability of property to capture at sea, until the adoption of the more liberal rule of the Declaration of Paris, in 1856.

General Acceptance of the Rule of the Consolato del Mare.—England adopted the rule at the organization of its admiralty courts during the reign of Edward III., and has consistently maintained it during her subsequent history. In a small number of treaties, made during the seventeenth and eighteenth centuries, the English government conceded the principle that free ships make free goods; but these concessions were of a temporary character, and in nearly all cases were terminated by a positive disavowal of the milder rule. France, after observing the rule of the *Consolato* for nearly five hundred years, repudiated it in the Maritime Ordinances of 1681. By that instrument the rule of capture was stated to be, that the goods of an enemy in a neutral vessel, and the goods of a friend in an enemy's vessel, were alike liable to capture; thus establishing the rule that enemy ships make enemy goods. This continued to be the practice of France, subject to some modification in her conventional law, until the Declaration of Paris. The practice of Spain, during the period of her maritime supremacy, was similarly severe. The policy of the United States, as indicated in the decisions of the Supreme Court, has been substantially the same as that of England. "The two distinct propositions, 1. That enemy's goods, found on board a neutral ship, may lawfully be seized as prize of war; and, 2. That the goods of a neutral, found on board of an enemy's vessel, are to be restored, have also been explicitly incorporated into the jurisprudence of the United States, and declared by the Supreme Court to be founded on the law of nations. The rule, it was observed by the court, rested on the simple and intelligible principle that war gave a full right to capture the goods of an enemy, but gave no right to capture the goods of a friend. The neutral flag constituted no protection to enemy's property, and the belligerent flag communicated no hostile character to neutral property. The character of the property depended upon the fact of ownership, and not upon the character of the vehicle in which it was found. Nations, indeed, had changed this simple and natural principle of public law by conventions between themselves, in whole or in part, as they believed it to be for their interest; but the one proposition, that free ships should make free goods, did not necessarily imply the converse proposition, that enemy's ships should make enemy's goods. If a treaty established the one proposition, and was silent as to the other, the other stood precisely as if there had been no stipulation, and upon the ancient rule."[1] The policy of the different departments of the United States government upon the question of maritime capture has not been the same. The courts of the United States, being to some extent controlled by the English precedents in prize cases, have, in the main, followed the English rule. The political departments, on the other hand, have constantly endeavored to secure the greatest possible immunity from capture for private property at sea, and to that end have endeavored to obtain, by treaty and otherwise, international consent, not only to the rule that free ships make free goods, but that *all* private property at sea, not contraband of war, should be exempt from capture and confiscation in time of war.[2]

3. *The Principle of Free Ships, Free Goods.*—The principle that *free ships make free goods* was first rec-

---

[1] The Nereide, Cranch, vol. ix., pp. 388–395, 428, cited by Phillimore, vol. iii., pp. 317, 318.

[2] The principle of free ships, free goods, was incorporated in the treaties between the United States and France in 1778 and 1800; with the United Provinces in 1782; with Sweden in 1783, 1816, and 1827; with Prussia in 1785 and 1828; with Spain in 1795.

ognized by Holland during the early part of the seventeenth century, and was the result of the peculiar situation of that state as a European power. Its military strength on land was far less in amount than that of the great states by which it was surrounded, and was never more than sufficient to the task of securing its independent political existence. The contrary, however, was the case at sea, where the maritime power of the republic was exceeded, if at all, by that of England alone. The maintenance of its position as a maritime and commercial power thus became a matter of the first importance, and was so recognized by the succession of able statesmen who directed the state policy of the United Provinces during the seventeenth and eighteenth centuries. Having but little military strength, it was desirable that Holland should remain neutral in all European wars. It was still more desirable, however, that its immense carrying trade should be exempt from the effects of war at sea. But this exemption could only be obtained by securing the adoption of the rule that *free ships made free goods*, as the rule then prevailing was that of the *Consolato del Mare*, by which the ownership of property determined its liability to capture. For the adoption of a new rule on the subject of maritime capture the general consent of nations was necessary, and that consent could only be obtained by treaty stipulations. The efforts of the Dutch government were therefore directed to that end, and, as a result, a number of treaties were negotiated in which the rule of *free ships, free goods*, was recognized, and the liability to capture was determined by the *nationality of the vessel*, and not by *the ownership of the goods*, as in the ancient rules.

As Holland was more generally neutral than belligerent, the adoption of the latter principle, in its fullest extent, would be, in the main, advantageous to her interests. She would gain more, as a neutral, by the adoption of the rule of *free ships, free goods*, than she would lose, as a belligerent, by the adoption of the rule of *enemy ships, enemy goods*. For this reason, in some of her treaties both of these principles were connected, and the liability of merchandise to capture on the high seas was determined by the nationality of the vessel, rather than by the ownership of the cargo.[1] The principle of free ships, free goods, was accepted by many of the less important commercial states of Europe. It was generally adopted by the Baltic powers, by France, in the Treaty of Ryswick, in 1657, and even by England, in a few treaties negotiated between the years 1658 and 1756. From the year 1715 onward, the maritime importance of Holland steadily declined; and as that state was no longer directly interested in the maintenance of the new rule, the treaties upon which it had been based were not renewed, or were suffered to lapse; and it appeared less frequently in the new treaties which were negotiated, from time to time, upon the subject of maritime capture. From the Peace of Paris, in 1763, until the outbreak of the Crimean War, in 1853, the maritime preponderance of England was sufficient to prevent the general adoption of any principle of capture, more liberal, or less severe, than that contained in the rule of the *Consolato del Mare*, the justice of which the British government had always maintained.

At the outbreak of the Crimean War the British

---

[1] For lists of these treaties see Phillimore, vol. iii., pp. 324 *et seq.*

government announced that, for the period of that war, it would "waive the right of seizing enemy's property laden on board a neutral vessel, unless it be contraband of war." A similar waiver was made by the French government. In both cases the concession was declared to be due to a desire to render the war "as little onerous as possible to the powers with which they remained at peace."[1]

4. *The Declaration of Paris.*—The Treaty of Paris, which terminated the Crimean War, was signed on March 30, 1856. The representatives of the powers that had been parties to the treaty, at the suggestion of Count Walewski, the French plenipotentiary, assembled in conference for the purpose of discussing the rules of maritime capture, and, on the 16th of April following, adopted a body of rules modifying the existing rules of capture, which has since been known as the Declaration of Paris. The rules adopted were four in number:

(*a.*) Privateering is, and remains, abolished.

(*b.*) The neutral flag covers enemy's goods, with the exception of contraband of war.

(*c.*) Neutral goods, with the exception of contraband of war, are not liable to capture under the enemy's flag.

(*d.*) Blockades, to be binding, must be effective, that is to say, maintained by a force sufficient really to prevent access to the coast of the enemy.

The declaration was signed by plenipotentiaries representing Great Britain, France, Russia, Austria, Sardinia, Prussia, and Turkey; and the signatory powers

---

[1] Joint Declaration of March 28, 1854, made by England and France.

further agreed to bring the declaration to the knowledge of the states which had not taken part in the Congress of Paris, and to invite them to accede to it. Between the years 1856 and 1861 the principles of the declaration had been accepted by all the European powers except Spain, and by all those on the western continent except Mexico and the United States. The three powers, which refused to adopt the proposed rules, agreed in rejecting the rule abandoning the practice of privateering; and, as the declaration had to be accepted as an entirety, these states were thus prevented from formally accepting the three rules to which they entertained no objection. When the Declaration of Paris was submitted to the government of the United States for adoption, it was replied, in behalf of that power, that, in their proposed form, the rules could not be accepted as a whole. The policy of the United States had always been to maintain a small naval establishment, and its important commercial interests would not permit it to resign the right of increasing its power at sea, at the outbreak of war, by the acceptance into its naval service of a force of privateers. It was observed, however, that if a rule were added to the Declaration exempting all private property from capture at sea, in time of war, the necessity for the employment of such an additional force would disappear, and the United States would gladly accede to the proposed rules. At the outbreak of the War of the Rebellion an attempt was made by the United States to become a party to the Declaration of Paris, but, as it was understood that its acceptance was to include the Confederate States as well, the attempt was not persisted in.

Binding Force of the Declaration.—The rules of the Declaration of Paris upon the subject of maritime capture, although binding upon the signatory powers alone, have been generally accepted as the rule of International Law upon the subjects of which they treat, and it is highly improbable that a severer rule will be adopted at any time in the future. The adoption of a milder rule is as little probable. Upon several occasions it has been suggested to amend them, in the direction of greater liberality, by the adoption of a rule exempting all private property from capture at sea. These suggestions have not been favorably received by the great maritime powers, however, and there is no indication, at present, that the rules of the Declaration will be relaxed in such a way as to give to private property, at sea, any greater immunity from capture than it now enjoys.

At different times the justice of the rules of the Declaration of Paris has been discussed, especially in England, and the opinion has been advanced that that power had unwisely surrendered a valuable right, without receiving in return any corresponding advantage. It is difficult to see how this ground can be maintained. The loss of private property at sea, however great in amount, rarely affects, to any material extent, the military resources of a powerful belligerent, and so, rarely contributes to bring to an end an existing war. It would be impossible to invent a more effective method of not only crippling, but absolutely destroying, the merchant marine of a state, than was resorted to, with the most complete success, by the government of the Confederate States during the War of the Rebellion. But the destruction wrought by the Confederate cruisers in no material way impaired the military strength of the United States, or changed the result of the war in the slightest degree. If it was intended, by the destruction of vast amounts of private property, to affect the course of the Federal government, that intention signally failed of execution. On the other hand, it is at least probable that the business revival of the Southern States has been, to an appreciable degree, injuriously affected by the change in carrying trade, which resulted from the destruction of the American merchant marine during the War of the Rebellion. The position of England in this matter is still more difficult to understand. The English navy, efficient and powerful as it may be, is not omnipotent, and, as the experience of the United States has shown, the enormous commercial marine of England would, in the event of war, be liable to capture and destruction, as a result of the depredations of a relatively small number of fast-steaming cruisers, whose operations are more difficult to check than is generally supposed. The power of a state to efficiently police the sea, and to protect its merchant marine, by preventing or punishing depredations against it, is largely overestimated. At no time in history has the supremacy of England at sea been more unquestioned than during the period of Napoleonic wars, at the beginning of this century; and yet, on two conspicuous occasions, when the fullest warning of the enemy's purposes and intentions had been given, a hostile fleet was able, without particular or exceptional difficulty, to evade the whole maritime power of England.[1]

---

[1] One of these occurred in 1796, when General Hoche succeeded

5. *Effect of Claims to Exclusive Dominion upon the Development of the Neutral Theory.*—As the assertion and enforcement of these claims have invariably had the effect of retarding the development of the true theory of neutral obligations, they will now be briefly discussed. If we examine the history of those cities and states which, at different times, have attained great maritime or commercial supremacy, it will be seen that they have always claimed exclusive commercial dominion over the seas and coasts with which they were the first to develop commercial intercourse. When the Greeks first began to interest themselves in foreign commerce they found the Phœnicians in possession of the most desirable coasts of the Mediterranean. They were, therefore, obliged to confine their commercial undertakings to new seas, or to parts of the Mediterranean which their rivals had not already appropriated. Neither of these people aspired to territorial, as distinguished from commercial, dominion. The possession of the sea-coast sufficed to secure the latter; with the former they had no concern. With the Romans the case was entirely different. They deemed mere commercial supremacy as of but slight importance, and claimed, and ultimately acquired, universal dominion. With the downfall of the Western Empire commerce greatly declined, and at times almost disappeared. With the revival of civilization, however, commercial intercourse was re-established, and was fostered and controlled by those cities of Italy and

---

in entering Bantry Bay, on the Irish coast; the other in 1798, when an enormous French fleet succeeded, during a period of more than six weeks, in evading a no less skilful naval commander than Lord Nelson. Thiers, vol. iv., pp. 67, 260 *et seq.*

Spain which were the first to engage in maritime pursuits, toward the close of the Dark Ages. These cities soon claimed exclusive dominion over certain waters for purposes of trade, and forbade all commerce with such coasts to the ships of other cities. Their right to such exclusive intercourse was denied, and numerous wars were undertaken, some in support of, and others in opposition to, these claims.

Venice was the first of the Mediterranean cities to attain to any considerable degree of commercial supremacy, and, so early as the twelfth century, asserted a right to the exclusive navigation of the Adriatic. This claim was sanctioned by Pope Alexander III., in 1177,[1] and was long maintained against all opposition. At a later period similar claims were advanced by Genoa and Pisa. The discovery of the sea route to India by Portugal, and of the western continent by Spain, largely reduced, and eventually destroyed, the commercial importance of the Mediterranean cities, and transferred the sovereignty of the seas to the two latter powers, by whom, in turn, the most extravagant claims were asserted to maritime dominion. As the claims brought forward by Spain and Portugal were in some degree conflicting, they were submitted to the pope, Alexander VII., who, in 1493, established, as a boundary between them, a meridian line passing through a point one hundred leagues west of the Azores Islands.[2] All of the earth's surface east of that line, which formed no part of the dominions of any Christian prince, was declared to belong to Portugal; while all to the west of the same line was, subject to a similar restriction,

---

[1] Azuni, vol. i., p. 76.   [2] *Ibid.*, p. 106.

19

decreed to Spain. Claims somewhat similar in character were advanced, at a later period, by England and Holland, only to encounter the most serious and obstinate resistance, which resulted in their final abandonment. The last instance of such a claim being advanced to any considerable portion of the high seas was that of Russia, who asserted the right of exclusive navigation of that part of the Pacific lying north of the fifty-fourth degree of north latitude, on the ground that it possessed the coasts of both continents above that line. This claim, however, was relinquished upon the representations of England and the United States, and has never been reasserted.[1]

If the claims which have been made, at different times, to exclusive maritime dominion be examined, it will be found that each of them is susceptible of being resolved into two parts:

(*a*.) A claim to a kind of territorial sovereignty over a portion of the high seas, with the adjacent coasts.

(*b*.) A claim to the right of exclusive commercial intercourse with the territories whose coasts were washed by the waters over which jurisdiction was asserted.

The first of these claims has been vigorously opposed since the middle of the seventeenth century, and with such success that all such claims have long since been abandoned, never to be reasserted.

The second continued to exist, and was long recognized as just and equitable. As new territories were acquired by different European powers, either by colo-

---

[1] See "Treaties and Conventions of the United States with Foreign Powers," Washington, 1871, pp. 733-735.

nization or by conquest, the exclusive privilege of trading with them was claimed by the parent or conquering state, and, tacitly or expressly, recognized by other states of the civilized world.

The Monopoly of Colonial Trade.— Although the claim of a parent state to a practical monopoly of colonial trade was finally recognized, such recognition was not conceded without opposition, nor was the colonial monopoly itself a source of unmixed benefit to the state enjoying it. In time of peace it was a fruitful source of revenue, and afforded a favorable market for the productions of the mother country. In the event of war, however, if the parent state occupied the position of a belligerent, its vessels engaged in the colonial trade became liable to capture and confiscation, and it was impossible to measure the resulting loss by the money value of the ships and cargoes which were captured by the enemy. A large part of the belligerent's commerce was destroyed, or diverted to other channels, and was but slowly revived after the peace. To obviate this attempts were made, at times, by several European states, to transfer their colonial trade to a neutral flag, during the period of hostilities. As this course deprived a belligerent of the right to injure his enemy, by a resort to one of the most powerful means of coercion then recognized by the laws of war, such transfers of trade were stoutly resisted, chiefly by the British government; whose maritime preponderance had become so firmly established by the middle of the eighteenth century as to enable it to enforce respect, in so far as its own interests were concerned, to whatever views of maritime warfare were deemed by it to be correct, and in accordance with International Law.

The Rule of 1756.—The view thus advanced by Great Britain was extended to all colonial trade with neutrals by the Rule of 1793, but was immediately opposed by France and Spain, and, at a later period, by the United States. A principle or rule, asserted, or even enforced, by one powerful state, is not a rule of International Law; to become such it must receive the sanction of all, or nearly all, of the civilized states of the world. The principle underlying the Rule of 1756 is now accepted, as applying to coasting trade, by the principal maritime powers. But the Rule of 1793 has received no such general sanction, and its enforcement, if persisted in, would have given rise to most serious complications. Its severity, however, was relaxed as practical free trade was gradually conceded to colonies; largely upon their demand to enter the markets of the world upon equal terms with the mother country.

6. *Development of the Theory of Neutrality among the Non-maritime States of Europe.*—The power and importance of the Mediterranean cities was entirely maritime, and was due to the energy and industry with which they prosecuted their commercial undertakings. They had but little power on land; they rarely asserted claims to territorial supremacy, and so were rarely engaged in wars, other than those caused by their conflicting commercial interests. It was for this reason that they progressed but little, in their development of the theory of neutrality, beyond the establishment of the rules regulating the subject of maritime capture. The relations of the great European states, which were gradually acquiring something of their present territorial form, were not such as to favor the development of any consistent or enduring theory of neutral obliga-

tion. Their relations were more generally hostile than peaceful; private and dynastic wars were common, and the brief periods during which hostilities were interrupted, or suspended, were usually devoted to the preparation of new schemes of conquest or dominion. Some progress must have been made, however, as the necessities of the great powers made peace occasionally desirable. But it was impossible for the conception of neutrality to obtain general recognition until the desire of the powers to remain at peace had acquired sufficient strength to become at least equal to the desire for war and conquest. In the absence of positive evidence, it is fair to presume that the rudiments of the theory were first recognized by those states which became neutral by reason of their distance from the theatre of war, and from a consequent lack of direct interest in the war, or its results. When the principle of the balance of power first began to be understood, it seems to have been regarded as possible to maintain it in no other way than by waging war against the state, or states, which threatened it. Indeed, it was not merely threatened, it was repeatedly attacked, and was in constant danger of overthrow, which could be effectively prevented only by force of arms. This state of affairs contributed powerfully to retard the growth of the theory of neutrality, since every important state in Europe was obliged to take part, as principal or ally, in the numerous wars which were undertaken whenever the equilibrium was disturbed.

Influence of England upon the Development of the Modern Theory of Neutrality.—The insular situation of England, so placed as to be secure from attack except by sea, enabled, and to some extent constrained, that power to adopt a policy of partial abstinence from interference in Continental affairs; and to decline taking part in Continental wars in which it had no important interests at stake. Not only was England able to decline participation in such wars, thus placing her in a position of practical neutrality, but her power on land and sea was so great as to enable her to insist upon her neutrality being respected by belligerents. She thus became, to a certain extent, an advocate of neutrality, and an example to other powers of the advantage of remaining neutral.

General Acceptance of the Modern Theory in the Seventeenth Century; its Later History. — Although its progress had been extremely slow, the principle of neutrality had received such general recognition by the middle of the seventeenth century, as to lead Grotius to devote a portion of his work to a discussion of the rights and duties of neutrals. From that time its progress was more rapid. The Treaty of Westphalia largely diminished the power and influence of the Pope in secular affairs, and enabled the intercourse of the European states to assume a more normal character. Wars became less frequent, and were more closely restricted, in their operations and effects, to the states which were immediately concerned in them. The states which chose to occupy the position of neutrals, at the outbreak of war, steadily increased in number; and were led to insist more strongly upon their rights being respected by belligerents.

It was during this period that the Dutch became interested in the amelioration of the rules of maritime capture. Their efforts were not permanently successful, however, and, as their influence declined, that of the United States began to be put forth in advocacy of the same cause. Their independence had no sooner been recognized than they began to assume importance as a commercial power. The tendencies of the new state were altogether peaceful. Its distance from Europe, not less than its peculiar governmental institutions, secured it an almost complete immunity from interference in European affairs, and enabled its people to devote their energies to projects of internal development, and to the extension of their already important commercial relations. The foreign policy of the United States was, from the first, one of strict non-participation in questions of strictly European concern. Every consideration, therefore, of material interest and territorial position, induced the new republic to occupy an attitude of neutrality in all wars of European origin. The justice and advantage of this policy were fully appreciated by those who directed its foreign affairs, and so thoroughly were the principles of neutral obligation understood by them, that the early proclamations of neutrality, issued by the United States, not only served to establish the permanent neutral policy of that power, but were soon generally accepted as furnishing an enduring standard of neutral right and duty.

7. *Gradations of Neutrality.*— The crude and imperfect views of neutral duty which formerly prevailed admitted of gradations, or degrees, of neutral obligation. These were, in substance, violations of neutrality, and, as such, are no longer sanctioned by the practice of nations. Such was the qualified neutrality of certain European states during the last century, by which the obligation to remain neutral was qualified by a previous treaty with one of the belligerents, stip-

ulating to furnish him with certain aid in men, money, or war material in the event of a particular war, or upon the occurrence of hostilities of any kind with any state. Such action would not now be tolerated; and a state entering into such treaty engagements would be regarded as an ally of the enemy so soon as it undertook to carry into effect its treaty stipulations.

Permanent Neutrality.—The status of permanent neutrality occupied by Switzerland and Belgium is in no way repugnant to International Law. The exceptional circumstances in each case are, to some extent, based upon the size and territorial position of these states, upon their inferior military power as compared with the great states by which they are surrounded, and to a certain extent, also, upon considerations having to do with the preservation of the European balance of power.

Armed Neutrality.—An armed neutrality is, in fact, an alliance of several powers, usually of a defensive character, though this is by no means essential. The purpose of such an alliance is to secure the maintenance of certain views of neutral right, which are believed to be in danger, or whose justice is likely to be questioned. The most striking historical examples of such alliances are those of the armed neutralities, of the northern European powers, of 1780 and 1800. These alliances were made to defend the principle of free ships, free goods, which had been adopted by treaties between the Baltic powers, and which was opposed by England; that power being, on both occasions, a belligerent. Although the purpose of the alliance was not effected on either occasion, the agitation of the question continued, and without doubt contributed materially to bring about the adoption of the Declaration of Paris. If the commercial interests of several nations are threatened by unjust or unlawful measures, on the part of a belligerent, which they deem unjust or dangerous, there can be no question of their right to secure their menaced interests by such combinations as seem best calculated to accomplish the purpose.

Strict Neutrality.—As at present understood, a state, in becoming neutral, occupies a position of strict neutrality. It rigidly abstains from aiding either belligerent, or from rendering to either of them any service, however slight or immaterial, which is calculated to assist him in his military operations. The friendly relations existing at the outbreak of the war are not interrupted, and it is to secure the continuance of such relations that a neutral state becomes charged with certain duties, during war, which do not exist during peace. These obligations are the measure of a neutral's duty in war. They are determined by International Law, and have the same binding force upon all states. A failure in the performance of these duties is an injury to the particular belligerent who suffers by the failure of a neutral state to fulfil its obligations. These obligations have to do, in part with the conduct of the neutral state in its capacity as a body corporate, and in part with the conduct of persons within its jurisdiction.

8. *Neutral Duty of a State.*—A state, in its corporate capacity, is not permitted to give any material aid to either belligerent, or to furnish money, ships, troops, subsistence, or munitions of war; or to render any assistance which is likely to be useful to such belligerent in his military operations. A neutral state,

therefore, cannot permit its ports, or territorial waters, to be used as a base of hostile operations, or as depots of supply of articles susceptible of warlike use. It is forbidden to allow the enlistment of men, or the organization or equipment, wholly or in part, of a hostile expedition, by sea or land, within its territorial limits.

Some of these acts being, in substance, acts of sovereignty, are forbidden alike in peace and war. Others are permitted in peace, but are forbidden in time of war. The principle underlying the latter class is this. Any substantial aid or service, which contributes to the success of the military operations of one belligerent, enables him to inflict an injury upon his enemy with whom the neutral is at peace. The neutral state, therefore, in a more or less direct manner, has injured, or contributed to injure, a friend. As every state is the exclusive judge as to what injuries it shall regard as furnishing just cause for war, a neutral state may in this way, by a single act of service, become a party to the war. It is easy to see, therefore, that, if it were permitted to render such services with impunity, every important war would, sooner or later, involve all neutral states in its operations, and so one of the chief purposes of International Law would fail of attainment. War would again become the rule, as in ancient times, and for much the same reason. Permanent peace would be impossible, and the relations of states would be subjected to a constant strain, which would seriously affect their prosperity and material development.

Neutral Duties.—A state in becoming a neutral cannot divest itself of the duties to other states, and to their individual subjects, which are incumbent upon it in time of peace. These continue in force, but certain precautions incident to, and made necessary by, the fact of war, must be observed in their performance.

Asylum to Troops and Ships.—A neutral is obliged to grant an asylum to individuals of the enemy, who come into its territorial limits to escape pursuit, or to find protection from acts of hostility. They become subject to neutral jurisdiction so soon as they enter its territory. If fleeing from an enemy, they are disarmed, and, at the discretion of the neutral government, may be removed to points in the interior, and may there be subjected to such measures of police supervision, or positive restraint, as it may deem necessary to secure respect for its neutrality. If in large numbers and without means of support, these fugitives are made the subject of treaty arrangements, and are usually supported at the expense of their own government. The French troops who fled to Belgium, after the battle of Sedan, were disarmed and conveyed to a point at some distance from the frontier, and the expense of their maintenance was ultimately defrayed by the French government.

Right of Asylum in the Case of Public and Private Vessels.—A similar right of asylum exists in the case of public and private armed vessels, and to merchant ships belonging to either belligerent. They may seek refuge in a neutral port from the perils of the sea, or from a superior force of the enemy. The protection of the neutral government is extended to them so soon as they come within its territorial waters; and it may resist, by force if need be, any hostile attempts that are directed against them while within its jurisdiction.

As the favor is that of asylum only, the asylum may terminate at the will of the neutral. When vessels of two belligerents are found in a neutral port, at the same time, it is within the power of the neutral to establish such regulations, in regard to their conduct and departure, as will make it impossible for an engagement to take place in the immediate vicinity of the port. This object is usually attained by the enforcement of the *twenty-four hour rule*, by which, when one belligerent vessel departs, the other is forbidden to sail within twenty-four hours. This rule has been so frequently and generally applied, in recent times, as to have received the universal sanction of nations.

Neutral Territory. — The territory and territorial waters of a neutral state are sacred from belligerent intrusion, save with the consent of the neutral government. Such consent may be granted, or denied, to both belligerents; but, according to the present rule, cannot be granted to either to the exclusion of the other. Captures made in neutral waters are restored, or indemnified, even after they have been condemned by a prize court, since such courts have no jurisdiction over prizes made, except on the high seas, or within the territorial waters of a belligerent. "It belongs, however, exclusively to the neutral government to raise objection to a title founded upon a capture made within neutral territory. So far as the adverse belligerent is concerned, he has no right to complain if the case be tried before a competent court.' The government of the owner of the captured property may, indeed, call the neutral to account for permitting a

---

[1] The Arrogante Barcelones, Wheaton, vol. vii., p. 496.

fraudulent, unworthy, or unnecessary violation of its jurisdiction, and such permission may, according to the circumstances, convert the neutral into a belligerent."[1]

The right of a public armed vessel of a belligerent to enter a neutral port, when not in distress, is usually conceded; and is presumed, unless notice to the contrary is formally given by the neutral government. They may be forbidden to enter certain ports, or to enter neutral territory at all except in distress, but the rule must bear equally upon both belligerents. Privateers may be denied entrance to neutral ports, especially if the neutral government is a party to the Declaration of Paris. The bringing in of prizes is still authorized by existing treaties, though the present tendency is to restrict the right within the narrowest limits, if not to deny it altogether. The condemnation or sale of such prizes by a neutral prize court, or by a belligerent prize court sitting in neutral territory, is no longer permitted.

A belligerent war ship which has been permitted to enter a neutral port, may procure there such supplies, not contraband of war, as may be permitted by the neutral government. The supply of coal is now made the subject of special regulation, and only a limited amount is allowed to be taken in.[2]

---

[1] Phillimore, vol. iii., p. 287.
[2] On Jan. 31, 1862, the British government adopted the rule that a belligerent armed vessel was to be permitted to receive, at any British port, a supply of coal sufficient to enable her to reach a port of her own country, or a nearer destination. A second supply was not to be given within three months, save with the express permission of the government.

9. *Responsibility of a Neutral State for the Acts of its Subjects.*—A different rule applies to the conduct of the subjects of a neutral state, than is applied to the neutral state itself, in its relations with the belligerents. It has been seen that the restrictions, to which neutral states are subject, are such as will prevent them from aiding either belligerent in his military operations, and, at the same time, be the smallest possible consistent with the purpose of the war. The subjects of a neutral state, however, at the outbreak of a war, are engaged in many different occupations, over some of which the belligerent is given jurisdiction to the extent of actual prohibition. They are also engaged in the production, manufacture, and sale of certain articles which become contraband of war if sold to an enemy, or found at sea *en route* to an enemy's port. In all other respects their undertakings are innocent, and are not interrupted, or affected, by the fact of war. The manufacture of contraband articles, and even their sale, in neutral jurisdiction, continues to be an innocent and lawful occupation. The neutral state itself ought not to be expected to interfere with the pursuits of its subjects, so long as they are not likely to compromise the position of neutrality which it assumed at the outbreak of the war. The power placed in the hands of the belligerents to blockade the ports of an enemy, to search neutral vessels on the high seas, and to seize and condemn such portions of their cargoes as are contraband of war, or are destined to a blockaded port, are ample to protect them from being injured by the acts of individuals. If they do not, or cannot, make their powers effective, they cannot, of right, expect neutral states to assist them in their en-

deavors. Nor can they expect neutrals to resort to severe police measures, against their own subjects, in a matter with which they have no direct concern.

View of England and the United States.—The principle involved was well stated by Mr. Webster in his reply to the Mexican government, which had complained of certain alleged violations of neutrality, on the part of individuals, in the supply of arms to Texas, then at war with Mexico. "It is not the practice of nations to prohibit their own subjects, by previous laws, from trafficking in articles contraband of war. Such trade is carried on at the risk of those engaged in it, under the liabilities and penalties prescribed by the law of nations or particular treaties. If it be true, therefore, that citizens of the United States have been engaged in a commerce by which Texas, an enemy of Mexico, has been supplied with arms and munitions of war, the government of the United States, nevertheless, was not bound to prevent it; could not have prevented it, without a manifest departure from the principles of neutrality, and is in no way answerable for the consequences. . . . The eighteenth article (of the treaty between the United States and Mexico) enumerates those commodities which shall be regarded as contraband of war; but neither that article, nor any other, imposes on either nation any duty of preventing, by previous regulation, commerce in such articles. Such commerce is left to its ordinary fate, according to the law of nations."[1]

Mr. Layard, the Solicitor-General of the British gov-

---

[1] Lawrence's Wheaton, p. 813, note, citing Webster's Works, vol vi., p. 452, "Letter of Webster to Thompson," July 8, 1842.

ernment, in a speech in the House of Commons, adopted the view above stated, and added, "The only law which enables Her Majesty's government to interfere in such cases is called the Foreign Enlistment Act, and the whole nature and scope of that act is sufficiently and shortly set out in its title. It is 'An act to prevent the enlisting and engagement of Her Majesty's subjects to serve in a foreign service, and the fitting out or equipping in Her Majesty's dominions, of vessels for warlike purposes, without Her Majesty's license.' That act does not touch, in any way whatever, private vessels which may carry cargoes, contraband, or not contraband, between this country and any port in a belligerent country, whether under blockade or not; and the government of this country, and the governments of our colonial possessions, have no power whatever to interfere with private vessels under such circumstances.

"It is perfectly true that in the queen's proclamation there is a general warning at the end, addressed to all the queen's subjects, that they are not, either in violation of their duty to the queen, as subjects of a neutral sovereign, or in violation or contravention of the law of nations, to do various things, one of which is carrying articles considered and deemed to be contraband of war, according to law or the modern usages of nations, for the use or service of either of the contending parties. That warning is addressed to them to apprise them that if they do these things they will have to undergo the penal consequences by the statute, or by the law of nations, in that behalf imposed or denounced. In those cases in which the statute is silent, the government is powerless, and the law of nations comes in.

"The law of nations exposes such persons to have their ships seized, and their goods taken and subjected to confiscation, and it further deprives them of the right to look to the government of their own country for protection. And this principle of non-interference in things which the law does not enable the government to deal with, so far from being a violation of the duty of neutrality—which the government is anxious to comply with—is in accordance with all the principles which have been laid down by jurists, and more especially by the great jurists of the United States."[1]

Continental View upon the Subject of Governmental Control of the Acts of Individuals.—The views above expressed are those which have long been held upon this subject in England and the United States. Most Continental writers are at variance with this, and contend that more or less of direct governmental interference is necessary. This difference of view arises from the fact that the governments of nearly all the Continental states of Europe are highly centralized in character, and all commercial undertakings are therefore subject to a more or less complete governmental supervision and control. This is the case in time of peace, and is an incident of internal administration. In time of war it is extremely easy for any of these governments to regulate, or even to effectually prohibit, contraband trade on the part of its subjects, if it is deemed desirable to do so as a matter of state policy. In England and the United States no such super-

---

[1] Lawrence's Wheaton, pp. 813, 814, citing remarks of Solicitor-General Layard in the House of Commons, Feb. 22, 1862. See also "Annual Message of President Pierce," 1854, "Executive Documents of the United States," 1854–1855.

vision exists in time of peace; and it could be established in time of war only as the result of legislation upon the subject, and could be maintained only at great expense, and at the constant risk of violating some of the existing constitutional guarantees of individual right.

10. *Neutral Rights.* — A neutral state, as such, receives no addition to its sovereign rights, either in number or extent, at the outbreak of war. It is at peace with both belligerents, and they have no more right to commit acts of hostility within its jurisdiction in time of war, than in time of peace. The neutral, therefore, may not only insist upon a complete immunity from such acts of belligerency, but may use force to compel respect to its sovereignty within the sphere of its exclusive jurisdiction, and to resist acts of aggression originating with either belligerent, and directed against the neutral state, or against the other belligerent, in neutral territory.

Violations of neutral right have occurred not infrequently in the past, and, as the sphere within which neutral rights are each year more strongly insisted upon is steadily increasing, such violations are likely to occur quite as frequently in the future. A neutral state may therefore insist—(1) upon an entire immunity from acts of belligerency within its territorial waters. A public vessel, by sailing through the coast sea of a neutral state, in no way violates its neutrality. This is especially true when the act is done in the simple prosecution of a voyage, and when not in pursuit of the enemy. It has been seen that a belligerent vessel, either public or private, is entitled to an asylum in the port of a neutral from danger of capture by an enemy as well as from the perils of the sea. An armed vessel, therefore, which pursues an enemy into neutral waters, or effects a capture there, has violated the sovereignty of the neutral state. It may be forcibly compelled to desist from the pursuit, and all captures made by it in neutral jurisdiction are illegal, and must be restored. The sovereignty of the neutral state has been invaded, and it may resort to such measures of prevention, or redress, as it may deem best suited to the emergency of the case.

(2.) A neutral state is entitled to a similar immunity from acts of belligerency on land. Troops fleeing from an enemy may seek an asylum in neutral territory. They must release their prisoners, however, give up all booty and captured property, and surrender their arms during the period of their sojourn upon neutral soil. The enemy must cease his pursuit at the neutral boundary. Should he continue it farther his act is one of invasion, and would be properly regarded as an act of hostility by the neutral state whose sovereignty is offended. Should either belligerent undertake to perform acts, within the territory of a friendly state, which are inconsistent with the neutrality of that state, the neutral may not only cause such acts to be immediately desisted from, but may punish the agents of the belligerent, if their acts are in violation of its municipal laws, or may forcibly eject them from its territory.

This subject is illustrated by the cases of the Chesapeake and the Florida.

Case of the Chesapeake.—The Chesapeake was one of a line of passenger steamers plying between the ports of New York and Portland, Maine. In 1863, while on her way between those points, she was forcibly seized by a number of her passengers, who claimed to be in the naval service of the Confederate States. In effecting the seizure several of the crew were killed and wounded, and the rest were set on shore. The vessel was navigated for a short time by its captors, but was finally abandoned by them, in an unfrequented bay on the coast of Nova Scotia. She was afterward found and seized, in British territorial waters, by a public armed vessel of the United States. The act was complained of by the British government as a violation of its neutrality, and a demand was made that the vessel be surrendered and the prisoners restored to British soil. The demand was acceded to by the United States, who disclaimed any intention of exercising any authority within the territorial jurisdiction of Great Britain. The government of the United States, in complying with the demand for the surrender of the property and persons, proposed that those who had been concerned in the forcible seizure of the vessel should be surrendered, with a view to their prosecution for the crime of piracy. The British government declined to consider this proposition until the captured persons had been returned to its territorial jurisdiction. The ship was afterward restored to its owners.[1]

Case of the Florida.—In 1864 the Confederate war steamer Florida entered the port of Bahia, Brazil, for the purpose of obtaining coal and provisions, and of effecting some necessary repairs. While thus engaged, the Wachusett, a public armed vessel of the United States, entered the same port. The Brazilian govern-

---

[1] Boyd's Wheaton, pp. 498, 499; Dana's Wheaton, p. 210, note.

ment, fearing a conflict, took such precautions as it deemed proper to prevent its occurrence, and, in accordance with its port regulations, assigned an anchoring-ground to each of the belligerent vessels. The commander of the Wachusett, taking advantage of the absence, at night, of a number of the officers and crew of the Florida, sent a boat's crew to attach a cable to the Confederate steamer, towed her out of the harbor, and conveyed her as a prize to the United States. This flagrant violation of neutral rights was at once complained of by the Brazilian government. The act was promptly disavowed by the United States. An apology was offered, and reparation made by saluting the Brazilian flag in the port of Bahia. The crew of the Florida were restored to Brazilian jurisdiction. The captured vessel foundered in Hampton Roads, under circumstances which were satisfactorily explained to the Brazilian government.[1] "The restitution of the ship having thus become impossible, the President expressed his regret that the sovereignty of Brazil had been violated, dismissed the consul at Bahia, who had advised the offence, and sent the commander of the Wachusett before a court-martial."[2]

NEUTRALITY LAWS.

11. Those municipal laws of a state which are intended to prevent violations of its neutrality in time of war are called, in general, *neutrality laws*. The title varies in different states, and in many cases is based upon

---

[1] Boyd's Wheaton, p. 499; Hall, p. 544; Dana's Wheaton, p. 209, note. See also Secretary Seward's letter of explanation, "Foreign Relations of the United States," 1863, 1864.

[2] Bernard, "Neutrality of England," etc., p. 433.

the particular violation of neutrality which was first made the subject of positive legislation.[1]

Neutral Obligation Determined by International, not Municipal, Law.—It has been seen that the neutral obligation of a state is determined by international, and not by municipal, law. The conduct of every state, which assumes the position of a neutral in war, is therefore measured by the standard of International Law. If it fails in the performance of a neutral duty, it cannot plead the inefficiency of its municipal laws in extenuation of its offence, nor will an exact and rigorous enforcement of such laws be regarded as a fulfilment of its obligation, if their provisions are not in accordance with the international standard. The neutrality laws of a state may therefore be, in point of efficiency, less than, equal to, or greater than the standard of neutral obligation as determined by the law of nations; or there may be no such municipal laws. In all these cases the responsibility of the state is precisely the same.

Most modern states, however, have covered this field of legislation more or less completely, either with positive laws, defining rules of conduct for persons subject to their jurisdiction, and imposing suitable penalties for their violation; or by general laws, or constitutional provisions, vesting discretionary powers in certain departments of government, to be used for the purpose of preventing violations of neutrality on the part of

---

[1] In England the first legislation on the subject was caused, in the time of James I., by the enlistment of recruits in England for service in other European armies. For this reason the British neutrality laws have received the name of the "Foreign Enlistment Act."

individuals. Violations of neutral duty by a state, in its corporate capacity, are questions of state policy that are rarely made the subject of municipal legislation. Neutrality laws, as such, have chiefly to do with the acts of individuals. They permit or forbid particular acts, and vest suitable powers of enforcement in certain officials, or departments of government.

English Neutrality Laws.—The first legislation in England on the subject of neutrality was had in the reign of James I. The statute was intended to regulate, rather than prohibit, the enlistment of British subjects in foreign services.[1] This statute was twice amended during the reign of George II., each time in the direction of greater severity.[2] The first general law on the subject of neutrality was the Foreign Enlistment Act passed in 1819, during the regency.[3] It remained in force until 1870, when the present act was passed.[4]

"The statute of 1819 was, with a few unimportant exceptions, never attempted to be enforced until the period of the American Civil War. Its deficiencies were then fully discovered, and the escape of the Alabama, the Treaty of Washington in 1871, and the Geneva Arbitration were the grave consequences."[5]

The neutrality laws now in force in the British empire are those contained in what is known as the Foreign Enlistment Act of 1870. They extend to all the dominions of Her Majesty, including the adjacent territorial waters. The act forbids British subjects to accept, or agree to accept, a commission in the mili-

---

[1] 3 James I., chap. 4.
[2] 9 George II., chap. 30; 29 George II., chap. 17.
[3] 59 George III., chap. 69.   [4] 33 and 34 Victoria, chap. 90.
[5] Phillimore, vol. iii., p. 244.

tary or naval service of a state at war with any state with which Her Majesty is at peace; to leave the realm with intent to engage in such service, or to induce another person to embark under false representations as to such service; and imposes a penalty upon any master of a ship who knowingly takes such persons on board ship, with intent to carry them to such state. It is also forbidden under severe penalties of fine and imprisonment—

(*a.*) "To build, or agree to build, or to cause to be built, any ship with intent or knowledge, or having reasonable cause to believe that the same shall or will be employed in the military or naval service of any foreign state at war with any friendly state.

(*b.*) "To issue or deliver any commission for any ship with intent or knowledge, or having reasonable cause to believe, that the same shall or will be employed in the military or naval service of any foreign state at war with any friendly state.

(*c.*) "To equip any ship, with intent or knowledge, or having reasonable cause to believe, that the same shall or will be employed in the military or naval service of any foreign state at war with any friendly state.

(*d.*) "To despatch, or cause, or allow to be despatched, any ship with intent or knowledge, or having reasonable cause to believe, that the same shall or will be employed in the military or naval service of any foreign state at war with a friendly state."

When a ship is built by the order of a foreign state, at war with a friendly state, the presumption is that it is intended for the naval service of the former state.

It is also forbidden to increase the armament, equipment, or force of such ships, or to aid in their construction or equipment, and it is also forbidden to fit out, or aid or assist in fitting out, any expedition against the dominions of a friendly state. The ships engaged in such acts are to be forfeited, and penalties of fine and imprisonment are to be imposed upon all persons violating any of the provisions of the act.[1]

The provisions of this act are of the most stringent character, and, if rigidly enforced, are calculated to prevent any act, on the part of any person within the jurisdiction of Great Britain, which can, in the remotest degree, compromise the neutrality of the British government.

Neutrality Laws of the United States.—The neutrality laws of the United States are chiefly contained in the acts of June 5, 1794, and April 20, 1818. By these acts it is declared a misdemeanor for any citizen of the United States to accept or exercise a commission to serve a foreign state in war against any friendly state; or to enlist, or enter himself, or hire or retain another person to enlist, or to go beyond the jurisdiction of the United States to enlist, or with intent to be enlisted, into such foreign service, or to fit out or arm; or to increase or augment the force of any armed vessel, with the intent that such vessel shall be employed in the service of a power at war with a friendly state; or to begin, set on foot, or provide or prepare the means for, any military expedition or enterprise against the territory of any foreign state with whom the United States is at peace.

The President is authorized to compel any foreign vessel to depart, which, by the law of nations or by

---

[1] 33 and 34 Victoria, chap. 90.

treaty, ought not to remain within the territorial waters of the United States, and is given power to use the public armed force to carry the provisions of the act into effect, and to enforce the observance of the neutral duties required by law.[1]

It is worthy of remark that the neutrality laws of the United States, though passed nearly seventy years ago, are at the present time fully in accordance with the standard of neutral obligation as determined by International Law.

The laws of both England and the United States are silent upon the question of the manufacture and sale of contraband of war, within their territorial jurisdiction, except in the case of building, arming, or equipping ships, fitted for, or adapted to, warlike uses. Dealing in contraband is forbidden in England, by proclamation, at the outbreak of a foreign war. It has never been forbidden in the United States. The policy of both governments has been to leave this question to be regulated by belligerents, in the exercise of the powers placed in their hands, for that purpose, by the law of nations.

Neutrality Laws of Other States.—The provisions of the French law on the subject of neutrality are those contained in Articles 84 and 85 of the Penal Code. The first of these imposes a penalty of banishment for any conduct of a subject which, without the approval of his government, exposes the state to a declaration of war. If war actually results, the punishment is increased to transportation. The second article punishes with banishment any acts, of a subject,

---

[1] "Revised Statutes of the United States," 1029–1031.

calculated to expose Frenchmen to reprisals. The precise acts which are so punishable are left to judicial determination, and, thus far, but three cases have arisen in which the laws were regarded as applicable. The responsibility of making suitable regulation on the subject of neutrality rests, in France, upon the government, and is usually made the subject of proclamation, whenever the outbreak of war makes it necessary for France to assume an attitude of neutrality. The task of the government in this respect is made easy of performance by the fact that the manufacture and sale of the most offensive forms of contraband of war, such as powder, fire-arms, ammunition, and projectiles, are made the subject of state regulation. It is, therefore, not difficult for the government, at the outbreak of war, to impose such additional restrictions upon the manufacture and sale of contraband articles as will effectually prevent violations of its neutrality. The absence of positive law on the subject enables France to adapt its neutrality regulations to the standard of International Law at any particular epoch; an advantage which is shared by all of the highly centralized governments on the continent of Europe. The law and practice of Belgium, Brazil, Italy, Holland, Russia, Spain, and Portugal are similar to those of France. Austria and Prussia have no laws upon the subject, and seem to need none, as ample powers to prevent violations of neutrality are vested in the respective governments. The laws of Denmark and Sweden are quite elaborate, resembling in many respects those of England and the United States.[1]

12. *Case of the Alabama.* — The most conspicuous

---
[1] "Report of English Neutrality Laws Commission of 1870," p. 40.

illustration, in recent times, of the failure of a state to observe its neutral obligations, is that afforded by the case of the Alabama.

The complainant in the case was the United States. The injury alleged was that certain aid had been obtained by the Confederate States in England during the rebellion.

The services which were made the ground of complaint are susceptible of classification under two heads:

(*a.*) The obtaining of arms and munitions of war by the Confederate States in England.

(*b.*) The fitting-out of hostile expeditions within English jurisdiction.

These causes of complaint will be discussed separately. The first of them furnished no reasonable ground of complaint to the United States; the second constituted a violation of the law of nations.

The Obtaining of Arms and Munitions of War.—The outbreak of the civil war in America found both parties to its operations but poorly prepared for a contest of the magnitude which that struggle immediately assumed, and both belligerents were obliged to have recourse to foreign markets for the supplies of arms and munitions necessary to enable them to place great armies in the field. "The demands of the war, as it advanced, were met in large measure by private manufacturers in the Northern States; but the export of arms and military stores went on freely and without intermission, so long as the struggle lasted, and the supplies drawn by the Federal government from [England] appear to have considerably exceeded in value those obtained by the South.

"An export trade, more or less considerable, in arms

and munitions of war, was carried on from England to both the northern and southern ports of the United States. Whether the goods were purchased in the English market by persons who came over for the purpose, or were shipped to order, or were consigned for sale in America on account of the shippers; whether the purchases were effected by agents of the two governments respectively or by private speculators, and whether these agents or speculators were American or English firms trading in New York or firms trading in Charleston, I do not know, and it is absolutely immaterial to inquire. None of these circumstances could affect in the slightest degree the character of the transaction. Articles of military use, when transported over sea, to the ports of either belligerent in neutral ships, are, during the transit, designated contraband, and may be captured under the neutral flag, the neutral carrier suffering the loss of his freight, and getting no compensation for the interruption of his voyage and the breaking-up of his cargo."[1]

---

[1] Bernard, "The Neutrality of Great Britain during the American Civil War," pp. 332, 333. In Sir Montague Bernard's able work, from which the above citation is made, the following table appears. It purports to give the total value of exports of arms and munitions of war to the United States and to the British West Indies during the period of the civil war. It is interesting as showing the amount of contraband trade that went on during that period.

Years.	Shipments to the United States.	Shipments to British West Indies.
1860	£45,076	£6,050
1861	119,555	59,110
1862	999,197	367,578
1863	425,081	200,402
1864	36,802	74,983
1865	23,625	29,420
1866	82,345	4,795

With these transactions, whatever part may have been taken in them by British subjects or others within British jurisdiction, International Law has nothing to do; and of these acts, whether of dealing in, or carrying contraband, or violating the blockade, the United States had no valid reason to complain. On the contrary, on at least two previous occasions, the last of them but a few years previous to the outbreak of the rebellion, citizens of the United States had themselves openly engaged in similar practices, with the full knowledge and presumed consent of their own government, as expressed in the annual message of its chief executive.[1]

The Fitting-out of Hostile Expeditions within English Jurisdiction.—" Among the most pressing needs of the Confederates was that of sea-going ships capable of being used for war. Such vessels as they possessed were, for the most part, very small. There was probably not one of these which could have ventured to engage a Federal cruiser of any class without certain destruction. In coast warfare they were able to achieve one or two brilliant, though unprofitable, successes. But the construction of a large sea-going steamer seems to have been beyond their power; their only ships were such as had fallen into their hands; and they either had not the materials and machinery for turning out marine steam-engines, or were unable to use them."[2]

To enable the Confederates to overcome this disparity of force at sea a scheme was projected of procur-

---

[1] Message of President Pierce, 1854, "Executive Documents of the United States," 1854, 1855.

[2] Bernard, "The Neutrality of Great Britain," etc., p. 336.

ing by purchase, in England, a number of war-steamers for the Confederate navy. This undertaking was quite different from those that had preceded it, inasmuch as it was proposed that these vessels, so soon as they had been completed and equipped 'for war, whether in England or elsewhere, should, without being sent to any port within the jurisdiction of the Confederacy, at once engage in hostile operations against the United States. With this end in view, agents were despatched to England with instructions to arrange for the purchase, or construction, of a number of swift and powerful steamers. These agents were to arrange all the details of purchase or manufacture of armament and equipment, and were to transfer them, when completed and ready for service, to certain designated officers of the Confederate navy.

These instructions were carried out in all their essential details. The ships, three in number, which were afterward known as the Florida, Alabama, and Shenandoah, were purchased or constructed in England. Their armament and equipment were obtained, and a portion of their crews enlisted, in British territory, without encountering any obstacles which do not seem to have been overcome without special difficulty. In every case the ships left England without guns or ammunition on board, and but partly manned; and in every case the articles needed to prepare the vessel for active service, and a part or the whole of the crew, were shipped from England by another vessel; the equipment being completed at a point previously agreed upon, usually in neutral waters, and never within British jurisdiction.

The question now arises as to what was the rule or

usage of International Law upon the subject of neutral duty in 1861; for by that rule the responsibility of England, as a neutral power, must be determined.

It has been seen that the neutral obligation of a state, at any time, is fixed and determined by *international*, and not by *municipal*, law. It has also been seen that that obligation is the same, whatever may be the provisions of municipal law upon the subject; indeed, it is not at all necessary that its municipal laws should contain any such provisions. Their existence presumes an intention, on the part of a state, to fulfil its neutral duties. Their absence may imply the contrary; or it may imply that some department of the government has sufficient power in the premises to make such provisions unnecessary. If they exist, and are inadequate to the purpose, their inadequacy cannot be pleaded in extenuation of a violation of neutral duty; if they do not exist, their absence cannot be alleged to excuse a failure to observe a neutral obligation; nor, finally, can their enforcement, by obscuring the real issue involved, or by distracting the attention of a neutral state from its real responsibility, at all diminish that responsibility, or change its character.

In this connection two questions arise. The first is, did war exist? If there was not in existence at that time an open, public war, there could be no belligerents, and consequently no neutrals; and, whatever may have been the relation existing between England and the United States, it was not that of a neutral to a belligerent. This question hardly admits of discussion. When insurrection or rebellion occurs in a state, two courses of proceeding are open to the central government, either of which may be pursued in its suppression. These are:

(*a.*) The method by Municipal Law, in which the attempt is made to restore the supremacy of the government by a rigid enforcement of the criminal law, military force being used to support the civil authority.

(*b.*) The method by International Law, involving the recognition of the insurgents as having belligerent rights, and the use of military force in accordance with the laws of war.

The United States chose the latter method. This made it necessary for other powers to follow its example, and to recognize the insurgents as belligerents, which they did by the issue of proclamations of neutrality. By the issue of such a proclamation England assumed the attitude of a neutral, and by so doing became charged with the duties, and vested with the rights, of a neutral state in time of war.

Standard of Neutral Obligation in 1861.—The next question is, what was the standard of neutral obligation, as at that time recognized and sanctioned by the law of nations? To the answer of this question it is, perhaps, fortunate that the injuries which made the rule necessary, and the deduction of the rule itself, were then relatively recent events, and so were presumably fresh in the minds of those by whom the government of England was carried on.

During the years between 1789 and 1794, England and France being then belligerents, several attempts were made, by agents of France in the United States, to fit out and arm certain ships to prey upon English commerce. Upon proper representation, in behalf of the latter power, the government of the United States took the most vigorous measures to bring about a discontinuance of the practice, and, to enable similar action to be taken in future cases of the same kind, the Neutrality Act of 1794 was passed.

During the period between 1816 and 1818 similar attempts were made to fit out and arm vessels, within the jurisdiction of the United States, to operate against Spanish commerce, under commissions, or letters of marque, from the revolted Spanish colonies in Central and South America. In this instance the Spanish minister "complained that some thirty vessels, specifically named, the property of American citizens, were thus preying on Spanish commerce. The representative of Portugal made similar complaints."[1] To remedy this wrong the United States Neutrality Act of 1818 was passed. It was more stringent in its provisions than had been that of 1794, and was, for that reason, better calculated to prevent acts on the part of individuals which were likely to compromise the neutrality of the United States.

Similar practices were resorted to in England, and, proper representations having been made by Spain, an attempt was made to remedy the wrong complained of, by the passage of the "Foreign Enlistment Act of 1819," the first British neutrality act which was intended to have general application, and to prevent and punish acts of individuals which might have the effect of compromising the foreign relations of Great Britain as a neutral power. This act was in force during the period of the Civil War.

---

[1] Opinion of Sir Alexander Cockburn in the Geneva case, "Foreign Relations of the United States," 1872, "Geneva Arbitration," vol. iv., p. 256.

Here are three instances in each of which a sovereign state, in the most solemn and formal manner, recognizes the fact that the acts of fitting-out and arming or equipping of expeditions, within its jurisdiction, for the purpose of carrying on hostilities against a friendly state, are not only unjust and wrong, but are so far opposed to the law and usage of nations as to constitute a serious violation of neutrality on the part of the government permitting them.

Conclusion as to Neutral Obligation.—In the face of these facts, it is useless to cite the opinions of text-writers. Their views and opinions are based upon such facts, and the rules deduced by them, to have value, must be supported by just such instances of international usage and intercourse. The conclusion based upon these facts must therefore be that, as the law of nations stood in 1861, the fitting-out, arming, or equipping, within the jurisdiction of a neutral state, of a vessel intended to carry on direct hostile operations against a friendly state, was a violation of International Law.

It has been seen that, during the continuance of the civil war, three war-steamers were obtained by the Confederate States, in England, by purchase and construction. Over the acts of those persons within its jurisdiction, who had to do with such purchase and construction, the British government had undisputed control. Its duty and responsibility in the premises should have been known to the individual members of the government; and the ease with which the American minister was able to obtain detailed information as to the purpose and ultimate destination of these vessels shows that no insuperable difficulties lay in the way of its obtaining similar knowledge, upon which to act in the performance of its neutral duty.

Manner in which the Neutral Duty of England was Performed.—In the performance of its duty as a neutral, however, the British government displayed not only a singular and unusual lack of energy and vigilance, but a more remarkable failure to discern the true point at issue. In a manner entirely in accordance with English tradition, it seems to have been taken for granted that a more or less vigorous enforcement of the existing neutrality laws would constitute a sufficient performance of its neutral duty, and a sufficient fulfilment of its neutral obligation. The action of the government, therefore, was not only confined to the enforcement of its neutrality law, but a peculiar construction was placed upon that law, by which it was deemed no violation of its provisions to construct a ship, even for an admitted warlike purpose, if no portion of its equipment and armament was contributed by its builders, or placed on board within British territorial jurisdiction.

Responsibility of England in the Case.—From what mistaken view of international duty such an idea was deduced it is not necessary to discuss here. Acts like those of which the United States complained were opposed to the usages of nations, because they constituted hostile attempts against a friendly power, and originated within neutral jurisdiction. A belligerent has no right, or color of right, to interfere in any manner with the internal administration of a sovereign state. He must judge of the attitude and intentions of that state by its acts, or by the acts of individuals which have originated within its territory. If an act of hostility originate in a neutral state, it matters not by whom it is committed, the neutral is entirely responsible for its effects and results, whatever they may be; and no other course is open to a belligerent than to hold such neutral to a strict accountability for events over which he has, and may exercise, a jurisdiction in every way adequate to his responsibility.

Later History of the Confederate Cruisers.—Of the three cruisers whose origin has been alluded to the career may be briefly told. The Florida, on Aug. 11, 1862, completed her armament in neutral West Indian waters, and entered upon her duty of destroying merchant vessels. Her career was terminated in October, 1864, by her illegal capture in the port of Bahia, Brazil.

The Alabama, in spite of the urgent remonstrances of the American minister, effected her departure from English waters on the 29th of July, 1862. Her armament and crew were placed on board at Angra Bay, in the Azores Islands, near the end of the following month. After a most eventful career, during which she succeeded in capturing or destroying fifty-eight merchant-vessels, she was defeated and sunk in an engagement with the United States steamer Kearsarge, off the port of Havre, France, on June 19, 1864.

The Shenandoah, a steamer formerly engaged in the China trade, attracted the attention of the Confederate agents in London by her speed and superior sailing qualities, as well as by her adaptability to the purposes which they had in view. She was, therefore, purchased, and on October 8, 1864, cleared from the Thames, ostensibly for Bombay. Her real destination, however, was the Island of Madeira, whither a tender had preceded her, containing her armament and crew. The transfer was effected in neutral jurisdiction, as in the preceding cases, about October 21st of the same year. The evidence submitted in the case of this vessel satisfied the Geneva Board of Arbitration that no responsibility attached to the British government for her conduct up to the date of her arrival at Melbourne, Australia. The circumstances attending her conduct there should have caused her detention, but did not, and for her acts, after the date of her departure from Melbourne, the British government was held responsible. The career of this vessel is remarkable from the fact that she continued to make captures, in the North Pacific, after the termination of hostilities in the civil war. Upon being notified of the peace in July, 1865, she was conveyed by her captain to Liverpool, and was there surrendered to the British government.[1]

Result of their Operations.—The result of the operations of these vessels and their tenders was, in effect, to destroy the merchant marine of the United States. Such of its ships as escaped capture or destruction were transferred to foreign flags, to secure an immunity from capture by acquiring the neutral character. The question continued an open one between the governments for a number of years, subjecting their relations to a constant strain, and at times taking such a turn as to render war between them a not unlikely occurrence. Several attempts at settlement were made, but without success, owing to the excited state of feeling at the time. The question was finally put in the way of adjustment by the negotiation of the Treaty of Washington, in 1871.

---

[1] For Captain Waddell's letter to the Secretary of Foreign Affairs, surrendering this vessel, see Bernard, pp. 434–436.

The Geneva Arbitration.

13. The most striking and successful example of the settlement of an international difference of the gravest character, by a resort to the principle of arbitration, is furnished by the adjustment of the dispute between the United States and England growing out of the Alabama claims.

Unsuccessful Attempts at Settlement.—It was impossible that a difference of such serious importance could long exist without endangering the friendly relations of the two powers, and, at different times between the years 1863 and 1869, efforts were made with a view to its adjustment. None of them, however, were successful. The first attempt was made, in 1863, by Mr. Adams, the United States minister to England. He submitted a proposition which was held under advisement, for a time, by the British cabinet, but was finally declined in 1865. Another effort was made in 1866, and negotiations were continued until, in January, 1868, they were broken off, apparently without hope of renewal. In 1869 they were again renewed by Mr. Reverdy Johnson, who had succeeded Mr. Adams as the American representative in England. An agreement was entered into, between Mr. Johnson and the Earl of Clarendon, by which the claims were to be referred to a commission selected by the interested powers. This agreement was not ratified by the United States Senate, a co-ordinate branch of the treaty-making power in that state, and thus, for the third time, the efforts at adjustment were abandoned.

The Treaty of Washington.—In 1870 a dispute arose between the United States and Canada, as to the rights of American citizens to participate in the fisheries in certain British territorial waters of North America. As the agitation of the question seemed likely to introduce a new element of difficulty into the complications already existing between the two governments, a proposal was submitted, through the British minister, to the government in Washington for the appointment of a *Joint Commission*. The commission was to be composed, in equal numbers, of members selected by each government, and was to be charged with the adjustment, not only of the fishing dispute, but of all questions which might affect the relations of the United States with the British possessions in North America. To this proposition a reply was made, in behalf of the United States, that the project of the commission would not be favorably considered, unless its powers were extended to include the settlement of the differences which had arisen, during the civil war, out of the acts committed by Confederate cruisers; which had given rise to the demands known as the Alabama Claims.[1]

The proposition of the United States was accepted, and an agreement was entered into providing for the organization of a commission of ten members, selected in equal numbers by the governments of England and the United States. The commission was to sit in the city of Washington, and was to address itself to the task of providing a means of adjusting all causes of difference then existing between the two countries.

The commission thus provided for met in Washington on March 4, 1871. Its labors terminated on May

---

[1] *Revue de Droit International*, tome iii., 1871, p. 113

8, with the completion and signature of the Treaty of Washington. That instrument provided for the reference of the Alabama Claims to a tribunal of arbitration to be composed of five members. Of these one was to be selected by each of the contracting parties, and one each by the King of Italy, the President of the Swiss Confederation, and the Emperor of Brazil. The tribunal was to meet in Geneva, on the earliest convenient day after the nomination of its members. A case was to be submitted, by each of the contracting parties; and within four months thereafter either party might, in its discretion, submit a counter case in reply to the evidence and correspondence adduced by the other in support of its claim.

The tribunal, in deciding the case, was to be guided by three rules which were incorporated in the treaty, and mutually agreed to by the litigant powers. The agreement on the part of Great Britain was qualified by the declaration that "Her Majesty's government cannot assent to the foregoing rules as a statement of principles of International Law which were in force at the time when the claims mentioned arose, but that Her Majesty's government, in order to evince its desire of strengthening the friendly relations between the two countries, and of making satisfactory provision for the future, agrees that in deciding the questions between the two countries arising out of these claims, the arbitrators should assume that Her Majesty's government had undertaken to act upon the principles set forth in the rules."[1]

The three rules are, "A neutral government is bound,

---

[1] "Treaties and Conventions of the United States," p. 416.

(*a.*) "To use due diligence to prevent the fitting-out, arming, equipping, within its jurisdiction, of any vessel which it has reasonable ground to believe is intended to cruise or carry on war against a power with which it is at peace; and also to use like diligence to prevent the departure from its jurisdiction of any vessel intended to cruise or carry on war as above, such vessel having been specially adapted, in whole or in part, within such jurisdiction, to warlike use."

(*b.*) "Not to permit or suffer either belligerent to make use of its ports or waters as a base of naval operations against the other, or for the purpose of the renewal or augmentation of military supplies or arms, or the recruitment of men."

(*c.*) "To exercise due diligence in its own ports and waters, and, as to all persons within its jurisdiction, to prevent any violations of the foregoing obligations and duties."

Decision and Award.—The decision of the tribunal was to be rendered, if possible, within three months after the arguments on both sides had been closed. It was to be in writing, prepared in duplicate, and signed by the arbitrators who assented to it. The question referred for decision, as to each vessel separately, was "whether Great Britain has, by any act of omission, failed to fulfil any of the duties set forth in the foregoing three rules, or recognized by the principles of International Law not inconsistent with such rules."[1]

"In case the tribunal finds that Great Britain has failed to fulfil any duty, or duties, as aforesaid, it may,

---

[1] "Treaties and Conventions of the United States," pp. 416, 417.

if it think proper, proceed to award a sum in gross, to be paid by Great Britain to the United States, for all the claims referred to it; and in such case the gross sum so awarded shall be paid in coin by the government of Great Britain to the government of the United States, at Washington, within twelve months after the date of the award."[1]

"In case the tribunal find that Great Britain has failed to fulfil any duty, or duties, as aforesaid, and does not award a sum in gross, the high contracting parties agree that a board of assessors shall be appointed to ascertain and determine what claims are valid, and what amount or amounts shall be paid by Great Britain to the United States on account of the liability arising from such failures, as to each vessel, according to the extent of such liability as determined by the arbitrators."[2]

Meeting of the Board of Arbitration.—The tribunal met at Geneva on December 15, 1871. The full powers of the arbitrators were exchanged, and the board was organized by the selection of Count Sclopis, the Italian representative, as president. The cases were submitted by the agents of the respective governments, and the tribunal directed that the counter cases, additional documents, correspondence, and evidence should be delivered to the secretary on or before April 15, 1872. After making some arrangements as to procedure, the tribunal, on the following day, adjourned to meet on June 15, 1872.

Indirect Claims.— In the case submitted by the

---

[1] "Treaties and Conventions of the United States," pp. 416, 417.
[2] *Ibid.*

United States certain claims appeared for damages due under the heads of—

1st. "The losses in the transfer of the American commercial marine to the British flag."

2d. "The enhanced rates of insurance."

3d. "The prolongation of the war, and the addition of a large sum to the cost of the war and the suppression of the rebellion." The consideration of these indirect claims by the tribunal was objected to by the agent of the British government; and the tribunal decided that, according to the rules of International Law applicable to such cases, they did not constitute a good foundation for an award, and should be wholly excluded from the consideration of the tribunal in making its award. This ruling was accepted by both of the governments interested.[1]

Decision of the Arbitrators.—A decision was reached by the tribunal at the session of September 9, 1872. It was concurred in and signed by four of the members, the English representative offering a dissenting opinion. On September 14, after directing that a copy of the decision should be delivered to each of the agents of the two governments, the tribunal was dissolved.

Decision and Award.—Before the members of the tribunal were able to apply the rules, furnished them in the treaty, to the decision of the case, they were obliged to place an interpretation upon some of the terms there used, and to define the rule of International Law upon certain points, which were involved

---

[1] "Foreign Relations of the United States," "Geneva Arbitration," vol. iv., p. 20.

in the judicial determination of questions not covered by the rules themselves. It was therefore decided—

(1.) That *due diligence* "ought to be exercised by neutral governments in exact proportion to the risks to which either of the belligerents may be exposed, from a failure to fulfil the obligations of neutrality on their part."

(2.) "The effects of a violation of neutrality committed by means of the construction, equipment, and armament of a vessel are not done away with by any commission which the government of the belligerent power, benefited by the violation of neutrality, may afterwards have granted to that vessel; and the ultimate step, by which the offence is completed, cannot be admissible as a ground for the absolution of the offender, nor can the consummation of his fraud become the means of establishing his innocence."

(3.) "The principle of exterritoriality has been admitted into the law of nations, not as an absolute right, but solely as a proceeding founded on the principle of courtesy and mutual deference between different nations, and therefore can never be appealed to for the protection of acts done in violation of neutrality."[1]

In the cases of the Alabama, of the Florida, and of the Shenandoah after her departure from Melbourne on February 18, 1865, the tribunal was of opinion that Great Britain had failed, by omission, to perform the duties prescribed in two or more of the rules of Article VI. of the Treaty of Washington.[2]

---

[1] "Foreign Relations of the United States," 1872, 1873, "Geneva Award," vol. iv., pp. 49, 50.

[2] The finding in the case of the Alabama was of a failure in re

The sum of $15,500,000 in gold was awarded to the United States as the indemnity to be paid by Great Britain, for the satisfaction of all the claims referred to the consideration of the tribunal; and, in accordance with the terms of Article XI. of the treaty, it was declared that "all the claims referred to in the treaty as submitted to the tribunal are hereby fully, perfectly, and finally settled."[1]

Results of the Geneva Arbitration.—The effect of the Geneva arbitration upon International Law has been much discussed, especially in connection with a clause in the treaty, which binds the high contracting parties "to observe these rules as between themselves in future, and to bring them to the knowledge of other maritime powers, and to invite them to accede to them."[2] Neither power is believed to have made any special or positive efforts to include other states in the operations of the treaty. In so far as the rules themselves are concerned, such action seems hardly necessary. Their effect has not been to change any existing rule of International Law, for the strict ob-

---

spect to the first and third rules; in the case of the Florida of the first, second, and third; in the case of the Shenandoah of the second and third respectively. The Tuscaloosa, a tender of the Alabama, and the Clarence, Tacony, and Archer, tenders of the Florida, were held to be involved in the lot of their principals. It was held in the cases of the Georgia, Sumter, Nashville, Tallahassee, and Chickamauga that Great Britain had not failed to observe the three rules. The cases of the Sallie, Jeff Davis, Music, Boston, and V. H. Joy, were excluded from consideration for want of evidence.—"Foreign Relations of the United States," 1872, 1873, "Geneva Arbitration," vol. iv., pp. 51, 53.

[1] *Ibid.*, p. 53.

[2] "Treaties and Conventions of the United States," p. 416.

servance of neutral obligation and duty would require substantial compliance with their provisions, by any neutral state, in time of war. Their chief effect has been to define and make clear a principle already existing, and so generally sanctioned by the usage of nations as to cause it to be regarded as a doctrine of International Law.

Not the least important of its effects, however, will be found to consist in the example afforded of two powerful states resorting to an amicable method of terminating a dispute which had aroused, in both nations, a feeling dangerously near to hostility; and which threatened, upon more than one occasion, to involve them in open war.

References.—For the old view of neutrality the student is referred to Vattel, book iii., chap. vii., §§ 103–111; Azuni, "Maritime Law," vol. ii., chaps. i.-v. For the views now generally accepted, see Hall, part iv., chaps. ii.-iv.; Boyd's Wheaton, §§ 405–501; Halleck, vol. ii., chaps. xxiv. and xxviii.; Creasy, pp. 570–683; Manning, book v., chaps. i.-vi., and viii.-xii.; Phillimore, vol. iii., pp. 225–386; Woolsey, §§ 163–192; Bernard, "The Neurtality of England;" Nys, "La Guerre Maritime," chaps. i., ii., and vi.; Glass, "Marine International Law," pp. 573–603; G. F. De Martens, vol. ii., §§ 305–314, and §§ 323–326; Klüber, §§ 279–287, and §§ 299–316; Heffter, pp. 269–286; Kusscrow, "Les Devoirs d'un Gouvernement Neutre," and Hautefeuille, vol. i., pp. 195–407; vol. ii., pp. 1–69, 289–462; vol. iii., pp. 214–276, and 432–449. For a discussion of the Alabama Case and the Geneva Arbitration, see Bernard, "Neutrality of England;" Cushing, "Treaty of Washington;" "The Alabama Question," by Professor Bluntschli, vol. ii., *Revue de Droit International*, pp. 452–485; "The Geneva Arbitration," vols. i.-iv.; "Foreign Relations of the United States," 1872; Gessner, "Sur la Réforme du Droit Maritime de la Guerre," in vol. viii. of *Revue de Droit International*, and Lorimer, "The Obligations of Neutrals."

CHAPTER XII.

CONTRABAND OF WAR.

1. The principle of forbidding, as a matter of state policy, the manufacture or sale of certain articles, or even the holding of them in legal possession, has been recognized by the municipal law of all states since the beginning of history. The origin of the rule of International Law on the subject of contraband of war, however, is relatively recent, and, in its present form, does not antedate the seventeenth century.[1]

Origin of the Practice.—The commercial cities of the Mediterranean had but little interest in asserting such a right against each other, since each of them claimed exclusive control of what it regarded as its own field of commerce, and was not disposed to surrender any portion of it, even in time of war. Moreover, a large part of their trade with the East, especially that of Venice and Genoa, was in articles which would now be regarded as contraband of war. It is, therefore, very

---

[1] So early as the thirteenth century it had become the usage for powerful sovereigns to forbid *all* trade with their enemies in time of war. Such an instance occurs in a treaty of Edward III., of England, with the Flemings, in 1370. Francis I., in 1543, forbade his allies and confederates to deliver munitions of war to his enemy. Grotius was the first writer of standard authority to discuss the subject. Although the transport of certain articles is forbidden in treaties of an earlier date, the Treaty of the Pyrenees, in 1659, and that of Utrecht, of 1713, seem to have been most effective in determining the present rule on the subject of contraband of war.

unlikely that they would have advocated, or even favorably considered, a principle, the application of which would have seriously injured, if it did not entirely destroy, a most lucrative branch of their commerce. The adoption of the modern rule was thus deferred until the northern and western European powers had begun to acquire maritime importance, and to carry on hostile undertakings against each other at sea.

So soon as interstate commerce became general it was seen that certain kinds of trade, if carried on during the existence of a war, were calculated to injure belligerents to such an extent as to make it necessary for them to cause, at least, their temporary discontinuance; and to justify them, in the exercise of the right of self-defence, in resorting to such measures of precaution as would neutralize their injurious effects. It was not difficult to find a remedy, when the trade complained of was carried on by a state in its corporate capacity, since it constituted a violation of neutrality, and was punishable as such.

Where the objectionable commercial undertakings originated with individuals, however, it was less easy to provide a remedy. On land it was soon found to be impossible to prevent contraband trade, unless the belligerent himself controlled the neutral frontier, or the neutral state was willing to resort to such elaborate police measures as would effectively prevent the conveyance of contraband articles across its boundaries. Its attempted regulation on land, therefore, was soon abandoned. At sea, however, the matter could be more easily regulated. The ships of neutrals could be searched, and, if contraband articles were found on board, a suitable penalty could be inflicted; or their introduction into the enemy's country could be prevented, by maintaining opposite his coasts a naval force of sufficient strength to make it difficult, or impossible, for neutral ships to obtain access to his harbors.

When such regulation was first undertaken, the attempt was made to forbid all traffic with an enemy. This claim, however, was soon abandoned, and the conveyance of contraband was regarded as a criminal act, involving the *persons* engaged in it, as well as their property, in the penalties imposed. In this form the rule was recognized by Grotius. The criminal feature was soon abandoned, so far as it affected the personal rights of those concerned, and the penalties were restricted to the contraband goods alone.

2. *Power of a Belligerent over Neutral Commerce in Time of War.*—The law of nations permits a belligerent to exercise a peculiar jurisdiction over neutral commerce in time of war. This jurisdiction is so extensive as to amount to an absolute prohibition of certain kinds of trade. It is limited, in its extent and operations, only by the zeal and energy which belligerents display in its exercise.

This jurisdiction extends—

(*a.*) To the prohibition of neutral trade with belligerents in certain articles susceptible of military use. The articles so forbidden to be transported are called *contraband of war*.

(*b.*) To the prohibition of all trade with certain ports or places, which are closed to such trade by an exercise of military force known as an *investment, siege*, or *blockade*.

(*c.*) To make these prohibitions effective, a belligerent is given the right to stop, and search, all neutral merchant vessels on the high seas, in his own territorial waters, or those of his enemy, for the purpose of determining the nationality of ships and goods, and of ascertaining whether they contain contraband of war. This is called the *Right of Search.*

These rights pertain to belligerent states alone. They come into existence at the outbreak of war, and are terminated by the treaty of peace. None of them exist, or may lawfully be exercised, in time of peace; and the enforcement of any one of them, during peace, would be regarded as a just cause of war by the state whose sovereign rights were injured by its exercise.

The Rules of Contraband Affect chiefly the Acts of Individuals.—The rules of International Law on the subject of contraband trade are directed chiefly against the acts of individuals. If a neutral state, in its corporate capacity, were to engage in contraband trade, it would be regarded as an act of hostility by the injured state, and would result in a declaration of war. An individual engaging in such trade, does so at the risk of losing the articles of merchandise which constitute his commercial venture. He does not involve his government, however, in the breach of neutrality of which he is himself guilty. If the municipal law of his own state forbids its subjects to take part in contraband trade, he may be punished by that government for a violation of its laws.

Character of Contraband Trade in Point of Legality.—International Law declares the acts of transporting contraband and breach of blockade to be unlawful, and denounces the penalty of confiscation upon the goods, and, in some cases, upon the ships engaged in such illicit trade. These rules of International Law are enforced by the belligerent who suffers by their violation, and the authorized penalties are imposed by his prize courts.

3. *Difficulty of the Attempt to Frame Rules for Determining what Articles are Contraband of War.*—It is difficult to lay down a rule the application of which shall, in every case, determine whether a particular article is, or is not, contraband of war. The attempt has frequently been made, but none of the rules suggested has, as yet, received that general sanction which is necessary to give it standing as a rule of International Law. "Grotius, in considering this subject, makes a distinction between those things which are useful only for purposes of war, those which are not so, and those which are susceptible of indiscriminate use in war and peace. The *first*, he agrees with all other text writers in prohibiting neutrals from carrying to the enemy, as well as in permitting the *second* to be so carried; the *third* class, such as money, provisions, ships' and naval stores, he sometimes prohibits and at others permits, according to the existing circumstances of the war."[1]

Difficulty of Stating a Precise Rule.—The question as to what is and what is not contraband cannot, as yet, be answered with precision. No complete list of articles which are to be deemed contraband under all

---

[1] Boyd's Wheaton, pp. 558, 559, citing Grotius; "De Jure Belli et Pac.," lib. iii., cap. i., § v, 1, 2, 3. The views of Bynkershoek and Vattel agree in substance with those of Grotius. The former, however, shows an inclination to extend Grotius's rules in the interest of belligerents, while the latter contends for a rule somewhat more favorable to neutrals. See Vattel, bk. iii., chap. vii., § 112, 113; Bynkershoek, "Quest. Jur. Pub.," lib. i., cap. 10.

circumstances has been drawn up, nor does it seem likely that it ever will be. That which is contraband under certain circumstances may not be so under others. The main point, in case of an article of doubtful use, is, whether it was intended for, or would probably be applied to, military purposes. The release or condemnation of the goods is, in every case, determined by the decision of this question.

Question Determined by Prize Courts.—In England and America the court before which the goods are brought will inquire into all the circumstances of the case; such as the destination of the ship, the purpose to which the goods seem intended to be applied, the character of the war, and so on, and will condemn or release them upon the evidence.[1] If, however, there are any treaty stipulations on the subject, or if the state before whose court the goods are brought has issued any definite list of contraband goods, the decision will, of course, be regulated accordingly. "*The liability to capture*," says Halleck, "*can only be determined by the rules of International Law, as interpreted and applied by the tribunals of the belligerent state*, to the operations of whose cruisers the neutral merchant is exposed."[2]

Field's Rule.—Mr. Field, in his proposed International Code, holds that "private property of any person whomsoever, and public property of a neutral nation, are contraband of war, when consisting of arti-

---

[1] Dana's Wheaton, note, p. 226; Calvo, vol. ii., § 1114; Abdy's Kent, p. 359.

[2] Boyd's Wheaton, pp. 575, 576; Halleck, chap. xxiv., § 19. See, also, on page 576 of the former work, the lists of contraband as determined by the English prize courts.

cles manufactured for, and primarily used for, military purposes in time of war, and actually destined for the use of the hostile nation in war, but not otherwise."[1]

Opinion of the Supreme Court of the United States.— The most recent authoritative opinion upon the subject, and the one which more nearly expresses the existing rule than any other, is that laid down by the Supreme Court of the United States in the case of the Peterhoff. The decision of the court was that "the classification of goods as contraband or not contraband has much perplexed text writers and jurists. A strictly accurate and satisfactory classification is, perhaps, impracticable; but that which is best supported by American and English decisions may be said to divide all merchandise into three classes: (1.) Articles manufactured and primarily or ordinarily used for military purposes in time of war. (2.) Articles which may be, and are, used for purposes of war or peace, according to circumstances. (3.) Articles exclusively used for peaceful purposes. Merchandise of the first class, destined to a belligerent country or places occupied by the army or navy of a belligerent, is always contraband; merchandise of the second class is contraband only when destined to the military or naval use of a belligerent; while merchandise of the third class is not contraband at all, though liable to seizure and condemnation for violation of blockade or siege."[2]

To these may be added the rule that no articles of merchandise are contraband of war so long as they remain in neutral territory, or are found on the high

---

[1] Field, "International Code," § 859.
[2] The Peterhoff, Wallace, vol. v., p. 58.

seas with a *bona fide* neutral destination. They acquire the character of contraband only when they are found, without the territorial waters of a neutral state, on board a ship which is destined to a hostile port.

Application of the Rules. — In the application of these rules, the first and third give rise to but little difficulty. Such discussion as has been had, with respect to the liability of merchandise to capture as contraband of war, has had to do chiefly with the second class, with reference to which there is a wide difference of opinion. This is observable, not only in the policy of states, but in the views of text writers. Those states which, at different periods, have enjoyed great maritime power, both in a commercial and a military sense, have usually advocated an extension of the list of contraband; while, on the other hand, those which have never attained to any considerable degree of maritime importance have opposed such an extension, and have contended for the greatest freedom of neutral trade. Of the former class England is the most conspicuous representative; next in order follow France and the United States. Holland, when an important maritime power, entertained a different view from that advocated by her when her maritime importance had been largely diminished.

Again, articles which are in dispute are differently regarded at different times, and under different circumstances of destination, as determined by the states which are parties to a particular war. So, too, articles which are undeniably contraband at a particular epoch gradually lose that character; on the other hand, articles formerly innocent, with the lapse of time and the march of improvement, acquire the character of contraband. Parts of marine steam machinery, previous to 1830, would have escaped capture. Plates of iron or steel, of suitable size for use as armor, would have enjoyed a similar immunity. At present both are everywhere regarded as contraband of war. However difficult it may be to prepare a list of contraband articles at any particular epoch, it is certainly much less difficult for a court to determine whether a certain article of captured merchandise is, or is not, contraband. In reaching such a determination the court takes into account the circumstances of capture, the necessities of the state to whose use it was destined, its condition, origin, and ownership. With these data the court is usually able to determine, with great accuracy, whether a particular article is, or is not, contraband of war.[1]

---

[1] The action of the court in the case of the Peterhoff may be cited as an example. A portion of the cargo of the ship consisted of stoutly-made shoes and cavalry boots. The ostensible destination of the cargo was Matamoras, a Mexican port. These articles were notoriously not worn or used, in Mexico, by any portion of the population; they were worn in the United States, and were especially needed for the equipment of the Confederate armies. Another portion of the cargo was composed of heavy woollen blankets, not adapted to the Mexican market, and of a kind entirely different, in pattern and weight, from those usually worn in Mexico. On the other hand, they closely resembled those made and sold, for military use, in the United States, and were adapted to the colder climate of that country. The court, in both instances, properly inferred that the goods were destined to the military service of the Confederacy. In the cargo of the Springbok a large quantity of gray cloth and metal buttons were found. The cloth was a heavy woollen material, altogether unsuited to the Nassau market, or for use in the manufacture of clothing in that climate. On the other hand, it was of the same color and quality as that officially adopted for the use of the Confederate armies. Some of the buttons bore as a device

Destination of Ships and Goods; how Determined.—
The destination of a vessel is determined from its papers. If the ultimate destination and all intermediate ports of call are neutral, the ship is said to have a neutral destination. If the port of final destination, or any intermediate port of call, be hostile, then her destination is hostile. If the purpose of the master to visit an intermediate hostile port be contingent only, and if he has abandoned his purpose in the course of the voyage, the burden of proof is with him to establish such abandonment of the hostile destination. In this case he will have to overthrow the presumption, as to destination, which is created by the ship's papers.

The destination of the goods is usually, but not invariably, determined from that of the ship. If the destination of the ship be neutral, that of the goods is neutral; if it be hostile, that of the goods is hostile. Until the American civil war the presumption by which the destination of the goods was deduced from that of the ship was generally regarded as conclusive. During the course of that war, however, the Supreme

---

the letter C; others the letter A; others the letter I; still others the letters C. S. N. These buttons were not usual articles of commerce in Nassau, the ostensible destination of the ship. The Confederate army regulations prescribed that such buttons should be worn by, and should designate the uniforms of, its cavalry, artillery, and infantry. Its navy regulations prescribed the use of buttons bearing the letters C. S. N. Goods bearing the name of the same makers, and in some cases of the same shippers, had been found and condemned in previous cargoes of contraband. These facts created a presumption, against the articles, which the claimants did not attempt to rebut by evidence of a legitimate neutral destination.—The Peterhoff, Wallace, vol. v., p. 58; The Springbok, *ibid.*, p. 1. See, also, Dana's Wheaton, p. 632, note.

Court of the United States rendered several decisions, the effect of which was to extend considerably the rights of belligerents at the expense of those of neutrals. As the new rule is likely to receive considerable support in future wars, it is important to understand its relation to the old rule of International Law upon the same subject. The rule laid down by the court was that the destination of the *goods*, rather than that of the *ship*, was to be inquired into by the court, in determining the liability to capture. If the result of such inquiry showed that the goods were destined to the military use of a belligerent, they were held liable to condemnation, even though they were ostensibly destined to a neutral port. The application of the rule is illustrated by the cases of the Springbok and Peterhoff.

Case of the Springbok.—The Springbok was a neutral ship, of English ownership, which sailed from London in December, 1862, having on board a cargo made up in great part of contraband of war. The destination of the vessel, as indicated by her custom-house certificate, certificate of clearance, and manifest of cargo was Nassau, N. P., a British, and therefore neutral, port. On February 3, 1863, she was captured by a public armed vessel of the United States, on the high seas, about one hundred and fifty miles east of her port of destination. She was conveyed to New York as a prize, and ship and cargo were there condemned by the United States District Court, a tribunal having original jurisdiction in the case. An appeal was taken to the Supreme Court, where the decree was reversed as to the ship, but affirmed as to the cargo. The decision of the court with regard to the ship was, that when "the papers of a vessel sailing under a charter party are all genuine and regular, and show a voyage between ports neutral within the meaning of International Law, and when the aspects of the case generally are, as respects the vessel, otherwise fair, the vessel will not be condemned because the neutral port to which it is sailing has been constantly and notoriously used as a port of call and transshipment by persons engaged in the systematic violation of blockade, and in the conveyance of contraband of war, and was meant by the owners of the cargo carried on this ship to be so used in regard to it."¹ The Springbok was held to come within the rule. "Her papers were regular, and they all showed that the voyage in which she was captured was from London to Nassau, both neutral ports within the definition of neutrality furnished by International Law. The papers, too, were all genuine, and there was no concealment of any of them, and no spoliation. Her owners were neutral, and do not appear to have had any interest in the cargo; and there is no sufficient proof that they had any knowledge of its alleged unlawful destination."²

The case of the cargo was quite different. The cargo of the ship consisted of over two thousand packages. Of these the bills of lading disclosed the contents of less than one third, and concealed the contents of over two thirds, of the entire cargo. The manifest and bills of lading named no consignee, but described the cargo as deliverable to order. The real owners of the cargo were found to be certain firms in London, all of whom had been the owners of similar packages of

---

¹ The Springbok, Wallace, vol. v., p. 1. ² *Ibid.*

merchandise which had been captured on a previous occasion, and condemned as contraband.¹ The court inferred from these facts the intention of concealing from the scrutiny of American cruisers the contraband character of a considerable part of the cargo. The motive of such concealment being "the apprehension of the claimants that the disclosure of their names, as owners, would lead to the seizure of the ship in order to the condemnation of the cargo."

The concealments above mentioned were not of themselves regarded by the court as sufficient to warrant the condemnation of the cargo. "If the real intention of the owners of the cargo was that the cargo should be unloaded at Nassau, and incorporated by real sale into the common stock of that island," the cargo should have been "restored, notwithstanding the misconduct of concealment. What, then, was the real intention?" This was inferred by the court, in part from the ship's papers, and in part from the character of the cargo. The manifest and bills of lading showed that the consignment was to order. This was regarded by the court as a negation that any sale was made, or intended to be made, at Nassau. The final destination of the cargo, therefore, was not Nassau, but some ulterior port, and must be inferred from the character of the cargo. A small part of this cargo consisted of articles which were contraband by the narrowest definition of the term. A considerable part consisted of articles useful and necessary in war—such as army cloth, blankets, boots and shoes—and therefore con-

---

[1] The Gertrude, "Blatchford's Prize Cases" (U. S. Dist. Court), p. 374; The Stephen Hart, ibid., p. 387.

traband within the construction of English and American prize courts. These being contraband, the residue of the cargo, belonging to the same owners, was included in the decree of condemnation.[1]

Case of the Peterhoff.—The case of the Peterhoff, in some respects, resembles that of the Springbok. The Peterhoff was a steamer which sailed from London with proper documents and ship's papers, indicating her destination to be Matamoras, Mexico. The Rio Grande, for a portion of its course, separates the territory of the United States from that of Mexico. The city of Matamoras is situated on the lower waters of the river, about forty miles from its mouth, and directly opposite the city of Brownsville, in the United States. The Peterhoff never reached her destination, but was captured, near the Island of St. Thomas, by the United States steamer Vanderbilt, on suspicion that her destination was the blockaded coast of the states in rebellion, and that her cargo consisted in part of contraband of war. She was taken to New York, where ship and cargo were condemned as prize. An appeal was taken to the Supreme Court by claimants interested in the vessel and a portion of the cargo.

The court, in reaching a decision, found it necessary to pass upon the question of the right of a belligerent to blockade a boundary river, in order to determine whether the ship was liable for breach of blockade or for carrying contraband of war.

Upon this point the ruling was, that when a navigable river separates two sovereign states, neither belligerent, in the exercise of his right of blockade, can in-

---

[1] The Springbok, Wallace, vol. v., p. 1.

terrupt commerce with the other state, if neutral, by preventing access to any ports of such neutral state as are situated upon the boundary river at any point of its course. As the *bona fide* destination of the ship, as indicated by its papers, was Matamoras, a neutral port, it was therefore decided that the ship was not, and, under the circumstances could not be, liable to condemnation for breach of blockade.

As to the cargo, the decision was that the destination of such part of it as was contraband of war, according to the rules already cited,[1] was not the neutral port of Matamoras, and "that these articles, at least, were destined for the use of the rebel forces then occupying Brownsville and other places in the vicinity. Contraband merchandise is subject to a different rule in respect to ulterior destination from that which applies to merchandise not contraband. The latter is liable to capture only when a violation of blockade is intended; the former when destined to a hostile country, or to the actual military or naval use of the enemy, whether blockaded or not. The trade of neutrals with belligerents, in articles not contraband, is absolutely free, except interrupted by a blockade; the conveyance by neutrals to belligerents of contraband articles is always unlawful, and such articles may always be seized during transit by sea. Hence, while articles, not contraband, might be sent to Matamoras and beyond to the rebel region, where the communication was not interrupted by blockade, articles of a contraband character, destined in fact to a state in rebellion,

---

[1] Lawrence's Wheaton, pp. 772-776, note; The Commercen, Wheaton, vol. i., p. 382; Dana's Wheaton, p. 629, note; Parsons, "Maritime Law," pp. 93, 94.

CONTRABAND OF WAR. 351

or for the use of the rebel military forces, were liable to capture though primarily destined for Matamoras."[1] The rule that the ownership of a portion of the contraband cargo rendered articles not contraband, but belonging to the same owners, liable to condemnation, was enforced as in the case of the Springbok.[2]

4. *The Doctrine of Continuous Voyages.*—In both of these cases the doctrine of *continuous voyages*, originated by the English prize courts at the beginning of this century, was recognized by the court in reaching a decree of condemnation. By this doctrine the ultimate destination of a cargo is held to determine its liability to capture. If such destination is a neutral port, and if the cargo is intended to be sold there, and taken up as a part of the general stock in trade, the cargo is not liable to condemnation. If, however, a neutral port is made a new base of operations, and the goods are intended to be finally delivered at a blockaded port; or if they are contraband of war, and are destined to the ultimate military use of a belligerent, then the alleged neutral destination will not avail. The principle of continuous voyages is thus seen to have been extended by the Supreme Court in its application to the cases of the Springbok and Peterhoff, although the fundamental principle involved, as announced by Lord Stowell in his original decision, has undergone no material change.[3] The later decision

---

[1] Wallace, vol. v., p. 35.

[2] The English cases of the Stert, Robinson, "Admiralty Reports," vol. iv., p. 65, and the Jonge Pieter, *ibid.*, vol. iii., p. 297, were cited by the court as precedents applicable to the case.

[3] For a full account of the decision of Lord Stowell upon the subject of continuous voyages, see the Polly, Robinson, "Admiralty

regards the goods if contraband, and destined to an enemy's use, or to a blockaded port, as still liable to capture, even when they were to have been discharged at a neutral port, with a view to reshipment to the belligerent destination.'

Difference between the Old and New Rules.—The rule thus laid down by the Supreme Court of the United States is undoubtedly at variance with the provisions of International Law on the same subject, as they were accepted and understood at the outbreak of the civil war. Neither has the new rule received that general recognition which it must receive to entitle it to consideration as a rule of International Law. The development of steam navigation, however, has been such as greatly to facilitate the operations of blockade-running and carrying of contraband. So important has this development been, that a belligerent would now suffer great injury were he to adhere to the old rule on the subject, which received international sanction at a time when maritime commerce was carried on in sailing vessels, and before the application of steam to purposes of navigation had become an accepted fact. Some modification of the old rule is, therefore, both

---

Reports," vol. ii., p. 369, and the William, *ibid.*, vol. v., p. 395. See, also, Phillimore, vol. iii., p. 394; and Boyd's Wheaton, pp. 589–592.

[1] In the case of the Springbok the British government was applied to by the owners of the contraband cargo to demand restitution of the goods from the American government, or compensation for their seizure. The case was referred to the law officers of the crown, and their opinion was that the seizure was illegal. The case was referred to a mixed commission, and the claim was rejected, but no reason was given by the commission for its decision. See Creasy, pp. 619, 620, for a full and able discussion of the subject. See, also, Field's "International Code," § 859.

just and necessary, in order to place a belligerent in as good a situation as that which he formerly occupied. What that modification is to be can only be deduced from experience, of which a sufficient amount has not yet been acquired to justify such a deduction, or to warrant the statement of a modified rule. This much only is clear. A powerful belligerent will not, in the future, allow himself to be injured by articles of contraband which the enemy actually receives from ships having an ostensibly neutral destination; nor, on the other hand, will a powerful neutral allow the property of his subjects to be seized on the high seas when those goods, although partaking of the character of contraband, have a *bona fide* neutral destination. In the cases above cited the ultimate destination of the goods was so clearly hostile as to make it difficult, if not impossible, for the British government to maintain the position that the goods of its subjects had been seized in the prosecution of an entirely innocent voyage, and were so entitled to the protection which that government invariably accords to its subjects when their rights have been wrongfully invaded by a foreign state.

5. *Penalty for Contraband Trade.*—The conveyance of contraband of war is an offence against the law of nations. Over this offence the prize courts of a belligerent are given jurisdiction, and, in the decision of prize cases, these courts apply the rules, and impose the penalties, which are sanctioned by International Law.

The invariable penalty imposed for the carriage of contraband is that of forfeiture. In ordinary cases this penalty is applied to the contraband goods alone, and to the freight due upon them to the neutral carrier. The question as to whether it is to be extended to other parts of the cargo, or to the ship, is determined by the knowledge and intention of their owners, as presumed from the circumstances of the case. The ancient penalty for engaging in contraband trade involved the forfeiture of the ship and the non-contraband cargo. This rule has been relaxed, in modern times, in cases where such contraband articles make up a minor portion of the cargo, thus creating a presumption of innocence in favor of the carrier. In other cases the old presumption remains, and the burden of proof lies upon the owner of the ship to establish his innocence. Such presumption exists, as to the ship—

(*a.*) When the owner of the ship owns any part of the contraband cargo. If a part owner of the vessel be shown to have an interest in the contraband cargo his share only is forfeited.[1]

(*b.*) When the greater part of the cargo is contraband. In this case the presumption is that the owner of the ship knew of the use to which his property was put, and consented to such illegal use.[2]

(*c.*) When deceit is attempted by the use of false papers, or when a false destination is claimed.[3]

(*d.*) When contraband is carried in violation of treaty stipulation.[4]

The innocent cargo is exempt from forfeiture, unless its ownership is the same as that of the whole or a part of the contraband.

Duration of Penalty. — The offence of carrying contraband begins so soon as the ship passes into the

---

[1] Boyd's Wheaton, p. 584.   [2] *Ibid.*   [3] *Ibid.*   [4] *Ibid.*

high seas from the territorial waters of the neutral state. It is complete, and the liability to penalty no longer exists, when the articles have been delivered at their hostile destination. A ship cannot be captured on its return voyage, since there is no offence against International Law in carrying a cargo of any character from a belligerent to a neutral destination.[1]

Release of Neutral Ship upon the Surrender of Contraband Cargo.—In a few instances neutral ships have been released, and allowed to proceed to their destination, on condition that the contraband articles be surrendered to the captor. Although this practice has been recognized in a limited number of treaties, it is entirely opposed to the rule of law upon the subject, and has never received, nor is it likely to receive, general sanction. The surrendered articles must be carried before a prize court in order to secure a decree of condemnation, upon which alone a valid title can be based. The court, in the absence of the ship's papers, frequently finds itself unable to determine, from lack of evidence, whether the articles are, or are not, contraband of war; and, in the absence of the owner, the master of the ship has no legal power to surrender any portion of his cargo, except in accordance with the laws of war.

---

[1] It was held by Sir William Scott, in at least two cases, that the duration of the penalty was prolonged to the end of the return voyage when false papers had been used to evade seizure on the outward voyage. This view is properly questioned by Wheaton, on the ground that there must be a *delictum* at the moment of seizure. To subject the property to confiscation, while the offence no longer continues, would be to extend it indefinitely, not only to the return voyage, but to all future cargoes of the vessel, which would thus never be purified from the contagion communicated by the contraband articles.—Boyd's Wheaton, pp. 584, 585.

6. *Neutral Conveyance of Enemy's Troops and Despatches.*—It has been seen that the conveyance of contraband of war is an offence against the law of nations. Over this offence belligerents are given jurisdiction, and the penalties sanctioned are imposed by the prize courts of the belligerent parties to the war. A neutral individual who carries contraband to either belligerent assists that belligerent to a greater or less extent, depending upon the character and quantity of the goods transported. Troops and despatches are, therefore, the most noxious form of contraband of war, because, in point of directness and importance, the service rendered by the conveyance of either is much greater than that afforded by the conveyance of ordinary contraband. The assistance rendered to an enemy by a single cargo of munitions of war, though direct and material, is, at best, limited. The mischief that may result from the carriage of a single despatch, or general officer, may have a decisive effect upon the issue of a war. The penalty for engaging in contraband trade usually extends to a forfeiture of the contraband articles. The question as to the ship and non-contraband cargo is made to depend on the guilty knowledge of their owners. If they are forfeited it is because a presumption of such knowledge is created by the fact of ownership. When troops or despatches are carried to a hostile destination the presumption of guilt, created by such carriage, is so strong as to be regarded as conclusive; and the ship is invariably condemned as the instrument with which the offence against International Law has been committed.

Definition of Troops and Despatches in this Connection.—The term troops includes not only military persons, but all individuals having an official character in the service of a belligerent, whose assistance is material in the prosecution of the war, or whose detention is calculated to impair his military efficiency.

Despatches are official communications between official persons, in the military or civil service of a state, upon matters connected with the public business. All other communications, of whatever character, are unofficial, and therefore not subject to classification as despatches.

The Destination Important.—In the conveyance of troops and despatches the destination of the vessel is of importance as creating a presumption of guilt or innocence. If the destination is hostile, the guilt of the carrier is presumed; if such destination be neutral, the contrary is the case, and the burden of proof lies on the captor to establish guilty knowledge. If the ports of origin and destination are both hostile, an extreme case of guilt exists; if such ports are both neutral, it is difficult to see how guilty knowledge can be presumed on the part of the neutral carrier. As in every other case of maritime capture, questions as to the character of particular despatches, and the consequent liability of the carrier, are determined by the proper prize courts.

Cases of the Friendship and Greta.—Several condemnations of vessels for carrying troops were made by the English prize courts during the period between 1803 and 1815. A leading case was that of the Friendship, a vessel hired to bring to France eighty-four shipwrecked officers and sailors. It was confiscated because it appeared in the evidence that it was hired as a transport, was not permitted to take cargo, and was being used, as a transport, to convey these persons, as a part of the French army, to a belligerent destination. In another case a vessel sailed from Rotterdam to Lisbon, where it was ostensibly chartered, by a Portuguese subject, to carry cargoes or passengers to Macao; no cargo was shipped, but, after some time spent in fitting it for passengers with unusual care, three Dutch officers of rank embarked in it, not for Macao, but for Batavia. Lord Stowell, on the facts in the case, inferred that a contract had been made with the Dutch government before the vessel left Rotterdam, and condemned it.[1] The Greta was a neutral vessel, employed in carrying certain shipwrecked Russian soldiers from a port of Japan to a destination in Asiatic Russia. She was captured by an English cruiser, and condemned. Had she been captured in the act of conveying them from the place of the shipwreck, to any destination, her act, being one of humanity, would have been innocent. In the particular voyage upon which she was engaged, however, she was acting in the capacity of a transport.

Presumption in the Case of Hostile Despatches.— In the case of hostile despatches, the mere presence of such documents on board suffices to create a presumption of guilt on the part of the neutral carrier. So severely is this rule applied, that a neutral may not even plead compulsion as an excuse, it being held in such a case that his remedy, in the event of being compelled to render such service to a belligerent, is through his own government in the diplomatic way.

Despatches of a Belligerent to its Ministers and Consuls in Neutral States.—The despatches of a public

---

[1] Hall, p. 594; The Friendship, Robinson, "Admiralty Reports," vol. vi., p. 422; The Orozembo, *ibid.*, p. 433.

minister or consul, representing a belligerent in a neutral state, are an exception to this rule. "They are despatches from persons who are, in a peculiar manner, the favorite object of the protection of the law of nations, residing in a neutral country for the purpose of preserving the relations of amity between that state and their own government. On this ground a very material distinction arises with respect to the right of furnishing the conveyance. The neutral country has a right to preserve its relations with the enemy, and you are not at liberty to conclude that any communication between them can partake, in any degree, of the nature of hostility against you."[1]

Conveyance of Mails in the Ordinary Course of Business.—The question of conveying hostile despatches must not be confused with the carriage of mails by a neutral, in accordance with contracts or agreements, and in the way of ordinary business. Such contracts not only have the sanction of municipal law, but are not infrequently made the subjects of treaty stipulation. It is not easy to see how the master of a vessel can acquire any duties or responsibilities in connection with them, save for their speedy and safe delivery. A neutral master who aids a belligerent by carrying his despatches, with full knowledge of their contents, or under circumstances which create a presumption of such knowledge on his part, is justly held to the fullest responsibility for his act. The conveyance of mails, however, in the usual course of business, can give rise to no such presumption. The packages are delivered

---

[1] The Caroline, Robinson, "Admiralty Reports," vol. vi., p. 461 cited by Wheaton, p. 581.

to him either locked or sealed. He has, and can have, no knowledge of their contents, much less of the character of the letters enclosed in them. Responsibility for them on the part of the carrier, therefore, cannot exist, for no knowledge or intention can be presumed. The modern tendency is to facilitate mail communication in every way possible, to remove every obstacle to their prompt and safe delivery, and to guarantee, beyond question, the sacredness of private correspondence.[1]

Case of the Trent.—The Trent was one of a line of mail steamers employed in general mail and transportation service between Havana and London. On November 7, 1861, she sailed from Havana, having on board, among other passengers, four persons, Messrs. Mason and Slidell, and their secretaries, who were *en route* to Europe, where they were to be employed as diplomatic agents of the Confederate States. On November 8 the Trent was stopped on the high seas by the San Jacinto, a public armed vessel of the United States, whose commander, Captain Wilkes, sent on board a search party composed of an officer and a detachment of marines. The two envoys, with their secretaries, were seized by the search party, taken on board the San Jacinto, and conveyed to New York. The Trent was then released and allowed to proceed on her way.

So soon as the facts were brought to the attention of the British government, a demand was made upon

---

[1] The rule of International Law, however, still authorizes the examination of mails found on board vessels which have been regularly captured; Field, "International Code," § 862; Lushington, "Naval Prize Law," introduction, p. xii.

the United States for the restoration of the arrested persons. Their diplomatic character was not drawn in question, their surrender being demanded on the ground that they had been forcibly taken from a neutral vessel on the high seas, and in the prosecution of a voyage from one neutral port to another. They were surrendered by the United States upon the ground of the irregularity of their seizure.

Conclusions.—The case of the Trent illustrates certain principles of the law of maritime capture.

(*a.*) The Trent, being a neutral vessel, was liable to search upon the high seas, by any properly documented armed vessel in the service of a belligerent power.

(*b.*) If the commander of the searching vessel had found enemy despatches on board, or had reason to believe that such despatches were being carried, it was his duty to seize the vessel and send her to a port of the United States, with a view to a judicial determination of the question involved.

(*c.*) In the exercise of his belligerent right it was his duty to capture the vessel; or release her, after having executed the right of search. No intermediate course was possible. His action, therefore, in seizing certain persons, under any pretext, was without warrant of law.

(*d.*) The destination of the Trent was neutral, a fact which should have created a strong presumption of innocence. The fact that her port of origin was also neutral should have made the presumption conclusive as to innocence.[1]

---

[1] For able discussions of this case, see Dana's Wheaton, p. 648, note; Bernard, "Neutrality of Great Britain," pp. 157, 225; Nys, "La Guerre Maritime," p. 46. The case of Henry Laurens is, in many respects, the same as that of the Trent. Mr. Laurens was

7. *Occasional Contraband*.—During the disturbed period intervening between the outbreak of the French Revolution in 1789, and the Treaty of Vienna in 1815, the old usages of International Law were subjected to a severe and constant strain. This was due, in part, to the frequency and magnitude of the wars that were carried on, in which, at times, nearly all of the European states were participants; and, in part, to the great disparity that existed in the relative naval and military power of the principal belligerents. During the greater part of this period the military supremacy of France was successfully maintained against every effort to overthrow it by operations on land; on the other hand, the supremacy of England at sea was so firmly established as to secure even more general recognition. As these powers were generally opposed to each other, it is not remarkable that they should have attempted to interpret the rules of war, each in a sense favorable to its own interests; and, as the one was strong where the other was weak, neither was able to

---

sent, in 1780, upon a mission to Holland, with the authority of Congress to secure the recognition of the independence of the colonies, and to obtain a loan of money. He left Charleston in 1780, and reached Martinique, in the West Indies, in safety. From there he embarked in a Dutch packet, the Mercury, for Holland. He was thus on board a neutral vessel sailing between neutral ports. When three days out the Mercury was overhauled by the British ship Vestal. Mr. Laurens and his secretary were forcibly removed, their papers were seized, and they were conveyed as prisoners to St. Johns, Newfoundland, where they were committed, under a charge of high-treason, to the Tower of London. After the surrender at Yorktown their status was changed to that of prisoners of war, and Mr. Laurens was eventually exchanged for Lord Cornwallis.—Sparks, "Diplomatic Correspondence," vol. ii., p. 461; Upton, "Law of Nations Affecting Commerce during War," pp. 360, 361.

interpose an effectual check upon the pretensions of the other. The result was that the rules of capture, on land and sea, underwent a considerable modification in the interest of belligerents, and to the prejudice of the rights of neutrals, as those rights were then understood. This influence upon the law of maritime capture was the more powerful from the fact that the northern states of Europe, and, to a certain extent, the United States as well, entered into general commerce largely as producers of raw materials, which were consumed by the principal belligerents, and so were obliged to find a market in belligerent territory. Thus, while these states were generally neutral, they were not strong enough at sea, even when acting in concert, to assert effectively their views of neutrality, or even to successfully maintain their neutral rights.

Under these circumstances, not only was neutral commerce likely to suffer from any extension of the definition of contraband, but the commercial prosperity of neutral states was made to depend, in no small degree, upon that definition being closely restricted in its application to neutral property. Such an extension was effected by the application of the doctrine of *occasional contraband*, by the English prize courts, to cargoes of neutral merchandise. According to this rule articles were condemned which had previously either been exempt from seizure, or, if regarded as contraband, had acquired that character only in exceptional cases, where the circumstances pointed clearly to an undoubtedly hostile destination. The articles so condemned were those usually classified as naval stores and provisions; and neutral states resisted the application of the new rule, partly because of the extreme hardship of the case, and partly because it was not, and had never been, generally recognized as a rule of International Law.

The English prize courts admitted the force of the objection, and the irregularity of the practice, by a somewhat less rigorous application of the new rule, and certain mitigating circumstances were recognized as creating presumptions in favor of innocence. In their application of the modified rule it was held that if the goods were produce of a neutral state, and were shipped, as raw materials, to strictly commercial ports, these facts were allowed to weigh against condemnation, and in favor of restoration.

The Rule of Pre-emption.—At a later period the original doctrine was still further modified by the adoption of the *rule of pre-emption*, by which the prize courts, in some cases, decreed the purchase of the cargo at its value at the port of origin, with a fair mercantile profit, usually ten per cent., instead of condemning it as contraband of war. The rule, as modified, continued to be enforced until the close of the period of Napoleonic wars. Their justice was not discussed at the Congress of Vienna, and the Treaty of Vienna contained no provisions upon the subject of maritime capture, or contraband of war. They never received such general sanction as to entitle them to be accepted as rules of International Law. On the other hand, they were objected to from the first, and so seriously as to lead to the formation of alliances to resist their application. They are no longer seriously maintained as rules of international obligation; and it may safely be said that no modern state would permit the property of its subjects to be confiscated by the operation of rules the justice of which it did not recognize, or by the exercise of rights which were not sanctioned by International Law.

References.—For further information upon this subject the student is referred to Vattel, book iii., chap. vii., §§ 112, 113; Azuni, vol. ii., chap. ii., pp. 144–157; Hall, part iv., chaps. v., vi.; Wheaton, Boyd's edition, §§ 476–508; Halleck, chap. xxvi.; Manning, book v., chaps. vii., viii.; Phillimore, vol. iii., pp. 387–472; Wildman, vol. ii., pp. 210–245; Dahlgren, pp. 65–100; Woolsey, §§ 193–199; Nys, "La Guerre Maritime," chap. iii.; Glass, "Marine International Law," pp. 464–508; G. F. De Martens, vol. ii., §§ 314–319; Wheaton, "History of the Law of Nations," pp. 115, 134, and 313–401; Klüber, §§ 288–292; Heffter, pp. 296, 304; and Hautefeuille, vol. ii., pp. 69–189. See also the notes to the article "Contraband," in Dana's and Lawrence's editions of Wheaton.

CHAPTER XIII.

BLOCKADE.

1. The most effective restraint which the law of nations permits a belligerent to impose upon neutral commerce, is that involved in the exercise of the right of blockade. The rules of maritime capture permit him to seize upon the high seas certain contraband articles, which are destined to the enemy's use, or are calculated to aid that enemy in his military operations. But non-contraband articles are exempt from seizure, even though they have a belligerent destination, and the ship incurs no liability whatever. By the establishment of a blockade, however, he may not only prevent the introduction of contraband articles, but may absolutely prohibit access to his enemy's coast, and so, for the time, interrupt all commercial intercourse with the outside world.

Definition of a Blockade.—The interruption or suspension of neutral commerce which results from the forcible closing of a belligerent's ports or harbors is called a *blockade*.

What Places may be Blockaded.—A belligerent, in the exercise of this right, may choose any port or harbor of his enemy, any portion of his coast line, or any entrance to a river, gulf, or bay, situated entirely within the territorial limits of a hostile state. He may not, however, by the establishment of a blockade, deny access to a river, or other navigable water boundary, between the territory of his enemy and that of a neutral. He may prevent access to the blockaded coast by means of ships of war or by batteries on land, or, if the circumstances be favorable, both measures may be resorted to. He may, by an investment, blockade a fortified place on land; as an incident of siege operations, or with a view to its reduction by cutting off its supplies of food or water. The right of a belligerent to blockade an enemy's port arises from his right to besiege it. The *right* is the same in both cases; the two operations differ in purpose only; in the one case the reduction of the place is the object aimed at; in the other the interruption of commercial intercourse.

What is a Valid Blockade?—At one time considerable doubt existed as to the manner in which an enemy's ports should be closed, in order to constitute a blockade which should be valid at International Law. This was set at rest by the fourth article of the Declaration of Paris, which provides that "a blockade, to be binding, must be effective." To this declaration nearly all the civilized states of the world were signatory parties, and, as the United States has always maintained the principle announced in the declaration, that rule may now be accepted as the existing rule of International Law upon the subject.

How Established and Notified.—As an attempt to enter a blockaded port is a flagrant violation of International Law, involving both ship and cargo in the severest penalties, it is important that official information of its existence should be conveyed to neutrals, in order that they may know when intercourse with the place becomes illegal, and their liability to capture begins. This is important because none but effective blockades are recognized as lawful, and, until a *de facto* blockade is established, neutrals are under no obligation to relinquish their commercial intercourse with an enemy's port. In other words, a neutral vessel incurs no penalty by entering a port which is not actually blockaded by the ships or batteries of a belligerent. This notification is given [1]—

(*a.*) *By proclamation*, announcing the date upon which a blockade will be established at a particular port. If a force, adequate to the maintenance of the blockade, be not stationed opposite the blockaded port on the date mentioned in the proclamation, a neutral vessel incurs no penalty by entering or leaving the port. This is the practice of England and the United States.

(*b.*) *By Notification, or Endorsement.*— This is, in substance, a warning given to neutral ships which are about to enter a blockaded port. The notification is given by ships of the blockading squadron, and is, or should be, endorsed on the ship's papers of the vessel notified, or warned away. An attempt to enter after such notification constitutes a breach of blockade, and renders the vessel liable to seizure and condemnation.

(*c.*) *By Proclamation and Notification.*—This is a combination of the preceding methods. A proclamation is first issued, fixing the date upon which the blockade will be established. A neutral vessel approaching the port after that date is warned off by the blockading squadron, and is only regarded as liable to capture if, after such warning, an attempt be made to enter. This rule is advocated by France, and was outlined by

---

[1] Dahlgren, "International Law," pp. 26, 61.

the President of the United States, in his proclamation of April 19, 1861. The prize courts of the United States have ruled that the second notification is not legally necessary.

It is thus seen that a mere notification, by proclamation or otherwise, not accompanied by the presence of a squadron, or by the establishment of batteries at the blockaded port, does not constitute a valid blockade at International Law. On the other hand, if a *de facto* blockade be established by a belligerent at an enemy's port, it must be respected by neutrals as having the sanction of International Law. Neutral vessels attempting to enter, or desiring, in good faith, to ascertain whether such a blockade exists, are entitled to a notification or warning. An attempt to enter by night, or by the use of force or deception; or a refusal to stop, or to observe the signals and warning guns of the blockading squadron, renders the vessel liable to capture; the presumption being that a breach of blockade is intended. By far the greater number of attempts to break blockade are made in this way.[1]

The presence of a blockading squadron makes either ingress or egress unlawful. Vessels in port at the date when the blockade begins are permitted to leave, with whatever cargo they may have on board at that time. In strictness, they may not complete their lading, after the blockade has been formally established, and they have been held liable to capture for so doing. As the object of a simple blockade is the interruption of *commercial* intercourse only, the public armed vessels of neutral powers are usually permitted to enter and leave

---

[1] Dahlgren, p. 51

a blockaded port. Their visit is for a public purpose; they do not carry in or bring out merchandise, and so cannot interfere with the purpose for which the blockade was established. Moreover, a refusal to permit them to enter may inflict unnecessary hardship upon a neutral government, or its subjects, without, in any way, contributing to the purpose for which the war was undertaken.[1]

2. *Penalty for Breach of Blockade.*—The penalty for breach of blockade consists in the forfeiture of the ship and cargo. As the offence consists in carrying on commercial intercourse with a blockaded port, the forfeiture includes everything which is engaged in the illegal venture. "If their owners are different, the vessel may be condemned irrespectively of the latter, which is not confiscated when the person to whom it belongs is ignorant at the time of shipment that the port of destination is blockaded, or if the master of the vessel deviates to a blockaded harbor. If, however, such deviation takes place to a port the blockade of which was known before the ship sailed, the act is supposed to be in the service of the cargo, and the complicity of the owner is assumed."[2]

Cases of Innocent Entrance to Blockaded Ports.— Hall mentions a few instances in which merchant vessels may pass into, or out of, a blockaded port without breach of blockade.

(*a.*) When a maritime blockade does not form part

---

[1] Hall, "International Law," p. 627; the Adonis, Robertson, "Admiralty Reports," vol. v., p. 258; the Mariana Flora, Wheaton, vol. vii., p. 59; the Alexander, Robertson, "Admiralty Reports," vol. iv., p. 93.

[2] Dahlgren, pp. 54–61; Hall, p. 628.

of a combined operation by sea and land, internal means of transport by canals, which enable a ship to gain the open sea at a point which is not blockaded, may be legitimately used. The blockade is limited in its effect by its own physical imperfection. Thus, during a blockade of Holland, a vessel and cargo sent to Embden, which was in neutral territory, and issuing from that port, was not condemned.[1]

(b.) If a vessel is driven into a blockaded port by such distress of weather, or want of provisions, or water, as to render entrance an unavoidable necessity, she may issue again, provided her cargo remains intact.[2] And a ship which has been allowed by a blockading force to enter, within its sight, is justified in assuming a like permission to come out; but the privilege is not extended to cargo taken on board in the blockaded port.[3]

Duration of the Penalty.—The penalty begins when a vessel clears from a neutral port with a hostile destination against which a blockade has been regularly established, and of the existence of which the neutral has, or is presumed to have, sufficient knowledge. An official proclamation of a blockade, made by a belligerent and communicated to neutral powers, would constitute such a presumption of knowledge. If, on the other hand, the blockade existed without proclamation, the presumption would be in favor of the neutral vessel, and it would be entitled to a warning in approaching the blockaded port.[4]

---

[1] The Stert, Robertson, "Admiralty Reports," vol. iv., p. 65.
[2] The Hurtige, Hane, *ibid.*, vol. iii., p. 326.
[3] *Ibid.*, vol. iii., p. 160; Hall, "International Law," p. 628.
[4] Dahlgren, pp. 43–54.

The former rule was that, if the distance between the ports of origin and destination was so great as to require a considerable time in the prosecution of the voyage, a neutral was entitled to the presumption that the blockade had been raised during the continuance of his voyage, and so was entitled to a warning if the blockade existed at the time of his arrival at the port of destination. The introduction of steam and the telegraph, however, have made it practically impossible for such a state of affairs to exist at the present time. Indeed, as blockade running is now carried on in swift steamers, specially constructed for the purpose, no defence is usually attempted in the case of a vessel captured in the act.

Breach of Blockade by Egress.—When the offence is one of egress the penalty continues until the vessel reaches the territorial waters of a neutral state. The liability to capture also ceases when the blockade is raised during the return voyage, since the offence exists only so long as the blockade exists.[1]

3. *Termination of Blockade.* — A blockade ceases when it is discontinued by the belligerent who establishes it, or is raised by an exercise of force on the part of the belligerent against whom it is declared. In the latter case the right of intercourse with the port is revived in favor of neutrals, and continues to exist until the blockade is formally and effectively re-established.

If the vessels of a blockading squadron are dispersed by a storm, the binding character of the blockade undergoes no change. The vessels of the squad-

---

[1] Dahlgren, p. 54.

ron return to their stations, the blockade is resumed without notice, and neutral vessels approach at their peril.

4. *Pacific Blockade.*—The right to establish what is called a *pacific blockade* has been asserted, on several occasions, since the beginning of this century. It has never been regarded as a war measure; nor does it resemble, except in name, the belligerent right of blockade which is sanctioned by International Law. Pacific blockades have always been made the subject of protest by neutrals, as unduly interfering with neutral trade. That such an operation is not a war measure, is shown by the action of prize courts in "refusing to condemn as prize because war did not exist."[1] It must, therefore, be regarded as a measure falling short of war, and must be justified, in any particular case, by the injury suffered by the state which resorts to it as a measure of obtaining redress. The first instance of such a blockade was that declared by England, Russia, and France against the Greek ports of Turkey, in 1827. Others were declared by England and France against the Argentine Republic, in 1838, and by France against Mexico, in 1837. The former of these was maintained for ten years, the latter for less than two, terminating with the capture of the Castle of San Juan de Ulloa, in 1838.

References.—For a discussion of this subject, see Hall, chap. viii.; Boyd's Wheaton, §§ 509–523; Halleck, vol. ii., chap. xxv.; Manning, bk. v., chap. ix.; Wildman, vol. ii., pp. 178–210; Dahlgren, pp. 25–65 and 129–142; Woolsey, §§ 202–207; Nys, "La Guerre Maritime," chap. iv.; Glass, "Marine International Law,"

---

[1] Dahlgren, "International Law," p. 27.

pp. 423-462; G. F. De Martens, vol. ii., § 320; Klüber, §§ 297, 298; Heffter, pp. 289-294; Hautefeuille, "Droits des Nations Neutres," vol. ii., pp. 189-272; Ortolan, "Diplomatie de la Mer," and Wheaton's "History," etc., pp. 137-144. See, also, the valuable notes on this subject, under the article "Blockade," in Dana's and Lawrence's editions of Wheaton.

CHAPTER XIV.
THE RIGHT OF SEARCH.

1. THE belligerent rights which have already been discussed—of capturing enemy property at sea, of seizing contraband of war, and of blockading the coasts and harbors of an enemy—could none of them be made effective were not belligerents also accorded the right to stop and search all neutral merchant vessels on the high seas, for the purpose of ascertaining their nationality and destination, the character and ownership of their cargoes, and to effect their capture, should the result of such examination show a liability to capture to exist.

2. *Definition of the Right; when and where Exercised.*—The right to stop and examine neutral vessels on the high seas is called the *belligerent right of search.* It comes into existence at the outbreak of war, and is terminated by the treaty of peace. Neutral merchant vessels, of whatsoever character, are at all times subject to its exercise, and must submit to search when required to do so by a properly documented armed vessel of either belligerent. If they refuse, or resist, they are subject to seizure and condemnation. If the right be exercised by a belligerent in a manner not warranted by the law of nations, or in violation of the terms of a treaty, the remedy must be sought through the neutral government under whose flag the ship sails.

As to place, the right of search may be exercised wherever a capture may lawfully be made, *i. e.*, on the high seas, or within the territorial waters of either belligerent, but never in neutral waters.

Manner in which the Right is Exercised.—The manner in which the right of search is to be exercised is determined by the usage of nations, except in those cases in which it has been made the subject of treaty stipulation. Many such treaties are in existence, and they specify, in considerable detail, the manner in which the search shall be conducted by war ships carrying the flags of the signatory powers. The duty of submitting is only incumbent upon neutral merchant vessels. Public armed vessels are not subject to visitation, either in time of peace or war, and the merchant vessels of a belligerent are justified in resorting to any measures, either of flight, resistance, or deception, which are calculated to enable them to escape search and inevitable capture. The right may be exercised by the regularly commissioned ships of war of a belligerent, or by duly authorized privateers in the service of those states which still retain the right to use that species of naval force in time of war.

Under ordinary circumstances, a man-of-war, in executing the right of search, hoists its national color, and fires an unshotted gun, as a signal to heave to. This is called the *coup d'assurance*, or affirming gun; and it is the duty of the neutral ship, on receiving this signal, to heave to at once, and hoist her proper national flag. Should the signal not be obeyed, and should the failure to obey indicate an intention to resist search, the belligerent cruiser is justified in resorting to such measures of force as will compel obedience to its summons. An attempt at flight, unaccompanied by resistance, has been held not to involve the ship making it in the penalty for resisting search.

The distance at which the searching vessel shall remain is determined by the judgment of her commanding officer, based upon the circumstances of wind and tide, upon the character of the vessel to be searched, and the necessity of remaining within easy supporting distance of the boat's crew by whom the search is carried on. The distance at which a man-of-war shall remain, when not regulated by treaty, is now a matter of but little importance. It was not so, however, in former times, when the right of search was executed by privateers, whose methods of search and capture were not above suspicion, and when piracy was a crime of much more frequent occurrence than at present.[1]

Duty of Boarding Party.—An officer is sent on board to conduct the search. He is accompanied by a boat's crew, and by one or two persons to assist him in the performance of his duty. The purpose of the search may be—

(*a*.) To ascertain from the ship's papers the nationality and destination of the vessel.

(*b*.) To ascertain from the same source the character and destination of the cargo.

(*c*.) When the papers do not contain satisfactory information as to the character and destination of the ship and cargo, to ascertain those facts by actual inspection.[2]

---

[1] The limitation as to the strength of the search party can be traced to a similar origin, and, like the former, is now less strongly insisted upon than formerly.

[2] Dahlgren, "International Law," p. 100.

If the ship's papers are in regular form, and show a *bona fide* neutral origin and destination of ship and cargo, the fact of the search having been made is noted upon them by endorsement, the search party retires, and the vessel is allowed to proceed on its voyage.

If the papers indicate a hostile destination, the manifests, invoices, and bills of lading are examined, to ascertain whether there are contraband articles on board. If such be found, or if the vessel be destined to a blockaded port, the ship is declared a prize, her papers are sealed, and she is sent into port under a prize master for adjudication. A similar course is pursued, if there is sufficient ground for believing that her papers are false; if any of them are concealed, or have been destroyed, with a view to evade examination, or if spoliation has been practised.

A practice has obtained to some extent of releasing a neutral ship, and allowing it to continue its voyage on condition that the contraband part of the cargo be surrendered. This method of procedure is irregular, without warrant of law, and is likely to lead to serious complications. The captor, by assuming some of its functions, greatly embarrasses the proper prize court in its action upon the captured property. The ship's papers, which, in most cases, constitute all the evidence upon which the court bases its decree, remain with the neutral vessel, and the court is obliged to proceed in the case without sufficient information. The master, under his general authority as such, cannot effect a legal surrender of a portion of his cargo in such a way as to bind the owners. His action, therefore, in a doubtful case, leaves to the owners the right of demanding, through their government, the restoration of the surrendered cargo. For these reasons the practice should not be resorted to unless authorized by treaty, or unless the owner, either personally or by his duly authorized representative, gives a legal consent to the proposed surrender.

3. *The Right of Visitation.*—The belligerent right of search has never been seriously questioned, and is accepted by all nations as a fact inseparably connected with the existence of war. A right somewhat resembling it, called the *right of visitation*, has been asserted to exist in time of peace, but has never received universal sanction, and is now generally abandoned, save in a few cases, where it maintains a lingering existence by treaty. In the long controversy which was carried on as to the assumed legality of this right, during the early part of the present century, England and the United States were the principal contestants.

It was maintained, on the part of the British government, that the rights of search and visitation were entirely distinct from each other, having a different origin and purpose. The *right of search* was peculiar to a state of war. The *right of visitation* existed in peace, and consisted in such an examination of merchant vessels, on the high seas, as was necessary to determine their nationality, the sufficiency and regularity of their papers, and the legality of the undertaking in which they were engaged.

On the part of the United States, it was contested that the right of search was an incident of belligerency; that it existed only during the continuance of war, and not only did not exist in time of peace, but an attempt to exercise it was an invasion of sovereignty which, if not disclaimed, would constitute a just cause for war.

The controversy was brought to an end, in 1858, by a formal renunciation, on the part of the British government, of the right of visitation in time of peace, except in cases where it was authorized by treaty stipulations. Of the justice and expediency of this abandonment there can be little question. The crimes of piracy and the slave-trade, the prevalence of which furnished the only reason for its existence, have practically disappeared. Its continued exercise, therefore, is unnecessary, giving rise to constant complaint and frequent international misunderstanding; nor can any good purpose be accomplished by it which could not be attained by the use of other and less questionable means. It lies within the power of every maritime state to establish and maintain such constant police supervision over its merchant marine as will prevent its register from being improperly used, and its flag from covering transactions which are not authorized by its municipal laws, or sanctioned by the law of nations.[1]

Impressment of Seamen.—During the naval wars succeeding the French Revolution the British government, in exercising the right of search, made a practice of extracting certain persons from neutral vessels, claiming that they were British subjects, and so liable to impressment into its naval service.[2] The exercise of this right, which never received the sanction of

---

[1] Halleck, vol. ii., pp. 268-283.

[2] The practice of impressing seamen was not restricted to American merchant vessels alone, but was exercised on public vessels as well. In 1798 the British war ship Carnatic, seventy-four guns, boarded an American war vessel off Havana. See, also, the case of the President, Halleck, vol. ii., p. 303, note; Brenton, "Naval History of Great Britain," pp. 200-203.

International Law, bore with peculiar hardship upon vessels sailing under the American flag; and manned largely by persons of the same race, and speaking the same language, as those by whom the search was conducted, and upon whose decision, in the matter of nationality, the question of seizure largely depended. On the part of Great Britain, it was alleged that an important naval war was being carried on,[1] of the justice of which there could be no question, and whose ultimate success involved the maintenance of enormous armaments at sea. To maintain its position, the British government had been obliged to impose heavy burdens upon the property and personal services of its subjects,[2] many of whom had attempted to evade their obligation by taking service in the merchant marine of neutral powers. The continued exercise of this right, in the face of repeated protests, led to the war of 1812, between England and the United States; which was terminated, however, without a definite settlement of this important question. The controversy was revived at a later period, and was exhaustively discussed by representatives of both governments in a long and ably conducted diplomatic correspondence. It was terminated, so far as the American government was concerned, by an announcement of policy contained in a letter of Mr. Webster to Lord Ashburton, bearing date of August 8, 1842. "The American government,"

---

[1] It has been estimated that at one time over seventy thousand British subjects were employed in the naval and merchant services of foreign powers.—Ashton, "Old Times."

[2] Article 45 of the "British Navy Regulations" of 1787 required commanders of English men-of-war to demand English seamen out of foreign ships wherever met with.—Halleck, vol. ii., p. 302, note.

says Mr. Webster, "is prepared to say that the practice of impressing seamen from American vessels cannot hereafter be allowed to take place. That practice is founded on principles which it does not recognize, and is invariably attended by consequences so unjust, so injurious, and of such formidable magnitude, as cannot be submitted to. In the early disputes between the two governments on this so long contested topic, the distinguished person to whose hands were first committed the seals of this department declared that the simplest rule will be, that the vessel, being American, shall be evidence that the seamen on board are such. Fifty years' experience, the utter failure of many negotiations, and a careful reconsideration, now had, of the whole subject, at a moment when the passions are laid, and no present interest or emergency exists to bias the judgment, have fully convinced this government that this is not only the simplest and best, but the only rule which can be adopted and observed consistently with the rights and honor of the United States and the security of their citizens.[1] That rule announces, therefore, what will hereafter be the principle maintained by their government. *In every regularly documented American merchant vessel the crew who navigate it will find their protection in the flag which floats over them.*"[2]

---

[1] The "United States Navy Regulations" (1876) contains the following provision: "Commanders of public vessels of war are not to suffer their vessels to be searched by any foreign power under any pretext, nor any officers or men to be taken out, so long as they have power of resistance. If force be used, resistance must be continued as long as possible. If overcome, they are to yield their vessel, but not their men without the vessel."—"United States Navy Regulations," ed. 1876, p. 41, par. 54.

[2] Secretary Webster to Lord Ashburton, Aug. 8, 1842; "Webster

4. *The Right of Convoy.*—At a time when the rules of maritime capture were rigidly and, at times, harshly and unjustly enforced, it is not remarkable that neutrals should have sought to mitigate their severity by advocating methods which, while securing to belligerents their existing rights, were also calculated to relieve neutral commerce from some of the burdens to which it was exposed in war. The most important attempt of this kind was that originated by the Baltic powers, toward the close of the last century, which has become known as the right of convoy. It was contended, in behalf of those powers, that the presence of a public armed vessel, with a fleet of neutral merchant ships, was sufficient to exempt them from search upon proper assurance being given, by the commanding officer of the armed vessel, that the ships under his convoy contained neither enemy goods nor contraband of war. In this form the right was first asserted by Sweden, and later by Holland, in the seventeenth century. The latter power, however, upon becoming a belligerent, changed its policy, and refused to recognize a practice for which it had formerly contended as a neutral. Renewed interest was shown in the subject between the years 1780 and 1800, during which period several treaties were entered into, chiefly by the Baltic powers, stipulating for the exemption from search of neutral vessels under neutral convoy.

The introduction of the new rule was vigorously opposed by Great Britain, a power at that time more interested than any other in the maintenance of bel-

---

Diplomatic and Official Papers," p. 101, cited by Halleck, vol. ii., pp. 303, 304.

ligerent rights at sea. The position assumed by that government was, in substance, stated by Sir William Scott, in the case of the Maria, and may be summarized as follows:

(*a.*) The laws of maritime capture give to a belligerent an incontestable right to stop and search, on the high seas, all neutral merchant vessels.

(*b.*) A search, to be lawful, must be exercised directly by the belligerent cruiser, a separate search being made in the case of each neutral vessel encountered.

(*c.*) A neutral government cannot interpose its authority between a belligerent armed vessel and a neutral merchant ship, by giving to one of its public vessels instructions which are calculated to abridge, in any manner, the belligerent right of search.

(*d.*) The resistance of a convoying ship amounts, in effect, to resistance to search on the part of the merchant vessels composing the convoy, and involves them in the penalty of condemnation for such resistance of search.[1]

As England was at that time sufficiently powerful at sea to maintain its view against the opposition of any existing state, the neutral powers regarded the emergency as one of such importance as to seriously threaten the very existence of their commerce. To protect their menaced interests, a treaty was negotiated which created the defensive alliance known as the Armed Neutrality of 1800, the purpose of which was to maintain the principle of convoy as described in the treaty. In 1801, however, Russia, though a party to the Armed Neutrality, entered into an agreement rec-

---

[1] Case of the Maria, Robinson, "Admiralty Reports," p. 340.

ognizing the right of a belligerent to visit neutral merchant vessels sailing under a convoy; and the constantly increasing maritime power of England sufficed to defer indefinitely the general adoption of the principle of convoy as a rule of International Law. Since the beginning of this century, the right has been stipulated for in a number of treaties, to which the Continental states of Europe have been parties. England alone refuses to recognize the right, even as a part of the conventional law of nations, as she has ever denied its existence as a custom based upon general international usage.

The views held as to the right of convoy by the different departments of the United States government have been at considerable variance. The political departments have uniformly recognized its existence, and have endeavored to secure its general acceptance by treaty. The United States Navy Regulations provide in considerable detail for the manner in which the right of convoy shall be exercised by its public armed vessels. If the convoyed vessel is bound to a belligerent port the commander of the convoy is to require proof that there are no contraband articles on board; and without such proof he is not to afford her protection against a belligerent cruiser, unless specially directed to do so. "He is not to permit the vessels under his protection to be searched, or detained, by any belligerent cruiser."[1] The judicial department, on the other hand, has followed the English precedents in denying the existence of the right of convoy as a rule, or principle, of International Law.

---

[1] "Navy Regulations of the United States," 1876, pp. 133, 134.

At the present time it is not believed that any serious objection would be offered, by any modern state, to the general adoption of the principle of convoy as a rule of International Law, under such restrictions as would be calculated to prevent abuse, and accompanied by such conditions as would secure to belligerents a right as effective as that which they now enjoy. That such a rule has not been adopted, or seriously advocated, is doubtless due to the fact that the necessity for its existence has passed away. The introduction of steam navigation involved an immediate and radical reorganization of the carrying trade of the world. The establishment of steamship lines, upon the old routes of commerce, has monopolized a trade which was formerly carried on in sailing vessels, and it is no longer regarded as desirable that even sailing vessels, in time of war, should move in fleets or convoys.

5. *Searches Authorized in Time of Peace.*—The right of search has been shown to be a belligerent right, and so existent only in time of war. In time of peace a right of visitation or search is recognized in the following cases:

(*a.*) *Search to Execute Revenue Laws.*—Merchant vessels coming into the jurisdiction of a state are subject to such inspection, and their cargoes to such examination and search, as are warranted by the municipal laws of that state, or are necessary to the enforcement of its sanitary and customs regulations. A vessel which attempts to evade such inspection, at any time during its sojourn, may be detained, and subjected to such penalties as are authorized by the laws of the offended state. It is questionable whether the right exists of pursuing such vessels upon the high seas, and of effecting their capture beyond the jurisdictional waters of the captor's state.[1] If such right exists at all, it is based upon international comity, and, in any particular case, its exercise must be justified by the emergency existing, in which event the government to which the offending vessel belongs may, and usually does, waive its strict rights in the premises, and declines to protect its subjects in wrong-doing.[2]

(*b.*) *Search on Suspicion of Piracy.*—Public armed vessels of any state are justified, when reasonable grounds of suspicion exist, in stopping vessels on the high seas which are believed to be engaged in piratical undertakings. If the search be made in good faith, and upon grounds warranting a suspicion of piracy, no claim for damage can be established, even in cases where the character of the ship visited proves to be legitimate.

(*c.*) *Search of Merchant Ships by War Vessels of the same State.*—The public armed vessels of a state may execute such visits of search and inspection, upon merchant vessels of the same nationality, as are authorized by the laws of the state under whose flag they sail. This is a question of municipal law pure and simple, and the search authorized may be as frequent or infrequent, as lax or as vigorous, as is deemed best by the government to which both vessels belong.

(*d.*) *Right of Approach to Verify Nationality.*— Public armed vessels, of whatever nationality, are also authorized to approach merchant vessels on the

---

[1] See opinion of Lord Stowell in the case of the Louis, Dodson, "Admiralty Reports," p. 246. See, also, the opinion of Sir Travers Twiss, in the case of the Cagliari, Boyd's Wheaton, p. 169.

[2] Lawrence's Wheaton, pp. 267-275.

high seas for the purpose of ascertaining their nationality. In the performance of this duty, except where suspicion of piracy exists, they are limited to hailing and the use of flags and signals. They board such vessels at their peril.

Case of the Virginius.—The question of search in peace is illustrated by the case of the Virginius. The Virginius was a steamer which had been specially constructed, in England, with a view to her employment as a blockade runner. While engaged in this service she was captured by one of the United States blockading squadrons, and was condemned and sold for violation of blockade. She afterward came into possession of the United States, in satisfaction of a debt, and on August 2, 1870, was sold, ostensibly to one Patterson, a resident of New York. At this sale a formal certificate of registry was issued, giving her the character of a merchant vessel of the United States. From this time, until 1873, she was engaged in various undertakings, some of which were of so questionable a character as to have involved the forfeiture of her register, had they been made known to the proper authority. No complaint appears to have been made to the government of the United States as to her character, or employment, during the period in question.

On October 30, 1873, she sailed from Jamaica for Port Limon, in Costa Rica, carrying the American flag, and provided with regular clearance papers from the American consul, at Kingston, Jamaica. On October 31, while on the high seas, about twenty miles distant from the island of Cuba, she was sighted and chased by the Spanish war steamer Tornado. After a pursuit of about eight hours she was captured, on the high seas, at a point about sixty miles distant from the coast of Cuba, and twenty-three miles from the island of Jamaica, in which direction she was steaming at the time. She was boarded by an officer of the Tornado, her officers, crew, and passengers were made prisoners, and she was sent under a prize crew to the Spanish port of Santiago de Cuba, where she arrived on the evening of November 1.

At nine o'clock on the morning of the following day a court-martial was convened for the trial of the captured persons, who were arraigned on a charge of piracy. The court-martial completed its labors at four o'clock in the afternoon of the same day. On the morning of November 4 four persons were executed, on the 7th twelve, on the 13th thirty-seven more, including a number of British subjects and citizens of the United States.

The attention of the Spanish government was immediately drawn to the occurrence, and protests against the action of its subordinate officials were made by the American consuls at Havana and Santiago de Cuba, but with so little effect that, on November 14, the United States minister to Spain was instructed to demand the restoration of the steamer, the return and delivery to the United States of the persons who had been captured, and the punishment of the officials who had been concerned in the capture of the vessel and the execution of her crew. He was also instructed to demand that the flag of the United States should be saluted in the harbor of Santiago de Cuba. After some correspondence between the two governments an agreement was entered into on November 29, between the Secretary of State and the Spanish minister in Washington, stipulating for the restoration of the vessel and the surrender of the survivors of the passengers and crew. It was also agreed that the flag of the United States should be saluted on the 25th day of December next ensuing. If, however, on or before that date, the Spanish government should prove that the Virginius was not entitled to her American register, the salute was to be spontaneously dispensed with; the United States agreeing to institute legal proceedings against the vessel, if it should be found that she had violated any law of the United States, and against any person who was shown to have been concerned in such violation.

The ship and survivors were surrendered at Santiago de Cuba on December 18, 1873; and, it having been made to appear, to the satisfaction of the United States, that the Virginius was not entitled to carry its flag and papers, the Spanish minister was formally notified that the salute would be dispensed with.

The following conclusions seem to be warranted by the facts in the case:

(*a*.) The Virginius was not a pirate, whatever may have been the character of the transaction in which she was engaged, and the Spanish authorities acted without warrant of International Law in proceeding against the crew and passengers for the crime of piracy.

(*b*.) The Spanish government would have been justified in resisting any acts of war or hostility directed against itself, and occurring within its territorial waters. It matters not with whom such acts or attempts originated, or by whom they were committed, whether subjects or aliens. Had the Virginius, therefore, been found in Spanish jurisdiction, engaged in landing, or attempting to land, her passengers upon the coast of Cuba, her forcible seizure would have been justified. Had resistance been offered, that resistance could have been overcome by force at any cost of life or property. The treatment of those on board would then have been determined, according to the nature and degree of their offences, by the municipal laws of Spain. If the provisions of that system of law had been affected or modified by treaty stipulations, guaranteeing to the citizens or subjects of foreign states certain rights and privileges in the event of their being charged with crime while in Spanish jurisdiction, the government of Spain would have been responsible for the observance of the treaty in all cases to which its provisions applied.

(c.) The pursuit and capture of the vessel on the high seas was an act of very doubtful validity, and could only have been justified, in any event, by the extreme urgency of the case, and then only in the exercise of the right of self-defence. In this instance it is extremely doubtful whether such an emergency existed as to justify a resort to force in self-defence. The Virginius was flying the American flag when sighted, and had not then entered Spanish waters; until she did so enter them she was not subject to visitation and search, still less to pursuit and capture.

(d.) The later conduct of the Spanish authorities in Cuba can only be characterized as unnecessary, not warranted by the emergency, and cruel and inhuman in the extreme. It was also contrary to the stipulations of treaties, and was grossly illegal even when judged by the standard of the municipal law of Spain. The Virginius was an unarmed merchant vessel. She offered, and was capable of offering, no resistance to search or capture. Her passengers, at the instant of capture, were not armed or organized, and so were incapable of levying war against the authority of Spain, whatever may have been their ultimate intention. So soon as the passengers and crew were made prisoners they were absolutely powerless to do harm, and the fact that the ship sailed under the American flag should have suggested such reasonable delay in the proceedings against them as would have sufficed to enable proper representations to be made to that government as to the service in which its flag and papers were being used.

(*e.*) The action of the Spanish authorities in this matter would not have been justified or recognized as lawful, had it been performed by a belligerent in time of war. Had a state of open war existed, and had the Virginius been captured at sea with enemy goods or contraband articles on board, the ship would not have been involved in the forfeiture, and her passengers and crew could not have been subjected to detention. Had she been captured in the act of violating a legal blockade, the ship and cargo alone would have been liable to forfeiture. Had she been engaged in carrying military persons to a hostile destination her contraband passengers only could have been made prisoners of war. The crew could have incurred no penal consequences for their share in the transaction.

References.—The student, for fuller discussion of this subject, is referred to Vattel, bk. iii., chap. vii., §§ 114–116; Halleck, vol. ii., chap. xxvii., with the references there given to the "American State Papers;" Boyd's Wheaton, pp. 169–173 and 607–622; Manning, bk. v., chap. xi.; Phillimore, vol. iii., pp. 522–558; Dahlgren, pp. 100–110; Woolsey, §§ 208–221; Glass, "Marine International

Law," pp. 509–552; Dana's Wheaton and Lawrence's Wheaton, with their references to the correspondence between the British and American governments upon the question of impressment and the rights of visitation and search; G. F. De Martens, vol. ii., § 321; Heffter, pp. 318–328; Wheaton, "History of the Law of Nations," pp. 145–151, 392–449, 599–713; Hautefeuille, vol. iii., pp. 1–208.

APPENDIX A.

PROFESSOR FRANCIS LIEBER'S INSTRUCTIONS FOR THE GOVERNMENT OF ARMIES OF THE UNITED STATES IN THE FIELD.

THE need of a positive code of instructions was severely felt during the early part of the Civil War in the United States. During the first two years of that war the Federal government had succeeded in placing in the field armies of unexampled size, composed, in great part, of men taken from civil pursuits; most of whom were unfamiliar with military affairs, and so utterly unacquainted with the usages of war. These armies were carrying on hostile operations, of every kind, over a wide area, and questions of considerable intricacy and difficulty were constantly arising, which required for their decision a knowledge of International Law which was not always possessed by those to whom these questions were submitted for decision. Conflicting decisions and rulings were of frequent occurrence, in different armies, and, at times, in different parts of the same field of operations; and great harm not infrequently resulted before these decisions could be reversed by competent authority.

To remedy this difficulty Professor Francis Lieber, an eminent jurist, who had been for many years an esteemed and honored citizen of the United States, was requested by the Secretary of War to prepare a code of instructions for the government of the armies in the field. This code, while conforming to the existing usages of war on land, was to contain such modifications as were necessary to adapt those usages to the peculiar circumstances of the contest then prevailing. The rules prepared by Dr. Lieber were submitted to a board of officers, by whom they were approved and recommended for adoption. They were published in 1863, and were made obligatory upon the armies of the United States by their publication in the form of a General Order of the War Department.

Although prepared nearly a quarter of a century ago, they are still in substantial accordance with the existing rules of International Law upon the subject of which they treat; and form the basis of Bluntschli's and other elaborate works upon the usages of war. They are accepted by text writers of authority as having standard and permanent value, and as expressing, with great accuracy, the usage and practice of nations in war.

There has been some misunderstanding, however, as to the force and significance of Professor Lieber's rules, to which it is proper to allude.

The war which existed at that time was strictly *internal* in character; and, although the belligerency of the states in rebellion had been recognized by the Federal government, the character of the contest, in many of its aspects, differed materially from an *external* war, in which the belligerent parties were independent states.

The war policy of the United States toward the insurrectionary forces was, in the main, in accordance with the laws of war, as those laws were then accepted and understood. Its enemies, however, were its own citizens, who, for the time, denied its sovereign authority, and refused obedience to its laws. Its right to suppress the rebellion, and its right to choose its method of doing so, were alike beyond dispute. In the exercise of this right it was at perfect liberty to choose any policy between the methods provided by its municipal laws, on the one hand, and those provided by the law of nations on the other.

As a matter of fact it chose a war policy lying between

the extremes above indicated. General operations in the field were carried on in accordance with the laws of war. In its treatment of the property of individuals in rebellion, in its view of occupation, and of occupied territory, and in its policy toward the residents of such occupied territory, it pursued a course which it deemed best suited to the task upon which it was then engaged—the suppression of a rebellion against its authority.

The rules, therefore, cannot fairly be said to contain a full expression of the views or future policy of that government upon the subject of external war. Should such a war occur, it is at least extremely probable that the United States would range itself with those powers, whose practice it is to maintain small permanent establishments, and whose policy is defensive rather than offensive.

(*General Orders No.* 100, *Adjutant General's Office*, 1863.)

INSTRUCTIONS FOR THE GOVERNMENT OF ARMIES OF THE UNITED STATES IN THE FIELD.

PREPARED BY FRANCIS LIEBER, LL.D., AND REVISED BY A BOARD OF OFFICERS OF THE UNITED STATES ARMY.

SECTION I.

MARTIAL LAW.—MILITARY JURISDICTION.—MILITARY NECESSITY.—RETALIATION.

1. A place, district, or country occupied by an enemy stands, in consequence of the occupation, under the Martial Law of the invading or occupying army, whether any proclamation declaring Martial Law, or any public warning to the inhabitants, has been issued or not. Martial

Law is the immediate and direct effect and consequence of occupation or conquest.

The presence of a hostile army proclaims its Martial Law.

2. Martial Law does not cease during the hostile occupation, except by special proclamation, ordered by the commander-in-chief, or by special mention in the treaty of peace concluding the war, when the occupation of a place or territory continues beyond the conclusion of peace as one of the conditions of the same.

3. Martial Law in a hostile country consists in the suspension, by the occupying military authority, of the criminal and civil law, and of the domestic administration and government in the occupied place or territory, and in the substitution of military rule and force for the same, as well as in the dictation of general laws, as far as military necessity requires this suspension, substitution, or dictation.

The commander of the forces may proclaim that the administration of all civil and penal law shall continue, either wholly or in part, as in times of peace, unless otherwise ordered by the military authority.

4. Martial Law is simply military authority exercised in accordance with the laws and usages of war. Military oppression is not Martial Law; it is the abuse of the power which that law confers. As Martial Law is executed by military force, it is incumbent upon those who administer it to be strictly guided by the principles of justice, honor, and humanity—virtues adorning a soldier even more than other men, for the very reason that he possesses the power of his arms against the unarmed.

5. Martial Law should be less stringent in places and countries fully occupied and fairly conquered. Much greater severity may be exercised in places or regions where actual hostilities exist, or are expected and must be prepared for. Its most complete sway is allowed—

even in the commander's own country—when face to face with the enemy, because of the absolute necessities of the case, and of the paramount duty to defend the country against invasion.

To save the country is paramount to all other considerations.

6. All civil and penal law shall continue to take its usual course in the enemy's places and territories under Martial Law, unless interrupted or stopped by order of the occupying military power; but all the functions of the hostile government — legislative, executive, or administrative — whether of a general, provincial, or local character, cease under Martial Law, or continue only with the sanction, or, if deemed necessary, the participation of the occupier or invader.

7. Martial Law extends to property, and to persons, whether they are subjects of the enemy or aliens to that government.

8. Consuls, among American and European nations, are not diplomatic agents. Nevertheless, their offices and persons will be subjected to Martial Law in cases of urgent necessity only; their property and business are not exempted. Any delinquency they commit against the established military rule may be punished as in the case of any other inhabitant, and such punishment furnishes no reasonable ground for international complaint.

9. The functions of ambassadors, ministers, or other diplomatic agents, accredited by neutral powers to the hostile government, cease, so far as regards the displaced government; but the conquering or occupying power usually recognizes them as temporarily accredited to itself.

10. Martial Law affects chiefly the police and collection of public revenue and taxes, whether imposed by the expelled government or by the invader, and refers mainly

to the support and efficiency of the army, its safety, and the safety of its operations.

11. The law of war does not only disclaim all cruelty and bad faith concerning engagements concluded with the enemy during the war, but also the breaking of stipulations solemnly contracted by the belligerents in time of peace, and avowedly intended to remain in force in case of war between the contracting powers.

It disclaims all extortions and other transactions for individual gain; all acts of private revenge, or connivance at such acts.

Offences to the contrary shall be severely punished, and especially so if committed by officers.

12. Whenever feasible, Martial Law is carried out in cases of individual offenders by military courts; but sentences of death shall be executed only with the approval of the chief executive, provided the urgency of the case does not require a speedier execution, and then only with the approval of the chief commander.

13. Military jurisdiction is of two kinds: first, that which is conferred and defined by statute; second, that which is derived from the common law of war. Military offences under the statute law must be tried in the manner therein directed; but military offences which do not come within the statute must be tried and punished under the common law of war. The character of the courts which exercise these jurisdictions depends upon the local laws of each particular country.

In the armies of the United States the first is exercised by courts-martial; while cases which do not come within the "Rules and Articles of War," or the jurisdiction conferred by statute on courts-martial, are tried by military commissions.

14. Military necessity, as understood by modern civilized nations, consists in the necessity of those measures

which are indispensable for securing the ends of the war, and which are lawful according to the modern law and usages of war.

15. Military necessity admits of all direct destruction of life or limb of *armed* enemies, and of other persons whose destruction is incidentally *unavoidable* in the armed contests of the war; it allows of the capturing of every armed enemy, and every enemy of importance to the hostile government, or of peculiar danger to the captor; it allows of all destruction of property, and obstruction of the ways and channels of traffic, travel, or communication, and of all withholding of sustenance or means of life from the enemy; of the appropriation of whatever an enemy's country affords necessary for the subsistence and safety of the army, and of such deception as does not involve the breaking of good faith either positively pledged, regarding agreements entered into during the war, or supposed by the modern law of war to exist. Men who take up arms against one another in public war do not cease on this account to be moral beings, responsible to one another, and to God.

16. Military necessity does not admit of cruelty; that is, the infliction of suffering for the sake of suffering or for revenge, nor of maiming or wounding except in fight, nor of torture to extort confessions. It does not admit of the use of poison in any way, nor of the wanton devastation of a district. It admits of deception, but disclaims acts of perfidy; and, in general, military necessity does not include any act of hostility which makes the return to peace unnecessarily difficult.

17. War is not carried on by arms alone. It is lawful to starve the hostile belligerent, armed or unarmed, so that it leads to the speedier subjection of the enemy.

18. When the commander of a besieged place expels the non-combatants, in order to lessen the number of those

who consume his stock of provisions, it is lawful, though an extreme measure, to drive them back, so as to hasten on the surrender.

19. Commanders, whenever admissible, inform the enemy of their intention to bombard a place, so that the non-combatants, and especially the women and children, may be removed before the bombardment commences. But it is no infraction of the common law of war to omit thus to inform the enemy. Surprise may be a necessity.

20. Public war is a state of armed hostility between sovereign nations or governments. It is a law and requisite of civilized existence that men live in political, continuous societies, forming organized units, called states or nations, whose constituents bear, enjoy, and suffer, advance and retrograde together, in peace and in war.

21. The citizen or native of a hostile country is thus an enemy, as one of the constituents of the hostile state or nation, and as such is subjected to the hardships of the war.

22. Nevertheless, as civilization has advanced during the last centuries, so has likewise steadily advanced, especially in war on land, the distinction between the private individual belonging to a hostile country and the hostile country itself, with its men in arms. The principle has been more and more acknowledged that the unarmed citizen is to be spared in person, property, and honor as much as the exigencies of war will admit.

23. Private citizens are no longer murdered, enslaved, or carried off to distant parts, and the inoffensive individual is as little disturbed in his private relations as the commander of the hostile troops can afford to grant in the overruling demands of a vigorous war.

24. The almost universal rule in remote times was, and continues to be with barbarous armies, that the private individual of the hostile country is destined to suffer every

privation of liberty and protection, and every disruption of family ties. Protection was, and still is with uncivilized people, the exception.

25. In modern regular wars of the Europeans, and their descendants in other portions of the globe, protection of the inoffensive citizen of the hostile country is the rule; privation, and disturbance of private relations, are the exceptions.

26. Commanding generals may cause the magistrates and civil officers of the hostile country to take the oath of temporary allegiance or an oath of fidelity to their own victorious government or rulers, and they may expel every one who declines to do so. But whether they do so or not, the people and their civil officers owe strict obedience to them as long as they hold sway over the district or country, at the peril of their lives.

27. The law of war can no more wholly dispense with retaliation than can the law of nations, of which it is a branch. Yet civilized nations acknowledge retaliation as the sternest feature of war. A reckless enemy often leaves to his opponent no other means of securing himself against the repetition of barbarous outrage.

28. Retaliation will, therefore, never be resorted to as a measure of mere revenge, but only as a means of protective retribution, and, moreover, cautiously and unavoidably; that is to say, retaliation shall only be resorted to after careful inquiry into the real occurrence, and the character of the misdeeds that may demand retribution.

Unjust or inconsiderate retaliation removes the belligerents farther and farther from the mitigating rules of a regular war, and by rapid steps leads them nearer to the internecine wars of savages.

29. Modern times are distinguished from earlier ages by the existence, at one and the same time, of many nations

and great governments related to one another in close intercourse.

Peace is their normal condition; war is the exception. The ultimate object of all modern war is a renewed state of peace.

The more vigorously wars are pursued, the better it is for humanity. Sharp wars are brief.

30. Ever since the formation and co-existence of modern nations, and ever since wars have become great national wars, war has come to be acknowledged not to be its own end, but the means to obtain great ends of state, or to consist in defence against wrong; and no conventional restriction of the modes adopted to injure the enemy is any longer admitted; but the law of war imposes many limitations and restrictions, on principles of justice, faith, and honor.

SECTION II.

PUBLIC AND PRIVATE PROPERTY OF THE ENEMY.—PROTECTION OF PERSONS, AND ESPECIALLY WOMEN; OF RELIGION, THE ARTS AND SCIENCES.—PUNISHMENT OF CRIMES AGAINST THE INHABITANTS OF HOSTILE COUNTRIES.

31. A victorious army appropriates all public money, seizes all public movable property until further direction by its government, and sequesters for its own benefit or that of its government all the revenues of real property belonging to the hostile government or nation. The title to such real property remains in abeyance during military occupation, and until the conquest is made complete.

32. A victorious army, by the martial power inherent in the same, may suspend, change, or abolish, as far as the martial power extends, the relations which arise from the services due, according to the existing laws of the invaded country, from one citizen, subject, or native of the same to another.

The commander of the army must leave it to the ultimate treaty of peace to settle the permanency of this change.

33. It is no longer considered lawful—on the contrary, it is held to be a serious breach of the law of war — to force the subjects of the enemy into the service of the victorious government, except the latter should proclaim, after a fair and complete conquest of the hostile country or district, that it is resolved to keep the country, district, or place permanently as its own, and make it a portion of its own country.

34. As a general rule, the property belonging to churches, to hospitals, or other establishments of an exclusively charitable character, to establishments of education, or foundations for the promotion of knowledge, whether public schools, universities, academies of learning or observatories, museums of the fine arts, or of a scientific character—such property is not to be considered public property in the sense of paragraph 31; but it may be taxed or used when the public service may require it.

35. Classical works of arts, libraries, scientific collections, or precious instruments, such as astronomical telescopes, as well as hospitals, must be secured against all avoidable injury, even when they are contained in fortified places while besieged or bombarded.

36. If such works of art, libraries, collections, or instruments belonging to a hostile nation or government, can be removed without injury, the ruler of the conquering state or nation may order them to be seized and removed for the benefit of the said nation. The ultimate ownership is to be settled by the ensuing treaty of peace.

In no case shall they be sold or given away, if captured by the armies of the United States, nor shall they ever be privately appropriated, or wantonly destroyed or injured.

37. The United States acknowledge and protect, in hos-

tile countries occupied by them, religion and morality; strictly private property; the persons of the inhabitants, especially those of women; and the sacredness of domestic relations. Offences to the contrary shall be rigorously punished.

This rule does not interfere with the right of the victorious invader to tax the people or their property, to levy forced loans, to billet soldiers, or to appropriate property, especially houses, land, boats or ships, and churches, for temporary and military uses.

38. Private property, unless forfeited by crimes or by offences of the owner, can be seized only by way of military necessity, for the support or other benefit of the army of the United States.

If the owner has not fled, the commanding officer will cause receipts to be given, which may serve the spoliated owner to obtain indemnity.

39. The salaries of civil officers of the hostile government who remain in the invaded territory, and continue the work of their office, and can continue it according to the circumstances arising out of the war—such as judges, administrative or police officers, offices of city or communal governments—are paid from the public revenue of the invaded territory, until the military government has reason wholly or partially to discontinue it. Salaries or incomes connected with purely honorary titles are always stopped.

40. There exists no law or body of authoritative rules of action between hostile armies, except that branch of the law of nature and nations which is called the law and usages of war on land.

41. All municipal law of the ground on which the armies stand, or of the countries to which they belong, is silent and of no effect between armies in the field.

42. Slavery, complicating and confounding the ideas of

property (that is of a *thing*), and of personality (that is of *humanity*), exists according to municipal law or local law only. The law of nature and nations has never acknowledged it. The digest of the Roman Law enacts the early dictum of the pagan jurist, that "so far as the law of nature is concerned, all men are equal." Fugitives escaping from a country in which they were slaves, villains, or serfs into another country, have, for centuries past, been held free and acknowledged free by judicial decisions of European countries, even though the municipal law of the country in which the slave had taken refuge acknowledged slavery within its own dominions.

43. Therefore, in a war between the United States and a belligerent which admits of slavery, if a person held in bondage by that belligerent be captured by or come as a fugitive under the protection of the military forces of the United States, such person is immediately entitled to the rights and privileges of a freeman. To return such person into slavery would amount to enslaving a free person, and neither the United States nor any officer under their authority can enslave any human being. Moreover, a person so made free by the law of war is under the shield of the law of nations, and the former owner or state can have, by the law of postliminy, no belligerent lien or claim of service.

44. All wanton violence committed against persons in the invaded country, all destruction of property not commanded by the authorized officer, all robbery, all pillage or sacking, even after taking a place by main force, all rape, wounding, maiming, or killing of such inhabitants, are prohibited under the penalty of death, or such other severe punishment as may seem adequate for the gravity of the offence.

A soldier, officer or private, in the act of committing such violence, and disobeying a superior ordering him to abstain from it, may be lawfully killed on the spot by such superior.

45. All captures and booty belong, according to the modern law of war, primarily to the government of the captor.

Prize money, whether on sea or land, can now only be claimed under local law.

46. Neither officers nor soldiers are allowed to make use of their position or power in the hostile country for private gain, not even for commercial transactions otherwise legitimate. Offences to the contrary committed by commissioned officers will be punished with cashiering or such other punishment as the nature of the offence may require; if by soldiers, they shall be punished according to the nature of the offence.

47. Crimes punishable by all penal codes, such as arson, murder, maiming, assaults, highway robbery, theft, burglary, fraud, forgery, and rape, if committed by an American soldier in a hostile country against its inhabitants, are not only punishable as at home, but in all cases in which death is not inflicted, the severer punishment shall be preferred.

SECTION III.

DESERTERS. — PRISONERS OF WAR. — HOSTAGES. — BOOTY ON THE BATTLE-FIELD.

48. Deserters from the American army, having entered the service of the enemy, suffer death if they fall again into the hands of the United States, whether by capture, or being delivered up to the American army; and if a deserter from the enemy, having taken service in the army of the United States, is captured by the enemy, and punished by them with death or otherwise, it is not a breach against the law and usages of war, requiring redress or retaliation.

49. A prisoner of war is a public enemy armed or at-

tached to the hostile army for active aid, who has fallen into the hands of the captor, either fighting or wounded, on the field or in the hospital, by individual surrender or by capitulation.

All soldiers, of whatever species of arms; all men who belong to the rising *en masse* of the hostile country; all those who are attached to the army for its efficiency and promote directly the object of the war, except such as are hereinafter provided for; all disabled men or officers on the field or elsewhere, if captured; all enemies who have thrown away their arms and ask for quarter, are prisoners of war, and as such exposed to the inconveniences as well as entitled to the privileges of a prisoner of war.

50. Moreover, citizens who accompany an army for whatever purpose, such as sutlers, editors, or reporters of journals, or contractors, if captured, may be made prisoners of war, and be detained as such.

The monarch and members of the hostile reigning family, male or female, the chief, and chief officers of the hostile government, its diplomatic agents, and all persons who are of particular and singular use and benefit to the hostile army or its government, are, if captured on belligerent ground, and if unprovided with a safe-conduct granted by the captor's government, prisoners of war.

51. If the people of that portion of an invaded country which is not yet occupied by the enemy, or of the whole country, at the approach of a hostile army, rise under a duly authorized levy, *en masse* to resist the invader, they are now treated as public enemies, and, if captured, are prisoners of war.

52. No belligerent has the right to declare that he will treat every captured man in arms of a levy *en masse* as a brigand or bandit.

If, however, the people of a country, or any portion of the same, already occupied by an army, rise against it, they are violators of the laws of war, and are not entitled to their protection.

53. The enemy's chaplains, officers of the medical staff, apothecaries, hospital nurses and servants, if they fall into the hands of the American army, are not prisoners of war, unless the commander has reasons to retain them. In this latter case, or if, at their own desire, they are allowed to remain with their captured companions, they are treated as prisoners of war, and may be exchanged if the commander sees fit.

54. A hostage is a person accepted as a pledge for the fulfilment of an agreement concluded between belligerents during the war, or in consequence of a war. Hostages are rare in the present age.

55. If a hostage is accepted, he is treated like a prisoner of war, according to rank and condition, as circumstances may admit.

56. A prisoner of war is subject to no punishment for being a public enemy, nor is any revenge wreaked upon him by the intentional infliction of any suffering, or disgrace, by cruel imprisonment, want of food, by mutilation, death, or any other barbarity.

57. So soon as a man is armed by a sovereign government, and takes the soldier's oath of fidelity, he is a belligerent; his killing, wounding, or other warlike acts, are no individual crimes or offences. No belligerent has a right to declare that enemies of a certain class, color, or condition, when properly organized as soldiers, will not be treated by him as public enemies.

58. The law of nations knows of no distinction of color, and if an enemy of the United States should enslave and sell any captured persons of their army, it would be a case for the severest retaliation, if not redressed upon complaint.

The United States cannot retaliate by enslavement;

therefore death must be the retaliation for this crime against the law of nations.

59. A prisoner of war remains answerable for his crimes committed against the captor's army or people, committed before he was captured, and for which he has not been punished by his own authorities.

All prisoners of war are liable to the infliction of retaliatory measures.

60. It is against the usage of modern war to resolve, in hatred and revenge, to give no quarter. No body of troops has the right to declare that it will not give, and therefore will not expect, quarter; but a commander is permitted to direct his troops to give no quarter, in great straits, when his own salvation makes it *impossible* to cumber himself with prisoners.

61. Troops that give no quarter have no right to kill enemies already disabled on the ground, or prisoners captured by other troops.

62. All troops of the enemy known or discovered to give no quarter in general, or to any portion of the army, receive none.

63. Troops who fight in the uniform of their enemies, without any plain, striking, and uniform mark of distinction of their own, can expect no quarter.

64. If American troops capture a train containing uniforms of the enemy, and the commander considers it advisable to distribute them for use among his men, some striking mark or sign must be adopted to distinguish the American soldier from the enemy.

65. The use of the enemy's national standard, flag, or other emblem of nationality, for the purpose of deceiving the enemy in battle, is an act of perfidy by which they lose all claim to the protection of the laws of war.

66. Quarter having been given to an enemy by American troops, under a misapprehension of his true character,

he may, nevertheless, be ordered to suffer death if, within three days after the battle, it be discovered that he belongs to a corps which gives no quarter.

67. The law of nations allows every sovereign government to make war upon another sovereign state, and, therefore, admits of no rules or laws different from those of regular warfare, regarding the treatment of prisoners of war, although they may belong to the army of a government which the captor may consider as a wanton and unjust assailant.

68. Modern wars are not internecine wars, in which the killing of the enemy is the object. The destruction of the enemy in modern war, and, indeed, modern war itself, are means to obtain that object of the belligerent which lies beyond the war.

Unnecessary or revengeful destruction of life is not lawful.

69. Outposts, sentinels, or pickets are not to be fired upon, except to drive them in, or when a positive order, special or general, has been issued to that effect.

70. The use of poison in any manner, be it to poison wells, or food, or arms, is wholly excluded from modern warfare. He that uses it puts himself out of the pale of the law and usages of war.

71. Whoever intentionally inflicts additional wounds on an enemy already wholly disabled, or kills such an enemy, or who orders or encourages soldiers to do so, shall suffer death, if duly convicted, whether he belongs to the army of the United States, or is an enemy captured after having committed his misdeed.

72. Money and other valuables on the person of a prisoner, such as watches or jewelry, as well as extra clothing, are regarded by the American army as the private property of the prisoner, and the appropriation of such valuables or money is considered dishonorable, and is prohibited.

Nevertheless, if *large* sums are found upon the persons of prisoners, or in their possession, they shall be taken from them, and the surplus, after providing for their own support, appropriated for the use of the army, under the direction of the commander, unless otherwise ordered by the government. Nor can prisoners claim, as private property, large sums found and captured in their train, although they had been placed in the private luggage of the prisoners.

73. All officers, when captured, must surrender their side-arms to the captor. They may be restored to the prisoner in marked cases, by the commander, to signalize admiration of his distinguished bravery, or approbation of his humane treatment of prisoners before his capture. The captured officer to whom they may be restored cannot wear them during captivity.

74. A prisoner of war being a public enemy, is the prisoner of the government, and not of the captor. No ransom can be paid by a prisoner of war to his individual captor, or to any officer in command. The government alone releases captives, according to rules prescribed by itself.

75. Prisoners of war are subject to confinement or imprisonment such as may be deemed necessary on account of safety, but they are to be subjected to no other intentional suffering or indignity. The confinement and mode of treating a prisoner may be varied during his captivity according to the demands of safety.

76. Prisoners of war shall be fed upon plain and wholesome food whenever practicable, and treated with humanity.

They may be required to work for the benefit of the captor's government, according to their rank and condition.

77. A prisoner of war who escapes may be shot, or oth-

erwise killed in his flight; but neither death nor any other punishment shall be inflicted upon him simply for his attempt to escape, which the law of war does not consider a crime. Stricter means of security shall be used after an unsuccessful attempt at escape.

If, however, a conspiracy is discovered, the purpose of which is a united or general escape, the conspirators may be rigorously punished, even with death; and capital punishment may also be inflicted upon prisoners of war discovered to have plotted rebellion against the authorities of the captors, whether in union with fellow-prisoners or other persons.

78. If prisoners of war, having given no pledge nor made any promise on their honor, forcibly or otherwise escape, and are captured again in battle, after having rejoined their own army, they shall not be punished for their escape, but shall be treated as simple prisoners of war, although they will be subjected to stricter confinement.

79. Every captured wounded enemy shall be medically treated, according to the ability of the medical staff.

80. Honorable men, when captured, will abstain from giving to the enemy information concerning their own army, and the modern law of war permits no longer the use of any violence against prisoners, in order to extort the desired information, or to punish them for having given false information.

SECTION IV.

PARTISANS. — ARMED ENEMIES NOT BELONGING TO THE HOSTILE ARMY. — SCOUTS. — ARMED PROWLERS. — WAR-REBELS.

81. Partisans are soldiers armed and wearing the uniform of their army, but belonging to a corps which acts detached from the main body for the purpose of making inroads into the territory occupied by the enemy. If

captured, they are entitled to all the privileges of the prisoner of war.

82. Men, or squads of men, who commit hostilities, whether by fighting, or inroads for destruction or plunder, or by raids of any kind, without commission, without being part and portion of the organized hostile army, and without sharing continuously in the war, but who do so with intermitting returns to their homes and vocations, or with the occasional assumption of the semblance of peaceful pursuits, divesting themselves of the character or appearance of soldiers—such men, or squads of men, are not public enemies, and therefore, if captured, are not entitled to the privileges of prisoners of war, but shall be treated summarily as highway robbers or pirates.

83. Scouts, or single soldiers, if disguised in the dress of the country, or in the uniform of the army hostile to their own, employed in obtaining information, if found within or lurking about the lines of the captor, are treated as spies, and suffer death.

84. Armed prowlers, by whatever names they may be called, or persons of the enemy's territory, who steal within the lines of the hostile army, for the purpose of robbing, killing, or of destroying bridges, roads, or canals, or of robbing or destroying the mail, or of cutting the telegraph wires, are not entitled to the privileges of the prisoner of war.

85. War-rebels are persons within an occupied territory who rise in arms against the occupying or conquering army, or against the authorities established by the same. If captured, they may suffer death, whether they rise singly, in small or large bands, and whether called upon to do so by their own, but expelled, government or not. They are not prisoners of war; nor are they, if discovered and secured before their conspiracy has matured to an actual rising, or to armed violence.

SECTION V.

SAFE-CONDUCT.—SPIES.—WAR-TRAITORS.—CAPTURED MESSENGERS.—ABUSE OF THE FLAG OF TRUCE.

86. All intercourse between the territories occupied by belligerent armies, whether by traffic, by letter, by travel, or in any other way, ceases. This is the general rule, to be observed without special proclamation.

Exceptions to this rule, whether by safe-conduct, or permission to trade on a small or large scale, or by exchanging mails, or by travel from one territory into the other, can take place only according to agreement approved by the government, or by the highest military authority.

Contraventions of this rule are highly punishable.

87. Ambassadors, and all other diplomatic agents of neutral powers, accredited to the enemy, may receive safe-conducts through the territories occupied by the belligerents, unless there are military reasons to the contrary, and unless they may reach the place of their destination conveniently by another route. It implies no international affront if the safe-conduct is declined. Such passes are usually given by the supreme authority of the state, and not by subordinate officers.

88. A spy is a person who secretly, in disguise or under false pretence, seeks information with the intention of communicating it to the enemy.

The spy is punishable with death by hanging by the neck, whether or not he succeed in obtaining the information or in conveying it to the enemy.

89. If a citizen of the United States obtains information in a legitimate manner, and betrays it to the enemy, be he a military or civil officer, or a private citizen, he shall suffer death.

90. A traitor under the law of war, or a war-traitor, is

a person in a place or district under martial law who, unauthorized by the military commander, gives information of any kind to the enemy, or holds intercourse with him.

91. The war-traitor is always severely punished. If his offence consists in betraying to the enemy anything concerning the condition, safety, operations, or plans of the troops holding or occupying the place or district, his punishment is death.

92. If the citizen or subject of a country or place invaded or conquered gives information to his own government, from which he is separated by the hostile army, or to the army of his government, he is a war-traitor, and death is the penalty of his offence.

93. All armies in the field stand in need of guides, and impress them if they cannot obtain them otherwise.

94. No person having been forced by the enemy to serve as guide is punishable for having done so.

95. If a citizen of a hostile and invaded district voluntarily serves as a guide to the enemy, or offers to do so, he is deemed a war-traitor, and shall suffer death.

96. A citizen serving voluntarily as a guide against his own country commits treason, and will be dealt with according to the law of his country.

97. Guides, when it is clearly proved that they have misled intentionally, may be put to death.

98. All unauthorized or secret communication with the enemy is considered treasonable by the law of war.

Foreign residents in an invaded or occupied territory, or foreign visitors in the same, can claim no immunity from this law. They may communicate with foreign parts, or with the inhabitants of the hostile country, so far as the military authority permits, but no further. Instant expulsion from the occupied territory would be the very least punishment for the infraction of this rule.

99. A messenger carrying written despatches or verbal

messages from one portion of the army, or from a besieged place, to another portion of the same army, or its government, if armed, and in the uniform of his army, and if captured while doing so, in the territory occupied by the enemy, is treated by the captor as a prisoner of war. If not in uniform, nor a soldier, the circumstances connected with his capture must determine the disposition that shall be made of him.

100. A messenger or agent who attempts to steal through the territory occupied by the enemy, to further, in any manner, the interests of the enemy, if captured, is not entitled to the privileges of the prisoner of war, and may be dealt with according to the circumstances of the case.

101. While deception in war is admitted as a just and necessary means of hostility, and is consistent with honorable warfare, the common law of war allows even capital punishment for clandestine or treacherous attempts to injure an enemy, because they are so dangerous, and it is so difficult to guard against them.

102. The law of war, like the criminal law regarding other offences, makes no difference on account of the difference of sexes, concerning the spy, the war-traitor, or the war-rebel.

103. Spies, war-traitors, and war-rebels are not exchanged according to the common law of war. The exchange of such persons would require a special cartel, authorized by the government, or, at a great distance from it, by the chief commander of the army in the field.

104. A successful spy or war-traitor, safely returned to his own army, and afterwards captured as an enemy, is not subject to punishment for his acts as a spy or war-traitor, but he may be held in closer custody as a person individually dangerous.

APPENDIX. 419

SECTION VI.

EXCHANGE OF PRISONERS.—FLAGS OF TRUCE.—FLAGS OF PROTECTION.

105. Exchanges of prisoners take place—number for number—rank for rank—wounded for wounded—with added condition for added condition—such, for instance, as not to serve for a certain period.

106. In exchanging prisoners of war, such numbers of persons of inferior rank may be substituted as an equivalent for one of superior rank as may be agreed upon by cartel, which requires the sanction of the government, or of the commander of the army in the field.

107. A prisoner of war is in honor bound truly to state to the captor his rank; and he is not to assume a lower rank than belongs to him, in order to cause a more advantageous exchange; nor a higher rank, for the purpose of obtaining better treatment.

Offences to the contrary have been justly punished by the commanders of released prisoners, and may be good cause for refusing to release such prisoners.

108. The surplus number of prisoners of war remaining after an exchange has taken place is sometimes released either for the payment of a stipulated sum of money, or, in urgent cases, of provision, clothing, or other necessaries.

Such arrangement, however, requires the sanction of the highest authority.

109. The exchange of prisoners of war is an act of convenience to both belligerents. If no general cartel has been concluded, it cannot be demanded by either of them. No belligerent is obliged to exchange prisoners of war.

A cartel is voidable so soon as either party has violated it.

110. No exchange of prisoners shall be made except

after complete capture, and after an accurate account of them, and a list of the captured officers, has been taken.

111. The bearer of a flag of truce cannot insist upon being admitted. He must always be admitted with great caution. Unnecessary frequency is carefully to be avoided.

112. If the bearer of a flag of truce offer himself during an engagement, he can be admitted as a very rare exception only. It is no breach of good faith to retain such a flag of truce, if admitted during the engagement. Firing is not required to cease on the appearance of a flag of truce in battle.

113. If the bearer of a flag of truce, presenting himself during an engagement, is killed or wounded, it furnishes no ground of complaint whatever.

114. If it be discovered, and fairly proved, that a flag of truce has been abused for surreptitiously obtaining military knowledge, the bearer of the flag thus abusing his sacred character is deemed a spy.

So sacred is the character of a flag of truce, and so necessary is its sacredness, that while its abuse is an especially heinous offence, great caution is requisite, on the other hand, in convicting the bearer of a flag of truce as a spy.

115. It is customary to designate by certain flags (usually yellow), the hospitals in places which are shelled, so that the besieging enemy may avoid firing on them. The same has been done in battles, when hospitals are situated within the field of the engagement.

116. Honorable belligerents often request that the hospitals within the territory of the enemy may be designated, so that they may be spared.

An honorable belligerent allows himself to be guided by flags, or signals of protection, as much as the contingencies and the necessities of the fight will permit.

117. It is justly considered an act of bad faith, of infamy or fiendishness, to deceive the enemy by flags of

protection. Such act of bad faith may be good cause for refusing to respect such flags.

118. The besieging belligerent has sometimes requested the besieged to designate the buildings containing collections of works of art, scientific museums, astronomical observatories, or precious libraries, so that their destruction may be avoided as much as possible.

SECTION VII.
THE PAROLE.

119. Prisoners of war may be released from captivity by exchange, and, under certain circumstances, also by parole.

120. The term *parole* designates the pledge of individual good faith and honor to do, or to omit doing, certain acts after he who gives his parole shall have been dismissed, wholly or partially, from the power of the captor.

121. The pledge of the parole is always an individual but not a private act.

122. The parole applies chiefly to prisoners of war whom the captor allows to return to their country, or to live in greater freedom within the captor's country or territory, on conditions stated in the parole.

123. Release of prisoners of war by exchange is the general rule; release by parole is the exception.

124. Breaking the parole is punished with death when the person breaking the parole is captured again.

Accurate lists, therefore, of the paroled persons must be kept by the belligerents.

125. When paroles are given and received, there must be an exchange of two written documents, in which the name and rank of the paroled individuals are accurately and truthfully stated.

126. Commissioned officers only are allowed to give their parole, and they can give it only with the permission

of their superior, as long as a superior in rank is within reach.

127. No non-commissioned officer or private can give his parole except through an officer. Individual paroles not given through an officer are not only void, but subject the individuals giving them to the punishment of death as deserters. The only admissible exception is where individuals, properly separated from their commands, have suffered long confinement without the possibility of being paroled through an officer.

128. No paroling on the battle-field, no paroling of entire bodies of troops after a battle, and no dismissal of large numbers of prisoners, with a general declaration that they are paroled, is permitted, or of any value.

129. In capitulations for the surrender of strong places or fortified camps, the commanding officer, in cases of urgent necessity, may agree that the troops under his command shall not fight again during the war, unless exchanged.

130. The usual pledge given in the parole is not to serve during the existing war, unless exchanged.

This pledge refers only to the active service in the field, against the paroling belligerent or his allies actively engaged in the same war. These cases of breaking the parole are patent acts, and can be visited with the punishment of death; but the pledge does not refer to internal service, such as recruiting or drilling the recruits, fortifying places not besieged, quelling civil commotions, fighting against belligerents unconnected with the paroling belligerents, or to civil or diplomatic service for which the paroled officer may be employed.

131. If the government does not approve of the parole, the paroled officer must return into captivity; and should the enemy refuse to receive him, he is free of his parole.

132. A belligerent government may declare, by a gen-

eral order, whether it will allow paroling, and on what conditions it will allow it. Such order is communicated to the enemy.

133. No prisoner of war can be forced by the hostile government to parole himself, and no government is obliged to parole prisoners of war, or to parole all captured officers if it paroles any. As the pledging of the parole is an individual act, so is paroling, on the other hand, an act of choice on the part of the belligerent.

134. The commander of an occupying army may require of the civil officers of the enemy, and of its citizens, any pledge he may consider necessary for the safety or security of his army; and upon their failure to give it, he may arrest, confine, or detain them.

SECTION VIII.

ARMISTICE.—CAPITULATION.

135. An armistice is the cessation of active hostilities for a period agreed upon between belligerents. It must be agreed upon in writing, and duly ratified by the highest authorities of the contending parties.

136. If an armistice be declared, without conditions, it extends no further than to require a total cessation of hostilities along the front of both belligerents.

If conditions be agreed upon, they should be clearly expressed, and must be rigidly adhered to by both parties. If either party violates any express condition, the armistice may be declared null and void by the other.

137. An armistice may be general, and valid for all points and lines of the belligerents; or special—that is, referring to certain troops or certain localities only.

An armistice may be concluded for a definite time; or for an indefinite time, during which either belligerent may resume hostilities on giving the notice agreed upon to the other.

138. The motives which induce the one or the other belligerent to conclude an armistice, whether it be expected to be preliminary to a treaty of peace, or to prepare during the armistice for a more vigorous prosecution of the war, do in no way affect the character of the armistice itself.

139. An armistice is binding upon the belligerents from the day of the agreed commencement; but the officers of the armies are responsible from the day only when they receive official information of its existence.

140. Commanding officers have the right to conclude armistices binding on the district over which their command extends; but such armistice is subject to the ratification of the superior authority, and ceases so soon as it is made known to the enemy that the armistice is not ratified, even if a certain time for the elapsing between giving notice of cessation and the resumption of hostilities should have been stipulated for.

141. It is incumbent upon the contracting parties of an armistice to stipulate what intercourse of persons or traffic between the inhabitants of the territories occupied by the hostile armies shall be allowed, if any.

If nothing is stipulated, the intercourse remains suspended, as during actual hostilities.

142. An armistice is not a partial or a temporary peace; it is only the suspension of military operations to the extent agreed upon by the parties.

143. When an armistice is concluded between a fortified place and the army besieging it, it is agreed by all the authorities on this subject that the besieger must cease all extension, perfection, or advance of his attacking works, as much so as from attacks by main force.

But as there is a difference of opinion among martial jurists, whether the besieged have the right to repair breaches or to erect new works of defence within the place during an armistice, this point should be determined by express agreement between the parties.

144. So soon as a capitulation is signed, the capitulator has no right to demolish, destroy, or injure the works, arms, stores, or ammunition in his possession, during the time which elapses between the signing and the execution of the capitulation, unless otherwise stipulated in the same.

145. When an armistice is clearly broken by one of the parties, the other party is released from all obligation to observe it.

146. Prisoners, taken in the act of breaking an armistice, must be treated as prisoners of war, the officer alone being responsible who gives the order for such a violation of an armistice. The highest authority of the belligerent aggrieved may demand redress for the infraction of an armistice.

147. Belligerents sometimes conclude an armistice while their plenipotentiaries are met to discuss the conditions of a treaty of peace; but plenipotentiaries may meet without a preliminary armistice; in the latter case, the war is carried on without any abatement.

SECTION IX.

ASSASSINATION.

148. The law of war does not allow proclaiming either an individual belonging to the hostile army, or a citizen, or a subject of the hostile government, an outlaw, who may be slain without trial by any captor, any more than the modern law of peace allows such international outlawry; on the contrary, it abhors such outrage. The sternest retaliation should follow the murder committed in consequence of such proclamation, made by whatever authority. Civilized nations look with horror upon offers of rewards for the assassination of enemies, as relapses into barbarism.

SECTION X.

INSURRECTION.—CIVIL WAR.—REBELLION.

149. Insurrection is the rising of people in arms against their government, or a portion of it, or against one or more of its laws, or against an officer or officers of the government. It may be confined to mere armed resistance, or it may have greater ends in view.

150. Civil war is war between two or more portions of a country or state, each contending for the mastery of the whole, and each claiming to be the legitimate government. The term is also sometimes applied to war of rebellion, when the rebellious provinces or portions of the state are contiguous to those containing the seat of government.

151. The term *rebellion* is applied to an insurrection of large extent, and is usually a war between the legitimate government of a country and portions or provinces of the same which seek to throw off their allegiance to it, and set up a government of their own.

152. When humanity induces the adoption of the rules of regular war toward rebels, whether the adoption is partial or entire, it does in no way whatever imply a partial or complete acknowledgment of their government, if they have set up one, or of them, as an independent or sovereign power. Neutrals have no right to make the adoption of the rules of war by the assailed government toward rebels the ground of their own acknowledgment of the revolted people as an independent power.

153. Treating captured rebels as prisoners of war, exchanging them, concluding of cartels, capitulations, or other warlike agreements with them; addressing officers of a rebel army by the rank they may have in the same; accepting flags of truce; or, on the other hand, proclaiming martial law in their territory, or levying war-taxes or forced loans, or doing any other act sanctioned or de-

manded by the law and usages of public war between sovereign belligerents, neither proves nor establishes an acknowledgment of the rebellious people, or of the government which they may have erected, as a public or sovereign power. Nor does the adoption of the rules of war toward rebels imply an engagement with them extending beyond the limits of these rules. It is victory in the field that ends the strife, and settles the future relations between the contending parties.

154. Treating, in the field, the rebellious enemy according to the law and usages of war, has never prevented the legitimate government from trying the leaders of the rebellion or chief rebels for high-treason, and from treating them accordingly, unless they are included in a general amnesty.

155. All enemies in regular war are divided into two general classes; that is to say, into combatants and non-combatants, or unarmed citizens of the hostile government.

The military commander of the legitimate government, in a war of rebellion, distinguishes between the loyal citizen in the revolted portion of the country and the disloyal citizen. The disloyal citizens may further be classified into those citizens known to sympathize with the rebellion, without positively aiding it, and those who, without taking up arms, give positive aid and comfort to the rebellious enemy, without being bodily forced thereto.

156. Common justice and plain expediency require that the military commander protect the manifestly loyal citizens, in revolted territories, against the hardships of the war, as much as the common misfortune of all war admits.

The commander will throw the burden of the war, as much as lies within his power, on the disloyal citizens of the revolted portion or province, subjecting them to a stricter police than the non-combatant enemies have to suffer in regular war; and if he deems it appropriate, or if his government demands of him, that every citizen shall, by an oath of allegiance, or by some other manifest act, declare his fidelity to the legitimate government, he may expel, transfer, imprison, or fine the revolted citizens who refuse to pledge themselves anew as citizens obedient to the law, and loyal to the government.

Whether it is expedient to do so, and whether reliance can be placed upon such oaths, the commander or his government have the right to decide.

157. Armed or unarmed resistance by citizens of the United States against the lawful movements of their troops, is levying war against the United States, and is therefore treason.

APPENDIX B.

THE GENEVA CONVENTION FOR THE AMELIORATION OF THE CONDITION OF THE SICK AND WOUNDED OF ARMIES IN THE FIELD.

Art. I.—Ambulances and military hospitals shall be acknowledged to be neuter, and, as such, shall be protected and respected by belligerents so long as any sick or wounded may be therein. Such neutrality shall cease if the ambulances or hospitals should be held by a military force.

Art. II.—Persons employed in hospitals and ambulances, comprising the staff for superintendence, medical service, administration, transport of wounded, as well as chaplains, shall participate in the benefit of neutrality, while so employed, and so long as there remain any wounded to bring in or to succor.

Art. III.—The persons designated in the preceding article may, even after occupation by the enemy, continue to fulfil their duties in the hospital or ambulance which they serve, or may withdraw in order to rejoin the corps to which they belong.

Under such circumstances, when these persons shall cease from their functions, they shall be delivered by the occupying army to the outposts of the enemy.

Art. IV.—As the equipment of military hospitals remains subject to the laws of war, persons attached to such hospitals cannot, in withdrawing, carry away any articles but such as are their private property.

Under the same circumstances an ambulance shall, on the contrary, retain its equipment.

Art. V.—Inhabitants of the country who may bring help to the wounded shall be respected, and shall remain free. The generals of the belligerent powers shall make it their care to inform the inhabitants of the appeal addressed to their humanity, and the neutrality which will be the consequence of it.

Any wounded man entertained and taken care of in a house shall be considered a protection thereto. Any inhabitant who shall have entertained wounded men in his house shall be exempted from the quartering of troops, as well as from a part of the contributions of war which may be imposed.

Art. VI.—Wounded or sick soldiers shall be entertained and taken care of, to whatever nation they may belong.

Commanders-in-chief shall have the power to deliver immediately, to the outposts of the enemy, soldiers who have been wounded in an engagement, when circumstances permit this to be done, and with the consent of both parties.

Those who are recognized, after their wounds are healed, as incapable of serving, shall be sent back to their own country.

The others may also be sent back, on condition of not bearing arms during the continuance of the war.

Evacuations, together with the persons under whose direction they shall take place, shall be protected by an absolute neutrality.

Art. VII.— A distinctive and uniform flag shall be adopted for hospitals, ambulances, and evacuations. It must on every occasion be accompanied by the national flag. An arm badge (brassard) shall also be allowed for individuals neutralized, but the delivery thereof shall be left to military authority.

The flag and arm badge shall bear a red cross on a white ground.

Art. VIII.—The details of execution of the present convention shall be regulated by the commanders-in-chief of belligerent armies, according to the instructions of their respective governments, and in conformity with the general principles laid down in this convention.

Art. IX.—The high contracting powers have agreed to communicate the present convention to those governments which have not found it convenient to send plenipotentiaries to the International Convention at Geneva, with an invitation to accede thereto; the protocol is for that purpose left open.

Art. X.—The present convention shall be ratified, and the ratifications exchanged at Berne, in four months, or sooner if possible.

ADDITIONAL ARTICLES.

Art. I.—The persons designated in Article II. of the Convention shall, after the occupation by the enemy, continue to fulfil their duties to the sick and wounded, according to their wants, in the ambulance or hospital which they serve. When they request to withdraw, the commander of the occupying troops shall fix the time of departure, which he shall only be allowed to delay for a short time in case of military necessity.

Art. II.—Arrangements will have to be made by the belligerent powers to assure to the neutralized person, fallen into the hands of the army of the enemy, the entire enjoyment of his salary.

Art. III.—Under the conditions provided for in Articles I. and IV. of the Convention, the name "ambulance" applies to field hospitals and other temporary establishments, which follow the troops on the field of battle to receive the sick and wounded.

Art. IV.—In conformity with the spirit of Article V. of the Convention, and to the reservations contained in the protocol of 1864, it is explained that for the appointment of the charges relative to the quartering of troops, and of the contributions of war, account only shall be taken in an equitable manner of the charitable zeal displayed by the inhabitants.

Art. V.—In addition to Article VI. of the Convention, it is stipulated that, with the reservation of officers whose detention might be important to the fate of arms, and within the limits fixed by the second paragraph of that article, the wounded who may fall into the hands of the enemy shall be sent back to their country, after they are cured, or sooner if possible, on condition, nevertheless, of not again bearing arms during the continuance of the war.

Art. VI.—The boats which, at their own risk and peril, during and after an engagement, pick up the shipwrecked or wounded, or which, having picked them up, convey them on board a neutral or hospital ship, shall enjoy, until the accomplishment of their mission, the character of neutrality, as far as the circumstances of the engagement and the position of the ships engaged will permit.

The appreciation of these circumstances is intrusted to the humanity of all the combatants. The wrecked and wounded thus picked up and saved must not serve again during the continuance of the war.

Art. VII.—The religious, medical, and hospital staff of any captured vessel are declared neutral, and, on leaving the ship, may remove the articles and surgical instruments which are their private property.

Art. VIII.—The staff designated in the preceding article must continue to fulfil their functions in the captured ship, assisting in the removal of the wounded made by the victorious party; they will then be at liberty to return to their country, in conformity with the second paragraph of the first additional article.

The stipulations of the second additional article are applicable to the pay and allowance of the staff.

Art. IX.—The military hospital ships remain under martial law in all that concerns their stores; they become the property of the captor, but the latter must not divert them from their special appropriation during the continuance of the war.

Art. X.—Any merchantman, to whatever nation she may belong, charged exclusively with removal of sick and wounded, is protected by neutrality, but the mere fact, noted on the ship's books, of the vessel having been visited by an enemy's cruiser, renders the sick and wounded incapable of serving during the continuance of the war. The cruiser shall even have the right of putting on board an officer in order to accompany the convoy, and thus verify the good faith of the operation.

If the merchant ship also carries a cargo, her neutrality will still protect it, provided that such cargo is not of a nature to be confiscated by the belligerent.

Art. XI.—Wounded or sick sailors and soldiers, when embarked, to whatever nation they belong, shall be protected and taken care of by their captors.

Their return to their own country is subject to the provisions of Article VI. of the Convention, and of the additional Article V.

Art. XII.—The distinctive flag to be used with the national flag, in order to indicate any vessel or boat which may claim the benefit of neutrality, in virtue of the principles of this Convention, is a white flag with a red cross. The belligerents may exercise in this respect any mode of verification which they may deem necessary.

Military hospital ships shall be distinguished by being painted white outside, with green strake.

Art. XIII.—The hospital ships which are equipped at the expense of the aid societies, recognized by the governments signing this Convention, and which are furnished with a commission emanating from the sovereign, who shall have given express authority for their being fitted out, and with a certificate from the proper naval authority that they have been placed under his control during their fitting-out and on their final departure, and that they were then appropriated solely to the purpose of their mission, shall be considered neutral, as well as the whole of their staff. They shall be recognized and protected by the belligerents.

They shall make themselves known by hoisting, together with their national flag, the white flag with a red cross. The distinctive mark of their staff, while performing their duties, shall be an armlet of the same colors. The outer painting of these hospital ships shall be white, with red strake.

These ships shall bear aid and assistance to wounded and wrecked belligerents, without distinction of nationality.

They must take care not to interfere in any way with the movements of the combatants. During and after the battle they must do their duty at their own risk and peril.

The belligerents shall have the right of controlling and visiting them; they will be at liberty to refuse their assistance, to order them to depart, and to detain them if the exigencies of the case require such a step.

The wounded and wrecked picked up by these ships cannot be reclaimed by either of the combatants, and they will be required not to serve during the continuance of the war.

Art. XIV.—In naval wars any strong presumption that either belligerent takes advantage of the benefits of neutrality, with any other view than the interest of the sick and wounded, gives the other belligerent, until proof to the contrary, the right of suspending the Convention as regards such belligerent.

Should this presumption become a certainty, notice may be given to such belligerent that the Convention is suspended with regard to him during the whole continuance of the war.

Art. XV.—The present act shall be drawn up in a single original copy which shall be deposited in the archives of the Swiss Confederation.

The Convention proper was signed at Geneva, Switzerland, August 2, 1864. It was signed by representatives of the following powers; *i. e.*, The Swiss Confederation, Baden, Belgium, Denmark, Spain, France, Hesse, Italy, the Netherlands, Portugal, Prussia, and Würtemberg. The ratifications of the contracting parties were exchanged at Geneva on June 22, 1865. In accordance with the invitation contained in the Ninth Article of the Convention, the following powers acceded to the Convention at various dates between 1864 and 1880. These were: Sweden, December 13, 1864; Greece, January 5-17, 1865; Great Britain, February 18, 1865; Mecklenburg-Schwerin, March 9, 1865; Turkey, July 5, 1865; Würtemberg, June 2, 1866; Hesse, June 22, 1866; Bavaria, June 30, 1866; Austria, July 21, 1866; Russia, May 10-22, 1867; Persia, December 5, 1874; Roumania, November 18-30, 1874; Salvador, December 30, 1874; Montenegro, November 17-29, 1875; Servia, March 24, 1876; Bolivia, October 16, 1879; Chili, November 15, 1879; Argentine Republic. November 25, 1879; Peru, April 22, 1880.

The Additional Articles were agreed to and signed at Geneva on October 20, 1868, by the duly accredited representatives of the following powers; *i. e.*, Great Britain, Austria, Baden, Bavaria, Belgium, Denmark, France, Italy, the Netherlands, the North German Confederation, Sweden, Norway, Switzerland, Turkey, and Würtemberg. The

Convention was acceded to by the United States on March 1, 1882.

In the published English text, from which this version of the Additional Articles is taken, the following paragraph appears in continuation of Article IX. It is not found in the original French text adopted by the Geneva Conference, October 20, 1868.

"The vessels not equipped for fighting which, during peace, the government shall have officially declared to be intended to serve as floating hospital ships, shall, however, enjoy during the war complete neutrality, both as regards stores, and also as regards their staff, provided their equipment is exclusively appropriated to the special service on which they are employed.

"By an instruction sent to the United States minister at Berne, January 20, 1883, the right is reserved to omit this paragraph from the English text, and to make any other necessary corrections, if at any time hereafter the Additional Articles shall be completed by the exchange of the ratifications thereof between the several signatory and adhering powers. The President of the United States, in his proclamation announcing the accession of that power to the Geneva Convention, reserves the promulgation of the Additional Articles until the exchange of the ratifications thereof, between the several contracting states, shall have been effected, and the said additional articles shall have acquired full force and effect as an international treaty."[1]

---

[1] Statutes of the United States, 1882–1883, pp. 126–137.

APPENDIX C.

THE DECLARATION OF PARIS.

DECLARATION RESPECTING MARITIME LAW, SIGNED BY THE PLENIPOTENTIARIES OF GREAT BRITAIN, AUSTRIA, FRANCE, PRUSSIA, RUSSIA, SARDINIA, AND TURKEY, ASSEMBLED IN CONGRESS AT PARIS, APRIL 16, 1856.

The Plenipotentiaries who signed the Treaty of Paris of the 30th of March, 1856, assembled in conference,— Considering:

That Maritime Law, in time of war, has long been the subject of deplorable disputes;

That the uncertainty of the law, and of the duties in such a matter, gives rise to differences of opinion between neutrals and belligerents which may occasion serious difficulties, and even conflicts;

That it is consequently advantageous to establish a uniform doctrine on so important a point;

That the Plenipotentiaries assembled in Congress at Paris cannot better respond to the intentions by which their governments are animated than by seeking to introduce into international relations fixed principles in this respect:

The above-mentioned Plenipotentiaries, being duly authorized, resolved to concert among themselves as to the means of attaining this object; and, having come to an agreement, have adopted the following solemn declaration:

1. Privateering is, and remains abolished.
2. The neutral flag covers enemy's goods, with the exception of contraband of war.

3. Neutral goods, with the exception of contraband of war, are not liable to capture under the enemy's flag.

4. Blockades, in order to be binding, must be effective, that is to say, maintained by a force sufficient really to prevent access to the coast of the enemy.

The Governments of the undersigned Plenipotentiaries engage to bring the present Declaration to the knowledge of the states which have not taken part in the Congress of Paris, and to invite them to accede to it.

Convinced that the maxims which they now proclaim cannot but be received with gratitude by the whole world, the undersigned Plenipotentiaries doubt not that the efforts of their governments to obtain the general adoption thereof will be crowned with full success.

The present Declaration is not and shall not be binding, except between those Powers who have acceded, or shall accede to it.

Done at Paris, April 16, 1856.

"This Declaration of the six powers of the Paris conference was communicated to other states, and it was stated, in a memorandum of the French minister of foreign affairs to the emperor, dated June 12, 1858, that the following powers had signified their full allegiance to the four principles, viz.: Baden, Bavaria, Bremen, Brazil, the duchy of Brunswick, Chili, the Argentine Republic, the Germanic Confederation, Denmark, the two Sicilies, Equador, the Roman states, Greece, Guatemala, Hayti, Hamburg, Hanover, the two Hesses, Lübeck, Mecklenburg-Strelitz, Mecklenburg-Schwerin, Nassau, Oldenburg, Parma, the Netherlands, Peru, Portugal, Saxony, Saxe-Altenburg, Saxe-Coburg-Gotha, Saxe-Meiningen, Saxe-Weimar, Sweden, Switzerland, Tuscany, and Würtemberg. The executive government of Uruguay also gave its full assent to all the four principles, subject to the ratification of the legislature. Spain and Mexico adopted the last three as their own, but, on account of the first article, declined acceding to the entire Declaration. The United States adopted the second, third, and fourth propositions, independently of the first, offering, however, to adopt that also, with the following amendment, or additional clause, "and the private property of subjects or citizens of a belligerent on the high seas, shall be exempt from seizure by the public armed vessels of the other belligerent, except it be contraband." The proposition thus extended has been accepted by Russia, and some other states have signified their approbation of it. There is reason to hope that all the maritime nations of Europe will eventually adopt the extension.[1] The reasons advanced by the United States for declining to accept the entire Declaration have been fully discussed elsewhere.[2]

---

[1] Halleck, vol. ii., p. 17. [2] Ante, p. 284.

APPENDIX D.

THE DECLARATION OF ST. PETERSBURG.

In December, 1868, a conference of delegates, representing nineteen states, assembled at St. Petersburg, upon the invitation of the Russian government, for the purpose of considering the existing rules of war. This body, which has become known as the International Military Commission, completed its labors on November 4–16 of the same year. As a result of its deliberations, the following Declaration was agreed to, and signed, by the duly authorized representatives of the states participating in the conference.[1]

DECLARATION.

"Considering that the progress of civilization should have the effect of alleviating, as much as possible, the calamities of war;

That the only legitimate object which states should endeavor to accomplish during war is to weaken the military force of the enemy;

That for this purpose, it is sufficient to disable the greatest possible number of men;

That this object would be exceeded by the employment of arms which uselessly aggravate the sufferings of disabled men, or render their death inevitable;

---

[1] Austria, Bavaria, Belgium, Denmark, France, Great Britain, Greece, Italy, the Netherlands, Persia, Portugal, Prussia, the North German Confederation, Russia, Sweden and Norway, Switzerland, Turkey, and Würtemberg.

That the employment of such arms would, therefore, be contrary to the laws of humanity;

The contracting parties engage, mutually, to renounce, in case of war among themselves, the employment, by their military or naval forces, of any projectile of less weight than four hundred grammes,[1] which is explosive, or is charged with fulminating or inflammable substances.

They agree to invite all the states which have not taken part in the deliberations of the International Military Commission, assembled at St. Petersburg, by sending delegates thereto, to accede to the present engagement.

This engagement is obligatory only upon the contracting or acceding parties thereto, in case of war between two or more of themselves; it is not applicable with regard to non-contracting powers, or powers that shall not have acceded to it.

It will also cease to be obligatory from the moment when, in a war between contracting or acceding parties, a non-contracting party, or a non-acceding party, shall join one of the belligerents.

The contracting or acceding parties reserve to themselves the right to come to an understanding, hereafter, whenever a precise proposition shall be drawn up, in view of future improvements which may be effected in the armament of troops, in order to maintain the principles which they have established, and to reconcile the necessities of war with the laws of humanity."

---

[1] Fourteen ounces avoirdupois.

APPENDIX E.

THE LAWS OF WAR ON LAND.

RECOMMENDED FOR ADOPTION BY THE INSTITUTE OF INTERNATIONAL LAW AT ITS SESSION IN OXFORD, SEPTEMBER 9, 1880.

At the Brussels session of the Institute, in 1879, a commission of fifteen members was appointed to prepare a code, or manual, of the rules of war on land. The task of collecting the materials, and preparing the proposed code, was intrusted to M. Gustave Moynier, of Geneva, Switzerland, the president of the International Society for the Relief of the Wounded in Time of War. The selection of M. Moynier for this purpose was a most fortunate one in every respect; and he addressed himself to his task with so much zeal and intelligence that, in February of the following year, he was able to submit to his colleagues a draft of the proposed manual. The rules prepared by M. Moynier were based upon the following authorities:

(*a*.) The Instructions for the Government of Armies in the Field, prepared by Dr. Francis Lieber, at the request of the United States government.

(*b*.) The Geneva Convention of August 22, 1864.

(*c*.) The Additional Articles of the Geneva Convention of October 20, 1868.

(*d*.) The Declaration of St. Petersburg of November 4–16, 1868.

(*e*.) The Declaration of Brussels of 1874.

(*f*.) The Official Manuals recently adopted by the governments of France, Russia, and Holland.

The code thus prepared was submitted to the members of the commission for examination and criticism. As a result the rules were entirely rewritten. A number of modifications and amendments, suggested by the members, were embodied in the work, which was again submitted to the commission for discussion and final action. It was approved by that body, and recommended for acceptance. On September 9, 1880, it was unanimously adopted by the Institute of International Law. By a later resolution of the Institute, the executive committee was instructed to bring the proposed rules to the notice of the different governments of Europe and America, with a view to their adoption, as a standard, to which their laws and regulations on the subject should be made to conform.

THE LAWS OF WAR ON LAND.

PART FIRST.

General Principles.

1. The state of war does not admit of acts of violence, save between the armed forces of belligerent states. Individuals who form no part of a belligerent armed force should abstain from such acts.

> *This rule implies a distinction between the individuals who compose the armed force of a state and its other citizens or subjects. A precise definition of the term "armed force" is therefore necessary.*

2. The armed force of a state includes:
    1st. The army proper, or permanent military establishment, including the militia and reserve forces.
    2d. The national guard, landsturm, free corps, and other bodies which fulfil the three following conditions; *i. e.*,
        (*a.*) They must be under the direction of responsible chiefs.

(*b*) They must have a uniform, or distinguishing mark, or badge, recognizable at a distance, and worn by individuals composing such corps.

(*c.*) They must carry arms openly.

3d. The crews of public armed ships, and other vessels used for warlike purposes.

4th. The inhabitants of non-occupied territory, who, at the approach of the enemy, take arms openly and spontaneously to resist an invader, even if they have not had time to organize.

3. Every belligerent armed force must carry on its military operations in accordance with the laws of war.

The only legitimate end that a state may have in war is to weaken the military strength of the enemy.

4. The laws of war do not recognize in belligerents an unlimited liberty as to the means of injuring the enemy. They are to abstain from all needless severity, as well as from all perfidious, unjust, or tyrannical acts.

5. Agreements made between belligerents during the continuance of war, such as armistices, capitulations, and the like, are to be scrupulously observed and respected.

6. No invaded territory is to be regarded as conquered until the end of the war. Until that time the invader exercises, in such territory, only a *de facto* power, essentially provisional in character.

PART SECOND.

APPLICATION OF GENERAL PRINCIPLES.

I. HOSTILITIES.

A. RULES OF CONDUCT WITH REGARD TO INDIVIDUALS.

(*a.*) *Inoffensive Populations.*

The contest being carried on by " armed forces " only.

7. It is forbidden to deal harshly with inoffensive populations.

(b.) Means of Injuring the Enemy.

8. It is forbidden,
   (*a.*) To make use of poison, in any form whatever.
   (*b.*) To make treacherous attempts upon the life of an enemy; as, for example, by keeping assassins in pay, or by feigning to surrender.
   (*c*) To attack an enemy by concealing the distinctive signs of an armed force.
   (*d.*) To use improperly the national flag, uniform, or other distinctive signs of the enemy; the flag of truce, or the distinctive signs of the Geneva Convention.
9. It is forbidden,
   (*a.*) To employ arms, projectiles, or materials of any kind, calculated to cause needless suffering, or to aggravate wounds—notably projectiles of less weight than four hundred grammes (fourteen ounces avoirdupois), which are explosive, or are charged with fulminating or explosive substances.
   (*b.*) To kill or injure an enemy who has surrendered, or who is disabled; or to declare in advance that quarter will not be given, even by those who do not ask it for themselves.

(c.) The Sick and Wounded, and the Sanitary Service.

The following provisions, extracted from the Geneva Convention, exempt the sick and wounded, and the *personnel* of the sanitary service, from many of the needless hardships to which they were formerly exposed:

10. Wounded or sick soldiers shall be collected together and cared for, to whatever nation they may belong.

11. Commanders-in-chief shall have power to deliver, immediately, to the outposts of the enemy, soldiers who

have been wounded in an engagement, when circumstances are such as to permit this to be done, and with the consent of both parties. Those who are recognized, after their wounds are healed, as incapable of serving, shall be sent back to their own country. The others may also be sent back, on condition of not again bearing arms during the continuance of the war. Evacuations, together with the persons under whose direction they take place, shall be protected by an absolute neutrality.

12. Persons employed in hospitals and ambulances, comprising the staff for superintendence, medical service, administration, transport of wounded, as well as chaplains, and the duly accredited agents of relief associations, who are authorized to assist the regular sanitary staff, shall participate in the benefit of neutrality while so employed, and so long as there remain any wounded to bring in or to succor.

13. The persons designated in the preceding article should, even after occupation by the enemy, continue to attend, according to their needs, the sick and wounded in the hospital, or ambulance, to which they are attached.

14. When they request to withdraw, the commander of the occupying troops shall fix the time of departure, which he shall only be allowed to delay, for a short time, in case of military necessity.

15. Suitable arrangements should be made to assure to neutralized persons, who have fallen into the hands of the enemy, the enjoyment of suitable salaries.

16. An arm-badge (brassard) shall be worn by neutralized individuals, but the delivery thereof shall be regulated by military authority.

17. The commanding generals of the belligerent powers should appeal to the humanity of the inhabitants, and should endeavor to induce them to assist the wounded, by pointing out to them the advantages that will result

from so doing. They should regard as inviolable those who respond to this appeal.

(d.) *The Dead.*

18. It is forbidden to rob, or mutilate, the bodies of the dead lying on the field of battle.

19. The bodies of the dead should not be buried until they have been carefully examined, and all articles which may serve to fix their identity, such as names, medals, numbers, pocket-books, etc., shall have been secured. The articles thus collected, from the bodies of the enemy's dead should be transmitted to their army or government.

(e.) *Who may be Made Prisoners of War.*

20. Individuals who form a part of the belligerent armed force of a state, if they fall into the hands of the enemy, are to be treated as prisoners of war, in conformity with articles 61–78 of these instructions. The same rule is observed in the case of messengers who carry official despatches openly; and towards aeronauts charged with observing the operations of an enemy, or with the maintenance of communications between the various parts of an army, or theatre of military operations.

21. Individuals who accompany an army, but who are not a part of the regular armed force of the state, such as correspondents, traders, sutlers, etc., and who fall into the hands of the enemy, may be detained for such length of time only as is warranted by strict military necessity.

(f.) *Spies.*

22. Spies, captured in the act, cannot demand to be treated as prisoners of war.

23. An individual may not be regarded as a spy, however, who, belonging to the armed force of either belligerent, penetrates, without disguise, into the zone of military

operations of the enemy. Nor does the term apply to aeronauts, or to couriers, or messengers, who carry openly, and without concealment, the official dispatches of the enemy.

24. No person, charged with being a spy, shall be punished for that offence, until the fact of his guilt shall have been established before a competent military tribunal.

25. A spy who succeeds in quitting the territory occupied by an enemy, incurs no penalty for his previous offence, should he at any future time fall into the hands of that enemy.

(*g.*) *Flags of Truce.*

26. The bearer of a flag of truce, who, with proper authority from one belligerent, presents himself to the other, for the purpose of communicating with him, is entitled to complete inviolability of person.

27. He may be accompanied by a drummer or trumpeter, by a color-bearer, and, if need be, by a guide and interpreter, all of whom shall be entitled to a similar inviolability of person.

28. The commander to whom a flag is sent, is not obliged to receive the flag under all circumstances.

29. The commander who receives a flag has a right to take such precautionary measures as will prevent his cause from being injured by the presence of an enemy within his lines.

30. If the bearer of a flag of truce abuse the trust reposed in him, he may be temporarily detained, and, if it be proven that he has taken advantage of his position to abet a treasonable act, he forfeits his character of inviolability.

B. RULES OF CONDUCT WITH REGARD TO THINGS.

(a.) Means of Injuring the Enemy.—Bombardments.

Certain precautions are made necessary by the rule that a belligerent must abstain from useless severity. In accordance with this principle,

31. It is forbidden,
- (*a.*) To pillage, even places taken by assault.
- (*b.*) To destroy public or private property, unless such destruction be commanded by urgent military necessity.
- (*c.*) To attack, or bombard, open or undefended towns.

32. The commander of an attacking force, save in cases of open assault, shall, before undertaking a bombardment, make due effort to give notice of his intention to the local authorities.

33. In case of bombardment all needful measures shall be taken to spare, if it be possible to do so, buildings devoted to religion and charity, to the arts and sciences, hospitals, and depots of sick and wounded. This on condition, however, that such places be not made use of, directly or indirectly, for purposes of defence.

34. It is the duty of the besieged to designate such buildings by suitable marks or signs, indicated, in advance, to the besieger.

(b.) Sanitary Establishments.

The arrangements for the relief of the wounded, which are made the subject of article 10 et seq. of the Geneva Convention, would be inadequate to their purpose, were not sanitary establishments granted equal protection. Hence, in accordance with the rules of the Geneva Convention,

35. Ambulances and military hospitals are recognized

as neutral, and, as such, are to be protected by belligerents, so long as any sick or wounded remain therein.

36. The same rule applies to buildings, or parts of buildings, in which the sick or wounded are gathered together, or cared for.

37. The neutrality of hospitals and ambulances ceases if they are guarded by a military force. This does not preclude the presence of an adequate police force.

38. As the equipment of military hospitals remains subject to the laws of war, persons attached to such hospitals cannot, in withdrawing, carry away any articles but such as are their private property. Under the same circumstances, an ambulance shall, on the contrary, retain its equipment.

39. Under the circumstances foreseen in the above paragraphs, the term *ambulance* is applied to field hospitals, and other temporary establishments, which follow the troops on the field of battle to receive the sick and wounded.

40. A distinctive and uniform flag is adopted for ambulances, hospitals, and evacuations. It bears a red cross on a white ground. It must, on all occasions, be accompanied by the national flag.

II. Occupied Territory.

A. Definition.

41. Territory is regarded as occupied when, as the consequence of its invasion by the enemy's forces, the state from which it has been taken has ceased, in fact, to exercise there its regular authority, and the invading state, alone, finds itself able to maintain order therein. The limits within which this state of affairs exists determine the extent and duration of the occupation.

B. Rules of Conduct with Respect to Persons.

42. It is the duty of the occupying military authority

to inform the inhabitants, at the earliest practicable moment, of the powers that he exercises, as well as to define the limits of the occupied territory.

43. The occupying authority should take all due and needful measures to assure order and public tranquillity.

44. To that end the invader should maintain the laws in force in the territory in time of peace, and should not modify, suspend, or replace them, unless it becomes absolutely necessary to do so.

45. The administrative officials and civil employees, of every grade, who consent to continue in the performance of their duties, should be supported and protected by the occupying authority. Their appointments are always revocable, and they have the right to resign their places at any time. They should be subjected to penalties only when they fail to perform duties freely accepted by them, and should be given over to justice only when they have betrayed them.

46. In case of urgency, the invader may demand the co-operation of the inhabitants, to enable him to provide for the necessities of local administration.

47. The population of an invaded district cannot be compelled to swear allegiance to the hostile power; but individuals who commit acts of hostility against the occupying authority are punishable.

48. The inhabitants of an occupied territory, who do not submit to the orders of the occupying authority, may be compelled to do so. The invader, however, cannot compel the inhabitants to assist him in his works of attack or defence, or to take part in military operations against their own country.

49. Family honor and rights, the lives of individuals, as well as their religious convictions, and the right of religious worship should be respected.

C. Rules of Conduct with Regard to Property.

(a.) *Public Property.*

Although the authority of the invader replaces that of the government of the occupied territory, his power is not absolute. So long as the fate of the territory remains in suspense—that is, until the peace—the invader is not free to dispose of property which still belongs to the enemy, and which is not of direct use to him in his military operations. From these principles the following rules are deduced:

50. The occupying authority may seize only the cash, public funds, and bills due or transferable, belonging to the state in its own right, depots of arms and supplies, and, in general, the movable property of the state, of such character as to be useful in military operations.

51. Means of transportation (railways, boats, etc.), as well as telegraph lines and landing cables, can only be appropriated to the use of the invader. Their destruction is forbidden, unless it be commanded by military necessity. They are to be restored, at the peace, in the condition in which they are at that time.

52. The invader can only act in the capacity of a provisional administrator in respect to real property; such as buildings, forests, agricultural establishments, etc., belonging to the enemy's state. He should protect these properties and see to their maintenance.

53. The property of communes, and that of establishments devoted to religious worship, and to the arts and sciences, cannot be seized. All destruction, or intentional defacement of such establishments, of historic monuments or archives, or of works of science or art, is formally prohibited, save when commanded by urgent military necessity.

(b.) *Private Property.*

If the powers of the invader are limited with respect to the public property of the enemy's state, with greater reason are they limited with respect to the private property of individuals.

54. Private property, whether belonging to individuals or corporations, is to be respected, and can be confiscated only under the limitations contained in the following articles.

55. Means of transportation (railways, boats, etc.), telegraphs, factories of arms and munitions of war, although belonging to private individuals or corporations, may be seized by an invader, but must be restored at peace; if possible, with suitable indemnities.

56. Impositions in kind (requisitions), levied upon communes, or the residents of invaded districts, should bear direct relation to the generally recognized necessities of war, and should be in proportion to the resources of the district. Requisitions can only be made, or levied, with the authority of the commanding officer of the occupied district.

57. The invader may levy, in the way of dues and imposts, only such as are already established for the benefit of the state revenues. He employs them to defray the expenses of administration of the occupied territory, contributing in the same proportion in which the legal government was bound.

58. The invader cannot levy extraordinary contributions of money, save as an equivalent for fines, or imposts not paid, or for payments not made in kind. Contributions in money can only be imposed by the order, and upon the responsibility, of the general-in-chief, or that of the superior civil authority established in the occupied territory; and then, as nearly as possible, in accordance with the rule of apportionment and assessment of existing imposts.

59. In the apportionment of burdens relating to the quartering of troops, and in the levying of requisitions and contributions of war, account is to be made of the charitable zeal displayed by the inhabitants in behalf of the wounded.

60. Impositions in kind, when they are not paid for in cash, and contributions of war, are authenticated by receipts. Measures should be taken to assure the regularity and *bona fide* character of these receipts.

III. Prisoners of War.

The confinement of prisoners of war is not in the nature of a penalty for crime; neither is it an act of vengeance. It is a temporary detention only, entirely without penal character. In the following provisions, therefore, regard has been had to the consideration due them as prisoners, and to the necessity of their secure detention.

61. Prisoners of war are the prisoners of the captor's government, and not of the individuals or corps who captured them.

62. They are subject to the laws and regulations in force in the army of the enemy.

63. They must be treated with humanity.

64. All articles in their personal possession, arms excepted, remain their private property.

65. Every prisoner of war is obliged to disclose, when duly interrogated upon the subject, his true name and grade. Should he fail to do so, he may be deprived of all, or a part, of the privileges accorded to prisoners of his rank and station.

66. Prisoners of war may be confined in towns, fortresses, camps, or other places, with an obligation not to go beyond certain specific limits; but they may only be imprisoned as an indispensable measure of security.

67. Every act of insubordination, on the part of a prisoner of war, authorizes the resort to suitable measures of severity on the part of the government in whose hands he is.

68. Prisoners of war attempting to escape may, after having been summoned to halt or surrender, be fired upon. If an escaped prisoner be recaptured, before being able to rejoin his own army or to quit the territory of his captor, he is only liable to disciplinary penalties; or he may be subjected to a more rigorous confinement. If, after having successfully effected his escape, he is again made a prisoner, he incurs no penalty for his previous escape. If, however, the prisoner so recaptured, or retaken, has given his parole not to attempt to escape, he may be deprived of his rights as a prisoner of war.

69. The government having prisoners of war in its hands, is obliged to support them. If there be no agreement between the belligerents upon this point, prisoners of war are placed, in all matters regarding food and clothing, upon the peace footing of the troops of the state which holds them in captivity.

70. Prisoners cannot be compelled to take any part whatsoever in operations of war. Neither can they be compelled to give information concerning their army or country.

71. They may be employed upon public works that have no direct connection with the captor's military operations; provided, however, that such labor is not detrimental to health, nor humiliating to their military rank, if they belong to the army; or to their official or social position, if they are civilians, not connected with any branch of the military service.

72. In the event of their being authorized to engage in private industries, their pay for such services may be collected by the authority in charge of them. The sums so

received may be employed in bettering their condition, or may be paid to them, at their release, subject to deduction, if that course be deemed expedient, of the expense of their maintenance.

IV. Termination of Captivity.

The right of detaining individuals in captivity exists only during the continuance of hostilities. Hence:

73. The captivity of prisoners of war ceases, as a matter of right, at the conclusion of peace; but their liberation is then regulated by agreement between the belligerents.

74. Captivity also ceases, in so far as sick or wounded prisoners are concerned, so soon as they are found to be unfit for military service. It is the duty of the captor, under such circumstances, to send them back to their country.

75. During the continuance of hostilities, prisoners of war may be released in accordance with cartels of exchange, agreed upon by the belligerents.

76. Without formal exchange, prisoners may be liberated on parole, provided they are not forbidden, by their own government, to give paroles. In such a case they are obliged, as a matter of military honor, to perform, with scrupulous exactness, the engagements which they have freely undertaken, and which should be clearly specified. On its part, their own government should not demand, or accept from them, any service contrary to, or inconsistent with, their plighted word.

77. A prisoner of war cannot be constrained to accept a release on parole. For a similar reason, the enemy's government is not obliged to accede to the demand of a prisoner of war to be released on parole.

78. Every prisoner of war, liberated on parole, who is recaptured in arms against the government to which he has given such parole, may be deprived of his rights and privileges as a prisoner of war; unless, since his liberation,

he has been included in an unconditional exchange of prisoners.

V. Troops Interned in Neutral Territory.

It is universally admitted that a neutral state cannot, without compromising its neutrality, lend aid to either belligerent, or permit them to make use of its territory. On the other hand, considerations of humanity dictate that asylum should not be refused to individuals who take refuge in neutral territory to escape death or captivity. From these principles the following provisions are deduced. They are calculated to reconcile, to some extent, the opposing interests involved.

79. It is the duty of a neutral state, within whose territory commands, or individuals, have taken refuge, to intern them at points as far removed as possible from the theatre of war. It should pursue a similar course toward those who make use of its territory for warlike operations, or to render military aid to either belligerent.

80. Interned troops may be guarded in camps, or fortified places. The neutral state decides whether officers are to be released, on parole, by taking an engagement not to quit neutral territory without authority.

81. In the event of there being no agreement with the belligerents concerning the maintenance of interned troops, the neutral state shall supply them with food and clothing, and the immediate aid demanded by humanity. It also takes such steps as it deems necessary to care for the arms and other public property brought into its territory by the interned troops. When peace has been concluded, or sooner, if possible, the expenses occasioned by the internment are reimbursed to the neutral state, by the belligerent state to whom the interned troops belong.

82. The provisions of the Geneva Convention of August

22, 1864 (Articles 10–18, 35–40, 59 and 74 above given), are applicable to the sanitary staff, as well as to the sick and wounded, who take refuge in, or are conveyed to, neutral territory.

83. Evacuations of sick and wounded, not prisoners of war, may pass through neutral territory, provided the *personnel* and material accompanying them are exclusively sanitary. It is the duty of the neutral state, through whose territory the evacuation is made, to take such measures of safety and necessary control as it may deem necessary to the rigorous performance of its neutral duty.

PART THIRD.

Penal Sanction.

If any of the foregoing rules be violated, the offending parties should be punished, after a judicial hearing, by the belligerent in whose hands they are.

84. Offenders against the laws of war are liable to the punishments specified in the penal, or criminal, law.

This mode of repression, however, is only applicable when the person of the offender can be secured. In the contrary case, the criminal law is powerless, and, if the injured party deem the misdeed so serious in character as to make it necessary to recall the enemy to a respect for law, no other resource remains than a resort to reprisals. Reprisals are an exception to the general rule of equity, that an innocent person ought not to suffer for the guilty. They are also at variance with the rule that each belligerent should conform to the rules of war, without reciprocity on the part of the enemy. This necessary rigor, however, is modified, to some extent, by the following restrictions:

85. Reprisals are formally prohibited in all cases in which the injury complained of has been repaired.

86. In all cases of serious importance, in which reprisals appear to be absolutely necessary, they shall not exceed, in kind or degree, nor in their mode of application, the exact violation of the law of war committed by the enemy. They can only be resorted to with the express authority of the general-in-chief. They must conform, in all cases, to the laws of humanity and morality.

This Manual is the latest, as it is in many respects the best, of the many attempts that have been made to frame a body of rules for the guidance of belligerents in war. In common with those that have preceded it, it possesses certain advantages which may be summarized as follows:

(*a.*) It expresses, with great accuracy and precision, the principles of International Law that underlie the rules of war; and states those rules, in considerable detail, as they existed at the date of its preparation.

(*b.*) In stating them, it places upon each the most favorable construction that it is capable of receiving—erring, if at all, upon the side of humanity.

(*c.*) Its publication tends, to a certain extent, to popularize knowledge upon a subject about which too little is known.

(*d.*) By drawing public attention to the existing methods of civilized war, it emphasizes its inevitable hardships and severities, encourages investigation and criticism, and affords an opportunity for their further amendment in the direction of greater humanity.

On the other hand, it is open to serious objections:

(*a.*) No code, or manual, can cover or include all the cases, or novel combinations of circumstances, that are likely to arise in war.

(*b.*) The interests of modern states, and so their military policies, are so diverse as to make it impossible for any rule, or set of rules, to apply to all states, or even to any considerable number of them, in the conduct of their military operations. This is illustrated by the divergent, and in many cases opposing, views upon the subjects of occupied territory, the employment of *levees en masse*, and the like, which are held by states of which England and Russia are the extreme types.

(*c.*) The rules are applied, in time of war, by the commanding generals of opposing armies in the field. Whenever a question of doubtful application arises, the rules are interpreted and applied to the case in point—not by a dispassionate tribunal—but by a party to the issue. His decision must, from the necessities of the case, be based upon a partial and one-sided representation of the facts in issue; and his ruling can hardly fail to be influenced, to an appreciable extent, by considerations of military policy and self-interest.

(*d.*) An invariable defect in most endeavors of this kind is that they attempt too much, and undertake to frame rules upon subjects as to which there is, as yet, no unanimity of opinion among modern states. A rule of International Law, to receive general acceptance, must be based upon general consent. If the policy of states varies as to a particular usage, it is impossible to frame a rule, as to that usage, which all states will agree to observe. The rules of the Geneva Convention, and those of the Declaration of St. Petersburg, have received practically unanimous recognition, because they had to do with practices concerning which all states were of the same opinion. The views held by different states as to the rights of military occupation and the government of occupied territory, and upon the subjects of requisitions and contributions of war, are so diverse, as to make it impossible to formulate a rule by which any considerable number of them will agree to be bound in the conduct of their military operations.

INDEX.

Adjustment of international disputes, 186.
Alabama, case of the, 315.
Alabama Claims, settlement of, 327.
Aliens, definition of the term, 112.
    Classification of, 112.
    Treatment of, in former times, 110.
    "   in modern times, 113.
    Restrictions upon, 115.
Allegiance, 100, 101.
    Doctrine of indelible, 110.
    Change of, how effected, 100.
    (*See* Naturalization, Expatriation.)
Alliances, 175.
    Offensive and defensive, 176.
    Equal and unequal, 176.
Ambassadors, 141.
    Origin of the modern institution, 141.
    The right of legation, 142.
    Right of sending and receiving, 142.
    Duty to receive, not absolute, 142.
    Classification of diplomatic agents, 143.
    Rank of ambassadors, 144.
    Titles of, 145.
    Manner of sending and receiving, 146.
    Reception of ambassadors, 146.
    Duties of ambassadors, 147.
    Diplomatic language, 147.
    Functions of, how suspended and terminated, 148.
    Privileges and immunities of ambassadors, 149.
    The fiction of exterritoriality, 150.
    Immunity from criminal jurisdiction, 151.
    Immunity from civil jurisdiction, 151.

    Immunity of hotel, 152.
    Privilege of religious worship, 153.
    Exemption from customs dues, etc., 153.
Amicable adjustment of disputes, 186.
Arbitration, 191.
    A means of adjusting international disputes, 191.
    A preliminary treaty necessary, 191.
    Character and composition of tribunal, 191.
    Rules of procedure, how provided, 192.
    Decision of tribunal, its character, 192.
    Its binding force, 192.
    Validity of, 192.
Asylum, right of, in war, 299.

Balance of power, 77.
    Interference in behalf of, 77.
    De Marten's statement of the principle of, 80.
    Vattel's statement of the principle of, 81.
    Senior's limitation of the right of interference, 81.
Belligerents, 200.
    Intercourse of, in war, 237.
    Obligation of, to respect the rules of war, 200.
Binding force of treaties, 169.
Bliss, James, case of the, 188.
Blockades, 366.
    Right of, a belligerent right, 366.
    What places may be blockaded, 366.
    Valid blockades, 367.
    How established and notified, 367.
    (*a*.) By proclamation, 368.

(b.) By notification and endorsement, 368.
(c.) By proclamation and notification, 368.
Penalty for breach of blockade, 370.
Duration of, 371.
" in breach by egress, 372.
Termination of blockades, 372.
Pacific blockades, 373.
Booty, 230.

Canon law, origin of, 11.
Capitulations, 239.
Captured property in war, 230.
On land (see Contributions and Requisitions), 230.
On the sea (see Maritime Capture), 259.
Cartels, 239.
Causes of war, 201.
Ceremonial—
Diplomatic, 89, 92, 146.
Maritime, 87.
Military, 91.
Observance of national anniversaries, 90.
Visits of ceremony, 91.
International agreement as to salutes, 90.
Chargés d'Affaires, 145.
Chesapeake, case of the, 307.
Chivalry, effect of the institution upon International Law, 10.
Citizen, definition of the term (see Subject), 98.
Classification of citizens, 99.
(a.) Native-born, 99.
(b.) Naturalized, 100.
Duty of allegiance, 98.
Right to protection, 98.
Citizenship, how determined, 98.
How distinguished from domicile, 117.
Civil wars, 199.
Closed seas, jurisdiction over, 87.
Combatants, 232.
Comity, duty of, 94.
Confederations, 32.
Test of the relative strength of, 32.
Rule for determining the strength of, 33.

Conflict of international rights, 186.
Methods of adjustment, 186.
(a.) Amicable adjustment by interested states, 186.
Duty of moderation, 189.
(b.) Mediation, 190.
(c.) Arbitration, 191.
Mediation and arbitration compared, 192.
Conflict of laws (see Private International Law), 132.
Consolato del Mare, 6.
Constitutional governments, 29.
Consular jurisdiction, 161.
How obtained, limits upon, 161.
Amount of, exercised by United States consuls, 162.
Consuls, 154.
Origin of the consular function, 154.
Classification of consular employees, 157.
Duties of, 156.
Privileges and immunities of, 157.
Method of appointment, the exequatur, 157, 159.
Method of appointment in the United States, 160.
Withdrawal of exequatur, 159.
Continuous voyages (see Contraband), 351.
Contraband of war, 336.
Origin of the practice, 336.
Definition of, 338.
Rules of, affect chiefly the acts of individuals, 339.
Character of contraband trade, 339.
Rules for determining contraband of war, 340.
Difficulty of framing, cause of the difficulty, 340.
Question decided by prize courts, 341.
Field's proposed rule, 341.
Rules of the Supreme Court of the United States, 342.
Application of, 343.
Destination of ships and goods, how determined, 345.
Doctrine of continuous voyages (see cases of the Springbok and Peterhoff), 345.
Difference between old and new

INDEX. 463

rules, probable consequences, 352.
Penalty for contraband trade, 353.
Rule as to contraband goods, 353.
Rule as to the ship, 354.
Rule as to innocent cargo, 354.
Release of neutral ship upon surrendry of contraband cargo, 355.
Duration of penalty, 354.
Neutral conveyance of enemy's troops and despatches, 356.
Definition of terms, 356.
Destination important, 357.
Cases of the Friendship and Greta, 357.
Presumption in the case of hostile despatches, 358.
Despatches of a belligerent government to its ambassadors and consuls in neutral states, 358.
Conveyance of mails in the ordinary course of business, 359.
Case of the Trent, 360.
Occasional contraband, 362.
Pre-emption, 364.
Contributions of war, 230.
Convoy, 383.
Council of Lyons, 13.
Councils of the Church (*see* Œcumenical Councils), 13.
Crimes—
Committed in foreign territory, jurisdiction over, 125.
Committed on the high seas, jurisdiction over, 125.
Criminal jurisdiction, right of, 123.
Views held as to, by various states, 124.
Custom, as a source of International Law, 25.
Customs of Amsterdam, 7.

Decisions—
Of boards of arbitration as a source of International Law, 20.
Of courts as a source of International Law, 23.
Declaration—
Of Paris, 284. (For text of the Declaration, *see* Appendix C, 437.)
Of St. Petersburg, 440.

Declaration of war—
Ancient and modern usage with respect to, 203.
right of, in whom vested, 201.
Despatches of enemy, carriage of, by neutral, 356.
Definition of, 357.
Destination of, important in determining liability of carrier, 357.
Destination, in contraband trade, how determined, 345.
Diplomatic agents (*see* Ambassadors), 141.
Correspondence of, as a source of International Law, 19.
Language, 147.
Divisions of International Law, 24.
1. The natural law of nations, 25.
2. The positive law of nations, 25.
(*a*.) The conventional law of nations, 25.
(*b*.) The customary law of nations, 25.
Domicile, 116.
Distinction between domicile and citizenship, 117.
Rules of, 118.

Effects of a state of war, 205.
Equality of states, 31.
Exchange of prisoners of war, 235.
Exterritoriality, 59, 150.
(*a*.) Application to ambassadors, 67, 150.
(*b*.) Application to armies in transit, 63.
(*c*.) Application to consuls in the East, 67.
(*d*.) Application to ships of war, 60.
(*e*.) Application to sovereigns, etc., 65.
Extradition, 123, 126.
Difference of view as to criminal jurisdiction, 124.
Methods of, 126.
Conditions of, 127.
Treaties of the United States on the subject of, 128.
Interstate, in the United States, 129.

Feudal system, 8.
    Effects of, on growth of International Law, 10.
Flags of truce, 238.
Florida, case of the, 308.
Foreign judgments, effects of, 138.
    Conditions respecting, 139.
Franconia, case of the, 41.
"Free ships, free goods," origin of the rule of, 281.
Friendship, case of the, 357.

Geneva arbitration, 327.
Government defined, 28.
    Forms of, 29.
    Right of a state to change form of, 33.
Greeks, International Law among the, 3.
Greta, case of the, 357.
Grotius, influence of, upon the science of International Law, 16.
    Theory of, respecting International Law, 17.
Guerillas, 214.
Guidon de la Mar, 5.

Hanseatic League, constitution of the, 7.
Heinrich's case, 102.
High seas, 42.
    Claims to dominion over portions of the, 43.
    Freedom of the, 43.
Humanity, duty of, 93.

Immunities of ambassadors, 150.
Imperfect rights, 92.
Impressment of seamen, 380.
Independence of states, principle of, 81.
    Grotius's view of, 17.
Intercourse, duty of, 94.
    Not a right, 95.
    Between belligerents in war, 237.
Interference, when justified, 74.
    (a.) To assist a state in suppressing rebellion, 75.
    (b.) In accordance with treaty stipulations, 76.
    (c.) In self-defence, 77.
    (d.) In behalf of the balance of power, 77.
International Law, 2.
    Difference between International and Municipal Law, 2.
    Divisions of, 24.
    History of, 3.
    Sources of, 18.
    Parties to, 26.
    Interpretation of treaties (see Treaties), 180.

Jugements of Oleron, 5.
Jurisdiction of states, 54.
    Where exercised, 54.
    In whom vested, 55.
    Where exclusive, 56.
    Exterritorial, when exercised, 56.
    Consular, 161.
Jurisdictional powers of government, 54.
    Classification of, 30, 54.
    (a.) Legislative, 55.
    (b.) Executive, 56.
    (c.) Judicial, 56.
Jus Feciale, 4.
Jus Gentium, 17.

Laconia, case of the, 188.
Language of diplomacy, 147, 170.
Law in general, 1.
    International, 2.
    Municipal, 1.
    Distinction between International and Municipal, 2.
Laws of Antwerp, 7.
Laws of war, 208.
    On land, 218.
    On the sea, 226.
Legislation, right of, 142.
Licenses to trade, in war, 240.
    By whom issued, 240.
    Conditions of, 240.
Lieber, Dr. Francis, rules of war prepared by (Appendix A), 395.

Marine League, the, jurisdiction over, 40.
Maritime capture, 259.
Maritime ceremonial, 87.
Maritime commerce, effect of, upon the development of International Law, 45.
Maritime Law, early codes of.
    (a.) The Consolato del Mare, 6.
    (b.) The Constitutions of the Hanseatic League, 7.
    (c.) The Customs of Amsterdam, 7.
    (d.) The Guidon de la Mar, 5.
    (e.) The Jugements of Oleron, 5.
    (f.) The Laws of Antwerp, 7.

(g.) The Maritime Law of Wisbuy, 7.
Maritime ordinances of Louis XIV., 6.
Martial law, 247.
Measures of redress, 193.
   (a.) Retorsion, 194.
   (b.) Reprisals, 195.
Mediation, 190.
Methods of adjusting international disputes, 186.
Military ceremonial on land, 91.
Most-favored-nation clause (see Treaties), 183.
Mutual respect, duty of, 83.
   To whom shown (see Maritime and Military Ceremonial), 85.

Nation, definition of the term, 28.
Nation and state, not synonymous, 28.
National character, 98.
   How determined in the case of an individual, 98.
   Change of, how effected (see Naturalization and Expatriation), 100.
Naturalization, 100.
   Conditions of, 101.
   How effected, 100.
   Heinrich's case, 102.
   Largomarsini's case, 105.
   Koszta's case, 103.
   Treaties of the United States on the subject of, 107.
Navigation—
   Of coast sea, 40.
   Of closed seas, 37.
   Of boundary rivers, 44.
   Of straits, 37.
   Of the high seas, 42.
Neutral, or neutral state, how defined, 276.
   Duty of, in time of war, 297.
   Responsibility of, in respect to the acts of its subjects, 302.
Neutral duties, 297.
   Duty of strict neutrality, 297.
   Asylum to troops and ships, 299.
   Responsibility of a neutral state for the acts of its subjects, 302.
   (a.) View of England and the United States, 303.
   (b.) View of Continental states, 305. (See case of the Alabama, 315.)

Neutral rights, 306.
   Immunity of neutral territory from acts of belligerency, 300, 306.
   Case of the Chesapeake, 307.
   Case of the Florida, 308.
Neutrality, 276.
   Origin and development of the neutral theory, 276.
   Rule of the Consolato del Mare, 279.
   Principle of "free ships, free goods," 281.
   Rule of the Declaration of Paris, 284.
   Claims to exclusive dominion of the sea, 288.
   Colonial monopoly, 291.
   Rule of 1756, 292.
   Development of the theory among the non-maritime states of Europe, 292.
   Influence of England, 293.
   General acceptance of the modern theory, its later history, 294.
   Gradations of neutrality, 295.
   Permament, 296.
   Armed, 296.
   Strict, 297.
Neutrality laws, 309.
   Neutral duty of a state determined by International, not Municipal Law, 310.
   Laws of England on the subject of, 311.
   Laws of the United States on the subject of, 313.
   Laws of other states on the subject of, 314.
Non-combatants in war, treatment of, 233.
Notice of a state of war, to whom given, 204.

Occasional contraband, 362.
Occupation, military, 244.
   Different views as to, 245.
   Present view of, 246.
   Martial law, or the state of siege, 247.
   Right of military occupation defined, 247.
Œcumenical councils, 13.
Offences against the laws of war, 241.
Oriental monarchies, existence of International Law among, 3.

Pacific blockades, 373.
Paroles, 236.
Parties to International Law, 26.
Peace, treaties of, 255.
Perfect rights or duties of states, 70.
    Definition of a perfect right, 70.
    Classification of, 70.
    The duty of mutual respect, 83.
    The duty of non-interference, 74.
    The enforcement of treaty stipulations, 74.
    Interference, when justified, 74.
    Protection of subjects, 72.
    The right of reputation, 73.
    The right of self-preservation, 70.
Peterhoff, case of the, 349.
Pope, decisions of the, in international controversies, 13.
Pope and emperor, position of, in the Middle Ages, 11.
Postliminy, rules of, 266.
Power of belligerents over neutral trade, 338.
Pre-emption, 364.
Prisoners of war, 233.
Private International Law, definition, 132.
    Relations of states and individuals at, 132.
    Practice of, based upon comity, or consent, 132.
    Origin of the practice, 133.
    Subjects treated of in, 136.
    Limitations upon the practice of, 137.
    Effect of foreign judgments, 138.
    Condition of reciprocity, 138.
    Why produced before the courts of a state, 139.
    When effective, 139.
    Practice of states in the matter of foreign judgments, 139.
Prize in war, 261.
Prize courts, 268.
Property, treatment of, in war, 226.
Property of the enemy, public and private, treatment of in war, 226.
Protocol, 183.

Quarter, in war, 222.
    Refusal of, not warranted, 222.

Ransom of captured vessels, 233.
Ransom contracts, 234.

Rebellions, 199.
Recapture of prizes at sea, 266.
Recez, 183.
Reprisals (*see* Means of Redress), 195.
Requisitions, 228.
Responsibility of a neutral state for the acts of its subjects, 302.
Retaliation in war, 251.
    Limitations upon the practice, 252.
Retorsion (*see* Means of Redress), 194.
Revival of commerce, effect of upon the development of International Law, 5.
Rhodian laws, 7.
Right of search, 375.
Rights of sovereign states, 28.
    Perfect rights, 70.
    Imperfect rights, 92.
River navigation, right of, 44.
    Cases of the Main, Meuse, Moselle, Neckar, Rhine, and Scheldt, 44.
    Cases of the Elbe, Douro, Po, Vistula, and Weser, 45.
    Case of the Danube, 45.
    Case of the Mississippi, 46.
    Case of the St. Lawrence, 49.
Rivers as boundaries, 35.
    Navigation of, not a perfect right, 44.
Roman Church, Influence of, upon the development of International Law, 11.
Roman empire, 11.
Roman Law, influence of, upon International Law, 19.
    As a source of International Law, 19.
    Early misconception as to, 21.
    Jus Feciale, 21.
    Jus Gentium, 20.
    Law of the XII. Tables, 20.
    Rules of, as to river boundaries, 35.
Romans, International Law among the, 4.
Rules of war on land.
    (*a.*) Dr. Lieber's Rules for the Government of Armies in the Field (Appendix A), 395.
    (*b.*) The Declaration of St. Petersburg (Appendix D), 440.
    (*c.*) Rules of the Institute of International Law (Appendix E), 442.

Safe-conducts, 239.
Safeguards, 239.

INDEX.   467

Salvage (*see* Recapture), 267.
Sea, claims to dominion over portions of the, 43.
   Jurisdiction over coast (*see* the Marine League), 40.
   Freedom of the, 43.
Sea laws, 5.
Search, the belligerent right of, 375.
   Definition of the right, 375.
   When and where exercised, 375.
   Manner in which the right is exercised, 376.
   Duty of boarding party, 377. (*See* Right of Visitation, 379.)
   Of merchant vessels in time of peace, when authorized, 386.
     (*a.*) To execute revenue laws, 386.
     (*b.*) On suspicion of piracy, 387.
     (*c.*) Inspection of merchant vessels by war vessels of the same nation, 387.
     (*d.*) Right of approach to verify nationality, 387. (*See* Case of the Virginius, 388.)
Seas, the high, 42.
Servitudes, 52.
   How created, 53.
   How terminated, 53.
   Positive, 53.
   Negative, 54.
   Examples, 53, 54.
Ship canals, 39.
   Jurisdiction over, 39.
   Neutrality of, in general, 39.
   Case of the proposed Nicaragua canal, 40.
   Case of the Panama canal, 40.
Sound dues, 38.
Sources of International Law, 18.
   Decisions of international courts, or boards of arbitration, 18.
   Decisions of municipal courts, 23.
   Diplomatic correspondence, 19.
   Divine law, the, 24.
   History — general histories, and histories of important epochs, 24.
   Municipal law of states, 24.
   Roman Law, the, 19.
   State papers, 19.
   Text-writers, 22.
Sovereignty of states, 28.
   How acquired, 34.

How lost, 34.
Test of a sovereign state, 33.
Classification of sovereign powers, 30.
The essential attributes of sovereignty, 31.
   (*a.*) Sovereignty, 31.
   (*b.*) Independence, 31.
   (*c.*) Equality, 31.
Spies in war, 241.
Springbok, case of the, 346.
State, the term defined, 28.
   Difference between the terms "state" and "nation," 28.
   Classification of states, 28.
     Sovereign, 32.
     Dependent, or semi-sovereign, 32.
     Confederate, 32.
     Belligerent, 200.
     Neutral, 276.
   Government of states, 28.
   Classification of, 29.
   Territory of a, 35.
St. Petersburg, Declaration of (Appendix D), 440.
Straits, 37.
   Jurisdiction over, 37.
   Rights of ownership and jurisdiction over, 37.
   Right of passage through, 38.
Subjects of states (*see* Citizens), 98.
   The terms "citizen" and "subject" synonymous, 98.
   Classification of, 99.
   Duty of allegiance, 98.
   Native-born, 99.
   Naturalized, 100.
   Right to protection, 98.

Temporary occupation in war, 244.
Territory, defined, 35.
   What constitutes the territory of a state, 35.
   Boundaries, 35.
   Rivers as boundaries, 35.
   Navigation of boundary rivers, 44.
Text-writers, works of, as a source of International Law, 22.
   Classification of, 22.
Thirty Years' War, influence of, upon development of International Law, 16.
Treaties and conventions, 165.
   Purpose of, 165.

Right to make treaties an incident of sovereignty, 165.
Contracts and agreements with individuals, 166.
Treaty-making power, 166.
Conditions essential to the validity of treaties, 167.
  (*a.*) Power of the contracting parties, 167.
  (*b.*) Consent of the contracting parties, 167.
  (*c.*) Possibility of execution, 168.
Binding force of treaties, 169.
Manner of negotiating treaties, 169.
  Language used, 170.
  Form and signature, 171.
Ratification of treaties, 172.
Classification of, according to their nature, 173.
  Transitory and permanent, 174.
Classification of, according to their objects, 174.
  Cartels and capitulations, 174.
  Treaties of alliance, 175.
  Treaties of guarantee, 176.
  Reciprocity treaties, 178.
  Treaties of peace, 257.
Termination of treaties, 179.
Rules for the interpretation of treaties, 180.
Terms used in treaties, 183.
Troops, neutral conveyance of enemy's, 356.
Truce, 253.

Usages of war, 208.
(*See* Appendices A, C, D, E.)

Virginius, case of the, 388.
Visitation, right of (*see* Right of Search), 379.

War, 198.
  The right of redress, 198.
  Definition and purpose, 198.
  Rightfulness of war, 199.
  Classification of, 199.
  The belligerent parties, 200.
  Right of declaring war, in whom vested, 201.
  Causes of war, 201.
  Responsibility for a resort to war, 202.
  Moral considerations involved, 202.
Declaration of war, and its effects, 203.
  Ancient and modern rule, 203.
  Notification of, to whom given, 204.
  Effect of, upon treaties, 204.
Effects of a state of war, 205.
  Upon subjects of an enemy in belligerent territory, 206.
  Upon property of enemy subjects in belligerent territory, 207.
Laws of war, 208.
  Their character and tendency, 208.
  Subjects discussed in, 210.
  Amount and kind of force that may be used, 210.
  Legal effects of a state of war upon the subjects of the belligerent states, 210.
  Who may lawfully carry on war, 211.
  Armed forces of a state, 211.
  Partisans, 211.
  Levees en masse, 212.
  Guerillas, 214.
  Forces that may not be used in war, 214.
Wars with savages, 215.
Forces employed at sea, 215.
  Naval establishments, regular and volunteer, 216.
  Privateers, 216.
  Letters of marque, 216.
Effect of modern inventions, and of improved methods of attack and defence, 218.
Methods of carrying on war, 218.
Rule of good faith; use of deceit, 219.
Attack of places, 219.
  Duty of the commanding officer in the matter of surrender, 221.
  Use of the enemy's uniform and flag, 222.
  Rule as to quarter, 222.
  Treatment of individuals of the enemy, 222.
  Forbidden practices, 223.
  Instruments of war, 223.

What instruments are forbidden, 224.
Torpedoes, mines, etc., 225.
The usages of war at sea, 226.
The public and private property of the enemy, 226.
Treatment of property on land, 226.
(a.) The public property of the enemy, 226.
(b.) The private property of enemy subjects, 227.
(c.) Requisitions, 228.
(d.) Contributions of war, 230.
(e.) Captured property on land; booty, 230.
Treatment of non-combatants in the theatre of war, 232.
Prisoners of war, 233.
Who may be made prisoners of war, 234.
Treatment of, 234.
Character of their confinement, 235.
Status of prisoners of war, how terminated, 235.
(a.) Exchange of prisoners, 235.
(b.) Paroles, 236.
By whom given, 236.
Conditions of parole, 237.
Breach of parole, 237.
Intercourse between belligerents, 237.
Flags of truce, 238.
Rules as to the use of flags, 238.
Cartels, 239.
Capitulations, 239.
Safe-conducts, 239.
Safeguards, 239.
Licenses to trade, 240.
Offences against the laws of war, 241.
(a.) Being a spy, 241.
(b.) Being a guerilla, 214, 242.
(c.) Crimes of violence, 243.
Right of temporary occupation, 244.
History of the different views of military occupation, 245.
Present view of occupation, 246.
Rights of occupation, 247.

Martial law, or the state of siege, how exercised, 247.
Difference of opinion as to the meaning of the term "occupation," 250.
Permanent occupation, 251.
Retaliation in war, 251.
Limitations upon the exercise of the right, 252.
The termination of war, 253.
Suspensions of hostilities—truces, 253.
(a.) Special truces, 253.
What may be done during a special truce, 253.
(b.) General truces, or armistices, 254.
Treaties of peace, 255.
In what respects different from ordinary treaties, 255.
How executed, 256.
When effective, 257.
Their binding force, 256.
Effects of treaties of peace, 257.
(a.) Upon the causes of the war, 257.
(b.) Upon individuals, 257.
(c.) Treatment of occupied territory, 258.
The rules of maritime capture, 259.
Their character and tendency, 259.
Forces that may be employed in maritime war, 260.
Prize, 260.
Title to prize, in whom vested, 261.
Duty of captor, 261.
Ransom of captured vessels, 263.
Ransom contracts, 264.
Hostages, 265.
Recapture and postliminy, 266.
Prize courts, 268.
Jurisdiction of, 269.
Law applied by, 270.
Procedure in prize cases, 271.
Right of appeal, 272.
Rules for determining nationality of ships and goods, 272.

THE END.

www.ingramcontent.com/pod-product-compliance
Lightning Source LLC
Chambersburg PA
CBHW021418300426
44114CB00010B/551